Frontiers of Globalization

Series Editor
Jan Nederveen Pieterse
Global Studies Department
University of California
Santa Barbara, CA, USA

With the onset of the twenty-first century, key components of the architecture of twentieth-century globalization have been crumbling. American hegemony has weakened politically and economically. Laissez-faire capitalism that shaped neoliberal globalization has proved to be crisis-prone and is giving way to a plurality of ways of organizing and regulating capitalism. With the rise of emerging societies, the driving forces of the world economy are shifting not merely geographically but structurally; industrializing societies, rather than postindustrial consumer societies, are again propelling the world economy. These changes involve major breaks: an era of multipolarity; the affirmation of the plurality of capitalisms; the emergence of new modernities; and the new patterns of East-South and South-South relations, in contrast to the North-South relations. These changes unfold on a global scale and cannot be properly understood on a national, regional or even international basis. Understanding these changes requires interdisciplinary and kaleidoscopic approaches that range from global political economy to cultural transformations. The series welcomes contributions to global studies that are innovative in topic, approach or theoretical framework. Amid the fin-de-regime of the millennium, with globalization in the throes of dramatic change, the series will cater to the growing interest in material on contemporary globalization and its ramifications. Proposals can be submitted by mail to the series editor: Jan Nederveen Pieterse, Mellichamp Professor of Global Studies and Sociology, Global & International Studies Program, University of California, Santa Barbara, CA 93106-7065, USA

Paul Bowles • Nathan Andrews
Editors

Extractive Bargains

Natural Resources and the State-Society Nexus

palgrave
macmillan

Editors
Paul Bowles
Global and International Studies
University of Northern British Columbia
Prince George, BC, Canada

Nathan Andrews
Department of Political Science
McMaster University
Hamilton, ON, Canada

Frontiers of Globalization
ISBN 978-3-031-32171-9 ISBN 978-3-031-32172-6 (eBook)
https://doi.org/10.1007/978-3-031-32172-6

This Palgrave Macmillan imprint is published by the registered company Springer Nature Switzerland AG.
The registered company address is: Gewerbestrasse 11, 6330 Cham, Switzerland

Acknowledgements

This volume arises from a workshop held at the University of Northern British Columbia (UNBC) in May 2022. We are grateful to all participants for their enthusiasm and comments. Mohammed Adam and Arturo Ramón Sepúlveda García provided excellent assistance and produced a rapporteurs' report for participants. Funding was provided by the Social Sciences and Humanities Research Council of Canada, and the Office of Research and Innovation, the Faculty of Indigenous Studies, Social Sciences and Humanities, and the Department of Global and International Studies at UNBC. Paul Bowles also benefitted from holding the Fulbright Canada Research Chair at the University of California Santa Barbara where fruitful discussions with Jan Nederveen Pieterse resulted in this volume appearing in the latter's *Frontiers of Globalization* series.

Praise for *Extractive Bargains*

"How do governments persuade people to accept a mine, or to close it? As geopolitical tensions and the green transition push forward a new phase of hyper-extractivism, states face many doubts around resource-based development and climate solutions. This impressive volume takes a deep dive into the ways states design and promote 'extractive bargains', exposing the search for a (post)extractive consensus within fluid state-society relations. A must-read on resource governance, supply security, and climate politics."

—Philippe Le Billon, *University of British Columbia and Institute for Advanced Study, Princeton*

"Extractivism has become an increasingly important concept in contemporary Global Development Studies. In this volume, Paul Bowles and Nathan Andrews present a highly sophisticated and nuanced framework of analysis to assess the varied role of the state in pursuit of extractive bargains. They have assembled an excellent team of scholars to assess sixteen case studies, from both Global North and South, representing a range of complex processes in state-society relations, including a broad assemblage of actors, power structures, institutions and coalitions. The book makes a major contribution to the burgeoning study of extractivisms, and illustrates in detail how extractive bargains in the state-society nexus do not have a singular or predetermined outcome."

—Barry K. Gills, *Professor of Global Development Studies, Helsinki University, Finland*

"Through a collaborative methodology, Andrews, Bowles and volume contributors offer a conceptually innovative typology of the kinds of conditions that facilitate, normalize and constrict extractive activities within and between states. The chapters are empirically rich, allowing scholars and advanced students to interrogate the parallels and variations uniting diverse global examples, including successful instances of national bans on the extraction of fossil fuels and international bargains in support of Green New Deals. Highly recommended!"

—Anna Zalik, *Associate Professor, Faculty of Environmental Studies, York University, Toronto, Canada*

Contents

Notes on Contributors

Moses Adjei is a postdoctoral fellow in the School of Science and the Environment at Memorial University of Newfoundland, Canada. His research focuses on natural resource governance (fisheries), women and gender studies, health and well-being. His studies have been published in *Rural Sociology*, *Journal of Comparative Family Studies*, *Journal of Urban Affairs*, *Ocean and Coastal Management*, and *The Extractive Industries and Society*.

Maud Esi Amoafo was born and raised in Accra, Ghana, until she moved to Canada in 2020. She holds a Master of Arts Degree in Political Science from the University of Windsor and an honours Bachelor of Arts Degree in Political Science from the University of Ghana. Her master's thesis focused on improving Ghana's petroleum socio-economic outcomes through local content, policy development, and fiscal discipline in the management of petroleum revenues. She is passionate about research and her research interests include energy policy and natural resource extraction governance, particularly maximizing the developmental outcomes of extractive industries in Africa.

Diego Andreucci is a postdoctoral fellow at the University of Barcelona, Spain, working on the political ecology of resource extractivism and energy transitions in Latin America and southern Europe.

Nathan Andrews is an associate professor in the Department of Political Science at McMaster University, Canada. His research focuses on the global political economy of natural resource extraction, global governance, and development. His research is featured in publications in journals such as *International Affairs, Resources Policy, World Development, Third World Quarterly, Energy Research & Social Science*, including books such as *Gold Mining and the Discourses of Corporate Social Responsibility in Ghana* (Palgrave Macmillan, 2019), *Corporate Social Responsibility and Canada's Role in Africa's Extractive Sectors* (2020), and *Oil and Development in Ghana: Beyond the Resource Curse* (2021).

Clifford Gordon Atleo (he/him) is from the Ahousaht (Nuu-chah-nulth) and Kitselas (Tsimshian) First Nations, where he carries the Indigenous names: Chachim'multhnii, Niis Na'yaa, and Kam'ayaam. He is an assistant professor in the School of Resource and Environmental Management at Simon Fraser University, Canada, where he teaches and researches Indigenous governance, political economy, and resource relationships.

Jonathan Martin Boron (he/him) is Cayuga (Goyogo̱ hó:nǫ') of the Haudenosaunee Confederacy from Six Nations of the Grand River and of mixed German, Polish, and Irish settler heritage. He is a PhD candidate in the School of Resource and Environmental Management at Simon Fraser University, where his research focuses on pathways to self-determination in resource governance and land relations.

Paul Bowles is Professor of Global and International Studies at the University of Northern British Columbia, Canada, located on the unceded traditional territory of the Lheidli T'enneh. He has written widely on China's political economy, globalization, development, the international monetary system, and resource extraction. His work on these topics has appeared in journals such as *Review of International Political Economy, Journal of Development Studies, New Left Review, New Political Economy, Cambridge Journal of Economics, Journal of Political Ecology*, and *Extractive Industries and Society*. He is the author or editor of 11 books, the latest being *Capitalism* (3rd edition, 2023).

Angela Carter has a dual role as an associate professor in the Department of Political Science and Balsillie School of International Affairs at the University of Waterloo, Canada, and also as an Energy Transitions Specialist at the International Institute for Sustainable Development (IISD). She has established an interdisciplinary comparative research programme focused on environmental policies and politics surrounding Canadian fossil fuel development and on new international approaches to climate policy. She also serves as a member of the Net-Zero Advisory Council, Government of Newfoundland and Labrador.

Alem Cherinet is a governance advisor with more than fifteen years in project management, strategic advancement, capacity building, and organizational consulting. Her academic expertise is in the field of complex governance in dynamics of conflict, violence, and security. With an MA in Political Science and undergraduate degrees in both International Relations and Latin American Studies, she is recognized for specialties in brokering, negotiation, and identifying crucial mechanisms in problem solving.

Raphael Deberdt is a PhD candidate in the Department of Anthropology at the University of British Columbia, Canada. His research is inscribed in the subfield of mining anthropology and explores the impacts that extractive industries hold on local communities. He studies the role of artisanal miners in the cobalt industry in the Democratic Republic of the Congo (DRC) and their integration in global markets, particularly in the battery manufacturing sector.

Jeff Geipel is the founder and managing director for the Mining Shared Value initiative at Engineers Without Borders Canada. This initiative improves the development impacts of mineral extraction in host countries through increasing local procurement by the global mining industry. Through this work Jeff co-created the Mining Local Procurement Reporting Mechanism (LPRM) in partnership with GIZ, which is a publicly available framework to guide mining companies to increase and standardise reporting on local procurement and supplier due diligence processes. Before Engineers Without Borders, Jeff was the founder and first executive director of Fair Trade Vancouver, which became a model for municipal-based fair trade organizations across Canada. Jeff holds a Master's Degree in International Development from the London School of Economics.

Sarah Greene is a PhD candidate in the Global Governance programme at the Balsillie School of International Affairs, Canada. She specializes in global energy studies and Canada's role in global energy governance. Her current research explores the climate implications of the varying approaches of fossil fuel reliant states to pandemic recovery, as some seek to entrench oil production, further making the shift to decarbonization harder.

John P. Hayes is a PhD candidate in the Department of Political Science at McMaster University, Canada. He is also the research coordinator of the Extractive Resource Governance Program at The School of Public Policy, University of Calgary. He specializes in comparative public policy and international relations, focusing on issues of natural resource governance in the context of the Latin American mining sector. He is a SSHRC Canada Graduate Scholar (2018–2022) and recipient of the International Development Research Center Doctoral research award (2020).

Marie Jasser is a DOC-team fellow of the Austrian Academy of Sciences in the Department of Development Studies at the University of Vienna, Austria, and an associate researcher at the Universidad Nur in Santa Cruz de la Sierra, Bolivia. She is researching the role of social movements in land conflicts in the Plurinational State of Bolivia and coordinates the research group SolPan+ Bolivia.

Ulrik Jørgensen received his MSc in Electronics Engineering in 1979 and PhD in Innovation Economics in 1985; he is Retired Professor of Sustainable Transitions at Aalborg University, Copenhagen, Denmark, and is now an independent researcher and consultant at UJ Consult. Jørgensen has done research in science and technology studies, as well as in environmental, mining, construction, and energy technology and policy. His recent work has been focused on sustainable transition processes in society and the navigations by actors involved in transitions. He is involved in the design of professional master's programmes in environmental management, in sustainable design, and in Arctic engineering (in Greenland).

Karin Beland Lindahl is Associate Professor of Political Science at Luleå University of Technology, Sweden, and Head of Research at the Swedish Mountain and Sami Museum. She has more than 20 years of research experience in natural resource politics in Sweden, the EU, and internationally. Her research focuses on natural resource conflicts, governance of sustainable development and transition, natural resource policy, and actors' perceptions and practices. She is particularly interested in politics and policy addressing Indigenous land use and rights in Sweden and internationally.

Ciaran O'Faircheallaigh is Professor of Politics and Public Policy in the School of Government and International Relations at Griffith University, Brisbane, Australia. His research focuses on Indigenous governance and leadership, especially as it relates to large-scale resource development on Indigenous lands. In addition to his area of research, his teaching includes policy design, implementation, and evaluation. For over 30 years he has acted as a negotiator and advisor for Indigenous communities and organizations in Australia, Canada, Chile, and Papua New Guinea. Since 2017 he has worked with Conservational International (CI) on developing the negotiation capacity of CI's Indigenous partners in the Global South.

Jesse Salah Ovadia is an associate professor at the University of Windsor, Canada. His research focuses on the political economy of resource extraction and development in Africa as well as sustainable energy transitions. He is the author of *The Petro-Developmental State in Africa* (2016). He has consulted for organizations such as the World Bank, African Development Bank, African Climate Foundation, and others. His academic research has been published in journals such as *Third World Quarterly*, *New Political Economy*, *Resources Policy*, *Journal of Modern African Studies*, *Journal of Agrarian Change*, and *the Extractive Industries and Society*.

Margot W. Parkes is a professor in the School of Health Sciences at the University of Northern British Columbia, Canada, and an honorary professor at the University of Otago, New Zealand. Her work connects with others to demonstrate shared respect for land, air, and water as living systems, and as foundations for health, equity, and well-being, prioritizing research, education, and practice that amplify co-benefits for people, place, and planet. Parkes draws on her background in clinical medicine, public health, human ecology, ecohealth, and Indigenous and planetary health, focusing especially on cumulative social and ecological influences on health within watersheds, and in rural, remote, and Indigenous communities.

Isabella M. Radhuber is a postdoctoral researcher in the Research Network Latin America at the University of Vienna, Austria, and part of the Centre for the Study of Contemporary Solidarity (CeSCoS). She works on environment and health politics, crisis responses with a current focus on the COVID-19 pandemic, and global inequalities from a decolonial perspective; her regional focus is on Latin America and Europe.

Jamie L. Shenk is a political sociologist interested in the intersection of peace, conflict, and environmental politics with a regional focus on Latin America. She is currently a Democracy Postdoctoral Fellow at Harvard Kennedy School's Ash Center for Democratic Governance and Innovation. She holds a PhD (DPhil) in Sociology from the University of Oxford and an MSc in Latin American Studies from the same university. Her work is published or forthcoming in *Comparative Politics* and *Journal of Peace Research*.

Darcy Tetreault is a professor and researcher in the Department of Development Studies (*Unidad Académcia en Estudios del Desarrollo*) at the Autonomous University of Zacatecas (*Universidad Autónoma de Zacatecas*), Mexico. His approach to research involves ongoing collaboration with popular forms of organized resistance to environmentally destructive projects and with collective efforts from below to construct alternatives. Areas of interests include extractivism, social environmental conflicts, agrarian transformation, and peasant and Indigenous movements, with a focus on Mexico and from the perspective of critical development studies, political ecology, and ecological Marxism.

Henry Veltmeyer is a senior research professor at the Universidad Autónoma de Zacatecas, Mexico, and Professor Emeritus of International Development Studies (IDS) at Saint Mary's University. In 2020 he was awarded the distinction Emeritus National Researcher by Conacyt, Mexico's National Research Council. In addition to holding a senior research fellowship in advanced Latin American Studies at the University of Guadalajara, he is the co-editor of Critical Development Studies book series. He has authored and edited over 50 books on the political economy of international development, including *The New Extractivism: A Model for Latin America or the New Imperialism?* (2014).

Jing Vivian Zhan is a professor in the Department of Government and Public Administration at the Chinese University of Hong Kong, Hong Kong. Her research interests span comparative political economy, contemporary Chinese politics, and research methodology, with a focus on the political economy of natural resources, local governance, intergovernmental relations, and development. She is the author of *China's Contained Resource Curse: How Minerals Shape State-Capital-Labor Relations* (2022) and dozens of articles in journals such as *the China Quarterly, Environmental and Resource Economics, Extractive Industries & Society, Geopolitics,* and *Policy Studies Journal.*

List of Figures

List of Tables

Part I

Theorizing and Contextualizing Extractive Bargains

1

Extractive Bargains and the State-Society Nexus: One World, Many Bargains

Paul Bowles and Nathan Andrews

Introduction

As the world confronts climate change, environmental degradation, rampant social and economic inequalities, wars and insecurity, extractive activities have come under increasing scrutiny (Bridge, 2004); the uncertainty over the future of fossil fuel and mineral extraction has perhaps

We are grateful to all participants, paper presenters and session chairs, at the Extractive Bargains workshop for their engagement with, and comments on, various versions of this introductory chapter. We are also grateful to participants at a seminar held in the Department of Global Development Studies at the University of Helsinki. The chapter has been immeasurably improved as a result of these inputs.

P. Bowles (✉)
Global and International Studies, University of Northern British Columbia, Prince George, BC, Canada
e-mail: paul.bowles@unbc.ca

N. Andrews
Department of Political Science, McMaster University, Hamilton, ON, Canada
e-mail: nandrews@mcmaster.ca

P. Bowles, N. Andrews (eds.), *Extractive Bargains*, Frontiers of Globalization,
https://doi.org/10.1007/978-3-031-32172-6_1

never been greater. When an increased global recognition of the rights of Indigenous peoples is added, then it is evident that how extraction takes place has become a source of major contention with states finding themselves at the centre of conflicting pressures from extractive capital and civil society forces.

There are many studies of how resistance to extraction is taking place around the world (Arboleda, 2020; Svampa, 2019; Kroger, 2020; Willow, 2018) and how corporations are responding through a plethora of corporate social responsibility (CSR) initiatives designed to placate their critics (Farkes, 2015). Relatively less attention has been paid to analysing how states have responded. This volume seeks to fill a part of that gap.

States have the authority to regulate extractive activities, set the terms for their approval or rejection and determine who has the opportunity or right to be involved in review processes and decision-making bodies. States decide who owns sub-surface rights and who therefore has the ability to use, transfer or lease those lands and waters for extractive activity. States also have the legal and military mechanisms to enforce their decisions if needed. In making their policies, states are subject to a multitude of pressures. All states operate in a global capitalist system that conditions and constrains their policy options; extractive industries are dominated by global capitalist firms. States have differing degrees of internal coherence and face a variety of domestic constituencies. In some cases, such constituencies have little power to affect state action and policy; in other cases, they have significantly more power to provide input and to shape, or to initiate disruption of, state policies on extraction. At the very least, states are critical actors in determining the extent and forms of the extractive activities which take place within their borders. For this reason alone, analysis of state behaviour and policy is important. Chagnon et al. (2022) argue more forcefully that "the state is central in birthing extractivism". Ehrnström-Fuentes and Kröger (2018) have also shown that the state plays a fundamental role in birthing extractive investment even when extractivism is largely based on multinational capital.

Historically, the state has been tasked with promoting economic growth and development and resource extraction has been a key feature of that for many of them. This has typically been accompanied by an optimism that a state's natural resource endowment has the potential to contribute positively to economic growth or development broadly defined (Bebbington et al., 2008; Kemp, 2010; O'Faircheallaigh, 2017; Andrews et al., 2022). The mounting evidence of a "resource curse" has significantly undermined this claim (see Morrison, 2013; Papyrakis, 2017; Williams & Le Billon, 2017; Andrews & Siakwah, 2021), but many resource-rich countries continue to rely on the notion that more is actually more: the idea that the more resources a state controls or exploits, the better its chances of making significant gains over time that could trickle down to address key societal needs.

The standard case made for extractive activities relies upon this assumption and extraction is seen as having the ability to generate employment and provide revenues to various actors in the form of incomes, tax and royalty payments, and export earnings.[1] This economic case has, however, been weakened as the limited jobs available from a capital-intensive industry often operating as an "enclave" have been evident, as royalty regimes have been diluted as states have competed with each other to attract capital, and as export earnings have been captured or dissipated by elites. Accompanying the realization that in many cases the economic benefits of extractive activities have been overstated has been the increasing recognition of the environmental and social costs of extraction and the intensification of resistance to extractive activities in many parts of the world. Appealing to the direct economic benefits of extractive activities has therefore become a more tenuous approach for many states pursuing extraction policies.

States have increasingly responded by making larger claims for extraction. That is, they have sought to persuade their citizens that extractive activities can bring more than the limited economic benefits that have typified many countries' experiences to date. In this way, states have sought to re-imagine extractive activities as presenting an opportunity for broader societal goals to be met. In this way, states are designing and promoting "extractive bargains", a search for an acceptance by a wide range of social actors of the state's preferred extractive policies in exchange for delivering on wider societal goals. There is something of a paradox

[1] For instance, see the Extractives for Development (E4D) project by UNU-WIDER: https://www.wider.unu.edu/project/extractives-development-e4d.

here in that as the direct benefits of extraction have been perceived as declining, and its costs escalating, the claims made on behalf of extraction by states have in many ways become larger and bolder. The idea of the "extractive bargain" assists us in examining what forms these claims take, who gains from them and whether they offer the prospect for improved social and environmental outcomes or not.

Previous work has looked at "extractive political settlements" (see Winato & Diprose, 2020), while Ali (2022) has referred to the "grand bargain" initiated, but subsequently abandoned, by President Correa of Ecuador which offered "not extracting oil from the highly biodiverse Yasuni National Park in the Amazonian reforest" in exchange for \$3.6 billion from the international community. Gunster (2019) has referred to the "spectacular failure" of the "grand bargain" offered by some Canadian political leaders "in which support for a modest carbon tax afforded 'social licence' for new pipelines and tar sands expansion". We draw inspiration from these ideas and seek to move beyond them in several important ways. Work on political settlements has tended to be primarily elite-based and rather static, while work on "grand bargains" has been piecemeal and under-theorized. In this volume, we seek to lay out more fully and comparatively the concept and utility of "extractive bargains" as an analytical framework. As we explain further below, for us extractive bargains are ubiquitous, complex and dynamic.

We define extractive bargains as the ways in which states attempt to convince different stakeholders and seek to establish some degree of consensus with societal actors about the need to pursue particular policies on resource extraction, whether that be the continuation, expansion or even reduction of extraction, for societal good. The purpose of examining state-society relations in the context of extractive bargains is not to reify the state or to suggest that it exists separate from society but to examine how it responds to, and seeks to shape, the actions of other social actors whether corporations, classes, social movements, Indigenous nations and groups or simply public opinion. Our conceptualization of state-society relations denotes a complex iteration of the broader assemblage of actors, power structures, institutions and coalitions that contribute to the justification for and material manifestations of resource extraction. This perspective challenges the tendency to see the state as a coherent or homogeneous entity working alongside other equally distinct entities. Exploring the state-society nexus as extractive bargains requires us to imagine a plethora of complex social forces and connections that operate through multiple channels to promote and/or resist extractivism. In other words, extractive bargains are dynamic and there is a dialectical process between states and social actors in the search for consensus as bargains constantly shift in their emphasis and scope.

Our primary objective in this book is to examine in detail and comparatively the ways in which different states have sought to construct these extractive bargains. We do so by examining case studies from 16 countries from both the Global North and Global South and including some majority Indigenous states. In selecting countries as case studies, we were conscious of finding countries where bargains may be said to have been offered. In some states, this is demonstrably not the case and the use of state violence is the standard response to civil society opposition. Of course, violence comes in different forms and is often present when examining natural resource extraction (Shapiro & McNeish, 2021). But violence is not the only, or necessarily the primary, mechanism which is used and in many states various efforts are made to obtain legitimacy; it is these states which are candidates for inclusion as case studies. We also selected cases where the direct benefits in terms of employment and tax revenue are not, in themselves, deemed sufficient to ensure public support for the extractive activity and other societal benefits have been promoted. These criteria guided us in our selection of case studies which include Australia, Bolivia, Canada, China, Colombia, Denmark, Ecuador, France, Ghana, Greenland, Ireland, Mexico, the Philippines, South Africa, Sweden and Tanzania.

Our starting point therefore is the lacuna in the study of the intricate position of states in extractivism despite their role in navigating the plethora of societal and private actors and structures of power. While being cognizant of the challenges of methodological nationalism (i.e. maintaining the prevalence of the state as a primary unit of analysis), within the context of this book we see the extractive bargains conceptualization as an innovative way of unpacking the different strategies taken by states to negotiate support for various kinds of extractive (and even post-extractive) activities. A bargains approach is a particularly productive way of understanding policy framings and choices, why and how they come about, the ways in which they are challenged or resisted and the strategies being used to justify such choices as serving the broader societal good. At the very least, this book highlights how the process of negotiating such bargains is neither straightforward nor consistent across a number of important cases in the Global South and Global North.

The next section provides a more detailed conceptualization of the central notion of an extractive bargain by examining varieties of analytical and normative bargains. In setting the scene in this way, we also highlight some of the key insights from the case study chapters which follow.

Conceptualizing Extractive Bargains

Underpinning the concept of an extractive bargain is the idea that policies concerning natural resource extraction are contestable and negotiable. The focus of this book is how states seek to negotiate with non-state actors to gain support for their preferred policies. The state's aim is to achieve a degree of consensus for, or at least a broad coalition in support of, its approach. From this several implications arise.

The first is that the state is an actor in its own right with its own interests—a proposition consistent with a number of theoretical traditions. It can be argued the state in capitalist society performs many functions which are critical to the process of capital accumulation including the protection of private rights, both legally and by force, and by facilitating and financing the infrastructure needed to support accumulation. But the state also operates with a degree of "relative autonomy" from capital to use the term developed by Marxist political economist Poulantzas (1968), when analysing state-society relations. As such, the state has the potential to regulate and control factions of capital, including powerful extractive capital. This is not to deny that extractive corporations and states often sing from the same hymn sheet especially when it comes to particular projects (see e.g. Cervantes & Zalik, 2018; Gilbert & Zalik, 2019; MacPhail & Bowles, 2021) or seek to construct discourses conducive to viewing land as a resource available for capital accumulation (Le Billon & Sommerville, 2017). But, at the state level, it is not necessarily or always the case that the state can be reduced to a mouthpiece for capital. To some examining the politics of the state in the economically successful developmental states of

East Asia, for example, it was precisely the state's ability to discipline and structure capital (as well as labour) that was identified as a critical component in the explanation for their success (Amsden, 1989; Wade, 1990). These successes provided those states with a degree of legitimacy. All states seek to find legitimacy and do so in many ways such as the provision of economic growth as in the East Asian case but also from addressing inequalities and providing social goods as found in Nordic social democracies. The state's position as a facilitator of capitalist accumulation and as an institution requiring societal legitimacy results in it having to navigate complex and contradictory pressures to ensure its own continuity. Striking societal bargains is one mechanism it can use to achieve this.

The second is that a bargain is not pre-determined and can lead to multiple outcomes depending on the power, agency and skill of the negotiating actors. The concept of a bargain implies that all actors have some power to influence the outcome even if there may be asymmetrical power differences. Bargains may be difficult to conclude and may not endure over time. They can be fluid, continually shifting in their terms as power shifts within states and society. The fact that there is a state-society bargain, or attempts to find one, does not therefore imply the absence of contestation or resistance. Part of each bargain are formidable social forces that may be considered "entrepreneurs" or "anti-preneurs" whose respective support for and/or opposition to bargains condition the bargain's potential to remain intact or shift over time. In short, the search for consensus is often elusive. As such, there is the prospect of continual struggle over how the state will construct its bargains.

The third is that in analysing state-society relations, it is necessary to disaggregate the actors involved. Extractive bargains can usefully be understood as societal level narratives designed by states to gain support for their extractive policies. But just as society is not homogenous neither is the state a unitary actor. The executive and legislative branches of government, the civil servants in the ministries which perform the day-to-day functions of government, the judiciary and the various forces of "law and order", all have their own interests and influence the design and implementation of bargains. In this context it is typically a branch of government which enunciates the bargain, seeking societal support, and changes in government often bring with them changes in the narratives. While governments and their policies are therefore crucial to the analysis of bargains, we argue that it is necessary to consider the broader concept of the state since other state actors, such as the judiciary and different ministries, for example, can and do play important roles in interpreting and implementing the bargain offered by political leaders, roles which may influence how the bargain is perceived by broader social actors.

In moving on to examine the content of specific extractive bargains, it is evident that state responses to extraction take many forms and need to be contextualized; we make use of the idea of Varieties of Extractive Bargains to capture and assess these responses. We propose to examine Varieties of Extractive Bargains along two axes. The first is the analytical and in which the content and social basis for bargains in specific state-level locations are identified, analysed and categorized. The second is a normative assessment of bargains and their ability to meet the challenges of a world beset with inequality, injustice and environmental crises at multiple scales. This requires the placement of bargains on a spectrum and analysing how each can be moved towards the progressive end of that spectrum.

Varieties of Extractive Bargains I: Analytical Types

The attempts to construct new state-society bargains to justify particular resource extraction policies have taken many forms. We identify six major state-level bargains here based on the country case studies and one which operates at other levels (as summarized in Table 1.1). The identification of these six "ideal types" was the result of an interactive and iterative process between the editors and the country specialist authors. The editors initially set out the framework of extractive bargains and suggested a number of possible types asking country authors to assess how their cases might fit within this framework. This led to some types of analytical bargain gaining support but country experiences suggested other types of bargain were in play or that countries differed from our initial placement. This led to further iterations until Table 1.1 was derived, a collaborative effort involving all authors.

It should be noted, and as will become clear in the examples provided, each type of bargain comes in several different forms and that, while we

Table 1.1 Analytical varieties of extractive bargains

Type of extractive bargain	Level	Goal/focus of bargain	Examples
Climate bargains	State	State offers climate-related commitments in exchange for resource extraction that appears somewhat consistent with a vision for "sustainable development"	Global North (e.g. Canada, Sweden[a], Australia)
Post-extractive bargains	State	Commitments to potentially abandon extraction including to reduce reliance on non-renewable sources of energy as a way to address the current and future ecological crisis.	Global North (e.g. France[a], Denmark[a], Ireland[a]) and Global South (e.g. Costa Rica)
Indigenous-focused bargains	State	Specific arrangements made to address Indigenous communities which take many forms (from IBAs to plurinationalism)	Global North (e.g. Australia[a], Canada[a]) and Global South (e.g. Bolivia[a], Ecuador[a], Philippines[a], South Africa[a])
Social redistribution bargains	State	Expanded resource extraction to be permitted in exchange for expected rents being directly committed to poverty reduction initiatives. May take specific forms in conflict zones as a "peace bargain".	Global South (e.g. Colombia[a], 'Pink Tide', China[a]) and Global North (e.g. Sweden[a])

(*continued*)

Table 1.1 (continued)

Type of extractive bargain	Level	Goal/focus of bargain	Examples
Independence bargains	State	Resource extraction used as a way to support political and economic independence. May be part of compensatory mechanism for possible disruptions to trade and other cross-border economic activities such as geopolitical tensions.	Global North (e.g. Greenland[a], Germany) and Global South (e.g. Mexico[a])
Developmentalist bargains	State	Justifying ongoing resource extraction as a means to harness resource wealth for broad-based national development projects and structural change. Considerable country specific variation.	Global South (e.g. China[a], Ghana[a], Tanzania[a], Zambia, Zimbabwe)
Parallel bargains	Global, subnational	Global architecture used to integrate national green strategies. Sub-national governments address particular issues.	Mainly Global North at global level[a]

[a]Denotes subject of chapter case study

can identify a number of distinct conceptual ideal types of bargains, they may be invoked at different times by the same state and/or a state may commonly invoke more than one at the same point in time in an attempt to appeal to different social actors. Furthermore, while the type of bargain can be identified, many of the case studies reveal there are large gaps between what is promised and what is delivered, and opposition and resistance to the bargains on offer remain significant.

One bargain may be termed a *climate bargain*. In this version of an extractive bargain, states justify their policies and seek to gain support for them by pointing to their climate benefits. For example, in Canada, the limits of the "staples trap" (Innis, 1999; Haley, 2011; Bowles & MacPhail,

2018) have led to new justifications for natural resource extraction which seek to balance this with climate commitments. Thus, Trudeau's Liberal government initiated a full public review of the way in which projects are assessed by the National Energy Board, introduced a national carbon tax and committed to meet GHG emission targets. In return, the state has sought support for the expansion of large fossil fuel mega-projects, such as those in the tar sands as well as so-called "transition fuels" such as natural gas, including the infrastructure necessary to get the product to market justifying them as consistent with its climate commitments. Sweden, the largest exporter of minerals in Europe, has a corporatist political system which encourages and facilitates consensus-based tripartite decision-making but has found it necessary to add a green twist to its arguments in support of continued extraction and "sustainable development" as Karin Beland Lindahl demonstrates in her chapter. In Greenland too, Ulrik Jørgenson argues, the global climate benefits of rare earth extraction have provided a justification in proposals for some mining projects. Thus, climate bargains have been used to support continued and expanded extraction in the context of both fossil fuels and the critical minerals needed for a transition to renewable energy.

Interestingly, Sarah Greene and Angela Carter show in their chapter how a form of climate bargain can also be used to "keep it in the ground". Analysing the examples of France, Ireland and Denmark, they show how states have sought to fashion extractive bargains which result in a ban on new fossil fuel projects in what may be termed a *post-extractive bargain*. While this can be seen as a subset of the climate bargain, we view it as sufficiently important and different from climate bargains which lead to continued extraction, to warrant its own category. It is found not only in three countries analysed here but also found in a number of other countries including Costa Rica, Belize, Bulgaria, Germany, the Netherlands, New Zealand, Portugal, Spain and Uruguay although the ban on extraction in a few of these countries refers to a technology (fracking) rather than all extraction. The post-extractive bargain is framed in terms of eschewing extraction activities in order to meet a higher-order cause such as climate change. It may also include social justice components such as the support for "green jobs" in order to compensate those who might otherwise lose from the implementation of the bargain. This form of bargain can extend beyond oil and gas to other resources, such as uranium, with Greenland's return to a "zero tolerance policy" illustrating how post-extractive bargains can extend beyond the climate goal; extraction is forgone in order to support the higher-order moral and political goal of a nuclear-free country (and world).

The continuing and expanding extraction of resources from Indigenous territories around the world has led to inevitable and rising conflicts (see Veltmeyer & Bowles, 2014; Rasch, 2017; Beland Lindahl et al., 2018; Wilson, 2019; Kuokkanen, 2019). As Indigenous rights have increasingly been recognized at the international level, for example with the adoption of the UN Declaration of the Rights of Indigenous Peoples (UNDRIP) in 2007, states have responded by proposing various forms of what might be termed *Indigenous-focused bargains*. These are designed to permit extraction to take place on Indigenous territories in return for specific benefits to Indigenous societies. As Ciaran O'Faircheallaigh demonstrates in his chapter, these have taken many different forms and led to a variety of outcomes across the world. He shows specifically how the bargain was framed, but not implemented, in the Philippines, how the outcomes of bargains differed from their intent in South Africa, and how Impact Benefit Agreements (IBAs) have been applied in Australia with varying outcomes. In their chapter, Cliff Atleo and Jonathan Boron argue that successful legal challenges by Indigenous nations in Canada have required the settler colonial state to pursue extractive bargains. However, outcomes vary and the continued dominance of Canadian law and priorities has meant there are and continue to be many instances where the bargains, including IBAs, have been used to essentially limit and remove Indigenous rights to land and disempower communities, a case of an Indigenous-focused bargain leading to outcomes which fundamentally undermine Indigenous communities' long-term viability in favour of the interests of the state and capital. Furthermore, as workshop participant Ricado Jacobs explained in his remarks, "indigeneity" has been used and manipulated by the state in South Africa as a way of privileging some groups, in essence striking a "retribalization bargain" with them, in order to enable a new round of capitalist extractive expansion. By promoting and incorporating (unelected) hereditary chiefs, Jacobs argued, the South African state is using "indigeneity" to enhance the power of chiefs who can be relied upon to support further extractive projects. A potentially profound form of an Indigenous-focused bargain is evident in the experience of extractivism in the plurinational states of Bolivia and Ecuador. Here, as Isabella M. Radhuber, Marie Jasser and Diego Andreucci show, the extractive bargain to reconcile postcolonial pluralism can open up the space for the plural economies important for the vitality of the diverse Indigenous and non-Indigenous societies alongside an expanding capitalist extractive sector (cf. Radcliffe & Radhuber, 2020; Radhuber & Radcliffe, 2022). In this way, a radically new way of reconciling internally socially diverse states and extractive activity is conceived, even if practice has fallen short. Plurinational states are enshrined in the Constitution, as are their plural economies, which encourage various forms of economic organization and activity and should particularly empower the Indigenous and communitarian. At the same time, the rights of nature have been incorporated into Constitutions thereby implying that resource extraction could be restrained according to socio-ecological principles.

Indigenous-focused bargains, therefore, utilize a variety of mechanisms designed to offer Indigenous communities sources of income, through IBAs, for example, and in some cases offer forms of political power, such as constitutional protections, in exchange for largely ongoing resource extraction.

There are also broader classes of bargains which can be termed *social redistribution bargains*. This type of bargain is often attributed to the so-called "Pink Tide" countries in Latin America and occurring with the global commodities boom on the first decade of the twenty-first century. Here some states sought to gain popular support for expanded resource extraction in return for revenues which "were funneled into a myriad of social programs for children, the elderly, and the poor, as well as infrastructure and other spending" (Perreault, 2022: see also Brand et al., 2016). The bargain offered is that dependence on external capital inflows and the environmental costs of resource extraction be borne in exchange for poverty reduction. In broad terms, the emphasis on social inclusion and on the benefits to all that this extractive bargain suggests also resonates with Beland Lindahl's analysis of mining in social democratic Sweden. Jamie Shenk's analysis of the extractive bargain in Colombia can be seen as a specific form of social redistribution bargain. Here, she argues that the war with the FARC and the subsequent peace settlement has led to the role of extractive activities being framed in terms of a *territorial peace bargain*. Perhaps ironically in view of the many conflicts which have arisen over extraction projects, such projects have been touted as contributing to post-conflict reconstruction and as a way of redistributing resources and power to former conflict areas.

The role of extractive activities in supporting state independence in various circumstances has led to examples of *independence bargains* where states appeal for public support for extraction to meet nationalist goals. In Greenland, for example, following the move to self-government in 2009 and with an over 80 per cent Indigenous population, resource extraction projects were touted as a way for the country to gain economic independence from Denmark. The 2009 decision to include sub-surface rights among those claimed by the new self-government opened up this possibility and it was seized upon with governments supporting oil and mineral exploration (see Kuokkanen, 2017; Cambou, 2020). However, as Ulrik Jørgensen documents in his chapter, this independence bargain was essentially rejected once the scale of new mining that would be required to meet the bargain's aim became clear and as a result of the opposition from social actors to one particular mine which has influenced national attitudes towards large-scale mining in general. The role of oil revenues in providing independence from global economic pressures has been an important part of the independence extractive bargain promoted in Mexico as Darcy Tetreault analyses. In fact, there is also a specific context for this in Mexico which extends beyond oil and includes mineral extraction. Mining activity in Mexico was spurred by the relaxation of restrictions on foreign direct investment in the sector which were part of the NAFTA agreement in 1994 (Palma, 2005). Mining was therefore viewed as part of the export-led growth model that Mexico adopted which brought with it the promise of higher living standards. Perhaps ironically, mining was subsequently promoted as a sector which could flourish in the wake of tariffs and a bleaker outlook for the manufacturing sector as fear of a trade war with the U.S. under former President Trump took hold. This led the Mexican state to emphasize mineral extraction as a compensatory mechanism for possible trade disruptions.

In this context, we may view *compensatory bargains* as a particular form of independence bargain. The idea of continued extraction as a compensatory mechanism for externally-induced disruptions has more recently been invoked in parts of the EU as it has sought to respond to the disruptions to its energy supply in the wake of the Russian invasion of Ukraine by increasing its energy independence.

In many countries of the Global South, it is perhaps not surprising to find a *developmentalist bargain* being promoted by states. Revenues from extraction are promoted as providing the means to support broad structural change of the economy thereby facilitating the development transition. This type of reasoning is common to many states which participated in the commodities boom and saw this as a way of becoming developmental states (Ovadia & Nem Singh, 2019). This is most obvious in Africa where, beginning with the Africa Mining Vision in 2009, which represents a regional consensus on effectively utilizing natural resources for development, many states have launched various plans and policies to make extraction provide the most benefit to the state to enable broader development goals to be met (Ovadia, 2016a; Nwapi & Andrews, 2017; Andrews & Nwapi, 2018). However, this comes against the long-standing concerns of limited domestic linkages, labour strife, corruption and environmental degradation. In response, many African states have, with the encouragement of international agencies such as the World Bank, included local content provisions as part of mining licences in an attempt to address the limits of "enclave development" and increase the potential for extractive projects to support broader developmental transitions (Campbell, 2004, 2008). Jesse Salah Ovadia and Maud Esi Amoafo demonstrate this in their chapter on Tanzania. In Ghana, the state only recently developed its oil industry. The responsibility for providing broader benefits was largely delegated to corporations as Moses Adjei and Nathan Andrews document. CSR policies essentially acted as a substitute for the state in constructing an extractive bargain illustrating how state roles can be delegated and subordinated to capital in extractive bargains especially in neoliberal contexts. These developmentalist extractive bargains have nevertheless been questioned given the contested politics and elite instrumentalization that underpin them (see Ovadia, 2016b; Gaynor, 2016; Bebbington et al., 2018; Oppong & Andrews, 2020). The need to address local concerns in the pursuit of extraction-supported state-level developmental goals is central to Jing Vivian Zhan's analysis of the extractive bargain made by the Chinese state. She documents how the central and local states have introduced a battery of regulations designed to ameliorate some of the worst negative consequences of mining on local communities—the "local resource curse" as Zhan calls it—and enhance the economic and social benefits of mining to local communities. The desire to maintain local stability is shared by many states but the specificities of the Chinese political economy mean that the developmentalist bargain to address it is manifested in distinct ways which rely on attempts to find "harmony" by promoting state-capital interactions and 'embedding' extractive capital at the local level. Pursuing a national developmentalist bargain but giving attention to environmental, economic, social and, to a more limited extent, political conditions in resource-rich cities, Zhan shows that even in an authoritarian state like China we can identify elements found in social redistribution bargains.

This review has identified some of many ways in which states have sought to construct extractive bargains to gain support for their extractive policies. The state is the main focus of our book but it is clear that extractive bargains are also sought at different scales of analysis. A participant at the workshop, Sarah Katz-Lavigne noted that subnational bargains in the DR Congo are occurring in a state which has received much attention as the supplier of cobalt to the global market and with instances of elite corruption and state violence well documented. At the local level, however, Katz-Lavigne pointed out that a variety of approaches are taken to the presence of artisanal miners, an often over-looked group in state mining policies. She explained what might be termed *parallel bargains* between local officials, corporations and local miners who operate in a grey legal zone. These parallel bargains complicate the definition of who is bargaining with whom and for whose benefit—further pointing to both the fluid and conflictual nature of bargains.

Extractive bargains can also operate at the global level and in our Chap. 14 we consider what type of global bargains are being considered to accompany the plethora of proposals and policies associated with Green New Deals. We argue that, at the global level, most of the Green New Deal proposals, rely on international *parallel bargains* rather than explicitly calling on new global bargains to accompany a global energy transition. This brief foray into the non-state level raises the interesting question for further research of whether and how different analytical bargains are pursued at different levels of authority within states (particularly relevant for federal states) and at the inter-state level.

There are, therefore, a range of extractive bargains that can be identified. Interestingly, many such as post-extractive and Indigenous-focused bargains, can be found in states located in both the Global North and Global South suggesting that there is scope for common ground and that global forces are producing comparable state-level bargains. However, others, such as developmental bargains are found primarily in the Global South and climate bargains are found primarily in the Global North in our (limited) sample suggesting that the distinction between Global North and Global South still has some analytical purchase. Even here though, it should be noted that the concept of the 'developmental state' has expanded to include states in the Global North attempting a 'green transition' (Bowles, 2020) and so there is also some convergence here as well. It is also interesting, from a comparative perspective, that the same type of analytical bargain can be found under different political regime types; independence bargains in social democratic Greenland and neo-authoritarian Mexico for example. In many cases, extractive bargains take on country specific forms, such as the territorial peace bargain as a form of social redistribution bargain in Colombia. This provides perhaps a unique example of a specific form a more general "ideal type" of bargain but it is also clear that many bargains take particular forms as a result of path dependence and national histories, an observation which is as relevant for countries as diverse as Ghana and Sweden. Taken together, what is striking is that very substantial claims have been made for extractive bargains including meeting climate, redistributive, national development and peace goals. One thing that the bargains all have in common is that they require close scrutiny and assessment; they receive this in the chapters which follow.

Varieties of Extractive Bargains II: Normative Analysis

A variety of extractive bargains can be identified not only in terms of the analytical types discussed above but also in normative terms. That is, the task we have set for this volume is, firstly, to identify and describe the various extractive bargains which states have sought and, secondly, to assess the ability of these bargains to meet the goal of promoting and achieving long-term environmental and social justice. To assess the bargains in this way first requires a closer examination and understanding of the nature of what we have hitherto typically called "extractive activities". More recently, these have been termed "extractivism". This term has been used in a number of different ways as explained by Chagnon et al. (2022). The term has been used to denote a phase of capitalism, a new phase of imperialism, and as form of accumulation distinct in its own workings. Chagnon et al. (2022) see it as an "organizing concept". They argue that "extractivism is based on socio-ecologically destructive processes of subjugation, depletion, and non-reciprocal relations, occurring at all levels of practices. It follows that extractivism is diametrically opposed to the concept and practices of sustainability (including ecological, social, and economic) if that concept is defined through criteria of stewardship, reciprocity, regeneration, and ensuring life for future generations".

This invites, indeed compels, us to examine further the dynamics of extractivism and the roles which particular bargains take in either reinforcing, reforming or replacing those dynamics. To start us on this investigation, Henry Veltmeyer's chapter provides a discussion of extractivism and poses the question of what "extraction after extractivism" might require. How we might get there depends on the starting point, the prospects for forming coalitions in favour of change, and questions of strategy. With respect to the latter, this involves calculations of whether bargains which seek to reform existing practices are sufficient to open spaces for coalition building and to lead to further change or whether they simply tinker around the edges and thereby reinforce existing unsustainable practices by failing to challenge them. The question of strategy also raises the thorny issue of whether and how the state can be used as an instrument for radical transformation and its relation to capital.

To apply this more concretely to the analysis of bargains, and to provide a more fine-grained analysis of them, we have conceptualized a spectrum along which extractive bargains may be found. The spectrum has bargains which provide for long-term environmental and social justice (the "practices of sustainability") at one end and bargains which then move through various degrees of incoherence to short-termism and bargains antithetical to long-term solutions at the other end ("extractivism" as defined by Chagnon et al., 2022). These are ideal types and they vary substantially when examining specific contexts. Yet, they help to frame an understanding of what a normative extractive bargain spectrum might look like as presented in Fig. 1.1.

The *Progressive* normative bargain is one in which extraction takes places in the context of meeting social and environmental justice goals. This may mean that some extractive projects are not undertaken, that a clear path to a just transition is identified and embraced, that extractive activities that are undertaken involve minimized environmental impacts and do not result in "sacrifice zones", that local affected communities are given important mechanisms of control over the activities, the economic benefits of extraction are fairly shared, and that long-term environmental and social sustainability are enhanced.

Constructive bargains are those where many of the elements are in place to achieve a progressive bargain but where some elements are missing and/or institutional designs are inadequate to realize the promise.

Contradictory bargains arise when some elements of a progressive bargain are in place and being implemented but other state policies and practices are working in the opposite direction so that extraction is taking place in a dualistic and contradictory way. Contradictory bargains may arise for several reasons. Firstly, the state, as a heterogeneous entity, may

Progressive **Constructive** **Contradictory** **Faustian**

←environmental and social justice in the long term

Incoherence and short termism→

Fig. 1.1 Normative spectrum of extractive bargains

have actors which are pulling in different directions be they different Ministries, or different branches such as the executive and the judiciary, for example. Secondly, it may be a case of cognitive dissonance where proclaimed goals may be progressive but where the actual practice is at odds with goals. The gap between objectives and practice is so large that it can only be bridged by cognitive dissonance—a failure to recognize the inability of policies to meet stated goals. To the extent that this is a deliberate process, it might also be termed "organized hypocrisy" to borrow a term used by Mörkenstam (2019).

The *Faustian* bargain is one in which a short-term bargain may be made between state elites and other (narrowly or more widely constructed) social groups which supports extractivism in the short term and which also severely compromises or destroys the possibilities for long-term social and environmental justice.

We find this a useful way of thinking about extractive bargains and take it as axiomatic that the goal should be the progressive bargain. However, few if any, states are close to achieving progressive bargains and extractive bargains are found along the spectrum as the case study chapters will show. It is important to locate specific state bargains along the spectrum because this helps in examining the political economy determinants of why the bargain is found at that particular part of the spectrum and what it would take to move in the direction of the progressive end of the spectrum. By political economy determinants, we mean here considerations of, *inter alia*, class interests and power, state composition and autonomy, sectoral composition and coherence, national histories and location in the global political economy, the extent of Indigenous rights, and civil society strength. In the transition from one part of the bargain spectrum to another, more progressive part, it is necessary to examine which actors have the agency and capacity to realize such a movement.

Examining extractive bargains through this normative lens not only enables us to see pathways to progressive bargains but also forces us to ask: Who are the bargains for? Which societal actors are implicitly or explicitly being asked to accept the bargain? and Which actors are excluded from the bargain, that is, are some labour, environmental or Indigenous groups being excluded, for example, or are some concerns, such as the gendered implications of resource projects, being ignored? Once these questions are asked it is also possible to reveal more precisely what type of normative bargain is being advanced. The normative analysis therefore allows authors to assess bargains at the level of the state and to place them on the spectrum indicated in Fig. 1.1 but also allows authors to pinpoint the differences that might be found within any bargain for different societal actors, an exercise useful in itself and important for identifying the challenges that need to be overcome before a coalition for progressive state-level bargains can be forged.

Concluding Remarks

A number of themes emerge from our case studies in terms of the normative analysis. These can be summarized as:

1. Bargains of the same analytical type can range significantly in their normative position. An example of this can be found with Indigenous-focused bargains. In the Canadian case, for example, Atleo and Boron argue that the extractive bargain offered by the settler colonial state has ambiguous implications for Indigenous communities and can, in some circumstances, lead to forms of dispossession. Further along the spectrum, however, Radhuber et al. argue that the constitutionally recognized plural economies approach inspired by Indigenous agendas for plurinational states in Ecuador and Bolivia has the potential to be a progressive bargain, *if* institutional foundations can be established which empower Indigenous nations to have a greater role in practice in the plurinational state.
2. The same bargain can have different normative implications for different groups exposing blind spots or divide and rule strategies. In some cases, we may therefore find that the bargain may seem at the progressive end of the spectrum when judged by the interests of one set of actors but as closer to Faustian when viewed from another. This is indeed exactly the conclusion reached by Beland Lindahl in her chapter when she argues that the Swedish extractive bargain might be viewed as progressive when viewed from the perspective of the working

class but is Faustian for the Sami Indigenous population in a political economy which has a blind spot for Indigenous rights. Mexico offers a similar example where its independence bargain is advantageous to state elites and some sections of organized labour while leaving exposed the local communities on the extractive frontline.

3. The state is a complex institution and contradictory bargains often reveal different positions within the state apparatus which can be used as leverage. There are a number of examples which can be used to illustrate this point. Tanzania uses local content provisions (LCP) to good effect, according to Ovadia and Amoafo, in its quest to extend the industrialization agenda. However, it's Women's Economic Empowerment (WEE) objectives and institutional policy location have not been integrated with the LCPs with the result that women continue to be adversely affected by extractive activities. However, giving greater support for the WEE programme and locating it in economic ministries, would enable the developmentalist extractive bargain to become more progressive. In the case of Colombia, Shenk argues that the contradictions between the Peace Accord and the ownership of sub-surface rights set up inevitable contradictions and a failure to deliver on the empowerment of local communities promised in the Accord. To move the extractive bargain in the progressive direction requires the realignment of sub-surface ownership rights to match the conditions of the Peace Accord. In the Philippines, the contradictions of the extractive bargain, as illustrated by the disjuncture between the Indigenous Peoples' Rights Act and the Mining Act, resemble more an example of "organized hypocrisy" where the possibilities for change appear limited; Iindigenous resistance assisted by the local state and in part validated by the courts has had some success though. In Ghana, the contradictory position of the "privatized developmentalist" bargain points not just to the complexity of the state but to the complexity of state-corporate relations and the need to bring elements of the state back into the bargain.
4. Agency matters and can shift or create bargains in a more progressive direction. The post-extractive bargains analysed by Greene and Carter reveal how the sources of progressive change have both generalizable and country specific elements. The scaling-up and transnational

nature of some movements has been clearly important in some cases while, at the same time, the intervention of some key individuals and organizations whether it be in the executive branch of government, as in France, or in the faith movement, as in Ireland, have been important country specific factors. The ability of the opposition to uranium mining in Greenland, even as a by-product of rare earth extraction, to draw upon the historical record played an important role in its success. In Australia, the Philippines, and South Africa O'Faircheallaigh shows how the different political mobilization capacities of Indigenous communities have led to quite different outcomes arising from the framework for extractive bargains offered by the state.

5. The challenge of extraction beyond extractivism. The case studies presented in this volume provide examples of progressive elements in bargains and highlight some of the obstacles and social forces that must be overcome in order to move contradictory bargains in the progressive direction. However, the possibilities for designing extractive bargains which fully meet the goals of social and environmental justice depend critically on being able to challenge the logic of extractivism. Here, the task appears much more difficult as while it is possible to identify and work towards incremental change, a necessary and important purpose, to realize the transformative extractive bargain implied by the progressive end the normative spectrum poses not just questions of immediate strategy but also of longer-term vision. As Veltmeyer's chapter shows there is no consensus here even in the context of Latin America where the continent has long been subject to extractivism. In other words, moving towards the progressive end of the normative spectrum may become more difficult as more transformative changes are required. It might be argued on the basis of our review of extractive bargains that one point to highlight here is the challenge of integrating ecological and social justice dimensions; few, if any, of the bargains we have enumerated address both dimensions in a systematic way despite the need to do so. The chapters in this volume illustrate how the state can be engaged, challenged and supported to facilitate the movement along the spectrum but fashioning a progressive bargain, and the role that the state can play in this, remains a subject of enduring interest and importance.

To assist us in understanding of the complex ways in which extractive bargains play out on the ground, as it were, we conclude this volume with a set of short observations from experts on the idea and practices of extractive bargains. Contributions are from NGO practitioners, research institute policy analysts and academics with particular areas of interest. Their contributions provide valuable insights into how the idea of extractive bargains is seen on the ground and in specific thematic applications. Raphael Deberdt (IMPACT) and Jeff Geipel (Engineers Without Borders) describe some of their work and campaigns and how bargains are made and are open to contestation in practice. John Hayes and Alem Cherinet provide a perspective as policy analysts. Cliff Atleo writes from his vantage point as a scholar engaged with Indigenous issues and Margot Parkes from her interests in community health and the cumulative impacts of resource projects.

There is much that remains to be further examined using an extractive bargains framework, questions such as, are some bargains more enduring than others? Is there a hierarchy of bargains with some dominating others? Relatedly, are some extractive bargains, such as those based on developmentalism more difficult to confront and change than those based on climate or social redistribution considerations as some of our cases would seem to suggest? Does the calculus of bargains change if a country's extractive sector consists of predominantly nationally owned corporations or multinational corporations? How does the framing of the bargain and its dynamics vary between states with different political systems? What differentiates states in which extractive bargains are evident from those in which they are not? All of these are important questions for further research; we hope that this volume might act as a spur for the utility of posing them.

References

Ali, S. (2022, May 1). The Galapagos bargain: Conservation and the extractive imperative in Ecuador. *Sustainable Community*. Retrieved June 6, 2022, from https://sustainabilitycommunity.springernature.com/posts/the-galapagos-bargain-conservation-and-the-extractive-imperative-in-ecuador

Amsden, A. (1989). *Asia's next giant: South Korea and late industrialization*. Oxford University Press.

Andrews, N. J., Grant, A., & Ovadia, J. S. (Eds.). (2022). *Natural resource-based development in Africa: Panacea or Pandora's box?* University of Toronto Press.

Andrews, N. J., & Nwapi, C. (2018). Bringing the state back in again? The emerging developmental state in Africa's energy sector. *Energy Research & Social Science, 41*, 48–58.

Andrews, N. J., & Siakwah, P. (2021). *Oil and development in Ghana: Beyond the resource curse*. Routledge.

Arboleda, M. (2020). *Planetary mine: Territories of extraction under late capitalism*. Verso.

Bebbington, A., Abdulai, A.-G., Bebbington, D. H., Hinfelaar, M., & Sanborn, C. (2018). *Governing extractive industries: Politics, histories, ideas*. Oxford University Press.

Bebbington, A., Hinojosa, L., Bebbington, D. H., Burneo, M. L., & Warnaars, X. (2008). Contention and ambiguity: Mining and the possibilities of development. *Development and Change, 39*(6), 887–914.

Beland Lindahl, K., Johansson, A., Zachrissen, A., & Viklund, R. (2018). Competing pathways to sustainability? Exploring conflicts over mine establishments in the Swedish mountain region. *Journal of Environmental Management, 218*. https://doi.org/10.1016/j.jenvman.2018.04.063

Bowles, P. (2020). The developmental state and the study of globalizations. *Globalizations, 17*(8), 1421–1438. https://doi.org/10.1080/14747731.2020.1724245

Bowles, P., & MacPhail, F. (2018). Contesting natural resource development in Canada: The legacies and limits of the staples approach. *British Journal of Canadian Studies, 31*(2), 167–180.

Brand, U., Dietz, K., & Lang, M. (2016). Neo-extractivism in Latin America—One side of a new phase of global capitalist dynamics. *Ciencia Política, 11*(21), 125–159.

Bridge, G. (2004). Contested terrain: Mining and the environment. *Annual Review of Environment and Resources, 29*, 205–259.

Cambou, D. C. (2020). Disentangling the conundrum of self-determination and its implications in Greenland. *Polar Record, 56*. https://doi.org/10.1017/S0032247420000169

Campbell, B. (Ed.). (2004). *Regulating mining in Africa—For whose benefit?* Discussion Paper 26. Uppsala: Nordic Africa Institute.

Campbell, B. (2008). Regulation & legitimacy in the mining industry in Africa: Where does Canada stand? *Review of African Political Economy, 35*(117), 367–385.

Cervantes, A. H., & Zalik, A. (2018). Canadian capital and the denationalization of the Mexican energy sector. *Journal of Latin American Geography, 17*(3), 42–72.

Chagnon, C., et al. (2022). From extractivism to global extractivism: The evolution of an organizing concept. *The Journal of Peasant Studies*. Advance online publication. https://doi.org/10.1080/03066150.2022.2069015

Ehrnström-Fuentes, M., & Kröger, M. (2018). Birthing extractivism: The role of the state in forestry politics and development in Uruguay. *Journal of Rural Studies, 57*, 197–208.

Farkes, D. (2015). *Mountain movers: Mining, sustainability and the agents of change*. Routledge.

Gaynor, N. (2016). Challenges to decentralisation in the Democratic Republic of the Congo: Beyond the political settlement. *Journal of International Development, 28*(2), 198–213.

Gilbert, L., & Zalik, A. (2019). The limits of audit culture extractivism: Risk and reinsurance in Canadian oil transport by rail and pipeline. *The Extractive Industries and Society, 6*(3), 654–664.

Gunster, S. (2019, July 2). Extractive populism and the future of Canada. *The Monitor*. Canadian Centre for Policy Alternatives. Retrieved June 6, 2022, from https://policyalternatives.ca/publications/monitor/extractive-populism-and-future-canada

Haley, B. (2011). From staples trap to carbon trap: Canada's peculiar form of carbon lockin. *Studies in Political Economy, 88*(1), 97–132.

Innis, H. A. (1999). *The fur trade in Canada: An introduction to Canadian economic history*. University of Toronto Press.

Kemp, D. (2010). Mining and community development: Problems and possibilities of local-level practice. *Community Development Journal, 45*(2), 198–218.

Kroger, M. (2020). *Iron will: Global extractivism and mining resistance in Brazil and India*. University of Michigan Press.

Kuokkanen, R. (2017). The pursuit of Inuit sovereignty in Greenland. *Northern Public Affairs, 5*(2), 46–49.

Kuokkanen, R. (2019). At the intersection of Arctic indigenous governance and extractive industries: A survey of three cases. *The Extractive Industries and Society, 6*(1), 15–21.

Le Billon, P., & Sommerville, M. (2017). Landing capital and assembling 'investable land' in the extractive and agricultural sectors. *Geoforum, 82*, 212–224.

MacPhail, F., & Bowles, P. (2021). Fractured alliance: State-corporate actions and resistance to fossil fuel development in Northwest British Columbia. *Journal of Political Ecology, 28*(1), 488–510. https://doi.org/10.2458/jpe.2967
Mörkenstam, U. (2019). Organised hypocrisy? The implementation of the international indigenous rights regime in Sweden. *The International Journal of Human Rights, 23*(10), 1718–1741.
Morrison, K. M. (2013). Whither the resource curse? *Perspectives on Politics, 11*(4), 1117–1125.
Nwapi, C., & Andrews, N. J. (2017). A new developmental state in Africa: Evaluating recent state interventions vis-a-vis resource extraction in Kenya, Tanzania, and Rwanda. *McGill Journal of Sustainable Development Law, 13*, 223.
O'Faircheallaigh, C. (2017). *Mining and development: Foreign-financed mines in Australia, Ireland, Papua New Guinea and Zambia*. Routledge.
Oppong, N., & Andrews, N. J. (2020). Extractive industries transparency initiative and the politics of institutional innovation in Ghana's oil industry. *The Extractive Industries and Society, 7*(4), 1238–1245.
Ovadia, J. S. (2016a). Local content policies and petro-development in Sub-Saharan Africa: A comparative analysis. *Resources Policy, 49*, 20–30.
Ovadia, J. S. (2016b). *The petro-developmental state in Africa: Making oil work in Angola, Nigeria and the Gulf of Guinea*. Hurst.
Ovadia, J. S., & Nem Singh, J. T. (Eds.). (2019). *Developmental states beyond East Asia*. Routledge.
Palma, J. G. (2005). The seven main "stylized facts" of the Mexican economy since trade liberalization and NAFTA. *Industrial and Corporate Change, 14*(6), 941–991.
Papyrakis, E. (2017). The resource curse-what have we learned from two decades of intensive research: Introduction to the special issue. *The Journal of Development Studies, 53*(2), 175–185.
Perreault, T. (2022). Extraction and its others. *Latin American Research Review, 57*(3), 708–718. https://doi.org/10.1017/lar.2022.55
Poulantzas, N. (1968). *Political power and social classes*. Verso.
Radcliffe, S. A., & Radhuber, I. M. (2020). The political geographies of D/decolonization: Variegation and decolonial challenges of/in geography. *Political Geography, 78*, 102128.
Radhuber, I. M., & Radcliffe, S. A. (2022). Contested Sovereignties: Indigenous disputes over plurinational resource governance. *Environment and Planning E: Nature and Space*. https://doi.org/10.1177/25148486211068476

Rasch, E. D. (2017). Citizens, criminalization and violence in natural resource conflicts in Latin America. *European Review of Latin American and Caribbean Studies, 103*, 131–142.

Shapiro, J., & McNeish, J.-A. (2021). *Our extractive age: Expressions of violence and resistance*. Routledge.

Svampa, M. (2019). *Neo-extractivism in Latin America: Socio-environmental conflicts, the territorial turn, and new political narratives*. Cambridge University Press.

Veltmeyer, H., & Bowles, P. (2014). Extractivist resistance: The case of the Enbridge oil pipeline project in Northern British Columbia. *The Extractive Industries and Society, 1*(1), 59–68.

Wade, R. (1990). *Governing the market: Economic theory and the role of government in East Asian industrialization*. Princeton University Press.

Williams, A., & Le Billon, P. (Eds.). (2017). *Corruption, natural resources and development: From resource curse to political ecology*. Edward Elgar Publishing.

Willow, A. (2018). *Understanding ExtrACTIVISM: Culture and power in natural resource disputes*. Routledge.

Wilson, E. (2019). What is benefit sharing? Respecting indigenous rights and addressing inequities in Arctic resource projects. *Resources, 8*(2), 74.

Winato, P., & Diprose, R. (2020). Reordering the extractive political settlement: Resource nationalism, domestic ownership and transnational bargains in Indonesia. *The Extractive Industries and Society, 7*(4), 1534–1546.

2

From Extractivism to Sustainability: Scenarios and Lessons from Latin American

Henry Veltmeyer

Introduction

Natural resource extraction, or extractivism as it is now referred to in the literature, has long been a key factor in both the economic development strategies pursued by governments as a means of expanding the forces of production and as a modality of capital accumulation. But in recent years, with the advent of a neoliberal world order based on the perceived virtues of free market capitalism and a major primary commodities boom, this resource-based approach towards development has become the subject of an extended ongoing debate. At the centre of this debate are what have been theorised as various contradictory features of capitalist systems that are manifest in a systemic propensity towards crisis and the current multidimensional crisis which has reached global proportions

H. Veltmeyer (✉)
Universidad Autónoma de Zacatecas, Zacateca, Mexico

P. Bowles, N. Andrews (eds.), *Extractive Bargains*, Frontiers of Globalization,
https://doi.org/10.1007/978-3-031-32172-6_2

(Petras & Veltmeyer, 2013).[1] At issue in the debates that have surrounded these 'contradictions' are certain dynamics associated with forces of development and resistance that can be traced out in different regional and local contexts, particularly in Latin America on the periphery of the world system where these dynamics have played out most clearly. In the current era of sustainable development policies, socio-environmental conflicts involving multiple actors—including governments, local communities, indigenous populations, national or transnational companies, international organisations and NGOs and academic organisations—more than ever before are at the centre of the development agenda both in Latin America and elsewhere in the world system.

The purpose of this chapter is to explicate some of these development dynamics—particularly in regard to what has been described as the post-extractivist transition—a transition towards a more sustainable and inclusive form of national development. The argument advanced with respect to this 'development' and associated dynamics is constructed as follows. *Firstly*, I trace out the evolution of natural resource extraction as a development strategy, from an initial phase of European colonialism and extractive imperialism in the Americas at the turn into the fifteenth century to what Lenin, at the turn into the twentieth century, viewed as the most advanced stage of capitalist development—imperialism. Imperialism, as understood by Lenin, refers here to state power at the service of Capital—actions taken by the State to promote and advance the capitalist development of the forces of production. From there the chapter turns to the current neoliberal era of capitalist development characterised by the advance of resource-seeking 'extractive' capital (investments in the large-scale acquisition of land and the extraction of natural resources to the purpose of exporting them to capitalist markets in primary commodity form). *Secondly*, I trace out the diverse interpretations and different schools of thought on the contemporary dynamics of capitalist development, and the actions (the investment and extractive operations, and related public policies) taken on these ideas by the

[1] Although Harvey has identified 17 such contradictions, there is a broad consensus in regard to the particular relevance of the exploitative capital-labour relation: the centre-periphery structure of international relations; and the society-ecology relation in what Foster (2002), after Marx, describes as a 'metabolic rift'.

agencies and agents of capitalist development. These actions implicate both the multinational corporations in the extractive sector and a number of governments, mostly in South America, that have been at the centre of different experiments in neodevelopmentalism and post-development. *Thirdly*, I seek to decipher and reconstruct the dynamic relationships formed among the main stakeholders in the search for a more inclusive and sustainable form of resource-based development in the context of a process of active negotiation among the actors and stakeholder groups in the development process. The chapter concludes with several reflections on the fate of extractivism in what has been described (Gudynas, 2013) as the 'post-extractive transition' towards a more inclusive and sustainable form of post-neoliberal socialist development—the socialism of the twenty-first century, based on community-based development or communalism, as well as social and environmental justice, and respect for both human rights and those of nature ('living well', or *buen vivir*, in Andean cosmology). On this see García Linera (2013), Ranta (2018), and various contributors to *Pluriverse. A Post-development Dictionary*.

Extractivism as Imperialism and Capitalism

Extractivism—or extractivisms, as Gudynas (2017) would have it—can be traced back at least as far as the 1970s as a means of describing current developments in the mining and oil export sectors, primarily in Latin America. Although Chiasson-Lebel (2016), in a systematic review of the literature on extractivism and what is understood in the Latin American context as neoextractivism, notes that one of its very first appearances in academic and political discourse was in Bunker (1984). In any case, Gudynas notes that the term *extractivism* is promoted by large transnational corporations in what we would today describe as the 'extractive sector' of capitalist development (mining for minerals and metals, drilling for fossil fuels, etc.), as well as by multilateral banks and governments. However, groups and organisations in civil society, as well as environmentalists and political activists opposed to extractivism as a model of national development because of its negative and destructive social and environmental impacts, have also embraced the term. This scenario became more complex as of the mid-2000s, particularly in South America, where a series of left-leaning 'progressive' (post-neoliberal) governments formed in what has been described as a 'pink tide' of progressive regime change, opted for extractivism as a development strategy based on the extraction of minerals and fossil fuels and agri-food products, the exportation of these 'natural resources' in primary commodity form, and the channelling of the additional fiscal resources generated by export sales into a neodevelopmentalist neoextractive programme based on a social policy of poverty reduction (Svampa, 2019).

In the context of these developments—that is, the advance of resource-seeking *extractive* capital, a primary commodities boom in capitalist markets, and the emergence of a cycle of left-leaning 'progressive' policy regimes—the literature on extractivism and neoextractivism, grew very rapidly. For some years, these studies focused mostly on the 'extractive industries' associated with the mining of industrial minerals and the production of fossil fuels (oil and gas), but recently the concept of extractivism has been extended to the agricultural sector (agriculture understood broadly to include not only the harvesting of agri-food products but also logging and fish farming)—hence the recent concern with the development and resistance dynamics of agro-extraction or agroextractivism in the form of uni- or flex-crop plantation agriculture (McKay et al., 2021). Thus, the mining of fossil fuels or hydrocarbon forms of energy and plantation agri-food production constitute what economists regard as the extractive sector of the economy, whose development and resistance dynamics have been the object of study and major concern of both scholars and activists in the field of international development studies as well as political economy and social ecology. As discussed below, this concern is with the development and resistance dynamics of extractivism and capitalist development in the Global South on the periphery of what has been described as the 'world capitalist system' (Araghi, 2010).

Development and Resistance Dynamics of Extractivism

Extractivism, as we have come to understand it, that is, as a way of understanding development, can be traced back to the onset of European colonialism in the so-called New World of the Americas—the accumulation of state-sponsored merchant capital, or mercantilism, based on the pillage of precious metals (gold and silver) and plantation agriculture, and the transfer of this wealth of natural resources to the imperial centre to provide the financial resources needed to sustain both the state and the privileges of the ruling class. On the evolution of the mercantile era of extractivist imperialism and European colonialism see Girvan (2014).

With the advent of industrial capitalism in the nineteenth century—a 'development' predicated on the enclosure of the commons and the dispossession and proletarianisation of the peasantry—we can trace out a second phase in the capitalist development of the forces of production and a corresponding advance in the forces of resistance. Lenin dubbed this phase of capitalist development as the most advanced form of capitalism (= imperialism), characterised by the fusion of financial and industrial capital, the export of capital from the centre to the periphery of the world system, a territorial division of the world by the European capitalist powers led by the British imperial state, and an unequal exchange of natural resources in primary commodity form for industrial goods manufactured in the centre, what Latin American theorists in the post–Second World War would later conceive of as 'dependency theory' (Borón, 2008).

The third development-resistance cycle—'developmentalism'—unfolded in the wake of the Second World War under the aegis of the 'developmental state'. It was characterised by the accumulation and advance of industrial capital, the dispossession and proletarianisation of the peasantry, which led to the formation of a reserve army of surplus agricultural labour. The subsequent resistance and activism of the semiproletariat of rural landless workers (what was left of the peasantry on the Latin American periphery of the system) in the form of peasant-led and-based social movements led to the delegitimation and widespread rejection of neoliberalism in the 1990s in the Latin American periphery (on these dynamics see, inter alia, Petras & Veltmeyer, 2013). The fourth and latest development-resistance cycle was characterised by the expansion of resource-seeking 'extractive' capital in the development process, the emergence and formation (in South America) of a series of left-leaning 'progressive' (postneoliberal) policy regimes oriented towards 'neodevelopmentalism'[2] and 'neoextractivism', and the mobilisation of diverse forces of resistance by the communities on the extractive frontier of capitalist development[3]—resistance that took the multiple form of socioecological 'subterranean' localised movements mobilised by the destructive impacts of extractivism on livelihoods and the life-support ecosystem, and by violation of their human and territorial rights (Zibechi, 2012).

The advance of extractive capital and the extractivist dynamic of the development process (extractivism as a strategy of economic development), should be understood in its international, regional, and local contexts. In this regard, 'development' of the forces of production hinges on the complex set of political relationships formed between the companies in the extractive sector of capitalist development, the State (governments) formed in this process, and the local communities, both indigenous and non-indigenous—the major stakeholders, one might argue. With reference to the complexity of these political relationships there is considerable debate surrounding the dynamics involved in the advance of extractivism in the development process. With reference to this debate in this chapter we argue that this advance hinges on two major developments: the inclusionary activism of the state (what was once understood as developmentalism); and the state's capacity to negotiate a deal and come to terms with the forces of popular resistance against the advance of

[2] Neodevelopmentalism refers to a policy regime, designed by economists at the Economic Commission for Latin America and the Caribbean (ECLAC), of poverty reduction and inclusive development (Bresser-Pereira, 2007).

[3] The extractive frontier encompasses both the extractive industries formed in the process of capitalist development— the central concern of this chapter—and the local communities impacted by the operations of the companies that make up these industries. However, there is another dimension to this development process that falls outside the scope of this chapter: the illicit extractive economies formed in the underground of the capitalist development process, the economies based on the illicit industries of fishing, logging and mining, and the cultivation of coca, opium and other drug-producing crops. On the complex and variegated development dynamics of this underground economy, and its connections to the capitalist development and state formation process see Gutierrez (2021).

extractive capital. In the current context this implies a capacity of state officials and agents to come to terms with both the widespread rejection of the neoliberal agenda resulting from the activism of the peasant and indigenous movements in the 1990s (on this see, inter alia, Petras & Veltmeyer, 2013) and the community-based resistance on the extractive frontier. More specifically, the advance of extractivism, or neoextractivism, in the development process requires the active engagement of the State with both the companies and the local communities, that is, with the forces of capitalist development and the resistance in a process of negotiation in search of an extractive bargain (Bowles & Andrews, 2022).

Strategic Dimensions of Capital's Extractive Bargains

The advance of extractive capital in the development process is the result of different strategies pursued and actions taken to mobilise the forces of development and the resistance. This process implicates and engages three main sets of actors, namely, (1) organisations of monopoly capital in the form of the large multinational capitalist corporations that dominate the global economy and manage the productive process and the extractive industries, provide the needed investment capital, and operate the mines and other the extractive projects; (2) the governments that have legal and technical jurisdiction over the indigenous territories where many of the extractive projects are located, and thus are responsible for providing the companies an operating license and to regulate the industry and the production operations of the companies;[4] and (3) the communities that are strategically located on the waterways and the land underlying which are located the resources slated for extraction, exploitation and commercialisation. These three sets of 'actors' in diverse contexts are enmeshed in a complex web of dynamic social, production and

[4] A regulatory regime typically includes the requirement of an environmental assessment, a contract that lays out certain rules regarding the distribution of the surplus—profit, resource rent—between capital and the State, engagement of the communities affected, and protective measures regarding the environment, labour and so on.

political relationships that come into play at various stages of the extraction and production process.

Within this dynamic complex of relationships on the extractive frontier the State has jurisdiction and has generally assumed the right and responsibility of regulating the resource development process in which it necessarily has to engage both the companies and the local communities for the purpose of generating the fiscal revenues needed to finance government programmes of social and economic development. In doing so, if the governments formed on the Latin American periphery in the latest primary commodities boom on capitalist markets (Ocampo, 2007) are to serve as a reference point and guide, a coincidence of economic interest between the companies and the governments (windfall profits for the former, additional fiscal revenues for the latter) has generally led the government to take the side of the companies in their relation of political conflict with the local communities that are negatively impacted by their extractive operations. Studies of these dynamics have shown that this applies not only to governments such as those in Colombia and Mexico, which have continued to hoe the neoliberal line, but even the most 'progressive' post-neoliberal regimes such as Ecuador and Bolivia in the vanguard of transformative change and post-development.

Within the institutional and policy framework of the capitalist system, the resource extraction and development process hinges on the capacity of the multinational corporations in the sector to obtain from the governments that have jurisdiction over the extraction of natural resources a permit and concession to implement its extractive projects, which, by all accounts, is easily enough obtained, and from the communities implicated and impacted by these extractive operations, a social licence, which by many accounts, given the power in many cases of the resistance, is not so easily obtained. However, with the support and considerable resources of the imperial state at the centre of the system, and the dependence of the host governments on foreign investment and operating capital—the 'new dependency', as Borón (2008) and Sotelo (2009) see it—the companies overall have generally managed to advance and successfully implement their extractive projects.

The main strategy used by the companies over the past two decades to obtain both a political and social licence is a programme of corporate social responsibility (CSR), designed for corporate self-regulation related to a model of 'inclusive growth' (Sagebien & Lindsay, 2011). The CSR programme was designed specifically as a counterweight and alternative to the model of state-regulated 'inclusive development' designed by economists at CEPAL armed with a neostructuralist understanding of the development process.

The varying assessments that have been made of the CSR scheme in diverse contexts over at least two decades point towards a very mixed record and no clear indication as to the overall impact of CSR on obtaining the support of the communities and overcoming their resistance. But some research on this question (see Conde & Le Billon, 2017) suggests that poorly designed and implemented CSR activities potentially increase frustrations and distrust, which can constitute a source of further resistance, especially when they follow confrontational events during which a company had lost its legitimacy. With the ever-increasing exchange of information across networks and alliances, communities today are also frequently questioning the merits of the extractive 'development' model, its destructive impact on rural livelihoods and territorial rights, their lack of participation, and the CSR and compensation schemes and negative impact of mitigation measures offered by the mining companies. This suggests that the critical factor in regard to the question as to whether and which communities resist and which do not is not the actual strategy pursued by the companies but the context for this deployment, including here the prevalence of neoliberalism as an ideology and policy agenda, the power imbalance between companies and communities, and distributive inequities in the share of national production. The relevant point is that because of a coincidence of economic interest in almost all cases of political conflict between these two 'actors' the State invariably takes the side of the companies. Notorious instances of this truism are the cases of the left-leaning 'progressive' governments of Evo Morales in Bolivia and Rafael Correa in Ecuador. In both cases indigenous leaders and environmental activists in a series of confrontations and resource conflicts were branded as 'environmental terrorists' who are prepared to sacrifice the country's development prospects on the altar of political principle.

In any case, there is no question that the CSR strategy has served the international capitalist class well, although in a number of contexts it manifestly failed to overcome community resistance and the strategy might have reached the limits of its functionality vis-à-vis the dynamic of community-based resistance.

It is apparent that to overcome this and other forms and instances of community resistance the operating agents of extractive capitalism have searched for and experimented with other innovative counter-resistance strategies. Fernando Leiva (2022) and his associates have conducted some preliminary research on these innovations in the context of Chile, where extractive capital has shown itself to be surprisingly resilient in finding innovative ways of defeating community-based resistance. This has included the design and implementation of a new round of strategic measures that have led to a degree of local socio-cultural embedding of corporate capital, the dynamics of which have not only increased the bargaining power of the companies vis-à-vis the local communities but to some extent has allowed the companies to replace the State as the agency primarily responsible for not only securing legitimacy and social cohesion but also territorial management.

As noted above, the CSR programme and subsequent innovations seem to have generally served the companies well as a means of gaining access to the natural resources slated for extraction, exploitation and commercialisation. However, they have not served so well as a way of improving the situation of developing countries in the development process—to help place them on the road towards 'another development', a new world of social and environmental justice in which everyone can 'live well' in social solidarity and harmony with nature. To embark on this road—and navigate the post-extractivist transition—evidently requires a more complicated process of bargaining among the stakeholder groups; for the State and the local communities to achieve a better deal in their bargaining with Capital, with the State normally taking the lead.

Each of the three major groups of stakeholders in maximising the benefits and opportunities provided by an extractive model of national development have chips to put on the bargaining table—authorised access to the resources, in the case of the State; approval or acquiescence to the implementation of extractive projects, in the case of the communities; and exploitation of the resource and its commercialisation, in the case of the companies. However, the actual form of the extractive bargain sought and obtained, and the final outcome in terms of advancing extractivism in the development process and achieving progress in the form of economic development or reaching a 'new green deal' is often problematic, reflecting the relative bargaining power of the players. For example, in 2009 when the 'progressive' government formed by Rafael Correa in Ecuador sought to bargain with Chinese and Thai oil corporations over credits to be repaid with oil, the Asian companies ended up taking a large part of Ecuadorian crude exports in exchange for pouring a significant amount of foreign exchange into the state's coffers, but the deal jeopardised long-term development opportunities. (Orozco, 2018; Valencia, 2015).

Another issue is whether the communities in their bargaining with the companies can lever their stake in the resource extraction process to strike a favourable deal as an alternative to resistance and conflict. In this regard, many analysts, particularly those who approach the problem from a critical development perspective, fail to appreciate that in a not insignificant number of cases community leaders are generally concerned not only with protecting the ecosystem and preserving their cultural heritage and habitat from the negative socioecological impacts of extractivism, but they are often equally concerned to derive a share in the presumed or possible benefits. Hence, these leaders in many cases with this concern tend to strike a hard bargain, a good deal for the community in a process described by the editors of this book as 'extractive bargaining' and by Conde and Le Billon (2017) as 'community-driven participation'.

The point is that company-community relations should not be viewed solely through the prism of political conflict, but also as a process of active negotiation and bargaining. In this context (see McNeish, 2012) many communities seem to welcome the development and employment opportunities promised by the mining companies, even at the price of the associated dependency or the support of their negotiating partners. For example, McNeish (2012), in a study of community-company dynamics points to the evolving colonial nature and 'militant pragmatism' that sometimes (often?) drives community leaders to seek dialogue and negotiated settlements with the mining company as an alternative to resistance.

Several analytical probes into the dynamics of this bargaining process have allowed us to discern some dominant features and patterns. For one thing, it is evident that the companies have generally had greater success in negotiating a deal with the governments than with the communities, which reflects the greater bargaining power of the companies in their relationship with the often all-too-compliant governments. The latter's bargaining position is often compromised by their dependence on companies for capital, technology and marketing and governments acquiesce all too often at the expense of the communities.

Strategising the Post-extractive Transition

In the search for alternatives in the direction of sustainable resource development, both researchers and activists who are understandably concerned to move beyond the contradictions of capital and the destructive socioecological impacts of extractivism, and government officials in pursuit of an extractive bargain that would allow them to advance their development agenda, are very much divided on the question as to whether extractivism has a role to play in what Eduardo Gudynas among others have described as the post-extractivist transition towards a more inclusive, equitable and sustainable future.

Coinciding with the view of those engaged in the resistance struggle, many activist scholars concerned with the design for a post-development 'pluriverse' and what Escobar describes as 'new ecologies for the 21st Century', have reached a virtual consensus on the need to move beyond extractivism as a modality and condition of capitalist development (Kothari et al., 2012). But the unsettled question remains as to whether extractivism has a role to play in what is bound to be a very narrow pathway in the post-extractivist transition—a transition that by some accounts given by these scholars will have to be navigated within a hybrid institutional and policy framework that combines elements of both capitalism and socialism—the 'socialism of the 21st century', as some (echoing Hugo Chávez) have argued.

We can identify three basic positions on this question of a post-extractive transition—extraction after extractivism, as it were. One is associated with the policy forums, foundations and think tanks constructed by the guardians of the capitalist system. The concern and role of these forums and organisations, whose scale of operations are commensurate with the globalising dynamics of capitalism, is to secure and guarantee the stable functioning of the capitalist world system, providing the world order with a source of legitimacy as well as rules of governance. Today there exist a myriad of such organisations, including international financial institutions such as the World Bank that are rooted in and committed to disseminating a belief in the virtues of free market capitalism (neoliberalism)—the ideological foundation of the new world order established in the 1980s as a means of liberating the 'forces of freedom' (capitalism, the market) from the regulatory constraints of the development state.

In regard to the dynamics of extractive capitalism in the current era, the guardians of the world capitalist system, armed with this ideology, constructed both a set of rules and principles governing international relations, as well as a theoretical model of 'inclusive growth' based on the agency of the private sector—mining companies and other multinational corporations in the extractive sector. For an example of this model, elaborated in a global network of right-wing policy forums, see Canada, House of Commons (2012). This model, used to guide public policy and international relations regarding mining and resource development, is predicated on the idea that a developing society's natural resource wealth provides unparalleled economic opportunities for expanding production and generating a process of sustainable and inclusive growth.

A second position on the future of extractivism is that it is more of a curse than a blessing (Acosta, 2009). This idea has led to a debate among economists regarding extractivism as a 'resource curse',[5] but it has been articulated most clearly and forcefully by a coalition formed by various regional and a global network of indigenous communities, environmental activists and researchers in the tradition of critical development studies. The position taken by these groups is that the contradictions of

[5] The notion of a 'resource curse' (see Acosta, 2009) refers to the fact that so many resource-rich countries are developmentally poor compared to resource-poor countries whose wealth depends on manufacturing and industries. Diverse explanations are given to explain this phenomenon, including the fact that resource extraction in many contexts supports just 1 direct job and 16 indirect jobs per million dollars of output compared to 25 direct and 22 indirect jobs for manufacturing (Morley, 2017). That is, manufacturing has a distinct comparative advantage over extractivism as a development pathway.

capital, especially the society-ecology contradiction, provide an insurmountable obstacle to the possibility of carving out a pathway towards sustainable and inclusive development. Extractivism as we have come to know it, that is, as a modality of development in which profits are inevitably placed before people, in this view is inherently unsustainable.

Extractivism, like capitalism in its origins and subsequent evolution as a world system, has functioned as a contemporary form of enclosure, denying local inhabitants and communities access to the commons, serving as a mechanism of dispossession—'accumulation by dispossession' as Harvey (2003) has it—resulting in the forced displacement of large contingents of the rural poor and what remains of the traditional peasantry of small-scale independent producers who have been forced to migrate in the search of an alternative way of life based on labour rather than agriculture. If this 'development', and the negative socioecological conditions of extractivism that have brought it about, are viewed as the price of progress, the inevitable costs of development as the ideologues of capitalism, neoliberalism and extractivism admit, then they cannot be mitigated or managed, not even by a turn away from fossil fuels towards renewable resources and 'green technologies'. The associated costs, which are disproportionately borne by the rural poor and the communities on the extractive frontier, exceed by far any perceived benefits, which moreover are highly concentrated, benefiting primarily the capitalist enterprises in the extractive sector for whom the natural resource wealth extracted from indigenous territories is a source of windfall profits.

A third perspective on this question (the fate of extractivism in a post-neoliberal transition) is that there is indeed a role for extractivism in this transition, but that it is contingent on the construction by developing societies on the periphery of the world system of a new industrial and energy policy that is respectful of both the territorial rights of the indigenous communities on the extractive frontier—and what these communities, self-identified as custodians of Nature or Mother Earth, understand as the 'rights of nature'.

The conclusion drawn by Nem Singh and Bourgouin (2013), and other researchers looking into the possible retention of extractivism in an alternative model of sustainable development—for example, Moreno-Brid and Garry (2022) and Puyana (2022)—is that it is not only possible but indeed necessary to combine a new industrial and energy policy designed for a more sustainable and inclusive form of capitalist development with a progressive regime of natural resource extraction—neoextractivism, as we have come to understand it (Svampa, 2019).

At issue in the argument advanced by these friendly critics of extractivism is the question of how and under what conditions to secure the insertion of Latin America and other peripheral regions into the global value chains of the extractive industries formed in the advance of extractive capital in the development process. Gereffi (2018), in this regard, in his book *Global Value Chains and Development* (pp. 11–13, 44–49) compares the differences in the way Latin America and East Asia were inserted in the global value chains of diverse extractive industries. Resource-rich Latin America, he notes, was inserted through production-driven value chains where the idea is to promote state expansion in domestic markets. Resource-poor East Asia, by contrast was incorporated through buyer-driven commodity chains. Consequently, these avenues of incorporation produced very different state-business relations, which for Gereffi explains the differential successes of the two regions in combining extractivism with industrialism as a way of transforming extractivism into a model of sustainable development.

Gereffi and Nem Singh, like Moreno-Brid and Garry (2022) and Puyana (2022) in the Mexican context, argue the need to combine extractivism with new industrial and energy policies that take advantage of the region's natural resource wealth while mitigating the destructive aspects of extractivism by substituting renewable resources for fossil fuels, incorporating advanced 'green' technologies, and the active engagement of local communities in the development process. This proposed solution to the extractivist problematic hinges on the ability of companies to negotiate technology transfers and to innovate and combine indigenous and the most advanced 'green' technologies, and for the governments to provide an appropriate institutional and policy framework for the extraction and sustainable development of natural resources—which for many activist scholars entails a new form of socialism—and their incorporation into an effective strategy of sustainable resource-based industrialisation.

Nevertheless, there is no consensus on this issue of continued resource extraction in the post-extractive 'green' transition. For example, Gudynas in his many writings has articulated an alternative dissenting view (e.g. see Gudynas, 2013, 2017). Gudynas argues in a Latin America committed to the goal of social and environmental justice that there is no place for extractivism as we have come to know it, that is, as a modality of capital accumulation and development.

His point is that no matter what policy and institutional reforms are put into place, the systemic workings of extractive capitalism, as well as its local impacts and spillover effects on public policies, are simply incompatible with the goals of social equity and environmental justice. On the other hand, this does not mean that there is no role for natural resource extraction in the transition towards a more socially inclusive and sustainable alternative future. On this point, he argues that it is important to clearly distinguish between extractivism as a modality of capital accumulation and economic activities and practices such as mining and agriculture on the one hand—and the appropriation of renewable natural resources under conditions of respect for both territorial rights and the right of communities to sustainable livelihoods on the other. For example, not all mining is extractivism as we know it, that is, as a mode of appropriation and profit-making within the institutional and policy dynamics of the capitalist system. Nor does resource extraction, or the appropriation of Latin America's natural resource wealth, necessarily entail the predatory practices—the usurpation of the lands and lives of the indigenous population—associated with extractivism in the Latin American context. Indeed, in the post-extractivist transition and beyond there is undoubtedly a place for some forms of sustainable natural resource extraction involving mining and agriculture/forestry, fish farming, and maybe even some types of hydrocarbon exploitation.

In lieu of a Conclusion: Whither Extractivism?

To end this brief excursus into extractivism, I conclude that what is needed is a closer look at the development and social dynamics of natural resource extraction, and further research into these dynamics from a critical development perspective. However, in consideration of the preponderance of the evidence provided by different studies, and mindful of the complexity and diversity of these extractivisms, it is possible to come to several tentative conclusions.

Given that dependence on the extraction of natural resources seems inevitable from a short- and even medium-term perspective, commodity-based economies will face the need to increase the sustainability and productivity of their extractive sectors, a very tall order under the circumstances and only possible in the context of a post-extractivist transition towards what Gudynas describes as the 'new extractivism of the 21st century'.

Many countries in the current context have failed to strike a balance between the purported economic and fiscal benefits of extractive industry growth and the heavy social and environmental costs in terms of environmental degradation, community displacement and social conflict, all of which are particularly acute at the local level.

Extractivism is an indissoluble part of today's varieties of capitalism, but as a modality of capitalist development it cannot provide a pathway towards another world of inclusive, equitable and sustainable development. A pathway towards an alternative more inclusive and sustainable form of post-development will not only require a new 'green deal' and a 'progressive' extractive bargain that fully engages the major stakeholders in the development process but a revolutionary transformation of both society and development on a global scale. This is because of an inherent contradiction to working within systems to counter the injustices and damages they cause. It will also require the agency and mobilisation of the diverse forces of resistance on both the extractive frontier and the broader political front and include the protagonism of the communities negatively impacted by the advances of extractive capital in the development process. The communities on the extractive frontier, both indigenous and non-indigenous, will need to be an integral part of any proposed solution to the extractivist problematic of capitalist development, to find a way out of the current crisis and chart a new course towards the new extractivism of the twenty-first century.

References

Acosta, A. (2009). *La maldición de la abundancia*. Ediciones Abya-Yala.

Araghi, F. (2010). Accumulation by displacement, global enclosures, food crisis and the economic contradictions of capitalism. *Review, 32*(1), 113–146.

Borón, A. (2008). Teorías de la dependencia, *Realidad Económica*, No. 238, agosto-septiembre.

Bresser-Pereira, L. C. (2007). Estado y Mercado en el Nuevo Desarrollismo, *Nueva Sociedad*, No. 210, Julio–Agosto.

Bowles, P., & N. Andrews. (2022). "Global Extractive Bargains for Green New Deals," Workshop 'Extractive Bargains: States, Natural Resources and the (Elusive) Search for Consensus,' UNBC, Prince George, British Colombia. May 5–6.

Bunker, S. G. (1984). Modes of extraction, unequal exchange, and the progressive underdevelopment of an extreme periphery: The Brazilian Amazon, 1600–1980. *American Journal of Sociology, 89*(5), 1017–1064.

Canada, House of Commons. (2012). *Driving inclusive economic growth: The role of the private sector in international development*. Report of the Standing Committee on Foreign Affairs and International Development, House of Commons, November. Ottawa: Public Works and Government Services.

Chiasson-Lebel, T. (2016). Neo-extractivism in Venezuela and Ecuador: A weapon of class conflict. *The Extractive Industries and Society, 3*(4).

Conde, M., & Le Billon, P. (2017). Why do some communities resist mining projects while others do not? *The Extractive Industries and Society, 4*.

Foster, J. B. (2002). Capitalism and ecology: The nature of the contradiction. *Monthly Review, 54*(4), 6–16.

García Linera, Á. (2013). Once again on so-called extractivism. *Monthly Review*, April 29, pp. 1–9.

Gereffi, G. (2018). *Global value chains and development: Redefining the contours of 21st century capitalism*. Cambridge University Press.

Girvan, N. (2014). Extractive imperialism in historical perspective. In J. Petras & H. Veltmeyer (Eds.), *Extractive Imperialism in the Americas*. Brill Books.

Gudynas, E. (2013). Transitions to post-extractivism: Directions, options, areas of action. In *Beyond development: Alternative visions from Latin America* (pp. 165–188). Transnational Institute.

Gudynas, E. (2017). Value, growth, development: South American lessons for a new ecopolitics. *Capitalism, Nature, Socialism, 30*(2), 1–10.

Gutierrez, E. (2021). The Paradox of Illicit Economies: How opium and coca transform agrarian markets, violence, and state formation in the developing world. PhD dissertation, Den Haag: Erasmus University Rotterdam's International Institute of Social Studies (EUR-ISS).

Harvey, D. (2003). *The new imperialism*. Oxford University Press.

Kothari, A., Salleh, A., Escobar, F. D., & Acosta, A. (Eds.). (2012). *Pluriverse. A post-development dictionary*. Tulika Books.

Leiva, F. (2022). Beyond corporate social responsibility: New territorial management strategies for defeating community-based resistance to extractivism. In H. Veltmeyer, & A. Ezquerro-Cañete, Eds.

McKay, B., Alonso-Fredejas, A., & Ezquerro-Cañete, A. (Eds.). (2021). *Agrarian extractivism in Latin America*. Routledge.

McNeish, J. A. (2012). More than beads and feathers: Resource extraction and the indigenous challenge in Latin America: New political spaces in Latin American Natural Resource Governance. In H. Haarstad (Ed.), *New political spaces in Latin American natural resource governance*. Palgrave Macmillan.

Moreno-Brid, J. C., & Garry, S. (2022). Challenges to transform extractivism into a progressive development path. In H. Veltmeyer & A. Ezquerro-Cañete (Eds.), *Extractive capitalism and resistance dynamics: Alternative scenarios from Latin America*. Routledge.

Morley, J. (2017). 'Beggars sitting on a sack of gold': Oil exploration in the Ecuadorian Amazon as Buen Vivir and sustainable development. *The International Journal of Human Rights, 21*(4), 405–441.

Nem Singh, J., & Bourgouin, F. (Eds.). (2013). *Resource governance and developmental states in the global south: Critical international political economy perspectives* (International Political Economy). Palgrave Macmillan.

Ocampo, J. A. (2007, December). The macroeconomics of Latin America's economic boom. *CEPAL Review, 93*.

Orozco, M. (2018). Ecuador vendió incluso el petróleo que no tenía en 2016. *El Comercio*, February 14. https://www.elcomercio.com/actualidad/ecuador-venta-petroleo-petrotailandia-petroecuador.html

Petras, J., & Veltmeyer, H. (2013). *Imperialism and capitalism in the 21st century: A system in crisis*. Ashgate.

Puyana, A., & Rodriguez Peña, I. (2022). The green energy transition: Expansion and intensification of extractivism. In H. Veltmeyer & A. Ezquerro-Cañete, Eds. (2022). *Extractive capitalism and resistance dynamics: Alternative scenarios from Latin America*. Routledge.

Ranta, E. (2018). *Vivir Bien as an alternative to neoliberal globalization*. Routledge.

Sagebien, J., & Lindsay, N. (2011). *Governance ecosystems: CSR in the Latin American mining sector*. Palgrave Macmillan.

Sotelo, A. (2009). Neo-imperialismo, dependencia e novas periferias. *A América Latina e os desafios da globalização*. Boitempo.

Svampa, M. (2019). *Neo-extractivism in Latin America: Socio-environmental conflicts, the territorial turn, and new political narratives*. Cambridge University Press.

Valencia, A. (2015). UPDATE 1-Ecuador signs $2.5 bln. oil supply deal with Thailand. *Reuters*, July 31. https://www.reuters.com/article/ecuador-petroecuador/update-1-ecuador-signs-2-5-bln-oil-supply-dealwith-thailand-idUSL1N10B2TA20150731

Zibechi, R. (2012). Territories in resistance. In *A cartography of Latin American social movements*. AK Press.

3

Extractive Bargains and Indigenous Peoples: A Comparative Perspective

Ciaran O'Faircheallaigh

Introduction

Applying the 'Extractive Bargains' framework developed by the editors (Bowles and Andrews, Chap. 1 this volume) to relations between states and Indigenous peoples reveals significant complexities. The first arises from the fact that the typology focuses on state policies and actions, as they have 'sought to construct extractive bargains which are designed to convince their citizens that continuing, expanding and even decreasing natural resource extraction can bring valuable societal benefits while minimizing the potential negative effects'. As the editors acknowledge the support for and/or opposition to bargains of societal actors 'condition the potential of bargains to remain intact or to shift over time' and, I would add, condition the potential for the state to achieve its desired bargain in the first place. In some contexts, Indigenous peoples have in fact refused to accept the bargain offered by the state and achieved a different result

C. O'Faircheallaigh (✉)
Griffith University, Brisbane, QLD, Australia
e-mail: ciaran.ofaircheallaigh@griffith.edu.au

P. Bowles, N. Andrews (eds.), *Extractive Bargains*, Frontiers of Globalization,
https://doi.org/10.1007/978-3-031-32172-6_3

in relation to extractive projects from that desired by the state (BankTrack, 2016; Zukulu, 2020). This raises the possibility that as a result of Indigenous agency *outcomes* in relation to extractivism might be consistent with a 'bargain' different from that sought by the state.

A second complexity arises from the fact that 'the state' is not a single coherent entity at a policy and operational level, as long acknowledged in the literature (Hill, 1997) and as recognised in Bowles and Andrews' (Chapter 1 in this volume) concept of a 'Contradictory Bargain' in which 'some elements of a progressive bargain are in place and being implemented but other state policies and practices are working in the opposite direction so that extraction is taking place in a dualistic and contradictory way'. In its approach to Indigenous peoples the state comprises multiple institutions and associated policies and practices (in Australia, for instance, see Dillon & Westbury, 2007). In some cases, the 'bargain' pursued by the 'political executive' (president or prime minister, cabinet, heads of major economic agencies) may be quite different from the 'bargain' reflected in decisions of the judiciary, and in policies and actions of line agencies responsible for environmental protection and protection of Indigenous or civil rights. Indeed, my research revealed several cases where Indigenous litigation resulted in judicial decisions that left governments unable to pursue specific extractivist projects.

A third source of complexity is the possible disjuncture between 'state policy' as reflected in formal documentation and institutional arrangements and the behaviour of state actors on the ground. In some of my case study countries, for instance the Philippines (see below), the gap between the two was very wide. One might therefore need to distinguish between the state's 'formal extractive bargain' and its 'actual extractive bargain'. I argue below that in the Philippines the first could be characterised as 'contradictory' or 'constructive', while state behaviour could be characterised as 'Faustian'.

A fourth complexity involves the impact of a temporal dimension on the analysis, as states or key state actors can move away or start moving away from one type of 'bargain' and towards another. Such transitions can be rapid. A final source of complexity is that state policy on extractivism does not operate in a silo, because the state's pursuit of goals in other policy areas may have consequences for its ability to achieve its preferred 'extractive bargain'.

Exploring these complexities offers fertile ground for examining the 'political economy determinants' the editors wish to explore, which include 'class interests and power, state composition and autonomy, sectoral composition and coherence, national histories and location in the global political economy, the extent of Indigenous rights, and civil society strength'. It is precisely the interaction of these 'determinants' that generates complexity.

My approach is to consider how Indigenous-focussed bargains in three quite different countries (the Philippines, South Africa and Australia) might be characterised in terms of the normative axis of the 'Extractive Bargains' typology identified in Chap. 1. I discuss the Philippines at greater length to provide a detailed illustration of my approach and consider examples from South Africa and Australia more briefly to show the range of bargains the state pursues and the diversity of outcomes that eventuate from its interactions with Indigenous peoples. The case studies analysed in this chapter draw upon a book to be published in 2023 by Oxford University Press, *Indigenous Peoples and Mining: A Global Perspective* (O'Faircheallaigh, in press).

The Philippines

The Philippines is composed of 7107 islands and islets spanning 1854 kilometres from north to south and stretching from China in the north to the Indonesian archipelago in the south. It was colonised by Spain (1521–1898) and the United States (1902–1936), and was occupied by the Japanese during World War II before becoming an independent country in 1946. It contains nearly 100 distinct Indigenous peoples who account for an estimated 12% of the population of around 101 million people recorded at the last census in 2015. The Philippines is rich in mineral resources including gold, copper, nickel and chromite. Nineteen large-scale mining projects were operating in the country in 2019 and the industry employs some 200,000 people.

The Philippines is one of the few countries that has introduced comprehensive legislation which aims to recognise the rights of Indigenous peoples, including in their interactions with extractive industry. The *Indigenous Peoples' Rights Act* (*IPRA*) *1997 (IPRA)* requires the state to 'protect the rights of ICCs/IPs [Indigenous Cultural Communities/ Indigenous Peoples] to their ancestral domains, to ensure their economic, social and cultural well-being and [to] recognize the applicability of customary laws governing property rights or relations …' (section (s) 1). The *Act* provides for the declaration of 'ancestral domains' which comprise 'lands, inland waters, coastal areas, and natural resources therein, held under a claim of ownership, occupied or possessed by ICCs/IPs … [They] shall include … mineral and other natural resources (s 3)' [and] 'the total environment including the spiritual and cultural bonds to the areas which the ICCs/IPs possess, occupy and use and to which they have claims of ownership' (s 4). The declaration of an Ancestral Domain confers on ICCs/IPs the 'right to develop, control and use lands and territories traditionally occupied, owned, or used' and 'to negotiate the terms and conditions for the exploration of natural resources in the areas …' (s 7(b)). The state undertakes to 'ensure that the employment of any form of force or coercion against ICCs/IPs shall be dealt with by law' (s 21). The *Act* establishes a National Commission on Indigenous Peoples (NCIP) to be the primary government agency responsible for the formulation and implementation of policies, plans and programmes to recognise, protect and promote the rights of ICCs/IPs, including through the recognition of Ancestral Domains.

In the years immediately prior to passage of the *IPRA*, the Philippine government, as part of a structural adjustment programme negotiated with the World Bank and the IMF, had substantially liberalised legislation governing mining to attract greater investment, especially foreign investment, into the industry. These changes were given effect through the *Philippine Mining Act of 1995* (the *Mining Act*), which remains in force today. Under the *Act*, 'Mineral resources are owned by the State and the exploration, development, utilization, and processing thereof shall be under its full control and supervision' (Chapter II). The *Act* included highly favourable tax treatment for the industry (Chapter XVI) and grants it rights to water and timber on lands containing mineral resources and to easement rights to lands adjacent to those containing mineral resources (Chapter XII). The *Mining Act* was favourably received by the international mining industry, and the number of foreign mining companies represented in the Philippines increased by 400% between 1994 and 1996 (Holden et al., 2011, p. 146).

There is obvious room for conflict between the *IPRA* and the *Mining Act*. The state's claim to own minerals and have 'full control and supervision of their development' is in tension with the *IPRA*'s statement that Indigenous peoples have 'the right to right to develop, control and use' their lands. The extensive rights in land afforded Indigenous peoples appear at odds with the priority and privileges offered by foreign mining companies, for instance, in relation to use of timber, water and lands adjacent to their mining concessions.

It would appear therefore that the Philippines constitutes a clear case of a *contradictory* bargain, one in which 'some elements of a progressive bargain are in place', represented by the *IPRA*, but 'other state policies and practices are working in the opposite direction', represented by the *Mining Act*. However, if we focus on the *practices* of successive Philippine governments, discussed in detail below in relation to two major resource projects, another picture emerges. These practices have involved unabashed support for mining and scant regard for Indigenous rights. This is reflected in the use of the Philippine armed forces and paramilitary groups they train to suppress Indigenous opposition to mining and to support mining company access to Indigenous land, in direct contravention of s. 21 of *IPRA*. The NCIP, the state agency supposedly responsible for supporting Indigenous rights, has offered official recognition to Indigenous individuals and groups supportive of mining and denied it to opponents of mining. The Philippine government has put pressure on the judiciary to reverse court rulings favourable to Indigenous peoples. These practices reflect a conviction among politicians that expansion of mining was and is essential to help address the Philippines' considerable economic challenges, and the close personal links between the mining industries and the political leadership. For example, former President Duterte's finance secretary, Carlos Dominguez, was previously a mining company executive, resigning just two weeks before Duterte's inauguration. Dominguez's brother Paul is a former president of Sagittarius Mines

Inc. (SMI), the company seeking to develop the giant Tampakan copper/gold deposit, discussed below (Calderon, 2021).

From the perspective of state practices rather than of legislation and formal policy, the Philippines appears to squarely match the concept of a Faustian bargain, in which state elites support extractivism in the short term and in a way which 'severely compromises or destroys the possibilities for long term social and environmental justice' (Bowles and Andrews this volume). A third perspective would focus on the final outcomes of extractive projects. Here outcomes have been variable, because of the intervention of Indigenous agency and the factors that shape its efficacy. Contrasting outcomes are offered by two projects in Mindanao, the Mount Canatuan project on the territory of Subanon Indigenous peoples and the Tampakan project on the lands of the B'laan peoples.

The Subanon and Mount Canatuan

Subanon territory lies in the Zamboanga Peninsula in the far west of Mindanao, and the Subanon live by farming, hunting and fishing. They maintain their Indigenous religious beliefs, which include the association of specific places with creation stories. Of particular importance to Subanon living in the Canatuan area is Mount Canatuan, which they wished to remain untouched. In 1993 members of the Subanon living in Canatuan began the process of seeking recognition of their legal ownership of Subanon territory, but a Certificate of Ancestral Domain Claim was not granted until June 2003. Long delays in processing applications for recognition of Indigenous rights reflected the government's failure to provide adequate resources to NCIP to implement its mandate on the ground, to such an extent that NCIP officers regularly had to rely on mining companies for transport (World Bank, 2007, pp. 33, 37–39).

In 1994, a Canadian company Toronto Ventures Incorporated (TVI) purchased a prospecting permit to explore the Mount Canatuan area. In 1996 it was granted a Mineral Production Sharing Agreement (MPSA) allowing it to develop a copper/gold orebody it had located on Mount Canatuan, and from 2004 operated a profitable gold/copper mine. Local Subanon were strongly opposed to TVI's operation because of its negative environmental impacts on land and water and because they believed, correctly as it transpired, it would result in the destruction of Mount Canatuan. They were supported in their opposition by farmers and fishers downstream from the mine, by a large majority of local government councillors in the area and by the Catholic Church. Their opposition proved fruitless. This reflected long delays in legal processes Subanon landowners sought to use to gain recognition under the *IPRA* and to stop the project; and successful efforts by TVI, after it became clear that the customary leadership would not accept its project, to promote an alternative Subanon leadership group who lived outside the district and some of whom were employed by the company. TVI paid for the operational costs of this latter group and directed benefits payable to Indigenous landowners to its members. The NCIP also undermined the customary leadership, helping to organise a meeting in September 2002 in a regional centre of a day's travel from Canatuan which was dominated by TVI supporters and voted to support its project. In 2004 the Subanon's supreme judicial body, the *Gukom* of Seven Rivers, found that the group supporting TVI had no legitimacy in Subanon law, and instructed the NCIP to declare agreements between them and TVI null and void. The NCIP refused to accept the Gukom's instruction and insisted on treating the decision of the group supporting TVI as constituting free prior and informed consent by local Subanon for the company's operations (Alternative Law Group Inc. et al., 2009; Christian Aid and PIPlinks, 2004; Sanz, 2007, 2019).

Another contentious aspect of TVI's operations involved its use of security forces. For example, in September 1999, members of the Philippine National Police Mobile Group, ostensibly in the area as part of the government's military campaign against the Moro Islamic Liberation Front, violently dispersed a human barricade formed by Subanon attempting to prevent TVI from bringing drilling equipment onto their territory (Christian Aid and PIPlinks, 2004; Hamm et al., 2013).

Despite sustained opposition from Subanon of the Canatuan area and their allies, TVI continued its operations for over a decade and mined a large part of Mount Canatuan. The outcome in this case could certainly be regarded as consistent with a 'Faustian bargain'.

B'laan Communities and the Tampakan Project

Tampakan is regarded as the largest undeveloped copper and gold deposit in Southeast Asia and the Western Pacific, with reserves of 2.9 billion tonnes grading on average 0.6% copper and 0.2g/t gold. It is located on the territory of the B'laan Indigenous peoples in a mountainous region in the east of Mindanao. Tampakan was first discovered by the Australian company Western Mining Corporation (WMC) in the early 1990s. Its development would require the creation of a large open pit with an area of 500 hectares and a depth of 785 metres; clearing of some 5000 hectares of forest; and construction of a power plant, waste rock storage facility, tailings dam, a 100 km underground pipeline from the mine to the coast and a port. It would directly affect 11 B'laan communities and require resettlement of some 5000 people (Hamm et al., 2013; SMI, 2011).

Traditionally swidden farmers engaged in shifting cultivation across an extensive territory, the B'laan have been forced to adopt a sedentary lifestyle as they have lost land to forestry companies and been encircled by immigrant farmers from elsewhere in the Philippines.

B'laan people continue to rely heavily on a subsistence economy, which includes upland farming of rice and corn and hunting, gathering and fishing. Traditionally headmen referred to as *Bong To* and *Bong Fulong*, the latter title given to especially knowledgeable and wise leaders, play the key role in B'laan governance. Where headmen felt they could not decide upon an issue on their own, they would call a community meeting. In recent decades state agencies have created 'tribal councils' as a vehicle through which the state seeks to organise its relations with the B'laan, creating internal tensions where tribal council leaders are not *Bong To* or *Bong Fulong* (Davis, 1998; DINTEG and KALUHHAMIN, 2015, p. 5).

In March 1995 WMC signed a Financial and Technical Assistance Agreement (FTAA) with the Philippine government covering an area of some 99,000 hectares. The company undertook a concerted effort to engage with B'laan communities and obtain their consent to develop the project, investing substantially in community development activities, including health facilities, mobile clinics, education facilities and agricultural advice. It negotiated an agreement with certain B'laan communities under which, in return for their support for Tampakan, they would receive a royalty, a community quota for employment, financial assistance to students and emergency medical assistance. Despite the signing of this agreement attitudes among B'laan people towards the company and the project were divided. Some supported WMC on the basis that the project would deliver much needed education, health and transport service to the region, services which the Philippine government was unable to unwilling to provide. Others were concerned at WMC's practice of engaging with tribal councils rather than the traditional B'laan leadership and that the project, especially because of the extent of forest clearing required and the need to resettle thousands of people, threatened their connection to their land and its sacred places and their continued existence. B'laan and other groups outside the immediate project area were also concerned about the impact of the project on watersheds, downstream water quality, irrigation systems and fishponds. Opponents of the mine began attacking WMC property and employees and took refuge in the most remote B'laan communities when the police and military responded (DINTEG and KALUHHAMIN, 2015; Hamm et al., 2013; World Bank, 2007).

In 1997, a church-based Tribal Association La Bugal-B'laan sued DENR for violating the 1987 Philippine Constitution by awarding the Tampakan ore body to a foreign firm, WMC, with 100% equity. Seven years later in February 2004, the Philippine Supreme Court ruled in favour of the La Bugal-B'laan. The Court's decision would not come into effect until the expiration of a specified time period for lodging a motion for reconsideration. The Philippine government and mining interests quickly filed a motion, and in December 2004 the Supreme Court reversed its decision after extensive lobbying by mining industry interests and government officials, including the president, congressmen, senators and department secretaries (Tan, 2006). In the meantime, WMC had transferred its rights to explore and develop Tampakan to another corporation, Sagittarius Mines Inc. (SMI), controlled by the Swiss-based multinational mining company Xstrata, which in turn merged with the British/Swiss mining and commodity trading company Glencore in 2013.

SMI expanded exploration activities in the proposed project area, increased infrastructure development and worked to obtain the environmental and other approvals required for the project to proceed. As the company's plans became clearer, opposition to the Tampakan project grew not only among sections of the B'laan, but also among civil society groups, including the Catholic Church and environmental NGOs. One indication of this opposition was when the Government of South Cotabato in 2010 passed an Environment Code banning open-pit mining method in the province. In January 2012 DENR denied the company's application for an Environmental Clearance Certificate (ECC), citing the South Cotabato Environment Code prohibiting open pit mining. SMI appealed this decision, and after President Aquino issued an Executive Order requiring local governments to align their local ordinances with national policies, SMI's ECC was issued subject to several conditions, including attainment of free prior and informed consent from affected Indigenous communities.

Local resistance continued to escalate and become increasingly violent and included armed assaults on Philippine troops and auxiliaries providing security for SMI and attacks on SMI personnel, the latter resulting in three fatalities. Philippine troops increased their efforts to repress resistance to SMI's activities, and in October 2012 when searching for a B'laan leader, shot dead his wife and children. Despite armed repression, B'laan resistance to SMI's project continued unabated, supported by the Catholic Church and civil society groups which collected petitions and organise protests against the project. In June 2015 Glencore sold its stake in Tampakan to Philippine interests. In February 2017 President Duterte's Environment Secretary Gina Lopez cancelled SMI's Environmental Compliance Certificate (ECC) but in May 2019 the ECC was restored by the Office of the President. SMI received a further setback in October 2020 when a Philippine court dismissed a request by pro-mining groups for an injunction against the South Cotabato province's ban on open-cut mining. To date B'laan resistance has been successful and the Tampakan orebody remains undeveloped (BankTrack, 2016; Calderon, 2021; DINTEG and KALUHHAMIN, 2015; Franciscans International, 2014; Sarmiento, 2020).

In this case the stubborn resistance of the B'laan, assisted by civil society and elements of the Philippine state, in particular the provincial government, has prevented the development of a mining project that would have had severely negative impacts on the environment and on B'laan territories and people. In the process the B'laan have reaffirmed their right to control development on their territory and to maintain their way of life and reaffirmed the authority of their customary leaders. In this instance, as in Mount Canatuan, the practices of the 'central state' were Faustian, but one could argue that the *outcomes* reflect elements of a 'Progressive bargain' in that social and environmental justice goals have been met. This has occurred at significant cost to the B'laan, including loss of life. It has nevertheless occurred, highlighting the significance of Indigenous agency.

South Africa

South Africa displays clear signs of a 'contradictory bargain'. This is reflected in the tension between laws recognising Indigenous rights and those governing mineral development. In post-apartheid South Africa there has been a strong push to recognise the rights of those who lost their land, including Indigenous peoples. The status of customary land is recognised in the Constitution, recognition which is reflected in the *Interim Protection of Informal Land Right Act*, which has remained in force since 1996. This states (s 2) 'no person may be deprived of any informal right to land without his or her consent … Where land is held on a communal basis … a decision to dispose of any such right may only be taken by a majority of the holders of such rights …'. These provisions indicate that 'disposal' of communal customary rights in land to allow for mining can only occur with the consent of a majority of community members. On the other hand, South Africa's *Mineral and Petroleum Resources Development Act 2002*, though introduced six years later, did not take this requirement for consent into account. The *Act* (s 10) only requires 'Consultation with interested and affected parties', after which grant of a mining interest is at the discretion of the responsible government minister.

The conflict between these contradictory laws was dramatically illustrated when, in the early 2000s, an Australian company, Mineral Resources Commodities (MRC), sought to establish large-scale mineral sand mining on the traditional land of the Xolobeni Indigenous community, an AmaMpondo people who live on the Wild Coast of South Africa's Eastern Cape Province, an area of great natural beauty and cultural interest. The sands of the coastline where Xolobeni is located are rich in titanium minerals. In February 2002 Transworld Energy and Mineral Resources (TEM), a South African subsidiary of MRC, was awarded a prospecting permit for a coastal area 22 kilometres long and 1.5 kilometres inland from the high water mark. After MRC established substantial mineral sands reserves, the company formed a partnership with a local company, Xolobeni Empowerment Company (XolCo) as required under South African Black Empowerment law, with XolCo eventually taking a 26% stake in the project. By May 2004 TEM/MRC had commenced environmental impact assessment work in preparation for submitting applications for a mining lease and development approval (MRC, 2005).

The large majority of the Xolobeni community, most of whom live close to the proposed mining area, opposed MRC's mine from the start, viewing it as a fundamental threat to their environment, their land and their way of life. In July 2007 the community established the Amadiba Crisis Committee (ACC) to coordinate opposition to the project. While small in size, numbering fewer than 100 households, the Xolobeni community organised, with the help of several NGOs, a sophisticated campaign against the proposed mine. It developed alliances with local and international legal rights and environmental NGOs and documented the potential impact of mining on the area's environmental values and on the livelihoods of the Xolobeni. The ACC's campaign against mining began to attract extensive media attention in South Africa and overseas, attention which grew further in September 2007 when the King and Queen of AmaMpondo visited the traditional court or Komkulu of uMgungundlovu, attracting a crowd of some 2000 people (Zukulu, 2020).

In August 2008 South Africa's Department of Mineral Resources (DMR) awarded mining rights to MRC's subsidiary, TEM, despite the fact that the Xolobeni community was neither notified nor consulted before the licence was awarded. The ACC lodged an appeal with DMR challenging the grant of the mineral licence, in response to which the Minister for Mineral Resources suspended the mining rights and MRC halted work on the project for several years (MRC, 2011, p. 3). Long delays occurred in the DMR's processing of Xolobeni's appeal, but eventually in 2012 the Department cancelled MRC's mining right. At the same time the DMR confirmed its intention to grant MRC a replacement mining right, and in 2015 TEM lodged a further application for a mining licence and resumed impact assessment and development work.

By 2008 a number of community members, including the chief of the Xolobeni who had previously opposed the project, had begun to agitate in favour of mining. It later transpired that TEM had given this individual a four-wheel drive vehicle and other financial benefits and that he and other supporters had been appointed directors of TEM and XolCo. Opponents of MRC confronted the pro-mining chief in public meetings, holding him to account for his actions in supporting the proposed mine. Tensions escalated in Xolobeni in 2014 after a large number of community members acted to prevent MRC/TEM consultants from gaining access to the proposed mine site to undertake work for the environmental impact assessment without which TEM could not gain final approval. Supporters of the mine attacked its opponents on several occasions, and in May 2015 an interim court interdict was granted against several of the mine's supporters preventing them from assaulting members of the community and from bringing firearms to community meetings (High Court of South Africa, 2018, p. 9).

In 2016 the Xolobeni community lodged a claim in South Africa's High Court against the DMR, asking the Court to declare that the grant of a mining licence would be invalid unless DMR complied with provisions of the *Interim Protection of Informal Land Right Act 1996*, which prohibits expropriation of 'land or rights in land' without the consent of the community that owned the land. The DMR, several other government agencies and TEM opposed the claim, arguing that TEM was required only to consult with the community as required by the *Mineral and Petroleum Resource Development Act 2002*, and that MRC had fulfilled this requirement. Litigation lasted more than two years. In November 2018 the High Court handed down a judgement in favour of

Xolobeni, ruling that the DMR lacked any lawful authority to issue a Mining Licence to TEM and that 'in terms of the *Interim Protection of Informal Land Right Act 31 of 1996* the First Respondent [the Minister for Mineral Resources] is obliged to obtain the full and informed consent of the Applicants and the uMgungundlovu community, as the holder of the rights in land, prior to granting any mining right to the Fifth Respondent [TEM] …'. Costs were awarded against the Minister for Mineral Resources and the other respondents (High Court of South Africa, 2018, pp. 39–40).

As in the case of Tampakan, it can be argued that *outcomes* in this case reflect elements of a 'Progressive bargain' in that the Xolobeni's social and environmental justice goals have been met. Here also, Indigenous agency has been crucial in determining this outcome.

Australia

Australia is a federation, which immediately introduces a level of complexity, as the state's 'bargain' in relation to extraction can vary from one sub-national jurisdiction to another. An obvious example is the Aboriginal land rights legislation which applies to about half of the Northern Territory (the *Aboriginal Land Rights (Northern Territory) Act 1996*). This confers on Aboriginal Traditional Owners an effective right of veto over exploration and mining on their lands. This places them in a strong position to ensure a progressive bargain, one in which 'local affected communities are given important mechanisms of control over the activities, the economic benefits of extraction are fairly shared, and long term environmental and social sustainability are enhanced' (Bowles and Andrews this volume). If Traditional Owners believe that a certain project cannot 'enhance sustainability', they can stop it, meeting another element of the 'Progressive bargain' definition, that is 'that some extractive projects are not undertaken'. If Traditional Owners approve a project, they do so on the basis of what they see as a fair sharing of economic benefits. For instance, agreements negotiated with mining companies under this legislation typically provide for payments of royalties to Traditional Owners at a level comparable to those imposed by government (O'Faircheallaigh, 2016, p. 87).

In much of Australia extractive activity on Aboriginal land is governed by the federal *Native Title Act 1993*. This resulted from the Australian High Court's 1992 *Mabo* decision, which overturned the previous basis of land law in Australia, that any existing Indigenous rights in land were extinguished in 1788 when Britain claimed Australia as a colony. The *Native Title Act 1993* gave expression to the High Court decision by creating a system through which Aboriginal and Torres Strait landowners could achieve recognition of their inherent rights in land ('native title'), on two conditions. The first was that native title claimants could demonstrate an unbroken connection with their territory since the time of colonisation; the second was that there had been no valid grant in land by colonial, and later Australian, authorities which had the effect of extinguishing native title.

This recognition of inherent Indigenous rights in land could, in principle, have formed the basis for a 'progressive bargain', but for three factors. Virtually all land in Australia that was suitable for European agriculture had been granted to settlers and so native title had been extinguished. Much of what remained was desert (central Australia) or subject to a monsoonal climate (far north Australia). Second, the process of gaining recognition of native title places a heavy evidentiary burden on Aboriginal and Torres Strait Islander claimants, which some have failed to meet, and is expensive and time consuming. Third, where native title is recognised, it does not bring with it a veto of the type that applies to Aboriginal land in the Northern Territory. Rather it confers what is known as the 'Right to Negotiate'. When a company applies for a mining licence, it must negotiate in good faith with the holders of native title rights and seek their consent to mining. However, if agreement is not reached within six months, the company can go to a government Tribunal and ask that the mining licence be granted. In the overwhelming majority of cases, the Tribunal agrees. When it does so, the Tribunal is prohibited from requiring payment of a mining royalty to the native title holders as a condition of granting the licence, whereas a royalty can be included in any agreement between them and the mining company. This puts enormous pressure on native title holders to reach agreement because if they fail to do so, the project is likely to proceed in any case and they will not share in its economic benefits.

Highlighting the importance of including a focus on outcomes, my detailed analysis of 45 mining agreements in Australia (O'Faircheallaigh, 2016) showed that some native title agreements resulted in strongly positive outcomes for Aboriginal communities, including a major share in economic benefits, a capacity to influence project design and environmental and cultural heritage protection much more effective than that available under relevant legislation. These outcomes occurred where the communities involved had a capacity to mobilise politically and so bolster their limited legal rights, and they were almost always associated with strong regional political organisations which supported individual communities in negotiations in part by providing access to sophisticated legal, technical and economic advice. These outcomes could certainly be regarded as displaying elements of a progressive bargain. Where conditions were not favourable to Aboriginal political mobilisation, agreements offered few benefits and did little to augment protection of Aboriginal lands and culture, outcomes that are more consistent with a Faustian bargain. The 'bargain' in this latter case is of course reached under duress. If Aboriginal Traditional Owners do not enter an agreement under the *Native Title Act* mining can proceed in any case, they receive no economic benefits from exploitation of their land and resources and forego the opportunity to play some (limited) role in minimising cultural and environmental impacts created by extractive activity.

Australia could therefore be characterised as a patchwork quilt of bargains, with the category that is most apt depending on sub-national jurisdiction, legal regime and, critically, on the capacity of individual Aboriginal groups to mobilise politically. The Australian experience illustrates the complexities involved in characterising the nature of extractive bargains even in one country. It also highlights the profound implications for Indigenous peoples of whether a 'bargain' is 'progressive' or 'Faustian'. I have illustrated this latter point elsewhere (O'Faircheallaigh, 2021) in contrasting agreements negotiated for extractive activities of the same type (Liquefied Natural Gas projects), concluded at the same time, under the same legislation and involving some of the same corporations. In a case in the Kimberley region of northwest Western Australia which involved a high degree of Aboriginal political capacity and mobilisation, negotiated agreements included:

- A A$1.5 billion economic benefits package for affected Aboriginal Traditional Owners and communities, including annual payments linked to project scale, and substantial ongoing state government investments in additional community services and economic development initiatives
- Extensive funding for agreement implementation and monitoring of environmental impacts
- Prohibition of any further processing of offshore gas on Aboriginal land, and of any industrial projects using gas as a feedstock, along the entire Kimberley coastline
- A right for Aboriginal traditional owners to unilaterally require the developer to build a desalination plant if they fear adverse impacts from use of water from major aquifers

In contrast agreements negotiated in Queensland in a context of limited Aboriginal political capacity and mobilisation:

- Have limited financial benefits. In some cases, payments are made only during the first 10 years of projects that can have operational lives greater than 40 years.
- Contain no dedicated funding for agreement implementation of environmental monitoring.
- Offer no role to Traditional Owners in environmental management.
- Have no review clauses that might allow changes to what are highly disadvantageous agreements to the future (O'Faircheallaigh, 2021, p. 2).

These contrasting outcomes also point to the critical role of Indigenous agency in shaping the nature of the bargains entered into or facilitated by the state.

Conclusion

This analysis highlights the potential utility of an 'extractive bargains' approach, particularly in a comparative context. It suggests that an approach that conceives of 'bargains' in a matrix structure may be productive, with the types of 'bargains' on one axis and 'formal state policies', 'state practices' and 'outcomes from extractive projects' on the other. This would allow for a situation in which different assessments might be made regarding which 'bargain' best characterises formal policy, state practices and outcomes. It would also allow for the impact of Indigenous agency in bringing about outcomes not envisaged or desired by the state, increasing the explanatory power of the approach.

A final point involves the term 'bargain'. A comparative approach undertaken in an Indigenous context also indicates that it may be important to acknowledge the two uses of the word 'bargain', as a noun ('agreement on terms of a transaction') and a verb ('discuss terms of a transaction (with person for thing)') (*The Concise Oxford Dictionary*). A 'bargain' in the first sense may indeed occur, in some cases under duress, in which case the bargain is likely to be Faustian; in other cases because Indigenous people willingly reach agreement, in which case the bargain is likely to be progressive. Both scenarios occur under Australia's *Native Title Act 1993*. In other cases the state may offer 'terms of a transaction' to Indigenous people but no agreement may occur, resulting either in the state forcing its bargain on Indigenous peoples (the Subanon and Mount Canatuan in the Philippines, a Faustian outcome), or Indigenous peoples being able to resist the state and extraction activity does not occur (the B'laan and Tampakan, the Xolobeni and mineral sand mining, both showing elements of a progressive bargain). Indigenous agency constitutes a critical variable in determining which of these outcomes will eventuate, as do the action or inaction of state institutions, and especially the judiciary, in enforcing legal recognition of Indigenous rights.

References

Alternative Law Group Inc., et al. [13 authors]. (2009). Submission to the [United Nations] Committee on the Elimination of all forms of Racial Discrimination Philippines Indigenous Peoples ICERD Shadow Report. Retrieved May 17, 2021, from https://www2.ohchr.org/english/bodies/cerd/docs/ngos/PIP_Philippines75.pdf

BankTrack. (2016). Tampakan Copper and Gold Mine project Philippines. BankTrack. Retrieved May 27, 2021, from https://www.banktrack.org/project/tampakan_copper_and_gold_mine_project

Calderon, L. (2021). Tampakan, other giant mines could strike gold in wake of Duterte's new order. CNN Philippines. Retrieved May 27, 2021, from https://www.cnnphilippines.com/news/2021/4/26/Exclusive%2D%2DTampakan%2D%2Dother-giant-mines-could-strike-gold-in-wake-of-Duterte-s-new-order.html

Christian Aid and PIPlinks. (2004). *Breaking promises, making profits: Mining in the Philippines*. London: Christian Aid and PIPlinks.

Davis, S. L. (1998). Engaging the community at the Tampakan Copper Project: A community case study in resource development with Indigenous people. *Natural Resources Forum, 22*(4), 233–243.

Dillon, M., & Westbury, N. D. (2007). *Beyond humbug: Transforming government engagement with Indigenous Australia*. Seaview Press.

DINTEG and KALUHHAMIN. (2015). *Right to our mineral resources in our Ancestral Territories*. Baguio City and General Santos City: DINTEG and KALUHHAMIN.

Franciscans International. (2014). *The Tampakan Copper-Gold Project and human rights violations in the South Cotabato, Philippines*. Franciscans International. Retrieved May 27, 2021, from http://franciscansinternational.org/fileadmin/media/Business and HR/Statements/philippines report tampakancopyrevisedmay2014.pdf

Hamm, B., Schax, A., & Scheper, C. (2013). *Human rights impact assessment of the Tampakan Copper-Gold Project*. Aachen: Institute for Development and Peace.

High Court of South Africa. (2018). Beleni and others v Minister for Mineral Resources and others: High Court of South Africa, Case No. 73768/2016, 22 November. Retrieved February 9, 2022, from https://cer.org.za/wp-content/uploads/2018/11/Baleni-and-others-v-Minister-of-Mineral-Resources-and-others.pdf

Hill, M. (1997). *The policy process in the modern state*. Prentice Hall.

Holden, W., Nadeau, K., & Jacobson, R. D. (2011). Exemplifying accumulation by dispossession: Mining and Indigenous peoples in the Philippines. *Human Geography, 93*(2), 141–161.

MRC (Mineral Resources Commodities). (2005). *Annual Report 31 December 2004*. MRC. Retrieved February 4, 2022, from https://www.mineralcommodities.com/investors-media/annual-reports/

MRC. (2011). *Annual Report 2010*. MRC. Retrieved February 4, 2022, from https://www.mineralcommodities.com/investors-media/annual-reports/

O'Faircheallaigh, C. (2016). *Negotiations in the Indigenous world: Aboriginal peoples and extractive industry in Australia and Canada*. Routledge.

O'Faircheallaigh, C. (2021). Explaining outcomes from negotiated agreements in Australia and Canada. *Resources Policy, 70*, 1–7. https://doi.org/10.1016/j.resourpol.2020.101922

O'Faircheallaigh, C. (in press). *Indigenous peoples and mining: A global perspective*. Oxford University Press.

Sanz, P. (2007). The politics of consent: The state, multinational capital and the Subanon of Canatuan. In A. B. Gatmaytan (Ed.), *Negotiating autonomy: Case studies on Philippine Indigenous peoples' land rights* (pp. 109–135). IWGIA.

Sanz, P. (2019). Mining in other people's land: The unintended consequences of mineral liberalization in Subanon Land in Mindanao, Philippines. PhD thesis. Saskatoon: University of Saskatchewan.

Sarmiento, B. S. (2020, October 17). Church-led group revives campaign vs South Cotabato mining project. *Inquirer Mindanao*. Retrieved June 7, 2021, from https://newsinfo.inquirer.net/1349129/church-led-group-revives-campaign-vs-south-cotabato-mining-project

SMI (Sagittarius Mines Inc). (2011). SMI consults stakeholders on its proposed Tampakan Copper-Gold mining operation. Press release, 14 June. Manila: SMI.

Tan, A. K. (2006). All that glitters: Foreign investment in mining trumps the environment in the Philippines. *Pace Environmental Law Review, 23*(1), 182–208.

World Bank. (2007). *Indigenous peoples rights act: Legal and institutional frameworks, implementation and challenges in the Philippines*. Washington, DC: World Bank.

Zukulu, S. (2020). Mining in the Eastern Cape Province, South Africa: Indigenous negotiations case study. Washington, DC: Conservation International. Retrieved July 27, 2022, from https://www.conservation.org/docs/default-source/publication-pdfs/indigenous-negotiations-case-study-mining-in-eastern-cape-province-south-africa.pdf?Status=Master & sfvrsn=9296dd09_3

Part II

Global North Case Studies

4

The Legacy of Sweden's Social Democratic State for Extractive Bargains with Indigenous Sámi Reindeer Herding Communities

Karin Beland Lindahl

Introduction

The Swedish state, mining companies and Indigenous communities have interacted for centuries, and the Swedish state has justified its bargains in different ways. For most of this period, open local and Indigenous opposition or conflict has been rare (Tarras-Wahlberg, 2014). However, during the last decade, controversy has escalated, particularly in Sápmi, the traditional territory of the Indigenous Sámi (Beland Lindahl et al., 2018; Raitio et al., 2020; Fjellborg et al., 2022). A growing body of research has explored the causes and nature of these conflicts (Anshelm & Haikola, 2018; Beland Lindahl et al., 2018; Lawrence & Kløcker Larsen, 2017, 2019; Raitio et al., 2020; Zachrisson & Beland Lindahl, 2019; Fjellborg et al., 2022; MacPhail et al., 2022). Less attention has so far been paid to

K. Beland Lindahl (✉)
Unit of Political Science, Luleå University of Technology, Luleå, Sweden

Ájtte—Swedish Mountain and Sámi Museum, Jokkmokk, Sweden
e-mail: karin.beland.lindahl@ltu.se

P. Bowles, N. Andrews (eds.), *Extractive Bargains*, Frontiers of Globalization,
https://doi.org/10.1007/978-3-031-32172-6_4

the role of the state and its strategies to gain acceptance for its mineral policy. In this chapter, I explore how the Swedish state justifies its mineral policy and extractive bargains with Indigenous Sámi reindeer herding communities (Sámi RHCs). The conflict over the Kallak/Gállok mine project in Jokkmokk municipality, northern Sweden, serves as an empirical example. I am probing the underlying logic that characterizes the Swedish state's contemporary extractive bargaining strategies in light of a Swedish policy style that was moulded by forty years of uninterrupted social democratic rule.

Sweden is a highly regulated welfare state with a long tradition of mineral extraction. Starting around 1600, mineral extraction was part of the Swedish state's mechanism to colonize and populate northern Sweden (Sörlin, 1988). As the mines developed, Indigenous people were recruited, or forced, to transport the ore (Sehlin MacNeil, 2017; Lundmark, 2008), and mines were established on Indigenous territories. A second wave of larger scale state-led industrialization of Sápmi started at the end of the 1800s when mining, hydro-power production and forestry boomed in what was justified and marketed as the industrial development of northern Sweden, "the Land of the Future" (Sörlin, 1988). The non-Indigenous population increased rapidly, and resource extraction provided wage labour to communities previously relying on subsistence livelihoods. Several mining towns developed in the north.

By the 1990s the number of jobs in the mining sector decreased substantially due to rationalization and increasing global competition (Tano et al., 2016). Less local jobs, and declining economic returns, threatened to undermine the social contract between the state and the mining-dependent communities (Liljenäs, 1992). In response, the Swedish state deregulated the mining sector and opened it to international actors and investors (Tano et al., 2016; Tarras-Wahlberg, 2014). As a result, exploration boomed and multiple mining projects were launched (Tarras-Wahlberg, 2014; Knobblock & Pettersson, 2010). In response to what was perceived as a "mining boom", a nationwide mining-sceptical movement formed in the beginning of the 2010s. In 2012, the national organization Urbergsgruppen (literally, "Bedrock Group") was formally registered and has since then sided, or collaborated with, the Indigenous mining opposition represented by Sámi RHCs and other Sámi organizations (Zachrisson & Beland Lindahl, 2019). The state's response to increasing contestation and conflict has primarily focused on extended dialogue and collaboration.

This chapter explores extractive bargains between the Swedish state and Sámi RHCs during the recent period of increased opposition. I start by introducing the Kallak/Gállok iron mine project and the Swedish mineral extraction permit process which will serve as an empirical example of how the Swedish state negotiates contested extractive bargains with Indigenous groups. Second, I explore how bargains are described and justified in Swedish mineral policy and the Kallak/Gállok mining permit process, and trace the main ideas underlying the Swedish bargaining style. Based on the findings, I use the typology introduced in Chap. 1 to characterize the analytical type of bargain and conclude with a normative analysis of the identified bargain.

The Kallak Iron Mine Project and the Swedish Mineral Extraction Permit Process

The iron deposit in Kallak, or Gállok in the Sámi language, is located 40 km west of Jokkmokk in northern Sweden. Jokkmokk municipality hosts five Sámi RHCs which practice traditional reindeer herding on their territories. The British company Beowulf Mining PLC started to explore the area in 2006 and soon announced plans to establish a mine. The events following this announcement are thoroughly described in several other publications (see Beland Lindahl et al., 2018; MacPhail et al., 2022). In short, the affected Sámi RHCs, Jåhkågaska tjiellde, Sirges and Tuorpon, have resisted the project from its inception. In 2013, Beowulf's subsidiary, Jokkmokk Iron Mines AB (JIMAB), informed the authorities and rights holders about planned test mining (Mineral Inspectorate, 2013). This generated protests by activists and members of the affected Sámi RHCs which temporarily halted the operations.

Later the same year, JIMAB applied for a mining permit (JIMAB, 2013) and the Mineral Inspectorate (MI) referred the matter to the government, as required, when the assessments of the MI and the County

Administration Board (CAB) differ. The CAB had recommended against a permit referencing the negative impacts on reindeer herding (Mineral Inspectorate, 2015). In March 2022, the government approved the mining permit with a number of conditions to help protect reindeer herding (Swedish Government, 2022a). This decision articulates the bargain made by the Swedish state.

The Swedish mineral extraction permit process is divided into four steps, exploration permit, mining permit, environmental permit and land designation, and regulated by two main acts, the Minerals Act (1991:45) and the Environmental Code (1998:808, Bäckström, 2015; Raitio et al., 2020). The Kallak/Gállok project has just received a mining permit and is now proceeding to the next step. As part of the mining permit assessment, the impacts and benefits of mineral extraction were assessed in relation to other land uses, for example, reindeer herding (Environmental Code, chapter 3, section 10). The Swedish Environmental Impact Assessment (EIA) process reflects the stepwise permit process: EIAs are required both for mining and environmental permits.

Previous assessments of Sámi RHCs' participation in the mine permitting process highlight several weaknesses: an a priori assumption by Swedish state authorities that reindeer herding and mining can co-exist; a lack of a codified Swedish state duty to consult the Sámi;[1] a narrow scope and weak status of cumulative impact assessments in Swedish EIA legislation and practice; and a weak recognition of Sámi reindeer herding as a "property right" (Raitio et al., 2020). The Swedish constitution offers protection of Sámi rights and the key provision targets the state, but it is weak and cannot alone be invoked before courts. Chapter 1, section 2, of the constitution (*Instrument of Government*, 1974) reads:

> The opportunities of the Sámi people and ethnic, linguistic and religious minorities to preserve and develop a cultural and social life of their own shall be promoted.

[1] A new short act recognizing the state's duty to consult the Sámi was adopted on 1 March 2022, but did not exist at the time of assessment.

It was only after an amendment in 2010 that the Sámi now are mentioned as (Indigenous) "people", not merely a "minority" (Raitio et al., 2020).

Extractive Bargains in Sweden: Analytical Type

Swedish Mineral Policy and Its Applications in the Kallak/Gállok Case

The state's objectives and rationale guiding Swedish mineral extraction are expressed, not only in the legislation, but in policy and strategy documents of various kinds. To characterize and analyse the Swedish bargaining style, it is necessary to capture objectives and justifications and to analyse how they were implemented in a real-world bargaining situation, using the Kallak/Gállok case as an example.

Swedish Mineral Policy: Objectives and Justifying Ideas

Current mineral policy objectives, and their justifications, are articulated in Sweden's national Minerals Strategy and other more recent policy initiatives. The Minerals Strategy seeks to further strengthen Sweden's position as the leading mining state within the EU by increasing the competitiveness of the Swedish mineral industry, and ensuring that Swedish mineral assets are used in ways that are sustainable in the long term. "Sustainable" is here understood as "taking ecological, social and cultural dimensions into account so that nature and cultural environments are preserved and developed" (Swedish Ministry of Enterprise and Innovation, 2013, p. 4). In short, the state vision is to promote growth in all parts of the country by long-term sustainable use of Sweden's mineral resources—in harmony with environmental, nature and cultural values (p. 20). Production shall, according to the strategy, increase without compromising the achievement of environmental quality objectives, and in agreement with, and respect for, other businesses and values. (p. 22). In case of competing land uses, "...dialogue shall take place at an early phase and consensual solutions should be sought…synergies with other businesses should be aimed for" (p. 26). The strategy recognizes that the Sámi are an Indigenous people with rights to land and water; that reindeer herding is a precondition for Sámi culture which is protected in the Swedish constitution; and that increased mineral extraction is likely to impact reindeer herding in negative ways. The strategy concludes that with dialogue between mining companies and affected Sámi RHCs at an early stage of the planning process, mining sites can be planned in ways so that mining and reindeer herding can co-exist to the greatest possible extent (p. 27).

Reflecting the strategy's vision is the more recent communication platform, "Mining for Generations", which since 2016 is jointly run by the Swedish government and Business Sweden. It states:

> With the help of innovative mining solutions…minerals and metals can be extracted in a sustainable way: mines should be operated in an efficient way with respect for indigenous people and nature. (Mining for Generations, 2022a)

Referring to the state-owned company LKAB's long-standing presence in the northern town Kiruna, that is, in Sápmi, it concludes that it is possible to combine large-scale industrial production with long-term sustainability and consideration for the local community:

> Showing consideration and respecting each other's needs and rights leads to just one thing: joint success. (Mining for Generations, 2022b)

The Swedish government's vision to combine industrial development and growth with environmental and social benefits was further boosted when the "green transition" towards a low carbon economy appeared on the agenda. The transition is portrayed as an opportunity for Swedish companies to become "winners" and the industry to become world leading in innovative and sustainable production (Swedish Government, 2022b). Several state-led initiatives have been launched to support new industrialization, innovation and associated resource extraction (Swedish Ministry of Enterprise and Innovation, 2016; Swedish Government,

2017; Swedish Ministry of Environment and Energy, 2018). In this context, Sweden is often portrayed as a forerunner: a country which has succeeded to combine sustainability, good working conditions, responsibility, security and growth and now has a role to show the rest of the world that a fossil free world is possible (Swedish Ministry of Enterprise and Innovation, 2022, p. 18). *Collaboration* is seen as an essential, and unique, component of the Swedish success story: "...in a small export dependent country, we have to concentrate our resources" (ibid., preamble).

The collaborative and consensual approach expressed above is not new. The Environmental Code—or, rather, the preparatory works therein—postulates that combined land-uses are preferable. The Code (chapters 3 and 4) guides important parts of the mineral permitting process. Accordingly, co-existence is generally promoted rather than being assessed on a case-by-case basis. From this general political preference for co-existence, it logically follows that different public interests must necessarily tolerate restrictions on their own activities (Prop., 1985/86:3, p. 154). This, in turn, justifies encroachments on Sámi RHC pastures as necessary for the greater good (ibid.). Hence, an a priori assumption that mines and reindeer herding should, and can, co-exist is institutionalized.

In summary, the vision of the Swedish state is to expand Swedish mineral extraction, to supply Europe with raw materials and to increase the competitiveness of Swedish industry. The justifying rational is economic growth, employment, welfare—and sustainability—to the benefit of all Swedes in all parts of the country. Recently, increased extraction and a second wave of industrialization in Northern Sweden are also justified by environmental benefits in the form of reduced climate emissions and a green transition. The policy documents convey a predominantly optimistic narrative about synergies and win-wins. To the extent that conflicting interests, for example with Sámi reindeer herding, are mentioned, they are expected to be resolved through dialogue, collaboration, consensual solutions and co-existence—to the benefit of everybody.

Implementation in the Kallak/Gállok Case

How do these intentions play out in a controversial case where the state must bargain between its objective to expand mineral extraction and affected Sámi RHCs aspirations to protect their livelihood, reindeer herding, culture and rights? The Kallak/Gállok case is extensive and reviewed in many other contexts. This brief analysis will target three key aspects derived from the policy review above: (1) *dialogue and collaboration*; (2) *distribution of benefits*; and (3) *consensual solutions for co-existence.*

Dialogue, or collaboration, between the company and the affected Sámi RHCs never developed in the Kallak/Gállok case. Contact was undertaken by Beowulf on several occasions but, according to Jåhkågaska tjiellde on whose territory the planned mine will be located, meetings were cancelled, the company presented a subsequently contested reindeer husbandry impact assessment without input from the Sámi RHCs, and inappropriate statements were made in media. Trust eroded and when a new company leadership tried to establish better consultation, the RHC had little faith in the process. An additional issue was power imbalances and uneven distribution of resources to participate and influence in the assessment process (MacPhail et al., 2022). However, Jåhkågaska and the neighbouring RHC Sirges delivered several critical written statements to the relevant state authorities and to the government (Jåhkågaska tjiellde and Sirges, 2014, 2015, 2016, 2018).

According to the Swedish legislation, company consultations and the (EIA) are the sole responsibility of the proponent (Raitio et al., 2020). In this case, Beowulf/JIMAB's consultant produced a reindeer husbandry assessment based on literature and information from the CAB and two relatively peripheral Sámi RHCs (Hifab, 2013). Jåhkågaska tjiellde and Sirges, who are most affected, found the analysis seriously misrepresentative and developed their own assessment (Jåhkågaska tjiellde and Sirges, 2014).

Dialogue and collaboration, to the extent that it developed, were not sufficient to bridge the conflicting positions between the company and the affected Sámi RHCs, or the involved state authorities. Consequently, the case was referred to the government for a decision. The government decision takes account for the different perspectives and positions, including that of the affected Sámi RHCs, but gives priority to mineral extraction (Swedish Government, 2022a). The government justifies its bargain by attaching several conditions which, according to the government, will ensure that the concession "...will not lead to a situation where affected Sámi RHC's possibilities to conduct reindeer herding will be terminated" (p. 32). The conditions stipulate, among other things, more consultations with the aim at reaching consensus with the affected Sámi RHCs, but do not reflect the Sámi RHC's views in substance.

In sum, the consultations that took place were limited, did not offer the Sámi RHCs substantial influence, were not experienced as meaningful and the affected RHCs did not perceive the assessment process as legitimate. However, the communities' experiences of interacting with the CAB were more positive since the CAB's statement against the mining permit was seen as a step in the right direction.

As for *distribution of benefits*, the anticipated economic benefits are local jobs and tax revenues over a period of 25 years, regional industrial development and revenues to non-local shareholders and investors (MacPhail et al., 2022). The project is expected to produce magnetite concentrate to supply regional processing facilities and fossil-free steelmaking (Beowulf, 2021), or, more generally, contribute to the green transition (Swedish Government, 2022a). While tax revenues would boost the entire local community, the jobs will not primarily benefit those who are already occupied in reindeer herding and related businesses.

The negative impacts, on the other hand, will primarily affect Sámi RHCs and nearby villages. The company recognizes in their EIA that there will be a loss of grazing land, impacts on migration routes and disturbance on reindeer due to noise and traffic; however, these impacts are assessed as manageable (Hifab, 2013). In contrast, Jåhkågaska tjiellde and Sirges assess the effects as substantial and threatening the viability of reindeer herding in the area (Jåhkågaska tjiellde and Sirges, 2014). In short, the Sámi RHCs see no benefits from a mine and very high costs (MacPhail et al., 2022).

The balance between costs and benefits on a societal level is assessed in terms of different "national interests". The Kallak/Gállok area is a designated "national interest" for valuable substances and minerals *and* reindeer herding (Hifab, 2013; CAB, 2014). When the government approved the mining permit, it gave priority to the national interest for valuable substances and minerals with reference to expected positive benefits in the form of regional development, employment and growth. The government did not totally dismiss negative impacts on reindeer herding, but justified the bargain with its own assessment that the attached conditions will diminish the impacts to a tolerable level (Swedish Government, 2022a, p. 31).

The aspiration to develop *consensual solutions for co-existence* permeates the proponent's argumentation for the project. According to the EIA, mining and reindeer herding are compatible. Planning and localization of the mining activities will "as far as possible" take reindeer herding into consideration and the remaining impacts are assessed as moderate (Hifab, 2013). This assessment is challenged by the affected Sámi RHCs who perceive the two activities as incompatible (Jåhkågaska and Sirges, 2014). The RHCs have continuously argued that co-existence with a mine in the proposed location is impossible and that the "sacrifice" goes far beyond impacts in the immediate surroundings of the pit (Beland Lindahl et al., 2018). For them this is not an issue of compensation, but of choosing between alternative development pathways, a choice that comes down to a question of whose vision is to be realized at the expense of whose livelihood (MacPhail et al., 2022). The mining company and RHCs agree that something must be sacrificed to establish a mine. But, it is the company's assessment of the RHCs' sacrifices as "limited" that constitutes the rationale for concluding that the compromise is reasonable for realizing co-existence (ibid.).

This rationale was challenged by the CAB's assessment, but is reiterated and further developed in the government's decision to approve the mining permit. The government assesses the impacts on reindeer herding as "limited in scale and time" and argues that mining represents good overall management of the area's resources given the economic benefits at stake (Swedish Government, 2022a, p. 31). By attaching conditions aiming at minimizing the impacts, for example, fencing, motorized transportation of reindeers, constructions to facilitate passage and additional consultations, a consensual solution for co-existence is constructed (p. 3).

The Minister of Enterprise and innovation concluded: "one [the mining company] should be able to co-exist with reindeer husbandry in this area" (SVT Nyheter, 2022). However, the National Union of the Swedish Sámi, SSR, responded that transporting reindeers on trucks is not consistent with traditional reindeer herding which the Swedish state has made commitments to protect, and the Sámi RHCs do not have resources for additional consultative processes (Dagens Nyheter, 2022).

Tracing the Ideas Underlying the State's Bargaining Strategies

A prominent feature of the Swedish state's bargaining strategy is an a priori assumption that there is a strong correspondence between resource extraction, economic growth and welfare benefits for everybody. Moreover, dialogue, collaboration, consensual solutions and co-existence are identified as unique Swedish virtues that will produce desirable national inclusive welfare outcomes. These ideas are not new but reflect historic processes and experiences (see e.g. Swedish Ministry of Enterprise and Innovation, 2022). In the following, I trace this approach to bargains during an early social democratic era and argue that these approaches were institutionalized into a distinct Swedish corporativist policy style and that this policy style still shapes environmental politics and associated extractive bargains.

In 1932, the Social Democrats took over political power in Sweden, which they held for 44 years. They returned to power in 1982, lost it in 2006 but ruled in minority between 2014 and 2022. The social democratic party played a major role in shaping the modern Swedish welfare state, and a corner stone in the dominance of Swedish social democracy was the labour movement's ability to mobilize the majority of the working class (Jansson, 2020). The leaders of the Swedish labour organization consciously built an organizational identity promoting reformism and a unique spirit of negotiation and consensus. This strategy took shape at the beginning of the 1900s when European social democracy was torn apart by internal rivalry between reformist and revolutionary fractions (ibid.). So, when the Swedish Social Democrats took power in 1932, their goal was to reform society with the help of the state and the political system. The labour movement was prepared for class compromise in order to realize political reforms and the welfare state (Lundmark & Åmark, 2001; Jansson, 2020).

These developments resulted in a negotiated compromise between labour, that is, the working class's demand for economic redistribution, and capital, expressed as the business sector's demand to maintain a capitalist system (Lundmark & Åmark, 2001). The Swedish Labour Organization (LO) concluded a landmark labour market peace agreement, the Saltsjöbaden Agreement, in 1938. The agreement, which forced the labour market parties to negotiate whenever a conflict arose, became known internationally as the Swedish model and effectively ended open industrial relations conflicts (Jansson, 2020). It became the ultimate symbol of the willingness to make negotiated compromise, and in the mid-1950s the spirit of consensus was institutionalized in Swedish labour market politics and practices (ibid.).

According to Dahlkvist (1975, p. 204), this historical bargain was made possible by the coincidence of several historically unique conditions: (1) a historic economic depression in the 1930s which required state interventions; (2) the working class's short-sighted demands for reforms and security; and (3) the capitalistic business interests' need for political influence when parliamentary representation was inefficient due to the social democratic majority.

Hence, the needs of the working class, represented by LO, and capitalist business interests happened to converge with the tools that the social democratic ideology and party could provide. The social democratic ideology stressed a "productivist strategy" claiming a positive-sum relationship between equality and efficiency: optimal economic efficiency must rely on social rights and equality (Esping-Andersen & van Kersbergen, 1992).

The compromise of the 1930s paved the way for the realization of the Swedish post-war welfare state, "the People's Home". This metaphor was coined to illustrate the idea of the state as a democratic family in which all its members enjoyed equal status and participated collectively in decision making (Tilton, 1990, p. 128). The People's Home was in large measure achieved through corporativism and institutionalized a specific social democratic ideal about the relationship between the state and interest organizations (Rothstein, 1992). Important economic bargains were made by institutionalized interest organizations, that is, the labour unions, the employers organizations and the top capitalist interests, outside of parliament but with the state as an active enabler and supervisor (Dahlkvist, 1975). Rothstein (1992) concludes that no Swedish policy areas escaped the corporativist approach—until the 1980s this political culture was hardly questioned. Reflecting this history, a host of literature describes Swedish politics as the epitome of a consensual policy style founded on rational and anticipatory political behaviour (Hinnfors, 1995, 1997).

However, this social democratic approach developed under unique conditions which during the 1930s created mutually beneficial relationships between labour, employers and capital (Dahlkvist, 1975). In the 1970s, the economic crises and huge budget deficits in the public sector foiled the symbiotic relationship: the needs of the working class and the social democratic party no longer coincided with the needs of the business and capital owners (ibid.). Some researchers argue that this marked the end of the Swedish Model, while others emphasize the continuity of Swedish consensus politics and efforts to find compromise. Reflecting the latter, the Swedish Social Democrats launched a new so-called Third Way economic policy, this time a compromise between neoliberalism and the previously dominant Keynesianism (Lundberg & Åmark, 2001). The state's justification for the new approach was still the welfare state and the capacity to uphold its benefits for all, but in a new way. Now, global competitiveness and attractiveness to capital were framed as valuable assets; the welfare state was to ensure that as many citizens as possible would have a share in this new global economy (ibid., p. 173).

Indeed, the Swedish Social Democratic party has demonstrated a capacity to adapt their idea of a welfare state to new political challenges and realities. In a speech as the new leader of the party in March 1996, Göran Persson proclaimed the achievement of an ecologically sustainable society to be a new mission (Lundqvist, 2004). Two weeks later, as prime minister, he stated that Sweden should be "an internationally driving force and a forerunner in the endeavors to create an ecologically sustainable development" (Swedish Parliamentary Record 22 March 1996). To achieve this objective, he referred to the experience of building the welfare state, the People's Home:

> [Our party] once built the People's Home in broad consensus on the conditions for production, increased standards of living, and security for everyone. Now, we have a similar mission. We will realize the vision of a green welfare state. (Persson, 1997; Lundqvist, 2004)

As Lundqvist (2004) points out, it is important to note the path dependency of this strategy. The "Green People's Home" can be seen as instrumental in getting acceptance for the further "consensualization" of environmental politics. "Corporatist" governance through co-operation between national government and organized interests helped build the social welfare state and was now envisaged as the vehicle for building the sustainable society. New win-wins were constructed between the working class, the business sector/capital and environmental gains. Green jobs, economic growth and increased competitiveness on international markets were envisioned to go hand in hand with environmental benefits.

Analytical Type of Bargains

Returning to the analytical bargaining types outlined in Chap. 1, the Swedish type, in its most recent forms, can be seen as a kind of "climate bargain". The current vision of the Swedish state is to expand Swedish mineral extraction, to supply Europe with needed raw material and to increase the competitiveness of the Swedish industry. The justifying rational is increased economic growth, employment, welfare—and sustainability—to the benefit of all Swedes in all parts of the country, thereby also resonating in some ways with social redistribution bargains. "Sustainable development" captures the contemporary Swedish state's efforts to forge a justifying narrative which emphasizes win-wins between the working middle class, the business sector and capital owners and the state's ambition to take a lead in the transition towards a low carbon economy.

However, contemporary extractive bargains in Sweden are better understood in the context of the historic bargains that enabled the development of the Swedish welfare state, the People's Home. Although the former social democratic hegemony is broken, it created path dependencies and a specific policy style which continues to shape Swedish bargains. First, a corporativist and consensus-oriented policy style, emphasizing dialogue, collaboration, consensual solutions and compromise form an integrated part of the Swedish bargaining type. Second, an inherited productivist approach assuming a positive-sum relationship between social rights and equality—and economic growth, industrial production and competitiveness—permeate contemporary bargains and their assumptions about harmonious co-existence. In the 1930s, a precondition paving the way for this approach was a convergence of needs by the party's main constituency, the working class, the Swedish business and capital owners, and classical social democratic policy tools to tackle the then economic recession (Dahlkvist, 1975).

Today, the climate crises offer similar opportunities to seek bargains based on perceived "win-wins" between the workers, the business sector and a common societal vision to create welfare and a sustainable future. In this sense, the Swedish bargaining type addresses the climate crisis. However, it is not a clear-cut "climate bargain" and a more accurate characterization may be "sustainability and welfare for all". Welfare *for all* signals a core value about the importance of *delivering* and *distributing* socio-economic benefits in the form of jobs, income and welfare. Accordingly, Swedish bargains typically include a component, and northern version, of the "social redistribution bargains" described in Chap. 1.

Concluding Normative Analysis

Finally, I use the typology of extractive bargains outlined in Chap. 1 to conduct a normative analysis. A fair analysis requires attention to the state's objectives and justifying ideas, as laid out in Swedish mineral and environmental policy, *and* actual implementation, in this case in the Kallak/Gállok case.

As stipulated in Swedish mineral and environmental policy, the state's primary objective is to achieve economic competitiveness and growth by a sustainable use of Sweden's mineral resources—in harmony with environmental, nature and cultural values. In the most recent policy documents, synergies with climate mitigation benefits are increasingly stressed. Although governments of different political colours have subscribed to these objectives, the approach represents a classic Swedish Social Democratic approach claiming a positive-sum relationship between extraction/production, industrial efficiency and equality by ensuring fair distribution of benefits in the form of jobs and growth to people in all parts of the country. Hence, meeting (some) social justice goals, for example, jobs and growth for the working and middle class in urban *and* rural areas, is an integral part of the state's strategy. A path to "just transition" is also identified by constructing win-wins between social (job creation), economic (industrial competitiveness) and environmental benefits (reduced emissions) associated with a green transition. As stipulated by the Mineral Strategy (Swedish Ministry of Enterprise and Innovation, 2013), mineral extraction should be conducted "in harmony" with environmental, nature and cultural values, and hence environmental impacts minimized. Moreover, a traditional Swedish consensual policy style, a history of direct bargaining between corporately organized interest groups, an institutionalized "collaboration" culture and a corresponding emphasis on dialogue and consensus building in contemporary Swedish mineral policy could pave the way for an open and inclusive decision-making process in which affected local community actors are able to influence the outcomes of bargains. Considering these characteristics of the Swedish bargaining style, one could argue that Swedish extractive bargains are "progressive" or "constructive".

However, as evident in the government's decision about the mining permit—which constitutes the core of the bargain made in the Kallak/Gállok case—there are several problems with the implementation of this bargaining strategy when applied in the context of Indigenous peoples and mining. As outlined below, many of the pre-conditions that shaped the historically successful bargains and the Swedish policy style were fundamentally different, or not in place, when the government made its decision about a mining permit in Kallak/Gállok.

First, a positive-sum relationship between resource extraction, industrial efficiency, Sámi reindeer herding and social justice—from a Sámi point of view—is hard to see. In a context characterized by land use competition, the relationship between mineral extraction and reindeer herding is antagonistic rather than synergistic. Therefore, the interests of the Sámi RHCs were in conflict with the workers represented by their unions *and* the business and capital owners promoting extraction. In contrast to union interests which could be aligned with goals about economic and industrial efficiency, Sámi reindeer herding interests are rarely compatible with resource extraction.

Second, the assumption about a positive-sum relationship and harmonious co-existence, which permeates Swedish mineral policy and policy style, neglects the fact that ecological systems and natural resources have limits. The reality in a reindeer herding, and land use context, may be more of a zero-sum relationship. Accordingly, the state's and the Sámi RHCs' understandings of impacts, sacrifice zones and the capacity of reindeer herding to mitigate disturbances differ dramatically. Notwithstanding Sámi efforts to communicate their perspectives, the government's decision and the conditions in particular illustrate how the government pursued its a priori position that co-existence is possible. The conditions stipulate rather minor adjustments of the mining plans, referring solely to the government's own understanding of how reindeer herding and Sámi culture are affected.

Third, as illustrated by the Kallak/Gállok permit process, the meaning of dialogue, collaboration and consensual agreements—core components of the Swedish policy style—are problematic in a Sámi context. While the traditional egalitarian Swedish policy style developed in a context where strong interdependencies existed between the marginalized interest (the workers), their organizations (the unions) and the ruling party (the Social Democrats), no such interdependencies exist with the Sámi. Sámi organizations stood outside of the corporative structures that provided the unions with access to political decision making and influence. Although open for input in theory, the Swedish mineral permit process has proved rather closed to the Sámi RHCs. Meaningful dialogue and collaboration are typically hampered by uneven power relations, lack of capacity and insufficient resources, and the RHCs have difficulties in asserting influence in decision making (see also Raitio et al., 2020).

Fourth, Indigenous rights are not sufficiently integrated in the Swedish mineral and environmental legislation guiding the permitting process (Raitio et al., 2020). In contrast to many other policy areas where Sweden has demonstrated a progressive ambition to ensure equality and protect human rights, proper implementation of Sámi rights has lagged behind (ibid.). Consequently, the state can escape the duty to address Sámi rights in its bargains. In spite a few general statements about Sámi rights and culture, the government justified its mining permit decision in Kallak/Gállok without addressing the topic and without explaining if/how the decision was deemed consistent with stipulated Sámi rights.

Finally, path dependency and the Swedish policy style generally risk producing an environmental politics based on ecological modernization (Lundqvist, 2004) and an optimistic "more of everything" approach (see Beland Lindahl et al., 2017). Win-win solutions are seen as desirable and possible, and growth is expected to be generated to the benefit for all and the nation. Accordingly, goal conflicts that ought to be made visible, handled and addressed tend to be downplayed, or even neglected (ibid.). This tendency is evident in the Swedish mineral policy and in the government's decision in the Kallak/Gállok case. The bargain is portrayed as a compromise enabling benefits from a mine *and* a viable reindeer herding and Sámi culture in the same area. However, the critical land use and goal conflicts largely remain unaddressed.

Consequently, as applied in the context of the Kallak/Gállok case, the Swedish bargaining type hardly lives up to what the typology introduced in Chap. 1 defines as "progressive" or "constructive". It rather resembles the type labelled "cognitive dissonance", referring to situations when proclaimed goals may be progressive but the actual practice is at odds with goals. To what extent this failure reflects a deliberate process, that is "organized hypocrisy", is not clear. The cognitive dissonance may also be an effect of an unreflective and self-righteous political tradition embedded in the Swedish welfare state project, and a Swedish policy style formed by path dependency. While the traditional Swedish bargaining type may have served the working class well, its legacy on contemporary extractive bargains with Indigenous people rather seems to maintain and enforce social injustices. The Kallak/Gállok process has not yet come to an end but there is a risk that the final bargain ends up as a "Faustian" type: a bargain between state elites and other social groups which support extractivism in the short term, but severely compromises or destroys the possibilities for long-term social and environmental justice of the affected Sámi RHCs.

References

Anshelm, J., & Haikola, S. (2018). Depoliticization, repoliticization, and environmental concerns—Swedish mining politics as an instance of environmental politicization. *ACME: An International Journal for Critical Geographies, 17*(2), 561–596.

Bäckström, L. (2015). Svensk gruvrätt: En rättsvetenskaplig studie rörande förutsättningarna för utvinning av mineral. Doctoral dissertation, Luleå University of Technology, Luleå.

Beland Lindahl, K., Johansson, A., Zachrisson, A., & Viklund, R. (2018). Competing pathways to sustainability? Exploring conflicts over mine establishments in the Swedish mountain region. *Journal of Environmental Management, 218*, 402–415.

Beland Lindahl, K., Sténs, A., Sandström, C., Johansson, J., Lidskog, R., Ranius, T., & Roberge, J.-M. (2017). The Swedish forestry model: More of everything? *Forest Policy and Economics, 77*, 44–55.

Beowulf. (2021). Beowulf Mining plc Kallak 16 October 2020, ProHearings, Stockholm. Retrieved July 7, 2021, from https://beowulfmining.com/wp-content/uploads/2020/10/20201015-Beowulf-Mining-ProHearings-Presentation.pdf

County Administration Board. (2014). Samråd enligt 8 kap. 18§ minerallagen (1991:45), Ert dnr. BS 22-559-2013. 2014-10-01, CAB dnr. 543-5306-14.

Dagens Nyheter. (2022). Regeringen beviljar tillstånd för omstridd gruva i Kallak. Published March 22, 2022. Retrieved April 10, 2022, from https://www.dn.se/sverige/besked-om-kallakgruvan-vantas-pa-presskonferens/

Dahlkvist, M. (1975). Staten, socialdemokratin och socialismen—En inledande analys. Verdandi Debatt nr 75. Lund: Prisma.

Esping-Andersen, G., & van Kersbergen, K. (1992). Contemporary research on social democracy. *Annual Review of Sociology, 18*, 187–208.

Fjellborg, D., Beland Lindahl, K., & Zachrisson, A. (2022). What to do when the mining company comes to town? Mapping actions of anti-extraction movements in Sweden 2009–2019. *Resources Policy, 75*, 102514.

Hifab. (2013). *Miljökonsekvensbeskrivning—till ansökan om bearbetningskoncession för fyndigheten Kallak Norra*. Hifab AB.

Hinnfors, J. (1995). *På dagordningen? Svensk politisk stil i förändring*. Nerenius & Santcrus.

Hinnfors, J. (1997). Still the politics of compromise? Agenda setting strategy in Sweden. *Scandinavian Political Studies, 20*(2), 159–177.

Jåhkågaska tjiellde and Sirges. (2014). Yttrande avseende Jokkmokk Iron Mines AB:s kompletterande ansökan om bearbetningskonscession Dnr BS 22-559-2013. 2014-09-10, Dnr. 543-6255-13.

Jåhkågaska tjiellde and Sirges. (2015). Ärende N2015/1677/FÖF, Yttrande angående LS i NBs yttrande angående samhällekonomiska överväganden i rubricerat ärende. 2015-09-14, Ref. nr: 1022943.9.0032.

Jåhkågaska tjiellde and Sirges. (2016). Ärende N2015/1677/FÖF—Ansökan om bearbetningskoncession för området Kallak Nr 1 i Jokkmokks kommun. 2016-04-15.

Jåhkågaska tjiellde and Sirges. (2018). Yttrande i anledning av ansökan om bearbetningskoncession, Kallak nr. 1 i Jokkmokks kommun, ärende N2017-04553-FÖF. 2018-02-02.

Jansson, J. (2020). *Crafting the movement: Identity entrepreneurs in the Swedish trade union movement, 1920–1940*. ILR Press.

JIMAB. (2013). Ansökan om bearbetningskoncession för fyndigheten Kallak Norra belägen ca 2 km SO om byn Björkholmen, Jokkmokks kommun, Norrbottens län, 2013-04-25.

Knobblock, E., & Pettersson, Ö. (2010). Restructuring and risk-reduction in mining: Employment implications for northern Sweden. *Fennia—International Journal of Geography, 188*(1), 61–75.

Lawrence, R., & Kløcker Larsen, R. (2017). The politics of planning: Assessing the impacts of mining on Sami lands. *Third World Quarterly, 38*(5), 1164–1180.

Lawrence, R., & Kløcker Larsen, R. (2019). *Fighting to be herd: Impacts of the proposed Boliden copper mine in Laver, Älvsbyn, Sweden for the Semisjaur Njarg Sami reindeer herding community*. Stockholm Environmental Institute and Sydney Environmental Institute, Stockholm.

Liljenäs, I. (1992). From mine to outer space: The case of Kiruna—A town in Northern Sweden. In C. Neil, M. Tykkläinen, & J. Bradbury (Eds.), *Coping with closure. An international comparison of mine town experiences* (pp. 247–265). Routledge.

Lundmark, L. (2008). *Stulet land: svensk makt på samisk mark*. Ordfront.

Lundberg, U., & Åmark, K. (2001). Social rights and social security: The Swedish welfare state, 1900–2000. *Scandinavian Journal of History, 26*(3), 157–176.

Lundqvist, L. (2004). *Sweden and ecological governance: Straddling the fence*. Manchester University Press.

MacPhail, F., Beland Lindahl, K., & Bowles, P. (2022). Why do mines fail to obtain a social license to operate? Insights from the proposed Kallak Iron Mine (Sweden) and the Prosperity/New Prosperity Gold–Copper Mine (Canada). *Environmental Management*. https://doi.org/10.1007/s00267-021-01587-3

Mineral Inspectorate. (2013). Arbetsplan för provbrytning och undersökningsarbeten inom undersökningstillståndet Kallak nr 1, Jokkmokks kommun, Norrbottens län, 2013-03-22, dnr. BS 211-467-2013.

Mineral Inspectorate. (2015). Yttrande Ansökan om bearbetningskoncession för området Kallak K nr 1 i Jokkmokks kommun, Norrbottens län, 2015-02-13, dnr. BS 22-559-2013.

Mining for Generations. (2022a). About Mining for generations. Retrieved April 25, 2022, from http://www.miningforgenerations.com/about/

Mining for Generations. (2022b). Sustainability: Respect for divergent interests. Retrieved April 25, 2022, from http://www.miningforgenerations.com/coexistens-at-its-peak/

Persson, G. (1997). Så gör vi Sverige till ett föregångsland för ekologisk hållbarhet! Prime Minister's speech at SSU:s and Byggnads Environmental Seminar, 11 April. Earlier available under 'Statsministern', 'Tal m.m.', at www.sb.gov.se_info.rosenbad

Prop. (1985/86:3). Förslag till lag om hushållning med naturresurser m. m. (Government Bill).

Raitio, K., Allard, C., & Lawrence, R. (2020). Mineral extraction in Swedish Sápmi: The regulatory gap between Sami rights and Sweden's mining permitting practices. *Land Use Policy, 99*, 105001.

Rothstein, B. (1992). *Den korporativa staten*. Norstedts.

Sehlin MacNeil, K. (2017). *Extractive violence on Indigenous country: Sami and Aboriginal views on conflicts and power relations with extractive industries*. Umeå Doctoral dissertation, Umeå University.

Sirges. (2018). Yttrande avseende ärende N2017/04553/FÖF—Ansökan om bearbetningskoncession för området Kallak nr 1, Jokkmokks kommun. 2018-02-05.

Sörlin, S. (1988). *Framtidslandet. Debatten om Norrland och naturresurserna under det industriella genombrottet*. Carlssons.

SVT Nyheter. (2022). Ministern: "Vi har ställt 12 stycken väldigt starka krav". Published March 22, 2022. Retrieved April 25, 2022, from https://www.svt.se/nyheter/sapmi/ministern-vi-har-stallt-12-stycken-valdigt-starka-krav

Swedish Government. (2017). Energimyndighetens regleringsbrev för budgetåret 2018, anslag 1:20 Industriklivet, dnr M2017/03180/S [delvis].

Swedish Government. (2022a). Regeringsbeslut—Ansökan om bearbetningskoncession enligt minerallagen (1991:45) för området Kallak K nr 1 i Jokkmokks kommun, Norrbottens län, 2022-03-22, N2017/04553.

Swedish Government. (2022b). Smart industri—en nyindustrialiseringsstrategi för Sverige. Retrieved April 25, 2022, from https://www.regeringen.se/informationsmaterial/2016/01/smart-industri%2D%2D-en-nyindustrialiseringsstrategi-for-sverige/

Swedish Ministry of Enterprise and Innovation. (2013). *Sweden's minerals strategy: For sustainable use of Sweden's mineral resources that creates growth throughout the country*. Stockholm: Government Offices of Sweden.

Swedish Ministry of Enterprise and Innovation. (2016). *Smart industry—A strategy for new industrialization for Sweden*, N2016.06. Stockholm: Government Offices of Sweden.

Swedish Ministry of Enterprise and Innovation. (2022). *The future of Swedish industry: A strategy for green and digital transition*. Retrieved April 25, 2022, from https://www.regeringen.se/493912/contentassets/be7e3504e9d640b0b998b15fac9e4cda/framti dens-industri%2D%2D-en-strategi-om-gron-och-digital-omstallning.pdf

Swedish Ministry of Environment and Energy. (2018). *Anpassad miljöprövning för en grön omställning*. Ds 2018:38.

Tano, S., Pettersson, Ö., & Stjernström, O. (2016). Labour income effects of the recent "mining boom" in northern Sweden. *Resources Policy, 49*, 31–40.

Tarras-Wahlberg, N. H. (2014). Social license to mine in Sweden: Do companies go the extra mile to gain community acceptance? *Mineral Economics, 27*, 143.

Tilton, T. (1990). *The political theory of Swedish social democracy: Through the welfare state to socialism*. Clarendon Press.

Zachrisson, A., & Beland Lindahl, K. (2019). Political opportunity and mobilization: The evolution of a Swedish mining-sceptical movement. *Resources Policy, 64*, 101477.

5

Extractive Settler Colonialism: Navigating Extractive Bargains on Indigenous Territories in Canada

Clifford Gordon Atleo and Jonathan Martin Boron

Introduction

As people around the world deal with multiple interrelated crises—the increasingly severe impacts of climate change, the lingering COVID-19 pandemic, armed conflict, and related economic turmoil—the shift towards a post-carbon future has become urgent. Bowles and Andrews (Chaps. 1 and 14 in this volume) offer us insight into the massive shift in resource extraction as demand moves from fossil fuels to the minerals and metals needed to power a decarbonizing transition within the context of "extractive bargains." In this volume, many of our co-authors engage this concept within an asymmetric north-south dynamic that has been plagued by centuries of colonialism including the present incarnation of neoliberal extractivism.

C. G. Atleo (✉) • J. M. Boron
School of Resource and Environmental Management, Simon Fraser University, Burnaby, BC, Canada
e-mail: clifford_atleo@sfu.ca; Jonathan_boron@sfu.ca

P. Bowles, N. Andrews (eds.), *Extractive Bargains*, Frontiers of Globalization,
https://doi.org/10.1007/978-3-031-32172-6_5

In this chapter, we consider extractive bargains in Canada as they impact Indigenous nations struggling to re-assert their rights of self-determination. We begin with a summary of extractive settler colonialism that is, in many ways, unique to Canada. This is followed by an examination of the political, legal, and economic mechanisms utilized to navigate contestation over Indigenous lands, resources, and rights. We pay particular attention to the extractive bargains made in a predominantly fossil fuel-based economy and consider the potential impacts of the emerging post-carbon economy.

Extractive Settler Colonialism in Canada

The modern world that Indigenous peoples inhabit, experience, and navigate has been shaped by imperialism (Smith, 2021). While Marx and Engels predicted that internal contradictions would bring about the collapse of capitalism, Lenin asserted that imperialism would prolong capitalism's existence (Cohn, 2005). The growth of empires, particularly those emanating from Europe, was fuelled by capitalism's unquenchable necessity for incessant growth. In the centuries that followed Columbus' "discovery" of Taíno territory in 1492, countries like Mexico, the United States of America, and Canada were built by slave labour from the African continent on the stolen Indigenous lands of Turtle Island (North America). Some writers (Galeano, 1997; Altamirano-Jiménez, 2011) have characterized colonialism in the Global South as extractive.

Despite formal decolonization in the eighteenth and nineteenth centuries, much of the political economy of Latin America remains extractive intensive (Chagnon et al., 2022; Gudynas, 2020). Settler colonialism, on the other hand, is about permanent occupation of Indigenous lands and the establishment of colonial institutions that replicate social, political, economic, and legal traditions from Europe (Altamirano-Jiménez, 2011). Former Canadian Supreme Court Chief Justice Antonio Lamer captured the essence of settler colonialism when he succinctly asserted that settlers were here to stay (Asch, 2014). Exactly how Indigenous and settler societies would coexist has been an ongoing challenge since before Canada became a country. The realities of colonization have become less and less palatable, and the state and resource extractive industries have had to make new extractive bargains to accommodate the changing terrain and maintain legitimacy.

Canada is unique among wealthy liberal democracies in that it has maintained a resource-intensive staples economy that never matured or diversified to the extent that its fellow G7 countries have (Innis & Ray, 1999). Canada remains heavily dependent on the extraction and export of raw resources in ways that influence decisions about the environment, labour, taxation, and relations with Indigenous peoples (Mills & Tufts, 2019; Stanford, 2008; Watkins, 2007) making the colonialism in Canada both settler *and extractive* in nature. In 2009, former Prime Minister Stephen Harper claimed that Canada had no history of colonialism (Ljunggren, 2009). Completely ignoring the colonialism experienced by Indigenous peoples, Harper was referring to Canada's reputation abroad. Granted, its global imperial pedigree pales in comparison to its progenitor or its southern neighbour, but Canada does lead in a rather striking category relevant here. Seventy-five per cent of the world's mining companies are headquartered in Canada, and this is due to a calculated effort to create a hospitable regulatory environment for extractive industries (Deneault & Sacher, 2012).

Extractive settler colonialism has evolved in Canada in a variety of ways that impact Indigenous peoples and territories. We are mindful that Indigenous peoples are diverse and while many share some common experiences, colonization occurred at different times, paces, and intensities across Canada (Atleo & Boron, 2022). Treaties (or lack thereof) with the newcomers varied from coast to coast to coast. Some treaties were alliances between sovereign partners or "peace and friendship" covenants. Others have been interpreted by the state as land surrenders. And while significant portions of Canada fall under historical treaties, there are few treaties—historic or modern—in the majority of British Columbia (BC).[1] This has led to a substantial number of legal challenges over land

[1] Comprehensive claims agreements (CCAs—colloquially known as "modern day treaties") grew out of the 1975 federal comprehensive claims policy, which followed the 1973 *Calder* decision, where the Supreme Court of Canada was split on the existence and nature of Aboriginal Title regarding a land claim initiated by Nisga'a chief Frank Calder. CCAs are not treaties under international law, while many argue that "historic" treaties are.

title. After Canadian confederation in 1867 and the passing of the *Indian Act* in 1876, however, Indigenous nations began to fall under a common political-economic framework. Crucial to understanding extractive settler colonialism in Canada is that it is a structure of institutions and relationships (Wolfe, 2006) that remains ongoing (Lowman & Barker, 2015; Tully, 2000) and adaptive (Corntassel, 2012). We argue that Canada has been forced to adapt to changing legal, political, and economic realities brought about by the persistent assertion of Indigenous self-determination. Despite some successes for Indigenous peoples, Canada and extractive capital remain committed to finding new routes and mechanisms to continue exploiting resources.

While European settlement did not begin in earnest in BC until the mid-nineteenth century, change to Indigenous lives began immediately after contact. The Nuu-chah-nulth peoples on the west coast of Vancouver Island provide an illustrative example of how extractive bargains in the past might be informative for the future. Sailing for the British navy, Captain Cook arrived in Nuu-chah-nulth waters in 1778. He stayed for a month initiating a trading relationship with the Mowachaht/Muchalaht peoples that sparked the Pacific maritime fur trade, which profoundly altered Indigenous subsistence patterns and economies (Inglis & Haggarty, 2000). Extraction that began with sea otter pelts shifted to seals, whales, fish, and trees and would ultimately endanger all these species. While increasingly intensive extraction represented a long-term threat to territories and communities (Kuokkanen, 2011), Indigenous peoples would consistently try to *co-craft* change to support their ongoing self-determination struggle (Atleo, 2018; Reid, 2014). From first contact, relations with explorers, settlers, and colonizers have been marked by conflict *and* cooperation. Early conflicts included the burning of sailing ships and bombardment of Indigenous villages. Present-day conflicts, while still at times being violent (i.e. Kanehsatake/Oka Crisis, Esgenoopetitj/Burnt Church, Gustafsen Lake, Six Nations/Caledonia, Wet'suwet'en, Ipperwash, etc.), are just as likely to be resolved in settler courts (UBCIC, 2005). From the beginning, it has been about land (Wolfe, 2006). While many treaties have been negotiated, in practice, Canada has adopted the doctrine of *terra nullius* ("land belonging to no one").

Settler Government Law and Policy

While the focus of this chapter is on land and resources, we would be remiss if we did not address Canada's legacy of Indian residential schools, which devastated Indigenous families and communities. The Truth and Reconciliation Commission of Canada (2015) described the impacts on Indigenous peoples as cultural genocide. In addition to residential schools, Canada governed the lives of Indigenous peoples as wards of the state through the *Indian Act*, legislation which remains in place today. In 1969, the *Statement of the Government of Canada on Indian Policy, 1969* (commonly known as the "White Paper") called for an end to the *Indian Act* and the Department of Indian Affairs. The goal of the policy was to get rid of the "Indian Problem" by getting rid of Indians (as distinct peoples), absorbing them into a multicultural Canadian society, and getting Canada out of the Indian business.[2] This vision was consistent with then Prime Minister Pierre Trudeau's vision of a just, liberal society. Based on legitimate fears of assimilation, however, the response from Indigenous peoples led to a new era of cultural revitalization and political organizing. The policy paper was rescinded, but Dale Turner (2006) argues that White Paper liberalism continues to influence government political and economic policy.

Laws, Courts, and Negotiations

In 1927, the *Indian Act* was amended to make it illegal for Indigenous peoples to hire lawyers in the pursuit of land claims (Tennant, 1992), as Canada feared the judgements of its own courts. This provision was removed in 1951. The Nisga'a Land Committee was established in 1883, which sent numerous delegations to petition provincial and federal leaders, and even the King in England (Trosper, 2009). In 1967, Frank Calder, president of the Nisga'a Tribal Council, sued the government of BC to reclaim ownership of Nisga'a lands. The Supreme Court of Canada

[2] We normally use "Indigenous peoples" or specific names of Indigenous communities, but we use the somewhat archaic terms "Indian" and "Aboriginal" when referring to specific legal or legislative terms.

(SCC) ruled in 1973 for the first time that Aboriginal title *might* exist but dismissed the case on a technicality (Trosper, 2009). In 1975, Canada responded with its comprehensive claims policy and began negotiating land claims. Since *Calder*, a mixture of conflict, evolving common law, government policy, international declarations, and industry initiatives has shaped the nature and scope of Aboriginal title and its implications for extractive industries. Whether Indigenous peoples have engaged in conflict or cooperation there has long been a sense of inevitability of settler permanence and resource extraction (Raibmon, 2005). In response, Indigenous peoples have often adopted a relational approach to asserting their self-determination, with myriad strategies, including legal, political, and economic (Boron & Markey, 2020; Mitchell et al., 2019; Murphy, 2019).

In 1982, Canada patriated its constitution, which included section 35(1) that reads, "existing Aboriginal treaty rights of the Aboriginal peoples of Canada are hereby recognized and affirmed" (Turner, 2006, p. 3). The Nisga'a would negotiate for over 20 years culminating in an agreement in 2000 that included a cash settlement of nearly $200 million, self-government provisions, and 2019 square kilometres of land, representing 8 per cent of their original land claim. Embroiled in their own disputes over fisheries and forestry, the Gitxsan and Wet'suwet'en peoples launched their own Aboriginal title case, commonly known as *Delgamuukw* in 1987. BC Supreme Court Judge Allan McEachern ruled that Gitxsan and Wet'suwet'en title had been extinguished when BC joined confederation. The case was appealed, and the SCC ruled in 1997 that BC had no right to extinguish Aboriginal title. The court did not actually *award* title, however, sending the case back to the lower court, but it did affirm Aboriginal title as a right recognized by section 35(1) of the constitution. *Delgamuukw* also affirmed Settler land rights and characterized Aboriginal title as a *burden* on underlying Crown title (Borrows, 2007), placing the latter in the superior position and solidifying settler colonialism in Canada. The SCC also affirmed settler governments' right to infringe upon Aboriginal rights for a whole range of purposes relating to settlement and development (Pasternak, 2020). The *Delgamuukw* ruling also stated that the recognition of Aboriginal title included "an inescapable economic component" (Atleo et al., 2022, p. 159). Combined with the *Haida* and *Taku* cases in 2004, the recognition of Aboriginal rights and the Crown's ability to infringe with adequate "consultation and accommodation" became clearer, essentially leading to a new cost of doing business on Indigenous lands.

There is a common understanding in Canada that a "victory" for one First Nation in court is a victory for *only that First Nation*, while a "loss" has tended to mean a loss for all. Evolving Aboriginal case law has established that the burden of proof lies with individual First Nations to determine their exclusive use and occupancy within the boundaries of their territory, of a continuous nature, and to do so in a way that Indigenous land tenure and governance systems are legible within colonial courts (Pasternak, 2020). Despite the odds, one nation—*Tsihlqot'in*—has been able to prove title in 2014 after twenty-five years of litigation and tens of millions of dollars in legal fees. But it's uncommon for communities to have the resources to prove their title in courts. Most conflict over resource extraction now happens within the framework of consultation and accommodation established in *Haida*, requiring Settler governments to act when infringement might occur on Indigenous lands, whether title has been "proven" or not.

Momentum from the changes in the constitution and Aboriginal case law has also been bolstered at the international level.

The United Nations Declaration on the Rights of Indigenous Peoples (UNDRIP)

The Declaration on the Rights of Indigenous Peoples was passed by the United Nations General Assembly in 2007. Canada was the last country in the world to remove its objector status in 2015, however in 2016 Jody Wilson-Raybould, Canada's first Indigenous Attorney General, stated that simplistic adoption of the UNDRIP into Canadian law was "unworkable" (Kirkup, 2016). Canada passed UNDRIP legislation in 2021, but key aspects of implementation remain contentious. At the heart of the debate is the UNDRIP principle of free, prior, and informed consent (FPIC) and whether this amounts to an Indigenous veto. Canada has made clear that neither the declaration nor Canada's adoption of it into law amounts to an Indigenous veto as evidenced by Prime Minister Justin Trudeau's position on Trans Mountain when he stated, "We are going to get the pipeline built. It is a project in the national interest…This project will go ahead" (Snyder, 2018). Unfortunately, when Indigenous peoples hear "the national interest" in Canada, it usually means their rights are about to be infringed.

New Costs of Doing Business

The evolving Indigenous rights frameworks internationally and domestically and resistance movements from coast to coast have forced Canada to become more creative in negotiating extractive bargains. As Bowles and Andrews (Chap. 1 in this volume) point out, several implications arise as the state seeks consensus or support for its actions. The state's central motivation is to maintain and strengthen its legitimacy, while ensuring a favourable investment climate for resource extraction companies through risk mitigation.[3] Canada's jurisdictional legitimacy, its *terra nullius* claim to land, is inextricably tied to the denial and subjugation of Indigenous jurisdictional authority and self-determination. Addressing Indigenous rights and title, which specifically impinge on the state's ability to protect private property and provide resource development certainty, has become a paramount concern. Reconciling the zero-sum game is the issue at hand as it pertains to securing resource investment. A variety of state actors, including Canada's judiciary, have committed to a vision of this reconciliation, built on the premise of maintaining state supremacy by engaging in tactics of economic accommodation, coercion, and violent repression (Barker, 2009).

In an effort to position itself globally (and in the eyes of its own settler constituents) as a progressive, multicultural nation, state-sponsored reconciliation has become the new norm. Despite commitments to a new relationship, settler governments maintain the reputation of moving slowly, especially with respect to the implementation of UNDRIP. While

[3] For a deeper examination of Canada's risk mitigation as a part of this conversation, see Pasternak and Dafnos (2018).

we wait for BC to comply with UNDRIP standards that it has set out through its 2019 Declaration on the Rights of Indigenous Peoples Act (DRIPA), a complex web of supra-regulatory contractual agreements has grown over the past few decades (Scott, 2020). This is largely due to deficiencies of environmental assessment and regulatory processes that fail to properly assess the socio-economic and environmental implications of project impacts on Indigenous rights and the increased necessity to obtain consent (Boron & Markey, 2020; Galbraith et al., 2007). As Scott (2020) argues, instead of legislative reform, the state understands that the current status quo continues to hold space for extraction contracting, delaying the breakdown of the state's jurisdictional authority on Indigenous lands, which might inevitably lead to more radical political and economic changes. Supporting this reconciliatory mode of extractivism, the courts believe that negotiated contracts seem to be the optimal solution as well, especially in *Delgamuukw*: "Ultimately it is through negotiated settlements, with good faith and give and take on all sides, reinforced by the judgments of this Court, that we will achieve...the reconciliation of the pre-existence of aboriginal societies with the sovereignty of the Crown" (*Delgamuukw v British Columbia*). In this passage, we see how the court reinforces its legitimacy and supremacy within these extractive bargains, while suggesting the use of contract law as the most suitable way to deal with constitutionally protected Aboriginal rights. While disaggregated state actors may at times be at odds with each other within an extractive bargain, as suggested by Bowles and Andrews (Chap. 1 in this volume), all these actors work individually to legitimize the settler state and its interests.

A Settler-Colonial Vision of Reconciliation Through Agreement or Force

Resource agreements typically come in two forms: either agreements made between settler and Indigenous governments that denote a revenue share of the tax royalty (governmental revenue sharing agreements) or private contracts negotiated between resource extraction companies and Indigenous communities, generally referred to as Impact Benefit

Agreements (IBAs).[4] Usually negotiated during the consultation phase of a proposed project, IBAs are advertised as legal contracts that mitigate adverse environmental and social impacts of development, provide a share of economic benefits through revenue sharing mechanisms and employment and contracting opportunities, and initiate the consultative process that serves to satisfy the state's fiduciary responsibility to Indigenous communities. While some might argue that the shift towards IBAs is a shirking of settler governments' fiduciary duties, Scott (2020) argues that IBAs also provide another adaptive mechanism for granting corporations access to Indigenous territories.

IBAs can be effective mechanisms for Indigenous nations looking for a greater level of participation in a development project, where they provide a platform to raise and address issues outside state regulatory mechanisms and can provide greater involvement in decision-making throughout the project's lifecycle (Gunton & Markey, 2021). At the same time, it is important to note that IBAs allow private extraction companies to define and limit Aboriginal rights. To ensure a project is immune to any future changes to the nature of Aboriginal rights, provisions within these agreements are structured to ensure project certainty. Further, provisions within IBAs limit the ability of community members to express dissent for a project (Cameron & Levitan, 2014). When IBAs are signed without full community participation, it can result in an agreement that does not adequately reflect broader community objectives, and unequal benefit distribution (Gunton & Markey, 2021). Further, the signing of IBAs that do not have full community support are often nonetheless used by the resource company, the state, and media intent on ensuring the extractive bargain, to prove community consent has been obtained. This tactic causes strife and division within and across communities.

This has had disastrous implications for the Wet'suwet'en as they try to resist the TransCanada (TC) Energy-owned Coastal Gaslink pipeline in northern BC. The province awarded an environmental assessment (EA) certificate for the project, citing the fact that both the Province and TC

[4] These private contracts may be called by a variety of different names including mutual benefit agreements, participation agreements, and community benefit agreements, but all typically share a similar purpose.

Energy were in the process of negotiating financial benefit sharing arrangements with affected First Nation band governments[5] as an important accommodating factor in fulfilling its fiduciary obligations of consultation and accommodation.[6] The Office of the Wet'suwet'en, the traditional governing body that asserts title over the territory in which the project crosses, was initially consulted by TC Energy and participated in the provincial EA process, but their concerns and alternative pipeline route suggestions were ignored. When Wet'suwet'en hereditary leadership issued an eviction notice and set up blockades to stop the project from destroying a culturally sacred river known as Wedzin Kwa, the settler-colonial court issued an injunction based on the EA certificate that was enforced by militarized police to criminalize and forcefully remove Wet'suwet'en members and hereditary leaders at gunpoint.[7] This injunction is now being utilized by private security workers hired by TC Energy to restrict access of Wet'suwet'en people from their own territory (Simmons, 2022).

While our focus here has been primarily on private agreements, we can also make note of how resource revenue sharing agreements with the state also work to economically accommodate impacts to Indigenous land rights, while maintaining state authority over the way the Indigenous share of the royalties are spent. Typically, these agreements offer a share of resource tax royalties collected by the state, the structure of which is typically industry and jurisdiction specific. As Pasternak (2020) and Boron and Markey (2020) note, mining royalties within these types of agreements are a percentage allocation taken from state tax payments, where the tax payments are not tied to industry activity the way a revenue-based model is, so there is no increase in the percentage allocated to an Indigenous signatory when there is an increase in the rate or pace of extraction and wealth generated from their territory. An increase in

[5] The Elected Band Council system is a system of governance created by the state through the *Indian Act* to replace traditional governing systems within Indigenous communities. The creation and maintenance of this system have ignited division and contestation within communities surrounding who has authority to speak on behalf of a community.

[6] See *Reasons for Ministers Decision-Coastal Gaslink Pipeline Project, Oct. 23, 2014.*

[7] For more on this police unit known as CIRG—Community Industry Response Group, see Forester (2022).

extraction-related impacts does not mean an increase in the percentage of revenue allocated to impacted Indigenous communities. This revenue sharing model can be seen across other industries such as oil and gas, and are not Indigenous community specific (Markey et al., 2019). With this model, the amount of revenue sharing is heavily dependent upon the province's tax structure, which inherently ties the amount of wealth an Indigenous community generates through this agreement to state tax regime decisions. This means that resource development tax subsidies and incentive programmes that encourage extraction limit this percentage further. Along with these resource revenue generation limitations placed upon Indigenous signatories, governmental revenue sharing agreements also include provisions that limit how the Indigenous community handles and ultimately spends the revenues. In a study examining different types of mining agreements in Secwepemcúl'ecw (an unceded territory in the interior plateau of BC), Boron and Markey (2020) found this paternalism embedded in an economic and community development agreement, where the state required the First Nation signatories to prepare annual statements outlining community priorities, goals, and specific outcomes that they intended to fund to enhance the communities' social, cultural, and economic well-being. The failure to provide an annual statement or the failure of these activities to meet the state's definition of "social, cultural, and economic well-being" would give the state cause to terminate the agreement (Boron & Markey, 2020). It is also important for us to note that the paternalism embedded within these community development provisions are Indigenous community specific when compared to agreements with non-Indigenous municipalities within BC.[8]

While it has been argued that revenues generated through IBAs can provide a pathway for socio-economic well-being and self-sufficiency (Slowey, 2008), there are serious and valid concerns that participation creates new modes of dependency on staples extraction. Economic reconciliation envisioned by the state requires economic assimilation into extractive land relations, which can lead to economic path dependency and staples dynamics that plague resource-dependent regions globally.

[8] See Peace River Agreement as an example.

Further, combined pressures from state actors ensuring that extraction is inevitable can be too overwhelming for anyone to refuse. In an example from Treaty 8 territory, Garvie and Shaw (2016) highlight how some communities choose to participate because they feel they have no other option as development will occur regardless of their consent. This phenomenon is also captured by Atleo et al. (2022) in describing how ambivalence can be a response to fossil fuel development projects. When we consider the use of state force to remove Indigenous land defenders in the case of the Coastal Gaslink pipeline, this sentiment is starkly understood. Extractive bargains, made under duress and threat of violence, undoubtedly define a Faustian bargain. While we agree that extractive bargains may lead to a multitude of socio-economic outcomes, these outcomes may not align with community values and interests and are housed within an extractive capitalist framework that severely limits Indigenous communities' ability to achieve sustainable long-term community well-being.

From Stakeholders to Co-owners: Indigenous Equity Ownership in Oil and Gas

Between 1974 and 1976, the Mackenzie Valley Pipeline Inquiry held more than thirty hearings in Dene, Inuit, and non-Indigenous communities in the Northwest Territories (NWT) in an attempt to resolve conflicts between Indigenous groups opposing the construction of natural gas pipelines from the Beaufort Sea to Alberta and beyond. One of the most rousing speeches was delivered by a 28-year-old chief from Fort Good Hope First Nation named Frank T'seleie, who stated,

> There will be no pipeline because we no longer intend to allow our land and our future to be taken away from us and that we are destroyed to make someone else rich. There will be no pipeline because we, the Dene people, are awakening to see the truth of the system of genocide that has been imposed on us and we will not go back to sleep…We are only asking now, as we asked you then, to let us live our own lives, in our own way, on our own land, without forever being threatened by invasion and extinction. We do not want to have to fight and struggle forever just to survive as a people. (Atleo, 2021, p. 364)

Renowned Dene writer Richard Van Camp described T'seleie's testimony as one of the most important speeches of our time (Deerchild, 2021). It inspired generations of Indigenous activists and the original pipeline proposals were not successful. A Mackenzie Valley pipeline proposal was revived in the 2000s, led by Imperial Oil, but this time the consortium included a 33.3 per cent ownership stake held by the Aboriginal Pipeline Group, of which T'seleie was a director. Many of the Indigenous communities in the NWT had negotiated land claims settlements by this time and T'seleie stated simply and unapologetically, "Times have changed" (Laird, 2003). The more recent Trans Mountain Pipeline expansion that spans from the northern Alberta oilsands to southwestern BC has also reflected this potential evolution in extractive bargains. The original proponent, Texas-based company Kinder Morgan, and later the government of Canada, negotiated fifty-eight "mutual benefit agreements" with Indigenous groups in BC and Alberta (Atleo et al., 2022). Despite these IBAs, widespread opposition continued, and Kinder Morgan sold the pipeline to the government of Canada in 2018 for $4.5 billion. Since then, Suncor Energy's CEO and several First Nation leaders have called for an ownership stake in the pipeline (Lewis, 2018). Sadly, this may be the social licence—an Indigenous-focussed bargain—required to get the project completed.

A Few Thoughts on Indigenous Resistance

We hope we have made it clear that Indigenous responses to extractive settler colonialism have been varied and not monolithic. At times Indigenous peoples have resisted and at other times they have negotiated compromises, all with self-determination as an underlying motivation we argue. Indigenous nations have made their own extractive bargains, navigating changing political and economic circumstances and at times relying on and/or challenging their own deeply held values and principles. Instances of Indigenous resistance to egregious resource extraction on Turtle Island are too numerous to name, but some prominent recent cases include the Standing Rock Sioux opposition to the Dakota Access Pipeline, Wet'suwet'en opposition to the Coastal GasLink pipeline, and opposition by a number of First Nations (despite numerous IBAs) to the Trans Mountain Pipeline. Wet'suwet'en land defenders have long made it clear that they are not protesters or demonstrators. They are simply trying to defend their unceded homelands from invaders—be they industry, settler governments, or paramilitary police. In saying "no," to settler encroachment, Indigenous nations are simultaneously saying "yes" to their own traditional governments and laws (Coulthard, 2014). Even with the diversity of strategies, it is clear that Indigenous nations are doing anything and everything they can to revive and assert their rights of self-determination.

Extractive Bargaining in Canada's Decarbonized Economy

Thus far, we have attempted to shed light on the concept of extractive bargains as experienced by Indigenous nations navigating a predominantly fossil fuel-based economy. In this section we briefly consider how Indigenous nations might navigate the emerging post-carbon economy.

Clean, renewable energy is not new to Canada. Canada is the second largest producer of hydroelectricity in the world, accounting for 59.3 per cent of the country's electricity supply (Natural Resources Canada, n.d.). In BC, 98 per cent of electricity comes from renewable sources, with 91 per cent coming from hydroelectric facilities (BC Hydro, n.d.). And according to non-for-profit organization, Indigenous Clean Energy (ICE), there are nearly 200 medium-to-large renewable energy projects with Indigenous involvement and an estimated 1700–2100 micro or small renewable energy projects in place with Indigenous leadership/partnerships in Canada (Indigenous Clean Energy, n.d.).

Given that Indigenous peoples are disproportionately impacted by the adverse effects of climate change (United Nations, 2018), it is understandable that they have an interest in leading the shift towards a post-carbon future.

It is worth noting that most of the projects highlighted by ICE are smaller in scale, especially in comparison to the mega-dam projects that have devastated Indigenous lands and traditional livelihoods. Notably, large hydroelectric projects have been built on Indigenous lands in Manitoba, Quebec (Martin & Hoffman, 2008), and British Columbia (Windsor & McVey, 2005) that displaced communities, flooded hunting, trapping, and medicinal grounds, and impacted fisheries. Presently, BC Hydro is building the Site C dam on the Peace River, which was opposed by several Treaty 8 First Nations. Site C will have similarly grave consequences for Indigenous peoples and territories, in ways that some feel threaten their very existence (Leddy, 2020). Despite significant opposition by Indigenous nations, and the project running over-budget ($6.6 billion to $12 billion) and behind schedule, largely due to unexpected seismic concerns (Canadian Centre for Policy Alternatives, 2020), BC Hydro is forging ahead with Site C. In 2022, West Moberly First Nation ended a long battle against Site C by signing a "partial settlement agreement" with BC Hydro. Chief Roland Willson stated, "We're never going to be in agreement with Site C. That's never going to happen. And every time we drive by that development it's going to be a constant reminder of what's been done to us. Forcing us into this situation like this is not something to be proud of. They beat us into submission, basically" (Gilchrist, 2022). Site C demonstrates that it does not matter whether an energy development project is dirty or clean, renewable or not, Settler governments remain willing to sacrifice Indigenous lands and communities illustrative of a continuity of environmental racism in Canada.

As Bowles and Andrews argue in Chap. 14, meeting GHG reduction targets and transitioning to a decarbonized global economy will require a "substantial increase" in the mining of specific metals and minerals, much of which are located in the Global South. Indigenous peoples' experiences with mining in Canada are also fraught with conflict in addition to evolving extractive bargain mechanisms. There are countless cases where mining operations have had devastating impacts on Indigenous land and life and there are also cases where Indigenous nations have negotiated agreements in an attempt to mitigate harm and benefit economically. Long experience and early indications suggest that the struggle for Indigenous self-determination in an era of reconciliation and Green New Deals will remain a challenge (Molander, 2022). Indigenous territories, peoples, and livelihoods remain under threat, not despite, but also because of the emerging drive to decarbonize. But this need not be inevitable. Compelled internationally by UNDRIP, and recent domestic legislation to implement it, Canada and BC have a contemporary framework to respect Indigenous governance, jurisdiction and the principle of free, prior, and informed consent. But for this to be meaningful, Indigenous peoples must be able to say "no."

Conclusion

The way states utilize IBAs could be seen through a variety of analytical lenses. While undoubtedly IBAs are Indigenous-focussed bargains that limit and remove Indigenous rights to land and disempower communities, justifications for the necessity and usefulness of IBAs also incorporate arguments from social distribution and developmentalist bargains. Indigenous nations often turn to IBAs as a last resort, feeling that development will occur regardless of their consent. They accept the trade-off between the extraction and destruction of their territories in order to alleviate poverty and address socio-economic issues within their community that are a result of living under a settler-colonial regime. Further, rural resource-dependent regions, in which many Indigenous communities reside, have seen an ongoing decrease in state spending on infrastructure. As the neoliberal state of Canada shifts further towards the privatization of service provisions, many rural communities are left with a social and physical infrastructure deficit and a need to find their own way of addressing these developmental issues (Ryser et al., 2019).

Community Benefit Agreements such as IBAs are developmentalist bargains that offer such relief. However, these bargains may ultimately lead to outcomes that fundamentally undermine Indigenous communities' long-term viability in favour of the interests of the state and capital.

References

Altamirano-Jiménez, I. (2011). Settler colonialism, human rights and indigenous women. *Prairie Forum, 36*(2), 105–125.

Asch, M. (2014). *On being here to stay: Treaties and aboriginal rights in Canada*. University of Toronto Press.

Atleo, C. (2021). Between a rock and a hard place: Canada's carbon economy and indigenous ambivalence. In W. Carroll (Ed.), *Regime of obstruction: How corporate power blocks energy democracy*. AU Press.

Atleo, C., & Boron, J. (2022). Land is life: Indigenous relationships to territory and navigating settler colonial property regimes in Canada. *Land, 11*(5), 609.

Atleo, C. G. (2018). *Change and continuity in the political economy of the Ahousaht*. Unpublished doctoral thesis, University of Alberta.

Atleo, C. G. (Niis Na'yaa/Kam'ayaam/Chachim'multhnii), Crowe, T., Krawchenko, T., & Shaw, K. (2022). Indigenous ambivalence? It's not about the pipeline …: Indigenous responses to fossil fuel export projects in Western Canada. In H. Boudet & S. Hazboun (Eds.), *Public responses to fossil fuel export: Exporting energy and emissions in a time of transition*. Elsevier.

Barker, A. J. (2009). The contemporary reality of Canadian imperialism: Settler colonialism and the hybrid colonial state. *American Indian Quarterly, 33*(3), 325.

BC Hydro. (n.d.). *Our clean system*. BC Hydro. https://www.bchydro.com/toolbar/about/sustainability/our-clean-system.html

Boron, J., & Markey, S. (2020). Exerting sovereignty through relational self-determination: A case study of mineral development in Stk'emlupsemc te Secwépemc Territory. *Journal of Rural and Community Development, 15*(4), 151–174.

Borrows, J. (2007). *Recovering Canada: The resurgence of indigenous law*. University of Toronto Press.

Cameron, E., & Levitan, T. (2014). Impact and benefit agreements and the neoliberalization of resource governance and indigenous-state relations in Northern Canada. *Studies in Political Economy, 93*(1), 25–52.

Canadian Centre for Policy Alternatives. (2020, August 11). Thousands of earthquakes near Site C dam and mounting 'geotechnical problems' at project warrant public inquiry, CCPA says. *Canadian Centre for Policy Alternatives*. https://policyalternatives.ca/newsroom/news-releases/thousands-earthquakes-near-site-c-dam-and-mounting-"geotechnical-problems"

Chagnon, C. W., Durante, F., Gills, B. K., Hagolani-Albov, S. E., Hokkanen, S., Kangasluoma, S. M. J., Konttinen, H., Kröger, M., LaFleur, W., Ollinaho, O., & Vuola, M. P. S. (2022). From extractivism to global extractivism: The evolution of an organizing concept. *The Journal of Peasant Studies, 49*(4), 760–792.

Cohn, T. H. (2005). *Global political economy: Theory and practice*. Pearson.

Corntassel, J. (2012). Re-envisioning resurgence: Indigenous pathways to decolonization and sustainable self-determination. *Decolonization: Indigeneity, Education & Society, 1*(1), 86–101.

Coulthard, G. S. (2014). *Red skin, white masks: Rejecting the colonial politics of recognition*. University of Minnesota Press.

Deerchild, R. (Host). (2021, August 3). Like a Razor Slash (No. 4). [Audio podcast episode]. In *This Place*. CBC. https://www.cbc.ca/listen/cbc-podcasts/1020-this-place/episode/15858573-like-a-razor-slash

Delgamuukw v. British Columbia. 1997 SCC 23799.

Deneault, A., & Sacher, W. (2012). *Imperial Canada Inc.: Legal haven of choice for the world's mining industries* (F. A. Reed & R. Philpot, Trans.). Talonbooks.

Forester, B. (2022, June 16). Behind the thin blue line: Meet a secretive arm of the RCMP in B.C. *Aboriginal Peoples Television Network News (APTN News)*. https://www.aptnnews.ca/ourstories/cirg/

Galbraith, L., Bradshaw, B., & Rutherford, M. B. (2007). Towards a new supra-regulatory approach to environmental assessment in Northern Canada. *Impact Assessment and Project Appraisal, 25*(1), 27–41.

Galeano, E. (with Allende, I. 1997). *Open veins of Latin America: Five centuries of the pillage of a continent* (25th anniversary ed. C. Belfrage, Trans.). Monthly Review Press. (Original work published 1973).

Garvie, K. H., & Shaw, K. (2016). Shale gas development and community response: Perspectives from Treaty 8 territory, British Columbia. *Local Environment, 21*(8), 1009–1028.

Gilchrist, E. (2022, June 28). 'They beat us into submission': West Moberly's decades-long fight against Site C dam is over. *The Narwhal*. https://thenarwhal.ca/site-c-dam-settlement/

Gunton, C., & Markey, S. (2021). The role of community benefit agreements in natural resource governance and community development: Issues and prospects Resources Policy 73102152-10.1016/j.resourpol.2021.102152

Gudynas, E. (2020). *Extractivisms: Politics, economy and ecology*. Fernwood Publishing.

Indigenous Clean Energy. (n.d.). *Indigenous clean energy project map*. Indigenous Clean Energy. https://indigenouscleanenergy.com/connect-learn/indigenous-led-clean-energy-project-map/

Inglis, R., & Haggarty, J. C. (2000). Cook to Jewitt: Three decades of change in Nootka Sound. In A. L. Hoover (Ed.), *Nuu-chah-nulth voices, histories, objects and journeys* (pp. 92–106). Douglas & McIntyre.

Innis, H. A., & Ray, A. J. (1999). *The Fur trade in Canada: An introduction to Canadian economic history*. University of Toronto Press. (Original work published 1930).

Kirkup, K. (2016, July 20). Government supports Indigenous declaration without reservation: Wilson-Raybould. *CBC News*. https://www.cbc.ca/news/indigenous/government-supports-undrip-without-reservation-1.3687315

Kuokkanen, R. (2011). Indigenous economies, theories of subsistence, and women. *American Indian Quarterly, 35*(2), 215–240.

Laird, G. (2003). The big thaw: The Mackenzie pipeline, once spurned, promises energy security for North America and a reckoning for northern natives. *Report on Business Magazine, 20*(4), 74–82.

Leddy, L. C. (2020). Exposing the true costs of a 'Clean' energy megaproject in the Peace River Valley. *New Solutions, 30*(3), 255–256.

Lewis, J. (2018, June 6). Suncor CEO Touts indigenous partnerships for trans mountain pipeline. *Globe and Mail*.

Ljunggren, D. (2009, September 25). Every G20 nation wants to be Canada, insists PM. *Reuters*. https://www.reuters.com/article/columns-us-g20-canada-advantages-idUSTRE58P05Z20090926

Lowman, E. B., & Barker, A. J. (2015). *Settler: Identity and colonialism in the 21st century*. Fernwood.

Markey, S., Halseth, G., Ryser, L., Argent, N., & Boron, J. (2019). Bending the arc of the staples trap: Negotiating rural resource revenues in an age of policy incoherence. *Journal of Rural Studies, 67*(April), 25–36.

Martin, T., & Hoffman, S. M. (Eds.). (2008). *Power struggles: Hydro development and first nations in Manitoba and Quebec*. University of Manitoba Press.

Mills, S., & Tufts, S. (2019). Innis's ghost: Canada's changing resource economy. In M. P. Thomas, L. F. Vosko, C. Fanelli, & O. Lyubchenko (Eds.), *Change and continuity: Canadian political economy in the new millennium* (pp. 106–127). McGill-Queen's University Press.

Mitchell, T., Arseneau, C., Thomas, D., & Smith, P. (2019). Towards an indigenous-informed relational approach to free, prior, and informed consent (FPIC). *International Indigenous Policy Journal, 10*(4), 399–410.

Molander, M. (2022). *Renewables and reconciliation: Decolonizing climate policies for a just transition to a low-carbon future*. Unpublished masters project, Simon Fraser University.

Murphy, M. (2019). Indigenous peoples and the struggle for self-determination: A relational strategy. *Canadian Journal of Human Rights, 8*(1), 67–102.

Natural Resources Canada. (n.d.). *About electricity*. Natural Resources Canada. https://www.nrcan.gc.ca/our-natural-resources/energy-sources-distribution/electricity-infrastructure/about-electricity/7359

Pasternak, S. (2020). Assimilation and partition: How settler colonialism and racial capitalism co-produce the borders of indigenous economies. *The South Atlantic Quarterly, 119*(2), 301–324.

Pasternak, S., & Dafnos, T. (2018). How does a settler state secure the circuitry of capital? *Environment and Planning D: Society and Space, 36*(4), 739–757.

Raibmon, P. (2005). *Authentic Indians: Episodes of encounters from the late-nineteenth-century Northwest Coast*. Duke University Press.

Reid, J. L. (2014). *The sea is my country: The maritime world of the Makahs*. Yale University Press.

Ryser, L., Halseth, G., Markey, S., Gunton, C., & Argent, N. (2019). Path dependency or investing in place: Understanding the changing conditions for rural resource regions. *The Extractive Industries and Society, 6*(1), 29–40.

Scott, D. N. (2020). Extraction contracting: The struggle for control of indigenous lands. *The South Atlantic Quarterly, 119*(2), 269–299.

Simmons, M. (2022, November 8). You will be arrested: Coastal Gaslink security denies Wet'suwet'en Hereditary Chief access to monitor project construction. *The Narwal*. https://thenarwhal.ca/coastal-gaslink-security-denies-chief-access/

Slowey, G. (2008). *Navigating neoliberalism: Self-determination and the Mikisew Cree First Nation*. University of British Columbia Press.

Smith, L. T. (2021). *Decolonizing methodologies: Research and indigenous peoples* (3rd ed.). Zed Books.

Snyder, J. (2018, April 15). 'We Are Going to Get the Pipeline Built': Trudeau begins federal talks with Kinder Morgan to guarantee trans mountain. *National Post*.

Stanford, J. (2008). Staples, deindustrialization and Canadian foreign investment: Canada's journey back to the future. *Studies in Political Economy, 82*(Autumn), 7–34.

Tennant, P. (1992). *Aboriginal peoples and politics: The Indian land question in British Columbia, 1849–1989*. UBC Press.

Trosper, R. (2009). *Resilience, reciprocity and ecological economics: Northwest coast sustainability*. Routledge.

Truth and Reconciliation Commission of Canada. (2015). *Final report of the truth and reconciliation commission of Canada: Volume one: Summary* (Honouring the Truth, Reconciling for the Future). James Lorimer & Company Publishers.

Tully, J. (2000). The struggles of indigenous peoples for and of freedom. In D. Ivison, P. Patton, & W. Sanders (Eds.), *Political theory and the rights of indigenous peoples* (pp. 36–59). Cambridge University Press.

Turner, D. (2006). *This is not a peace pipe: Towards a critical indigenous philosophy*. University of Toronto Press.

UBCIC. (2005). *Stolen lands, broken promises: Researching the indigenous land question in British Columbia* (2nd ed.). Union of BC Indian Chiefs.

United Nations. (2018). Indigenous peoples disproportionately impacted by climate change, systematically targeted for defending freedoms, Speakers Tell Permanent Forum. *UN Permanent Forum on Indigenous Issues*.

Watkins, M. (2007). Comment: Staples Redux. *Studies in Political Economy, 79*(Spring), 213–226.

Windsor, J. E., & McVey, J. A. (2005). Annihilation of both place and sense of place: The experience of the Cheslatta T'En Canadian First Nation within the context of large-scale environmental projects. *Geographical Journal, 171*(2), 146–165.

Wolfe, P. (2006). Settler colonialism and the elimination of the native. *Journal of Genocide Research, 8*(4), 387–409.

6

Self-government and Resource Extraction in Greenland: From Independence to Diverse Bargains?

Ulrik Jørgensen

Introduction

The mining of mineral resources has been pursued in Greenland (Kalaallit Nunaat) since the nineteenth century and continues in the present. Greenland changed from being a colony after World War II (WWII) and formally became a normalized part of Denmark in 1953 when Greenland was assigned the status of a county similar to other counties in Denmark. After a period of rapid transformation and modernization, Greenland was given increased independence in two steps, first by the establishment of Home Rule (*hjemmestyre* in Danish) in 1979 and then by the legislative and economic power provided in the Self Government Agreement (*selvstyre*) in 2009. Still a part of the Danish Realm (*Rigsfællesskab*), the inhabitants of Greenland are still classified as Danish citizens, but now with independence in many areas of legislation and governance including

U. Jørgensen (✉)
Aalborg University, Aalborg, Denmark

Arctic Engineering, Sisimiut, Greenland
e-mail: ulrik@sts-research.dk

P. Bowles, N. Andrews (eds.), *Extractive Bargains*, Frontiers of Globalization,
https://doi.org/10.1007/978-3-031-32172-6_6

mineral and other resources, but with foreign affairs, justice, and military protection still under the jurisdiction of Denmark.

These changing political and legal conditions have had profound impacts on the governance and regulatory framework for resource extraction in Greenland. From being solely handled by Danish governments until 1979, it was a cooperative arrangement between Denmark and Greenland during the Home Rule period. After 2009 the governance of the subsurface mineral resources has been the responsibility of the Self-government with the only exception being that any royalties from large-scale mining have to be negotiated as part of the Danish annual grant to Greenland which covers approximately 50% of public spending.

The focus here is on mineral resource extraction in Greenland—a vast region of isolated settlements along the coastlines and a total population of only 56,000, 90% of whom are born in Greenland and from Inuit descent. There has been underwater oil exploration around Greenland though it has not resulted in any exploitation licenses. This is primarily due to a lack of feasible projects but protests related to the potential harm to critical marine ecologies in the Arctic have also increasingly played a part. The potential access to hydropower has supported the development of mining and mineral processing, but has so far only been used to supply electricity to several cities.

Greenland's main natural resource basis is fishing. Fish and other marine products account for more than 90% of exports. Consequently, fish exports together with Danish grants to the Self-government are the main sources of income for the country. Despite the dominant economic importance of fishing, mining potential in Greenland has played an equally important part in the political debates over development and economic prosperity in Greenland over the past recent 50 years; debates that have become even more controversial in the period of Home Rule and Self-government for the country's future economic prospects. The extractive bargains which have emerged in recent debates are analyzed in this chapter, illustrating how historical factors have shaped their framing and their societal acceptance or rejection.

Specifics of Mineral Resource Exploitation

The changing state and governance frameworks in Greenland provide a rich set of historic and contemporary cases of the mining of minerals to which a discussion of 'extractive bargains' can be applied. This framework defines a policy space comprising of the legal conditions for states to grant permission for mineral extraction to mining corporations and the building of societal legitimation and conditions in support of these activities (see Bowles and Andrews, Chap. 1 in this volume). The 'bargain' processes are consequently supported and challenged in a number of ways including over local society relations, the jurisdiction of mining companies, economic impacts, property and indigenous rights, environmental protection as well as the roles of international corporations, capital-state relations, and political strategies. While the formal bargains are made between state authorities and mining companies, these are dependent on a variety of other actors involved in the attempt to build a network of trust and legitimation to support and eventually become part of granting licenses. This aspect of 'extractive bargains', as well as the following general observations, provides the context for the analysis of extractive activities in Greenland.

The institutionalization of 'extractive bargains' demands the standardization of the procedures involved while specific conditions of mining in addition require diversity to take account of variations in geology, nature, social settlements, and infrastructure. Greenland with its vast area, disperse settlements, and island economies (Hendriksen, 2022) challenges the concept of 'extractive bargains' and therefore requires an understanding of diverse processes and consequently variations in the typology. These variations can also be found in Alaska, Canada, and Siberia, for example, but in these cases state formation as well as corporations have an established history of mining and may consequently have stronger institutions and more experience in support of standardized procedures reducing the variations of bargain types.

Mineral extraction projects operate in most cases within a specific temporality as from the outset they do not meet the principles of sustainability from the perspective of the intergenerational reproduction of resources.

Even in cases where a mining project accesses resources that can be exploited for many decades, they operate with a limited timeline. Consequently, environmental protection measures cannot focus only on the active period of mining operations but must include the long-term process of initiation and scaling up of operations as well as on measures for the locking down and providing an afterlife for the mine including a nature restoration program, which reflects the normative intention of 'progressive bargains'.

In the Arctic context, this raises important issues of representation and requires a powerful state-local society relationship to cope with seemingly vast uninhabited areas in combination with very sensitive ecosystems of importance for the global climate. This combination of finite and temporal exploitation has become a core part of policy discussions and regulatory efforts in Greenland and defines mineral resource exploitation in a distinct way differing from strategies operating with core notions of continuity, renewability, and ecosystem preservation.

The temporality of mining has at the same time increasingly influenced how states and mining corporations frame extractive bargains in support of shorter timelines for the extraction strategies of mining corporations. While raw materials exploitation has a history of being a dangerous and rogue industry—and still is in quite a number of places in the world—the restructuring and closing down of old mining districts and towns have given rise to a preference for, and acceptance of, the fly-in-fly-out strategy based on temporary mine sites in contrast to the emergence of mining cities. This strategy operates based on access to a mobile workforce, and it supports increased corporate jurisdiction at the mine site and its facilities.

Modern mining and raw materials processing industries depend on the knowledge and experience of an international and professionally specialized workforce. In combination with an integrated world market for raw materials, this has profound impacts on states in the non-industrialized world. These states, like Greenland, are faced with social and political contradictions and a pressure to accept 'Faustian bargains'. These challenges and controversies, along with the costs of operating mine sites in Greenland, have contributed to the current reluctant expansion of extractive activities in Greenland.

Self-government and the Quest for Independence

In its preparations for the constitutional change to Self-government, the Greenland central administration established during the Home Rule period had already focused on finding ways of increasing its export revenue. Mining and tourism were seen as obvious economic activities to investigate to avoid what was already then identified by the popular term as 'the death trap' of the economy of Greenland. Figure 6.1 illustrates the growing diversion between the income and expenditures of the Greenland state and has shaped the discussion of what changes are needed to take further steps toward independence.

The Self Government Agreement of 2009 implied that the size of the Danish grant to Greenland—which was approximately 5 billion Danish Kroner in 2022—would stay unchanged in the future adjusted only for the Danish rate of inflation. This pushed the new Greenland government to search for new sources of export revenue to match growing expenditures. Additional income would be needed to takeover government activities that were still funded by the grant from Denmark.

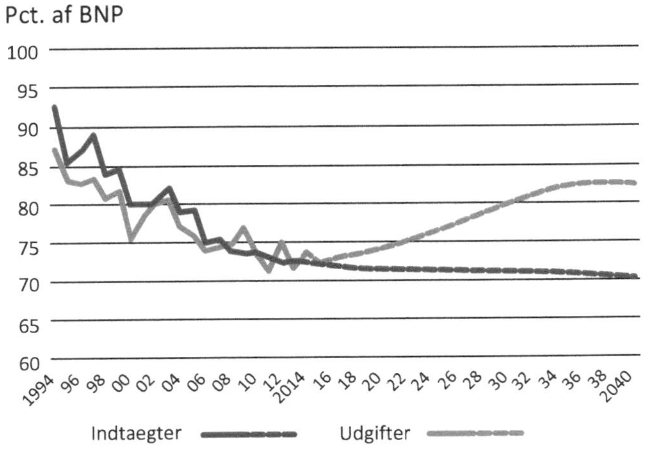

Fig. 6.1 Actual and projected income (*indtægter*) and expenditures (*udgifter*) of the Greenland government, 1994–2040. (Source: Economic Council 2013)

Expanding the government's income from taxing fishing—especially on trawlers—would be one obvious short-term action, while longer-term action would depend on tourism and the exploitation of minerals and oil. As oil explorations did not show promise, mining ended up being the focal area in the quest for independence.

Mining for Independence

The Self-government and its administration argued that Greenland should focus on attracting mining activities and large-scale mineral processing to Greenland. They argued that just five large mines would provide the tax revenues from mining corporations and their employees in Greenland to replace the Danish grants. Raw material extraction was viewed as an instrument for economic and political independence at the same time as being framed in a context of necessity and urgency. The population was being asked to accept mining in return for independence (Naalakkersuisut, 2014).

The Self-government took over the Bureau of Minerals and Petroleum (BMP) established during the Home Rule period when mineral exploitation was organized as a mutual responsibility of the Danish state and the Greenland administration. The procedures for Environmental Impact Assessment (EIA) and Social Impact Assessments (SIA) were constructed with help from international consultants and experts as the core elements in the process of granting exploitation licenses including formal hearing procedures involving local authorities and the local communities affected by the potential future mining activity (BMP, 2009a, 2009b). In the subsequent years, the special status of the BMP stayed unchanged including its jurisdiction over environmental matters and employment related to exploration activities.

To support the new strategy, a School of Mining and Minerals was established in 2010 in Sisimiut responsible for core drilling and machine operations. This was located adjacent to the vocational training for the construction sector at the School for Building Construction. The Arctic Engineering Education started in 2001 at the Arctic Centre run by the

Technical University of Denmark and was later complemented by a specialization in Raw Materials Engineering in 2010.

Failing Expectations

The great expectations of government were soon questioned and critiqued for overstating mining's potential. The Greenland Employer's Organization produced a different future scenario showing that around 30 mines would be needed to meet the tax revenue target set by the Self-government.

In 2014 a group of researchers from Denmark and Ilisimatusarfik, the university in Nuuk, published a report entitled 'To the Benefit of Greenland' which presented scenarios for a future with mining as an important economic activity in Greenland (Illisimartusafik and Copenhagen University, 2014).

They demonstrated that mining would not provide a 'fast track' toward independence and warned against hasty and consequently less favorable extractive bargains, especially in a period with low raw material prices in the world market, which provided the mining industry with a strong bargaining position. The report also argued for a long-term strategy to avoid short-termism based on tax incomes in an annual perspective and instead proposed a raw materials fund to secure long-term investment and rents.

Other voices such as Transparency Greenland advocated for caution based on international experience showing that mining projects often increased corruption and weakened democratic institutions. It also argued that the negotiation position of the Self-government was too weak in periods of low raw material prices and that hasty actions would create new dependencies that might even overshadow the dependency on Denmark within the Realm (Langhoff, 2013).

Nevertheless, the Self-government enacted legislation in 2013 on 'large scale projects' which allowed industrial projects to employ international workers at lower wage levels compared to Greenlanders and with special work permits as a way to attract international mining companies utilizing global migrant workers traveling for jobs and accepting the conditions that come with fly-in-fly-out schemes such as long working hours and barrack-like accommodation. This reflected the view among central politicians and the administration that they were forced to accept extractive bargains that introduced regulatory-sanctioned inequality in order to get the benefits of tax revenues and options for local employment at higher wage levels than migrant workers, thereby demonstrating the downside of 'independence bargains'.

Three large-scale projects were significant in the first attempts to attract new mining and large-scale industrial activities exemplified by the Alcoa smelter in the town of Manitsoq based on access to hydropower, the Isua iron mine in the inner fjord of Nuuk and the Kuannersuit rare earth and uranium mine close to the town of Narsaq. All three crystallized different aspects of extractive controversies.

The Alcoa smelter project in Manitsoq was based on shipping aluminum ore and other process materials to the town and using the access to climate-neutral electricity from a new hydropower station close to the inland ice cap. There was a potential for local jobs, but the project also was dependent on migrant workers being accommodated in closed and guarded communities close to Manitsoq replicating a model that the Alcoa corporation had established in Iceland. Local planning was initiated by the municipality opening for further discussion on the consequences of a large influx of migrant workers accommodated in closed camp-like facilities. The project was, however, soon abandoned by Alcoa preferring alternative location options.

The Isua mine close to Nuuk was initiated by London Mining which operated on behalf of a large Chinese mining corporation. The project went through several steps of the assessment procedures and was committed to employing and training a larger number of workers from Greenland, but at the same time was reluctant to scale down the size of their operations and instead chose a long-term extraction period. This reflected not least the unstable world market prices for iron ore, which in the end turned out to be decisive in London Mining canceling the project.

Last but not least, the most debated mining project ever in Greenland was the proposed Kuannersuit mine close to Narsaq in South Greenland. It comprises a huge deposit of rare earth minerals and a significant though not large uranium part (2.6% of the ore). This mineral deposit was originally explored as part of the Danish government's consideration of building nuclear power stations in Denmark after WWII. This did not lead to the development of a mine, however, as Danish energy policy changed away from nuclear energy. The project subsequently reappeared due to the increasing global demand for rare earth metals to support the energy transition abandoning fossil fuels and added a climate dimension to the proposed extractive bargain.

To reach a deeper understanding of how the controversies unfolded following the attempts to make mining a driver of independence, it is necessary to provide some background on the constitution of the new state of Greenland and the institutions and competencies to which it had access. In addition, the controversies reflect historically grounded social memories that are present in civil society with the established NGOs also being influential in how mining is viewed in relation to other societal concerns (Jørgensen, 2015).

The Transition from Colonial Status to Home Rule to Self-government

The actions of the new Self-government occurred against a background of colonial rule and radical social and institutional transformation that characterized the development of Greenland after WWII.

Following the emergence of fossil fuels and gas in Europe, the market for fat and oil from whales and seals faded in the nineteenth century. In search of other sources to cover Danish state expenditures in Greenland on its administration and institutions, the quite large cryolite mine of Ivittuut was opened in 1854 and operated until 1989, based on a concession given to the Cryolite Company. Cryolite was used as in the production of aluminum making it a strategic and valuable raw material. The ore was transported from Ivittuut for further processing outside of Greenland. The mine served solely Danish economic interests and demonstrated the power of the colonial state (Berry, 2013).

It was operated based on the colonial policy of not engaging the Inuit population in modern trade and industry and, for many years, workers at the mine were primarily recruited from outside of Greenland. While the official legitimation of this policy argued that this protected traditional culture and trade, its economic motivation was to make sure that the indigenous population continued hunting and fishing serving the colonial trade monopoly.

With a completely different purpose and local set up, a coal mine was opened in 1924 to supply the increased need to provide heating to the population of Greenland. In the settlement of Qullissat on the island of Disko on the west coast of Greenland, a rich coal deposit was well known and used by the people from the local settlements for heating and cooking. The exploitation of the coal was initiated on an industrial scale introducing mine shafts and modern technologies well-known from British and European mine sites. Coal was viewed as a local energy source for domestic use in Greenland.

Qullissat was organized as a diverse community with school, shop, hospital, and administration. The community had a fairly even gender composition and its population was primarily Greenlanders, although the municipal authorities and a part of the technical staff came from Denmark and a few from Britain.

The community maintained broad subsistence and commercial activities based on hunting, fishing, fish processing, and construction. It attracted people from all over the country. For a period, Qullissat was Greenland's second largest city with about 1200 inhabitants. Qullissat became the birthplace of the Greenland trade union movement, as well as a cultural centre for music and political debate. It is key that the dominant part of the workforce was Greenlanders and that the community was attractive to citizens not working in the mine. The coal mine can be viewed as an example of a radical change by introducing industrial working conditions in parallel with existing hunting and fishing practices and demonstrating that these two forms of livelihood in fact could coexist.

Acting as if the Danish administration for Greenland was still a colonial power, it closed down the Qullissat mine and the settlement in 1972. This resulted in much anger in the Greenlandic population. The decision to close the mine was made without consultation of the local population, and inhabitants were forcibly relocated and scattered in cities and settlements along the coast. This decision by the Danish government turned out to be an important driver in Greenland for the political mobilization leading to Home Rule in 1979. The memory of the forced closing of a seemingly well-functioning mining settlement continues to be a part of the Greenlandic population's skepticism concerning mining corporations and how mining is seen by the political authorities (Sørensen, 2013).

Modernizing Greenland

From the end of the colonial period and until the late 1970s, the Ministry of Greenland in Copenhagen was in charge of the economic and technical affairs for 'modernizing' Greenland society. Decisions concerning mineral resources continued to be handled by the Raw Materials Commission under the Ministry in Copenhagen—as all decisions about underground resources in Denmark were a state affair including all licenses for exploration and exploitation as well as royalties. The mineral richness of the mountains of Greenland was mapped in detail in a geological survey including mineral as well as hydropower potential carried out by the Danish Government's Greenland Geological Survey during the 1950s, illustrated in Fig. 6.2.

The motivation for the survey was the search for economic potential for the future development and modernization of Greenland, not least as a response to the preceding decades which witnessed poverty and worsening health conditions for the Inuit population and which spurred the Danish government to initiate a wide-ranging modernization project for Greenland, bringing an end to the former colonial policies of isolation. The transformation from a hunting-based society to an industrialized society utilizing the rich marine and mineral resources was core to the economic vision that in addition implied a process of urbanization/centralization of the population (Greenland Commission, 1950; Greenland Committee, 1964).

The Marmorilik Experience

The only large mining operation established in the modernization period was the Marmorilik zinc and lead mine in the Uummanaq district. From 1972 to 1980 the Canadian (and later Swedish) mining company Greenex

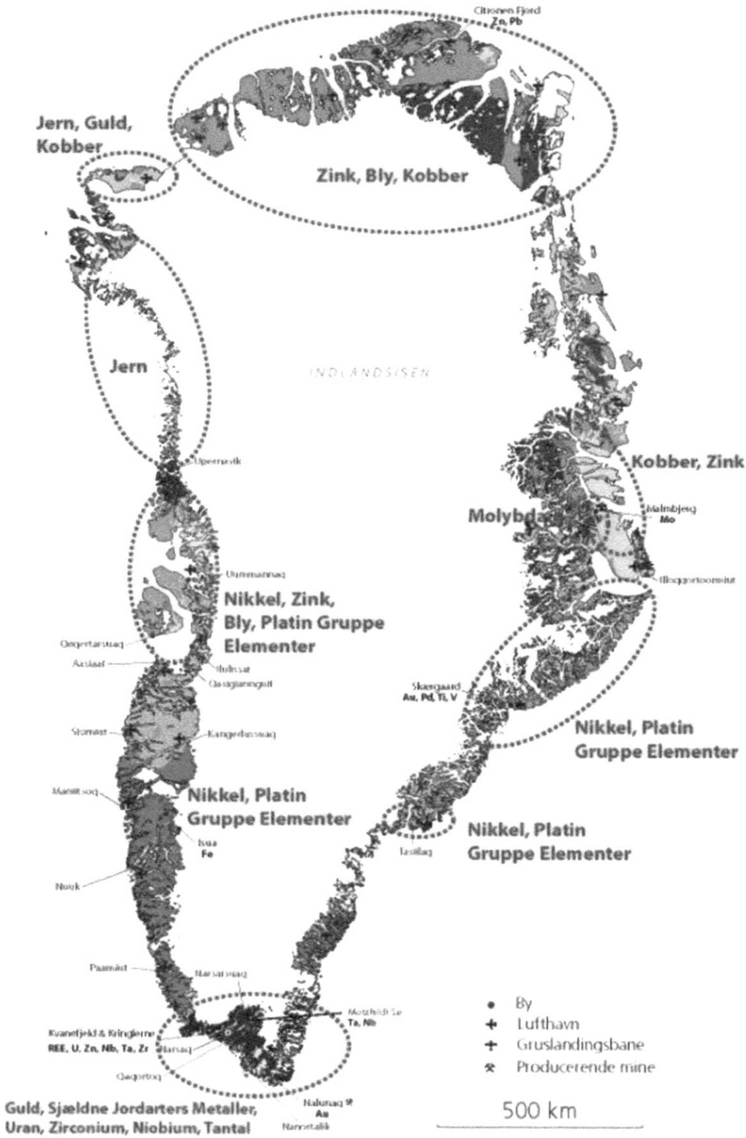

Fig. 6.2 Map of mineral resources in Greenland. (Source: GEUS—National Geological Survey for Denmark and Greenland)

operated the so-called Black Angel mine based on a license granted by the Greenland administration in Denmark. The mining operation was located at an inner fjord. Despite a smaller settlement located further out to sea, the exchanges and contacts with the mine were deliberately kept minimal. The mine was organized as a fly-in-fly-out operation with shifts of 14 days of work followed by 14 days off. Approximately 15% of the workers were born in Greenland and only 9% of the workforce were women (Dahl, 1977; Nordregio, 2009).

Until 1979 the workforce originating in Greenland, compared to that from Denmark, was discriminated against in terms of lower salaries and less employment security due to the birthplace criteria (*fødestedskriteriet* in Danish) (Poppel & Stenbæk, 2005). A conflict in 1977 resulted in giving equal conditions for migrant and local workers. A general strike in 1982 demonstrated the importance of the company's jurisdiction and power by using the Greenland police to force workers to leave the compound and Greenland. In addition, several controversies arose between the mining company and the settlement as ships loading ore from the mine cut up sea ice and disrupted local fishing and hunting activities (Dahl & Berg, 1977).

The environmental impacts of the mining operations resulted in heavy pollution as low-quality ore and tailings from the concentration of minerals were dumped in an inner fjord assumed to be isolated by an underwater barrier keeping the pollution from spreading. Instead, marine life became extinct in large parts of the inner fjord and pollution seeped into the outer fjord system (Hertz, 1995).

The Marmorilik mining endeavor demonstrated extraction lacking the reflection of social and environmental concerns and emphasizing the economic power and interests of state. Together with the completely different experience of the Qullissat mine, these experiences with mining became reference points for public skepticism concerning mining activities.

Home Rule and Mining Assessment

The political awakening and the demand for independence resulted in the Home Rule agreement of 1979 and the formation of a Greenlandic parliament (Inatsisartut) and government (Naalakkersuisut) taking over parts of the Danish government's administration of Greenland. From the early 1970s, building construction, infrastructure and the provision of energy, heating, and water, which was organized in the Greenland Technical Organization (GTO) started moving its activities to Greenland. But the Home Rule administration continued to be dependent of employing Danish civil servants leading to a continuation of existing routines and practices.

With the transition to Self-government in 2009, the Bureau of Minerals and Petroleum (BMP) in Nuuk took over the complete regulation of exploration licenses but continued until 2016 to have a special status in the Greenlandic Self-government administration with a mandate that included the assessment of environmental, business, and labor conditions at proposed mining sites. The procedures for granting exploitation licenses and the guidelines for how mining companies should provide documentation of their planned extractive operations were continued.

The guideline for EIAs envisages a mining activity as an intervention into existing environmental states, ecosystems, and habitats and in which the impacts have to be minimized. The aim of the EIA assessment is to identify the relevant environmental issues and to make public the choices made. The procedure implicitly assumes that EIAs operate in a society that has access to a pool of independent professionals and civil society groups with the capacity to present their cases and interests. In addition, the mining company has to provide an SIA. The SIA guidelines reproduce the concept embedded in the EIA. They operate with an initial state with the positive and negative impacts of introducing a mine assessed, including impacts on cultural identity, social inequality, and measures of employment, training, local company growth, and tax/royalty revenues which reduce what is considered the social impact and demonstrate the weakness of these guidelines (Jørgensen, 2003).

While in jurisdictions like Canada and Alaska the regulation of local rights is embedded in legislation protecting indigenous rights, the situation in Greenland is different. In Greenland there is no explicit distinction between the interests of government and the population as government represents the Greenlandic population of Inuit descent and consequently the interests of the 'indigenous' population.

Changing Perspectives on Extractive Activities

The idea of a 'fast track' to independence has—if not disappeared—been backgrounded due to the complex implications and changes for Greenland society enforcing this strategy would have. In parallel to the continuing controversies, a number of smaller-scale mining projects have been granted licenses to operate demonstrating that it is not mineral extraction per se that causes opposition. The location of the extractive activities, their social and environmental implications, and the general social legitimacy of these projects have become crucial for the specific bargain processes.

At the same time, further economic challenges have recently resulted from growing government investment in new airports and housing construction in the larger cities leading to a discussion of a possible renegotiation of the relationship between Greenland and Denmark within the Realm. These investments represent a wish to centralize population originating from economic ideas of making production, institutions, and infrastructures more efficient. This can be exemplified by the concentration of fish-processing facilities and locating most of the public companies in the larger cities. In consequence, there has been an increased urbanization and a growth of Nuuk, the capital of Greenland, and a few other cities with a population primarily employed in public institutions, public companies, and private companies in the construction, housing, and service sectors. This development path contradicts the fact that all the natural resources (marine and raw materials) that provide the actual productive income and export earnings of Greenland are widely distributed and often not close to the bigger cities (Hendriksen, 2013).

Similar centralization policies led to the opposition to the Danish dominance in Greenland and the calls for independence as a reaction against the impacts of the modernization period after WWII leading to the closure of half of the smaller settlements. The question of centralization now reappears as a controversy between a new Greenlandic elite comprising of those owning a large part of the fishing fleet and those employed in jobs provided by public institutions and business activities heavily dependent on public spending and the local, distributed populations still living partly from a subsistence economy and partly earning income from working primarily in fishing, tourism, and mining. The political divides are complex and produce a similarly diverse set of political views, but at the same time they become evident in the controversies and priorities in extractive bargains—not least in the conflicts over how to value, compare, and assess the income from taxes compared to distributed income, local influence, employment, environmental impacts, and alternatives to mining.

Kuannersuit and the Uranium Controversy

These controversies crystalized around the application for a license for the Kuannersuit mine and have impacted how all other mining projects are handled by government and in the ways local society and other stakeholders have been involved. This has resulted in a diverse set of extractive bargains being pursued. But first the Kuannersuit case will be presented in further detail, starting with the question of uranium.

When Denmark declared its interest in utilizing nuclear power, the Danish Atomic Energy Commission was established in 1956 to prepare for this transformation in Danish electricity production. Following that, uranium was discovered in South Greenland in 1955 and the Commission initiated further exploration resulting in 5000 tons of uranium ore being shipped to Denmark in the early 1970s from Kuannersiut (*Kvanefjeld* in Danish) in preparation for the first Danish Energy Plan in 1976 which envisioned the building of six nuclear power plants from 1985 and onward.

The erection of nuclear power plants in Denmark faced increasing opposition from the anti-nuclear war movement from the mid-1960s followed by dedicated energy movements arguing against nuclear power as a centralized and high-risk radioactive waste-producing solution. Fueled by the oil crisis in 1973, the focus changed to renewable energy and resulted in the Danish Parliament's termination of the plans for nuclear power in 1985.

In Greenland opposition grew as well, not least triggered by the presence of US airbases as a core part in the nuclear strategy due to Greenland's geographic position in between the US and the Soviet Union. In addition, the international regulation of uranium and nuclear material was established with the Treaty on the Non-Proliferation of Nuclear Weapons and, with it, a strict control of uranium production and distribution. The matter was further complicated when Greenland stepped out of the EEC treaty in 1985 leaving open the question of the eventual export control of uranium (Vestergaard & Thomasen, 2015).

While there might be contestations to whether a ban on producing uranium was ever formally decided upon, the general view held this was a reality with reference to a decision made by the Joint Commission for Minerals in Greenland in 1988. The ban was formally lifted in the Greenland parliament in October 2013, thereby making the exploration of the mineral potential of Kuannersuit possible in response to an application from the Australian-owned company Greenland Minerals and Energy in 2010. This reopened the controversy over uranium production in Greenland and the question of who had the responsibility in the Danish Realm in relation to international treaties (Bjørst, 2016).

The ban on uranium exploitation—phrased as the 'zero-tolerance policy'—was the result of arguments for a nuclear-weapon-free zone in the Danish Realm and of the risks of long-term contamination resulting from accidents. Taken up by the growing environmental movement in Greenland, they have argued for this being the ultimate reason not to exploit the uranium and consequently all other minerals in the Kuannersuit formation. They managed to make this question a Greenland-wide issue again in the elections of 2021 and which in the end has been one of the determining factors in not granting a license for the mine.

Employment Options and Environmental Risks

In addition, the environmental critique of the EIA pointed to the potential consequences for the local community including the risks of storms and a subsequent spread of contaminated dust to the nearby farming areas producing grass for sheep farming as well as potatoes and vegetables, the long-term contamination of the tailings pond, and the risk of cracks and movements in the rock formation leading to contamination of the fjord system and its fishing grounds (GME, 2018).

Unemployment in the Kujallec municipality covering South Greenland is high, and the declining population of the town of Narsaq has resulted from a long-term crisis of cod fishing, the centralization of municipal administration and diminishing tourism. In the proposal presented by the corporate proponent, GME, the mine would employ 600 workers in full operation of which at least 200 could be recruited among skilled Greenlanders and at the same time contribute with at least 800 million Kr. in tax revenue to the government. The employment promises interested local workers and the municipality.

In contrast, the farming communities rebelled against the mine with the argument that just a minor disaster could destroy their livelihoods and potentially endanger the use of the land for decades or centuries. This would also threaten the remaining tourism in South Greenland instead of building a future for this district on the growing opportunities resulting from climate change for agriculture as a source of self-supply for Greenland and the options for growth in tourism. The active involvement of farmers and local actors was important for these positions, but their spokespersons had to organize the protests at a nationwide scale which included demonstrations in Nuuk, access to national media, and enrolling the 'zero tolerance' argument in the political process (interview with farmers 2018).

To accommodate for the involvement of different stakeholders, the Self-government changed the procedures of the hearing processes and added additional support and funding for meetings involving the local population in Narsaq and several of the surrounding settlements and sheep farmers where a diverse group of experts had the task of explaining the pros and cons of the mining operations reflected in modified EIA and

SIA guidelines. Recognizing the obvious asymmetry between the knowledge of the local population on one side and the mining professionals and the public authorities on the other, these arrangements reflected the fact that most of the population did not meet the preconditions of a pre-informed public (Keskitalo et al., 2011).

In addition, a cooperation between environmental NGOs in Denmark and the environmental NGO Avataq in Greenland resulted in organizing a conference in March 2014 at the Parliament in Copenhagen where experts and indigenous people from other countries with experience of uranium mining discussed the Kuannersuit project. The outcome was very critical of the project (KNR, 2014).

Alternative Mining Options

While the Kuanneruit mine was denied a licence in 2021, other mining projects are in operation demonstrating other aspects of the societal response to mining and other facets of extractive bargains (Jørgensen et al., 2013).

One of the mines granted an early license was the Nalunaq gold mine in Kirkespirdalen in South Greenland, Nanortalik district operating from 2004 to 2013 and in periods since then. The mine continuously employed 80–100 people with more than 50% being local workers, especially in the service positions (Dahl, 2008). This is remarkable as the mine is located in one of the country's poorest districts with huge unemployment. Quite high numbers of Greenlanders including trained workers with mining or construction sector experience have worked at the Nalunaq mine, but only for shorter periods. Working at a mine is acceptable as an efficient way to earn money for specific purposes, but only few view this as a permanent job as it does not comply with the everyday life practices of most people prioritizing time spent frequently with family as well as hunting and fishing (Hendriksen, 2013).

Another example of an active mining licence is the ruby mine close to the small settlement of Qeqertarsuatsiaat. Here ruby gemstones have been collected by the locals using this as an additional source of income for a long time based on the legal rights given to them. The mining project has been underway since 2003 and True North Gems was granted a licence by the Self-government in 2014. The deposit is located 150 km south of Nuuk and 20 km southeast from the settlement with 205 inhabitants. Shortly after the licence was granted construction of the mine began, including processing plant in Nuuk, and is expected to be in operation for at least ten years. The phase of closure integrates the clean-up and termination of the project and forms part of the planning process. The mine is cooperating with the settlement and organizes weekly transport to the settlement and to Nuuk for people working at the mine site with the intention of employing 75% of the workforce from Greenland and preferably from the settlement and Nuuk (Rix, 2012).

On the opposite side of the fjord from Narsaq, and as a different part of the mineral formation that also covers the Kuannersuit mining field, lies another mining exploration site in the mountain called Kringlerne. The size of the rare earth deposit is smaller and its uranium content low. This site has been explored by the Australian mining company Tanbreez and has been granted a licence. The project raises issues both at local and global scales. The question is whether it is possible to organize a mining operation in a market dominated by Chinese companies without the involvement of their technology and expertise. At the local level this mining project is smaller in size and employment and has the potential of supporting infrastructural development in South Greenland.

The recent anorthosite mine at White Mountain in the Kangerlusuaq fjord south of Sisimiut and the new the Moriusaq project in Northeast Greenland located close to an abandoned settlement, though still used as an active hunting ground, share characteristics with a number of other newer mineral extraction projects such as the ruby mine in Qeqertarsuatsiaat and the gold mine in Nalunaq. They are all situated at a distance from existing settlements, though within sailing distance, making them function as connection points for providing Greenlandic workers to the mines.

A special extraction case is the Citronen Fjord large-scale mining project located in a 'remote' and completely unpopulated part of Northeast Greenland where a connection out of Greenland to Svalbard north of Norway may be the chosen option.

Toward a Future of Diverse Extractive Bargains in Greenland?

The involvement of state as well as the modes of operation and the relation to global markets of mining companies have changed historically. While several early extractive activities were determined by the economic interests of state with little local involvement in Greenland in line with this period of 'extractivism', the Qullissat coal mine was different in primarily supplying the domestic market and recruiting a predominantly Greenlandic workforce offering attractive working and living conditions resembling some of the national mining activities in the Nordic countries related to the creation of welfare states. Later and recent mining projects are typically organized by global companies operating on the world market. Consequently, the involvement of local communities does not provide an economic advantage to the mining corporations compared to building operations based on the fly-in-fly-out concept. In parallel, the general experience in Greenland so far is that working in mines is attractive only to smaller groups of especially professionally trained workers and engineers while supplying services to mines is attractive to a variety of local producers and companies.

What has been considered an economic advantage for Greenland, that is, raising wages and providing welfare state conditions to its population, is challenged by the disadvantage of having to compete with low-wage, efficient migrant workers. In addition, the specific conditions of Greenland with remote locations, costly transportation, and climate challenges have resulted in a slow and reluctant introduction of mining in Greenland.

The core vision of creating economic independence for Greenland by the Self-government based on a strategy of 'independence bargains' failed. The promised fast-track to independence was shown to be infeasible not least as a consequence of the opposition organized by local society actors and NGOs emphasizing the potential risk of being a 'Faustian bargain'. While not abandoned, this type of bargain has been reduced to being relevant only in cases of remotely located mine sites as exemplified by the Citronenfjord project that will only be operated as a fly-in-fly-out mine, but still operating with strict environmental and habitat protection requirements.

Among the other contemporary mining projects, specific local circumstances appear to have a huge impact on the type of societal and local population benefits that can be achieved from the exploitation of minerals. They reflect the intention of 'progressive bargains' and though resembling some of the specifics of 'indigenous-focused bargains' are better described as a 'locally embedded bargain' due to the identity of the Greenlandic state representing a Greenlandic population of indigenous Inuit descent.

While the standardized balancing scheme of extractive bargains tends to take an economic shape where revenues from the extractive activity are shared between state and society and the mining enterprise to cover investment, profits, taxes, and employment, the 'locally embedded bargains' tend to include a variety of different measures dependent on place and how the operations relate to civil society.

These diverse extractive bargains either may have the mining operations located in area with existing settlements that provide access to workforce and services and dependent on local infrastructure by boat or road connections or would provide an opportunity for the government and the municipalities to develop a strategy of flexible settlements and communities (settlement mobility instead of personal mobility). Based on the high mobility in Greenland between settlements in contrast to the lack of commuting options in most parts of Greenland, the potential of flexible settlements may prove to be an alternative to the fly-in-fly-out concept. The projects of Kringlerne, Nalunaq, Qeqertarsuatsiaat, and future mining projects, including the variations they represent, are examples of these new forms of extractive bargains emphasizing the social and infrastructure opportunities as the main legitimation of extractive endeavors.

References

Berry, D. A. (2013). Cryolite: Lessons from history for contemporary practice. *ARTEK event: Sustainability in mining in the Arctic*, Sisimiut. Arctic Center, Technical University of Denmark.

Bjørst, L. R. (2016). Saving or destroying the local community? Conflicting spatial storylines in the Greenlandic debate on uranium. *The Extractive Industries and Society, 2016*(3, Elsevier), 34–40.

BMP. (2009a). *Guidelines for preparing an Environmental Impact Assessment (EIA)*. Bureau of Minerals and Petroleum, Nuuk.
BMP. (2009b). *Guidelines for Social Impact Assessments for mining projects in Greenland*. Bureau of Minerals and Petroleum, Nuuk.
Dahl, J. (1977). *Miners in Umanaq Municipality* (in Danish). Kragestedet.
Dahl, J., & Berg, H. (1977). *Mining in a catcher society* (in Danish). Kragestedet.
Dahl, O. (2008). The Nalunaq Goldmine – fifth year (in Danish). *Geologisk Nyt* 4/08. Economic Council (2013). *The economy of Greenland*. The Economic Council.
GME. (2018). *Kvanefjeld project environmental impact assessment*. Greenland Minerals & Energy A/S.
Greenland Commission. (1950). *Greenland Commission report*. (in Danish).
Greenland Committee. (1964). *Report from the Greenland Committee 1960*, Report nr. 363. (in Danish).
Hendriksen, K. (2013). Greenland settlements – Economy and development dynamics, *Inussuk, Arktisk forskningsjournal 3*, Government of Greenland (in Danish).
Hendriksen, K. (2022). The island economy of Greenland (in Danish), *Trap Grønland* (pp. 232–234).
Hertz, O. (1995). *Ecology and living conditions in Uummannamiut*, Christian. Ejlers' Forlag. (in Danish).
Ilismatusarfik & Copenhagen University. (2014). *To the benefit of Greenland*. Udvalget for samfundsgavnlig udnyttelse af Grønlands naturressourcer.
Jørgensen, A. M. (2015). Miner og eftermæler: Qullissat og Marmorilik. *Tidsskriftet Grønland, 2015*, 3.
Jørgensen, U. (2003). The hidden networks of knowledge In ISO 14001. Paper. *Greening of Industry Network conference*, San Francisco.
Jørgensen, U. et al. (2013). Social and environmental conditions for mining in Greenland. *ARTEK Event: Sustainability in mining in the Arctic*, Sisimiut. Arctic Center, Technical University of Denmark.
Keskitalo, E. C. H., et al. (2011). Adaptive capacity determinants in developed states: Examples from the Nordic countries and Russia. *Regional Environmental Change, 11*, 579–592.
KNR. (2014). Recordings from the conference: *The impacts of uranium mining in Greenland and the rest og the world*. Organised by Avataq, The Danish Ecological Council, NOAH Friends of the Earth Denmark and Sustainable Energy. Greenlandic Broadcasting Corporation. https://knr.gl/da/radio/impacts-uranium-mining-greenland-and-rest-og-world-03042014

Langhoff, R. (2013). *Raw material activities in Greenland: With the people's mandate? Consultation processes and public involvement in the mineral resource area.* (In Danish) Inuit Circumpolar Council & World Wide Fund.

Naalakkersuisut. (2014). *Our raw materials shall create wealth. The oil and mineral strategy of Greenland. Summary*. (in Greenlandic). Naalakkersuisut, Nuuk.

Nordregio. (2009). *Mobility in Greenland* (in Danish). Nordregio.

Poppel, B., & Stenbæk, M. (2005). Birthplace criteria. In M. Nuttall (Ed.), *Encyclopedia of the Arctic* (Vol. 1, pp. 261–262). Routledge.

Report for Mineral Exploitation in Greenland.

Rix, T. K. (2012). *Mineplanning in the Aappaluttooq deposit* (in Danish). Thesis, Arctic Centre, Technical University of Denmark.

Sørensen, S. P. (2013). *Qullissat: The city that would not die* (in Danish). Frydenlund.

Vestergaard, C., & Thomasen, G. (2015). *Governing Uranium in the Danish Realm* (DIIS Report 2015:17). Danish Institute for International Studies.

7

Keeping Oil in the Soil: National Bans on Oil Extraction as the Future of Global Climate Policy?

Sarah Greene and Angela Carter

Introduction

As the climate crisis intensifies and fossil fuels are increasingly acknowledged as the lead source of emissions causing that crisis, calls to end fossil fuel extraction are growing. This supply-side effort to keep oil, gas, and coal

We would like to acknowledge the work of Dr. Justine Salam, who had a lead role in fieldwork and interviews on the France case. We also thank the editors for providing guidance that improved the work and Nadine Fladd for her support throughout all stages of the writing process.

S. Greene (✉)
Balsillie School of International Affairs, University of Waterloo, Waterloo, ON, Canada
e-mail: snorton@balsillieschool.ca

A. Carter
Department of Political Science and Balsillie School of International Affairs, University of Waterloo, Waterloo, ON, Canada

Energy Transitions, International Institute for Sustainable Development (IISD), Winnipeg, MB, Canada
e-mail: avcarter@uwaterloo.ca

P. Bowles, N. Andrews (eds.), *Extractive Bargains*, Frontiers of Globalization,
https://doi.org/10.1007/978-3-031-32172-6_7

Caron (2016)

in the ground is burgeoning at every level, from community efforts to block fossil fuel infrastructure to international climate negotiations, where recently, UN Secretary-General António Guterres observed that "investing in new fossil fuels infrastructure is moral and economic madness" (United Nations 2022, n.p.). This chapter explores a critical thread of the supply-side climate policy effort: How and why national governments are implementing bans on oil exploration and/or extraction?

Expanding national bans on oil extraction signals a new phase in the urgent effort to phase out fossil fuels, and such bans are opening a new avenue in climate policy. This possibly reflects what Bowles and Andrews, in Chap. 1 of this volume, describe as a "post-extractive bargain" whereby such efforts to phase out oil extraction are meant to address the ongoing or future ecological crisis. In this chapter, we describe the origins and progression of these "keep it in the ground" (KIIG) bans, then focus on how they developed in three recent front-running countries: France, Denmark, and Ireland. Next, drawing on our analysis of these three cases, we offer insights into common conditions that fostered the development of these KIIG bans in these countries, guided by a framework developed by Carter and McKenzie (2020). We conclude by noting how these bans are currently being amplified internationally, despite some barriers to scaling up, through promising new multilateral international initiatives.

The Road to National Bans on Fossil Fuel Extraction

For decades, global climate negotiations via the United Nations Framework Convention on Climate Change (UNFCCC) have focused on demand-side emission reductions, holding countries responsible for greenhouse gases (GHG) *emitted* only in their own territory, thereby ignoring nations' fossil fuel extraction and exportation to be burned elsewhere. Since its inception in 1992, the UNFCCC has concentrated entirely on controlling emissions where fossil fuels are consumed and has been silent on fossil fuel supply, leaving the question of extraction to the market (Aykut and Castro 2017; Greg Muttitt et al. 2016). This approach has not resulted in the required emission reductions to keep the aspirations of the Paris Agreement on Climate Change alive and limit temperature rise to 2.0 °C, ideally restricting warming to 1.5 °C, above pre-industrial levels by the end of the century (Intergovernmental Panel on Climate Change (IPCC) 2018; Jackson et al. 2019; Verkuijl et al. 2018).

In contrast, communities worldwide have long understood the need to rein in fossil fuel production, initially to protect ecological systems, human health, and community sovereignty and, more recently, to ensure a climate-safe future (Carter and McKenzie 2020). KIIG movements first appeared in the mid-1990s in Ecuador and Nigeria. Today, they are consolidating in the Fossil Fuel Non-Proliferation Treaty (FF-NPT), which has been widely endorsed by cities, subnational governments, organizations, municipal governments, 101 Nobel Laureates from around the world, and garnering increasing support from national governments and international institutions (Fossil Fuel Non-Proliferation Treaty 2022, Newell and Simms 2020). Since the mid-2010s, there has also been an upsurge in academic literature and engagement by research institutes with supply-side climate policy.[1]

Welsby et al. (2021) found that 58% of oil, 59% of fossil methane gas, and 89% of coal reserves must never be extracted, while global fossil fuel production must steadily decrease by 3% every year until 2050 to have just half a chance of keeping global temperatures below 1.5 °C.

Newer research indicates that keeping global temperature rise to a 1.5 °C limit means 90% of fossil fuel reserves must be kept in the ground (Allen and Coffin 2022). Meanwhile, governments and companies must "prematurely decommission" ongoing production, avoiding almost 40% of emissions from existing projects (Trout et al. 2022, p. 1). Yet, by 2030, governments anticipate producing more than double the amount of fossil fuels that would keep the global temperature within a 1.5 °C increase (SEI, IISD, ODI, E3G, and UNEP 2020).

Calls for curtailing supply are also building in international climate negotiations and are now foregrounded in reports by the IPCC. Oilwatch brought community activism against fossil fuels to the 1997 Kyoto Protocol negotiations, where it advocated for a fossil fuel extraction moratorium. The need to keep fossil fuels in the ground is now echoed at the highest levels of the United Nations (UN), notably by Secretary-General

[1] Key works include, for example, Asheim et al. 2019; Blondeel and Van de Graaf 2018; Carter 2020; Collier and Venables 2014; Erickson 2018; Gaulin and Billon 2020; Le Billon and Kristoffersen 2019; Piggot 2017; Piggot et al. 2018; Rempel and Gupta 2021; Trout et al. 2022; van Asselt 2021; Welsby et al. 2021.

Antonio Guterres, who acknowledged in 2019, "We simply have to stop digging and drilling" (United Nations Secretary-General 2019, n.p.). Then in 2021, the IPCC report, AR6 Climate Change 2021: The Physical Science Basis, documented that the burning of fossil fuels—oil, gas, and coal—has been responsible for about 64% of global emissions since 1750, and 86% over the last decade (IPCC 2021, p. 97; Arias et al. 2021; Aykut et al. 2017; Jackson et al. 2019; SEI, IISD, ODI, E3G, and UNEP 2020). In response, Guterres emphasized that this report "must sound a death knell for coal and fossil fuels, before they destroy our planet" (United Nations 2021, n.p.). The 2021 UN Climate Change Conference, COP26, in Glasgow, signalled the beginning of a breakthrough in international supply-side climate policy. For the first time in UN climate deliberations, the first draft of the "Glasgow Climate Pact" (later weakened[2]) advocated for the "phasing-out of coal and subsidies for fossil fuels" (UNFCCC 2021, p. 2). While there are daunting challenges ahead, there are now clear pathways towards an international agreement to leave fossil fuels in the ground (van Asselt and Newell 2022).

As community pressure, research, and international negotiations continue to turn towards curtailing oil and gas supply, a building wave of countries are proposing bans on oil and gas exploration and extraction (Carter and McKenzie 2020). Starting in 2017, following Costa Rica's 2002 example, national bans were proposed by Belize (a ban on offshore oil), Bulgaria (shale gas), Denmark (oil and gas), France (oil and gas), Germany (some forms of fracking; oil and gas drilling in the North Sea), Italy (18-month moratorium on offshore oil and gas exploration, now expired), Ireland (oil and gas), the Netherlands (gas), New Zealand (oil and gas), Portugal (oil and gas), Spain (oil and gas), and Uruguay (fracking) (SEI, IISD, ODI, E3G, and UNEP 2020). Sweden, Greenland, and Wales have also recently signalled their commitment to end new oil and gas exploration and production via their participation in the Beyond Oil and Gas Alliance (BOGA).

[2] The final text references the phasing *down*, not *out*, of *unabated* coal (it could still be used with carbon capture and storage), and the phase-out of fossil fuel subsidies that are *inefficient* (arguably all of them are) (UNFCCC 2021).

What is fostering the rise of these historically progressive, post-extractive bargains leading to such significant bans? Carter and McKenzie (2020) surveyed the burgeoning supply-side climate policy literature and identified several important conditions. KIIG policies could be expected to originate from small-scale, locally oriented campaigns focused on a singular impact or issue. Moreover, a diverse set of organizations across society, some of which are connected to international organizations with more resources and tested strategies, would likely coordinate support for broad KIIG policies. These horizontally connected (across a constituency) and vertically integrated (with international organizations) coalitions could then seize, or create, political openings that allow for improved policy influence. This would mean intervening in predictable or institutional processes, such as elections or consultation processes. Momentum for advancing fossil fuels bans can also come from amplifying exogenous unpredictable openings, such as climate disasters or the release of new research, or shifting political attention via organizing large-scale protests or civil demonstrations. Additionally, national KIIG policies would likely be fostered by "norm entrepreneurs"—well-placed individuals within and outside government who can lend legitimacy and credibility to grassroots KIIG movements (Green 2017; Piggot 2017). These entrepreneurs could offer enhanced political access to particular organizations and coalitions within the broader KIIG movement. Finally, Carter and McKenzie (2020) expect that emotionally resonant framing of the KIIG issue, messages that amplify a collective sense of (in)justice, emphasizes local risks and offer a clear, straightforward solution with a vision of an optimistic post-fossil fuel future, would be essential to the development of KIIG policies (Healy et al. 2019; Healy and Barry 2017).

How are these conditions playing out in the real world in some of the first countries to implement national bans on oil production? Here we reflect on our analysis of three recent first-mover countries, France, Denmark, and Ireland.

Vanessita (2012)

Tale of Three Bans

This section highlights some critical domestic, regional, and international events and influences that contributed to the development of national KIIG policy in each of the first-mover cases explored in this chapter. Bans on fossil fuel extraction in these three countries are an extension of more general approaches to improve energy security and reduce emissions given the climate crisis. As these countries ratcheted their climate policy ambition, they began to focus on phasing out fossil fuel extraction. Thus, each country became a first mover in historic policies aiming to keep fossil fuels in the ground to respond to the climate crisis (Fig. 7.1).

France enhanced its emission reduction ambition and effort to transition away from fossil fuel use over the last 15 years, considering both energy security and climate concern. France's emphasis on reducing hydrocarbon consumption and production was strengthened with the 2017 election of President Emmanuel Macron, who, during his campaign, committed to a "profound rupture" that would end France's fossil fuel dependence. As a result of France's recent energy and climate efforts,

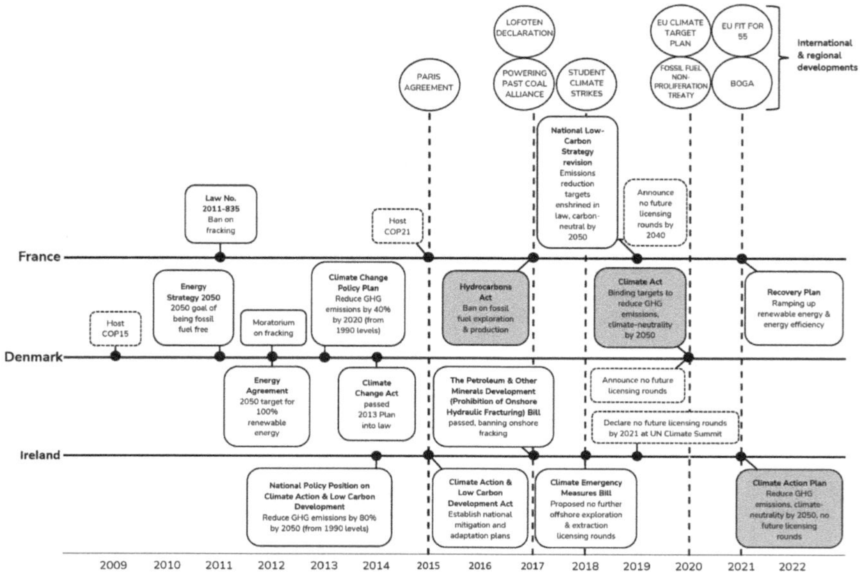

Fig. 7.1 Key national, regional, and international KIIG events and influences

it has successfully enhanced its climate performance, decoupling GDP and population growth from emissions growth. From 2005 to 2019, despite GDP increasing by 17% and the population by 7%, the "carbon intensity of the economy fell by 32%" (Yougova 2021, pp. 1–2). France's emissions fell by approximately 20% by 2020 from 1990 levels (International Energy Agency 2021, p. 41), and the country aims to improve upon this emissions reduction success via KIIG policies.

France's 2017 ban on fossil fuel exploration and production was central to the country's climate policy development. The 2017 Climate Plan, created to fulfil France's 2015 Paris Accord commitments, pledged to achieve carbon neutrality by 2050 through measures such as ending the sale of petrol and diesel vehicles by 2040, closing the last of France's coal-fired electricity plants by 2022, and phasing out fossil fuel extraction (International Energy Agency 2021). Nicolas Hulot, Minister of Ecological and Solidarity Transition, presented a bill to the Council of Ministers (Conseil des ministres) in September 2017 proposing a ban on fossil fuel extraction. After revisions by the Council of State (Conseil d'État), legislature, and senate, in December 2017, France's *Hydrocarbons Act*, known as the Hulot Law, was passed (L'Assemblée nationale 2017). The Hulot Law prohibits new permits for hydrocarbon exploration or production onshore and offshore, except mine gas, and no current licences will be eligible for renewal. All existing licences will end before 1 January 2040 (L'Assemblée nationale 2017, Art. L. 111-12). The legislation was intended to set a global example for keeping fossil fuels in the ground; through it, France became the first of a recent series of countries to explore what Bowles and Andrews define as a post-extractive bargain, implementing a national ban on fossil fuel exploration and production.

Denmark, for its part, is a global frontrunner in emission reductions, having cut emissions by 23% between 2005 and 2018 (Climate Change Performance Index 2021). The country is decreasing the carbon intensity of its energy mix through advancements in renewable energies, chiefly wind energy (Jørgensen et al. 2017). Though Denmark has a long history of bolstering its renewable energy portfolio, its efforts to move away from fossil fuels and sustain a post-extractive bargain were boosted by the 2011 Energy Strategy 2050, establishing the goal of being fully independent of fossil fuels by 2050 (International Energy Agency 2011). The 2012 Energy Agreement enhanced the share of renewable energy, particularly wind, to the broader target of 100% renewable energy by 2030 and committed Denmark to set plans to phase out all reliance on fossil fuels (International Energy Agency 2020). Following this, in 2020, Denmark announced to cease state-approved exploration in the North Sea and to phase out all fossil fuel extraction by 2050 (Danish Ministry of Climate, Energy and Utilities 2020).

In contrast to France and Denmark's climate reputations, Ireland had a reputation as a climate policy laggard with the worst climate policy in Western Europe and the second-worst in the European Union (EU) (Torney and O'Gorman 2019). However, starting in 2014, Ireland took key steps that committed it to creating a low-carbon economy by 2050 and joining the likes of France and Denmark in post-extractive bargains. Ireland first moved towards a national bill to keep fossil fuels in the ground in 2017 with a prohibition on onshore fracking (Oireachtas 2017). Then the 2018 Climate Emergency Measures

(CEM) bill proposed to immediately stop permitting licences for offshore oil and gas exploration and extractions if global atmospheric carbon exceeded 350 parts per million (Oireachtas 2018). The CEM lapsed before the 2020 election (Carter and McKenzie 2020). However, at the 2019 UN Climate Summit, Ireland announced that it would phase out offshore oil exploration licences (United Nations 2019), a proclamation that was later expanded to incorporate natural gas. This commitment was enacted via the Climate Action and Low Carbon Amendment Bill, which legislated a rapid reduction in GHG emissions of 51% by 2030 and net-zero emissions by 2050 (Oireachtas 2021). As part of this bill, the Irish Cabinet approved a ban on licences for new oil and natural gas exploration in 2021 (Oireachtas 2021). Upon announcing the ban, Minister for the Environment, Climate and Communications Eamon Ryan emphasized there would be no rounds of licensing in the future (O'Sullivan 2019).

Kickstarting KIIG bans

What conditions supported the development of these bans? Looking across these three cases, we preliminarily identify trends, attending to the development of broad-based movements, vertical connections to international organizations, domestically resonant framing, and well-placed norm/policy entrepreneurs. These are interacting conditions—constellations of factors—that we observe as combining to foster KIIG policy.

External Pressure

First, these oil bans developed in the context of rising external pressures to strengthen national climate policy. Notably, pressure came from EU membership. The EU pursues an emission reduction target of at least 50% below 1990 levels by 2030 through national reduction obligations (European Commission 2021). The focus is primarily on large emitters, such as power plants and the oil and gas sectors, and emissions from buildings, agriculture, and transportation (European Commission 2021).

Ireland, in particular, was under EU pressure to improve its climate policy and emissions reduction performance. Indeed, by the late 2010s, Ireland's failure to meet its emissions target risked EU non-compliance costs exceeding €500 million a year (O'Sullivan 2019).

External pressure to improve climate policy also came from reports produced by the international scientific community—notably the fall 2018 report from the IPCC (IPCC 2018). This report inspired or redoubled public awareness about climate change and mobilization, notably school strikes and climate protests sparked by Swedish teenager Greta Thunberg, who called for more serious climate policy across these countries.

Inspired by international strikes, school strikes in Ireland—with remarkable turnout across the country—influenced politicians to move the first ban bill (the CEM) to the committee stage. Likewise, in Denmark, public opinion appeared to shift in response to these internationally inspired climate marches and strikes throughout 2018 and 2019. Before Denmark's 2019 election, polls indicated that climate change was a top concern for 46% of voters, compared to 27% in 2017 (Holstein 2019).

Internal Pressure: The Pursuit of Energy Security/ Independence

Rising pressure to adopt bolder climate policies, often coming from outside these states, was joined by concerns for domestic energy security, notably in Denmark and France. Where Ireland's initially proposed fossil fuel extraction ban came as a response to mounting climate concerns, Denmark's and France's efforts to keep fossil fuels in the ground and replace them with renewable energy were motivated by the need to secure energy independence. The 1970s energy crisis was a catalyst for Denmark to develop a more decentralized energy system, aided by Denmark's small-scale entrepreneurial-oriented economy (Kooij et al. 2018). Denmark fostered the development of localized, municipality-owned energy systems, driving experimentation in renewable sources, particularly wind technology (Jørgensen et al. 2017). Denmark's early pursuits for energy security set the country on a trajectory that is now well aligned with climate action. Likewise, France's transition away from fossil fuels was motivated by energy security concerns, as embodied in the 2015 *Energy Transition Act* (République française 2015). France's emphasis on reducing hydrocarbon consumption and production has strengthened since the 2017 election of President Emmanuel Macron, who committed to ending France's consumption of fossil fuel energy.

Electoral Politics and Institutional Openings

Informed by the aforementioned external pressures, in both Ireland and Denmark, it was small political parties who initially advanced proposals to ban fossil fuel extraction. For Ireland, these proposals were bolstered via minority coalitions composed of the socialist Solidarity/People-before-Profit (PBP) party and the Greens. These smaller parties were able to advance ban legislation, thanks to minority coalition governments, the outcome of the long-reigning centre-right Fianna Fail party losing its hold on parliament in 2016 (McKenzie and Carter 2021). During the 2019 election campaign in Denmark, the parties on the left of the Social Democrats, the Socialist People's Party (SV), the Red-Green Alliance (RGA), and the Social Liberals established a coalition to implement bolder emission reductions. Following the elections, the Social Democrats leaned on the support of the aforementioned to form government. The Social Democrats united with the left-facing coalition on the commitment of acting to reach a 70% emission reduction. This included an agreement on the future of fossil fuel extraction in the North Sea, resulting in the cancellation of the ongoing and all future rounds of licensing for oil and gas extraction.

In contrast to smaller parties advancing KIIG policy, the governing party actively supported France's ban. Climate action was institutionalized via a "super-ministry," the Ministry of the Ecological Transition, responsible for energy, environment, and climate, while coordinating with other ministries on social issues, notably equality. In addition, the High Council on Climate, created in 2019, independently assesses the government's climate strategy and effectiveness; the government must provide an official response to its annual progress reports International Energy Agency 2021, p. 26. Meanwhile, the Ecological Defence Council, created in 2019, facilitates climate action across governments. Chaired by the President and involving all ministers with portfolios relevant to climate and environmental issues, the council develops ecological transition priorities and works to advance them across national policies (International Energy Agency 2021, p. 49). KIIG policy in France, while stemming from local campaigns as noted in the next section, was actively advanced by the leading political party.

Each of these three national governments created institutional openings for citizens to participate in and call for the further boosting of climate policy ambition with public awareness, and some opposition helped to solidify such state-society bargain towards post-extractivism. Climate policy advances in France were fostered partly by intensive public consultations, such as the National Debate on the Energy Transition in 2013 and the Citizen's Climate Convention, held in 2019 and 2020. The recommendations from these initiatives fed into policy development, such as the 2015 *Energy Transition Act* and the bold 2021 *Climate Resilience Act* that, for example, which prohibits short-haul flights where train service is available (International Energy Agency 2021, p. 28; République française 2021). In Denmark, the government commissions the Climate Change Council, a group of academics and experts, to advise on drafting policy and achieving climate goals. In 2020, this group advocated for ending any future exploration in the North Sea, substantiating a ban by citing the country's climate ambitions under the Paris Agreement. Also, under the new 2020 *Climate Act*, the Climate Citizens Assembly was created with 99 randomly selected citizens to provide recommendations to the government as to how to achieve the goals of the *Climate Act* (Danish Ministry of Climate, Energy and Utilities 2020). A Youth Climate Council, an independent youth-led advisory board to the climate minister, was also created in 2019 to advocate on behalf of Danish youth and influence climate policy decisions. Finally, in Ireland, one of the country's Citizens' Assemblies signalled a shift in public opinion towards a stronger climate policy. The assembly on climate change drew significant public attention and resulted in a special cross-party committee of parliament being struck to integrate the recommendations into the 2019 Climate Action Plan (Devaney et al. 2020). Through this initiative, researchers with close connections to the Irish climate justice movement were integrated into the Green and PBP parties and later brought forward KIIG policy through targeted bills.

Seeded from Local Campaigns and Advanced by Broad-Based Domestic Coalitions

While national electoral politics were critical in KIIG policy development, these bans were rooted in local and sometimes much older campaigns contesting fossil fuel development. The civil society capacity and networks developed in these struggles were then directed towards more general bans on oil. In France, public opposition to fracking—beginning in 2010, motivated initially by fears of impacts on water systems—was a gateway to considering the broader climate impact of this form of extraction, which helped open broader conversations about the consequences of a global fossil-fuelled capitalist system (de Sartre and Chailleux 2021). The anti-fracking mobilization created a "knockout" victory that framed France's subsequent KIIG policy (Chailleux 2016, p. 161). Yet the seeds of public pressure for KIIG policy run even deeper as anti-fracking coalitions remobilized older activist networks on globalization, GMOs, and nuclear energy (Chailleux 2016). Likewise, organized public opposition to fracking in Ireland—which began as a small campaign on the west coast to block a single offshore fracking project, initially led by local people concerned about safety, autonomy, property values, and water quality—resulted in a national anti-fracking bill. That legislation was a major stepping stone to a broader ban on oil development (McKenzie and Carter 2021). Reminiscent of Denmark's anti-nuclear movement in the 1970s and 1980s, Danish anti-fracking campaigns intensified in 2015 as concerns over public health—particularly regarding groundwater quality with Total's unauthorized use of Null Foam—merged with environmental activism. Danish anti-fracking campaigns similarly scaled up to nationwide denouncements of fossil fuel exploration and production as calls to end the use of fracking were matched with demands to cease fossil fuel production by any other means to maintain Denmark's "green" reputation and meet its climate commitments.

Within each country, KIIG policy was advanced by a broad range of actors coordinating their efforts via coalitions. For example, in France, well-coordinated citizen groups, organized in regional umbrella groups as well as national coordinating committees, communicated concerns about fossil fuel extraction to all levels of government for well over a decade.

The movement involved graduate students, professors, judges, retired mining personnel in areas proposed for oil development, lawyers, hydrologists, and citizens from across the political spectrum. Alliances with people in the agriculture sector were vital given the importance of that sector in France and the direct threats posed by oil and gas development. And in Ireland, faith groups, humanitarian and international development organizations, local community groups, environmentalists, academic/scientific researchers, and the youth wings of political parties collaborated to focus on preventing fossil fuel production.

Supported by International Connections

Meanwhile, local campaigns in all three countries were supported by well-connected international organizations that have bolstered domestic campaigns for KIIG policy. International connections offered guidance on movement strategy and messaging learned from other cases. France's oil ban was supported by a network of local, regional, national, and European environmental advocacy groups (Chailleux 2016), which grew from the anti-fracking campaign, informed by connections across Europe, the US, and countries in North Africa, South America, and Canada (Quebec). Groups like Friends of the Earth France (Les Amis de la Terre) were central in connecting French opposition to fossil fuels with citizen groups internationally. Denmark's ban was likewise advanced through connections with international organizations, most visible in the 2020 direct action taken by Greenpeace. Activists occupied one of Total's offshore drilling rigs in the North Sea, effectively shutting down production for 36 hours to protest future exploration and bring awareness to the environmental risks of fossil fuel extraction ventures. In Ireland, international connections were also vital in informing and advancing the KIIG movement. Irish movement actors connected with groups opposing Shell pipelines in the US, liquid natural gas facilities in Europe, coal extraction in Colombia, and fracking globally. Meanwhile, groups like Friends of the Earth Ireland maintained close ties with their European and international counterparts and acted as a connector to outside resources and international organizations like Oil Change International, 350.org, and the Global Catholic Climate Movement provided support.

Multi-Pronged Movement Strategy and Resonant Message Framing

In each of these cases, movements successfully pressed for KIIG policy by framing the need to keep fossil fuels in the ground in ways that resonated with the domestic context. For example, in Denmark, movement actors foregrounded just transition policies (support for economic diversification and job creation) in the Esbjerg region, where most offshore oil and gas activities were located. Social movements also called on politicians to leverage Denmark's leadership in renewable energy to assert itself as a global green energy frontrunner that could inspire other states to end their dependence on fossil fuels. As another example, in Ireland, the movement advocating

KIIG policy interpreted the scientific reality of the climate crisis and the need for a fossil fuel wind-down as issues of human rights, morality, and social justice, arguing that Ireland had a "moral obligation" to prevent fossil fuel extraction. The KIIG movement also repositioned debates about fossil fuel extraction within a broader conversation about the socio-economic future of Irish communities. As one local campaign organizer noted, "it's *for* something that you're campaigning. It's talking about home" (Ireland Interview #4, April 2019).

The movements in each country then spread these messages using a range of strategies to communicate directly with elected officials and to the general public, often through media-appealing actions. In France, movement actors used a range of methods learned from the anti-fracking effort, from neighbourhood meetings and door-to-door information sharing to direct actions such as an "anti-gaz de couche" [anti-fracking] camp at one proposed fracking site. One notable action included the group Houille…ouille-ouille! [Coal…Ouch, Ouch!] organizing a 100-kilometre caravan to expose the converging risks of fossil fuel projects. Meanwhile, movement actors engaged directly with elected officials from across the political spectrum at all levels of governance, from city halls to the national legislature. Movement actors identified elected officials who could channel people's concerns about oil development into policy action and provided research and policy recommendations to politicians. In Denmark, members of the Green Student Movement (GSM) composed letters to media outlets and politicians while also organizing direct actions, later with Extinction Rebellion advocates. Direct action included a bike demonstration to garner participation and mobilize people in the climate campaign to get the attention of politicians, stressing the urgency and necessity of ceasing all talks about tenders for more oil extraction from the North Sea. Accompanying this, the GMS has set up human chains around the Danish parliament in Copenhagen, such as the one that took place in the fall of 2018, expressing their concerns for the future and calling for aggressive carbon reduction activity before the opening of parliament. In Ireland, social movement actors also employed diverse strategies to raise public awareness about and pressure politicians to deliver KIIG policies. Some groups focused on producing scientific analyses that informed ban movement messaging. Others, like the Stop Climate Chaos Coalition and NGOs, like Not Here, Not Anywhere (NHNA), organized visual protests and direct actions that got media attention. To reach national politicians, groups organized multiple "mass lobbies" at critical moments in developing KIIG policy that brokered conversations between citizens concerned about fossil fuel development and their elected representatives outside the legislature. Catholic international development organization Trócaire, a lead group in Irish KIIG policy development, nurtured direct relationships with politicians from all parties, providing policy information to support KIIG policy.

Supported by Norm Entrepreneurs

Finally, each of these successful KIIG movements was supported by leading actors, domestic or international, or lent credibility to the call to keep fossil fuels in the ground. For example, in Ireland, the movement drew on the urgent statements made by Pope Francis about the climate crisis to bring legitimacy to their cause which resonated strongly in the country, given the predominance of Catholicism. Likewise helpful was the vocal support for the ban of former Irish President and UN Special Envoy for Climate Change Mary Robinson. In France, the ban was advanced, thanks to strong champions within the government, such as Nicolas Hulot, a well-known environmental advocate appointed Minister of

Ecological and Solidary Transition. Denmark similarly has high-ranking officials forwarding KIIG policy, such as Dan Jørgensen, Minister for Climate, Energy and Utilities. Norm entrepreneurs were also active in the Danish business community, such as the former CEO of Ørsted, Anders Eldrup. Eldrup resisted internal corporate pressure to keep with fossil fuels, especially its reputedly efficient coal production, and instead focused on renewable energy investments, pivoting the company away from fossil fuels.

What's Next? Leveraging First-Mover Bans

The national bans in France, Denmark, and Ireland arose, thanks to mounting external pressures and institutional openings, the scale-up of more localized campaigns against fossil fuel development, and coordination among a diverse set of organizations within the country that are connected with international organizations. These threads are accompanied by the presence of multi-pronged mobilization efforts that simultaneously reached the public and engaged with elected officials, well-tailored message framing, and assistance from norm entrepreneurs. This constellation of conditions might guide those seeking to advance progressive bargains and KIIG policies in other countries, drawing attention to the importance of, for example, supporting local campaigns against fossil fuel projects as a "gateway" to a general oil ban or of enacting strategies and framings that resonate with the specific concerns and values of the country.

However, while these bans are inspiring, KIIG policy faces formidable barriers, especially in jurisdictions where fossil fuel development is longstanding. In those cases, fossil fuel firms wield significant, coordinated political power and use their direct access to policymakers to forestall any attempt to wind down production; governments reliant on revenues from fossil fuel activity give industry preferential access in the policy development process as well as a range of benefits (notably subsidies) to support continued fossil fuel activity (Carter 2020). This arrangement has legitimacy where citizens perceive their communities as dependent on fossil fuel extraction for employment and revenue—in "petrocultures" (Szeman 2019), where people associate industrial activities with cultural identity, there is significant resistance to winding down oil. So far, national bans on oil extraction have been enacted primarily in countries without, or with only nascent, oil sectors—the clear exception is Denmark, the largest oil producer in the EU when it declared its ban. Amplifying KIIG policy in other deeply entrenched oil-producing states is an ongoing challenge, one that will require collaboration with labour movements on just transitions and the creation of climate jobs to develop a counter-constituency that can challenge oil's political and cultural dominance. This occurred in Denmark with jobs in the green energy sector proliferating and expected to continue to do so (Sperling et al. 2021), a forecast that is substantiated by recent assessments by key Danish labour unions that endorse the potential further renewable energy investment would have on employment and economic performance in Denmark. Moreover, calls for just transition were central in France, Denmark, and Ireland, where movement leaders advocated an oil wind-down intertwined with more social equity. In this way, movements for KIIG policies challenge the existing political-economic order and foreground how the energy transition must also enhance social justice.

While implementing KIIG policies in major oil-producing states will be challenging, it is also clear that the national bans enacted to date are contributing to the development of a burgeoning global norm to keep fossil fuels in the ground (Green 2018) and are scaling up to have tangible policy impact. These national bans have the potential to set a foundation for regulatory certainty and consistency, sending clear investment signals to energy markets to align with decarbonization. At the same time, they allow states to create global connections and knowledge sharing on how to keep fossil fuels in the ground. Most notably, they have led to the historic multilateral effort of Denmark and Costa Rica, two KIIG first-movers, to launch the BOGA at COP26 in Glasgow. BOGA is an alliance of states committed to ceasing all new oil and gas exploration and production; Ireland and France have joined, as has Québec, a momentous move as the province is the first North American BOGA member and from the deeply oil-entrenched Canadian petro-state. The rising wave of national bans on oil extraction is inspiring the kind of supply-side climate policy urgently needed to confront the source of the climate crisis.

References

Allen, T., & Coffin, M. (2022). Unburnable Carbon: Ten Years On The financial markets are still enabling a carbon bubble (p. 50). Carbon Tracker Initiative.

Arias, P. A., Bellouin, N., Coppola, E., Jones, R. G., Krinner, G., Marotzke, J., et al. (2021). *2021: Technical Summary* (pp. 33–144). Cambridge University Press: Intergovernmental Panel on Climate Change.

Asheim, G. B., Fæhn, T., Nyborg, K., Greaker, M., Hagem, C., Harstad, B., et al. (2019). The case for a supply-side climate treaty. *Science, 365*(6451), 325–327. https://doi.org/10.1126/science.aax5011

van Asselt, H. (2021). Governing fossil fuel production in the age of climate disruption: Towards an international law of 'leaving it in the ground.' Earth System Governance, 9. https://doi.org/10.1016/j.esg.2021.100118.

van Asselt, H., & Newell, P. (2022). Pathways to an International Agreement to Leave Fossil Fuels in the Ground. *Global Environmental Politics, 1–20*, 1. https://doi.org/10.1162/glep_a_00674

Aykut, S. C., & Castro, M. (2017). The end of fossil fuels? : Understanding the partial climatisation of global energy debates. In S. C. Aykut, J. Foyer, & E. Morena (Eds.), *Globalising the Climate: COP21 and the climatisation of global debates*. https://doi.org/10.4324/9781315560595-10

Aykut, S. C., Foyer, J., & Morena, E. (Eds.). (2017). *Globalising the climate: COP21 and the climatisation of global debates*. Routledge, Taylor & Francis Group.

Blondeel, M., & Van de Graaf, T. (2018). Toward a global coal mining moratorium? A comparative analysis of coal mining policies in the USA, China, India and Australia. *Climatic Change, 150*(1–2), 89–101. https://doi.org/10.1007/s10584-017-2135-5

Carter, A. (2020). *Fossilized: Environmental Policy in Canada's Petro-Provinces During the Last Oil Boom*. UBC Press.

Carter, A., & McKenzie, J. (2020). Amplifying "Keep It in the Ground" First-Movers: Toward a Comparative Framework. *Society & Natural Resources*. https://doi.org/10.1080/08941920.2020.1772924

Chailleux, S. (2016). *Non au gaz de schiste ! : cadrages et débordements de la controverse sur les hydrocarbures non conventionnels en France et au Québec* (p. 423). Science politique, Université de Bordeaux.

Climate Change Performance Index. (2021). CCPI Countries and Rankings: Denmark. https://ccpi.org/country/dnk/.

Collier, P., & Venables, A. J. (2014). Closing coal: economic and moral incentives. *Oxford Review of Economic Policy, 30*(3), 492–512. https://doi.org/10.1093/oxrep/gru024

Danish Ministry of Climate, Energy and Utilities. (2020, June 26). Climate Act. https://storage.googleapis.com/cclow-staging/gow3goc4p5jszb41rhjdrtv1et44?GoogleAccessId=laws-and-pathways-staging%40soy-truth-247515.iam.gserviceaccount.com&Expires=1645584100&Signature=MlQQl9WjCLURehmHFK8PpRtGZSHipAg0bndyyo1DLmSSRlOb%2FkvyxqKU2BlK9eic86g98fko8cmw9HfSArLCvrvFgv%2BZvAXQm9jWm%2F0C8hrC7h7Iln1w814zfls8XhFOoeygTUtJXetgf7fgsiy2sd%2FvL5BQ6TuuaRsYGIA%2BQciEjqkMzlfq3ZqbTjzL8Kxp18FslrdgVNT4UBYOGiid9DIt3YkdnM%2FvwOwRg0qN842ueLQP1d5bRoVAETvM%2BBgUGkHwIcXJzEd3UOwlblj%2BlLos%2FnZh%2Fe%2B4dkde80nEz%2BzyxMS65nNDLP-aDv6ZFcdztJRiXV84%2BjM%2BijaiuvYdDdA%3D%3D&response-content-disposition=inline%3B+filename%3D%22Climate+Act_Denmark+-+WEBTILGAENGELIG-A.pdf%22%3B+filename%2A%3DUTF-8%27%27Climate%2520Act_Denmark%2520-%2520WEBTILG%25C3%2586NGELIG-A.pdf&response-content-type=application%2Fpdf.

Devaney, L., Torney, D., Brereton, P., & Coleman, M. (2020). Ireland's Citizens' Assembly on Climate Change: Lessons for Deliberative Public Engagement and Communication. *Environmental Communication, 14*(2), 141–146. https://doi.org/10.1080/17524032.2019.1708429

Erickson, P. (2018). *Confronting carbon lock-in: Canada's oil sands* (p. 12). Stockholm Environment Institute.

European Commission. (2021). 2030 Climate Target Plan. Climate Action. https://ec.europa.eu/clima/eu-action/european-green-deal/2030-climate-target-plan_en.

Fossil Fuel Non-Proliferation Treaty. (2022). The Fossil Fuel Non-Proliferation Treaty. https://fossilfueltreaty.org/.

Gaulin, N., & Billon, P. L. (2020). Climate change and fossil fuel production cuts: assessing global supply-side constraints and policy implications. *Climate Policy, 1*, 1–14. https://doi.org/10.1080/14693062.2020.1725409

Green, F. (2017). The normative foundations of climate legislation. In *Trends in Climate Change Legislation* (pp. 85–107). Edward Elgar Publishing. https://doi.org/10.4337/9781786435781.00014

Green, F. (2018). Anti-fossil fuel norms. *Climatic Change, 150*(1–2), 103–116.

Greg Muttitt, H. M. K., Stockman, L., Kretzmann, S., Scott, A., & Turnbull, D. (2016). The Sky's Limit: Why the Paris climate goals require a managed decline of fossil fuel production. *Oil Change International.* http://priceofoil.org/content/uploads/2016/09/OCI_the_skys_limit_2016_FINAL_2.pdf.

Healy, N., & Barry, J. (2017). Politicizing energy justice and energy system transitions: Fossil fuel divestment and a "just transition". *Energy Policy, 108*, 451–459. https://doi.org/10.1016/j.enpol.2017.06.014

Healy, N., Stephens, J. C., & Malin, S. A. (2019). Embodied energy injustices: Unveiling and politicizing the transboundary harms of fossil fuel extractivism and fossil fuel supply chains. *Energy Research & Social Science, 48*, 219–234. https://doi.org/10.1016/j.erss.2018.09.016

Holstein, E. (2019, May). Ny måling: Den grønne dagsorden tager en suveræn førsteplads. Altinget.dk. https://www.altinget.dk/artikel/ny-maaling-den-groenne-dagsorden-tager-en-suveraen-foersteplads.

International Energy Agency. (2011). *Energy Policies of IEA Countries: Denmark 2011 Review* (p. 158). International Energy Agency. https://iea.blob.core.windows.net/assets/3df26d26-9271-490b-ae10-1e9a14350412/EnergyPoliciesofIEACountriesDenmark2011.pdf.

International Energy Agency. (2020). Danish Energy Agreement for 2012–2020 – Policies. https://www.iea.org/policies/606-danish-energy-agreement-for-2012-2020.

International Energy Agency. (2021). *France 2021 Energy Policy Review* (p. 211). International Energy Agency. https://iea.blob.core.windows.net/assets/7b3b4b9d-6db3-4dcf-a0a5-a9993d7dd1d6/France2021.pdf.

IPCC. (2018). *Global Warming of 1.5°C: IPCC Special Report on impacts of global warming of 1.5°C above pre-industrial levels in context of strengthening response to climate change, sustainable development, and efforts to eradicate poverty* (1st ed.). Cambridge University Press. https://doi.org/10.1017/9781009157940

IPCC. (2021). *Climate Change 2021: The Physical Science Basis* (p. 2391). Cambridge University Press.

Jackson, R. B., Friedlingstein, P., Andrew, R. M., Canadell, J. G., Le Quéré, C., & Peters, G. P. (2019). Persistent fossil fuel growth threatens the Paris Agreement and planetary health. *Environmental Research Letters, 14*(12), 121001. https://doi.org/10.1088/1748-9326/ab57b3

Jørgensen, M. S., Jørgensen, U., & Jensen, J. S. (2017). Navigations and governance in the Danish energy transition reflecting changing Arenas of Development, controversies and policy mixes. *Energy Research & Social Science, 33*, 173–185. https://doi.org/10.1016/j.erss.2017.09.034

Kooij, H.-J., Oteman, M., Veenman, S., Sperling, K., Magnusson, D., Palm, J., & Hvelplund, F. (2018). Between grassroots and treetops: Community power and institutional dependence in the renewable energy sector in Denmark, Sweden and the Netherlands. *Energy Research & Social Science, 37*, 52–64. https://doi.org/10.1016/j.erss.2017.09.019

L'Assemblée nationale. (2017). LOI n° 2017-1839 du 30 décembre 2017 mettant fin à la recherche ainsi qu'à l'exploitation des hydrocarbures et portant diverses dispositions relatives à l'énergie et à l'environnement (1). 2017–1839.

Le Billon, P., & Kristoffersen, B. (2019). Just cuts for fossil fuels? Supply-side carbon constraints and energy transition. *Environment and Planning A: Economy and Space, 0308518X1881670*. https://doi.org/10.1177/0308518X18816702

McKenzie, J., & Carter, A. V. (2021). Stepping stones to keep fossil fuels in the ground: Insights for a global wind down from Ireland. *The Extractive Industries and Society, 8*(4), 101002. https://doi.org/10.1016/j.exis.2021.101002

Newell, P., & Simms, A. (2020). Towards a fossil fuel non-proliferation treaty. *Climate Policy, 1*, 1–12. https://doi.org/10.1080/14693062.2019.1636759

O'Sullivan, K. (2019, June 13). Ireland would face multibillion EU fines over emissions target failure. The Irish Times. https://www.irishtimes.com/business/transport-and-tourism/ireland-would-face-multibillion-eu-fines-over-emissions-target-failure-1.3924909.

Oireachtas. Petroleum and Other Minerals Development (Prohibition of Onshore Hydraulic Fracturing) Act 2017. Pub. L. No. 15 of 2017 (2017). https://data.oireachtas.ie/ie/oireachtas/act/2017/15/eng/enacted/a1517.pdf.

Oireachtas. Petroleum and Other Minerals Development (Amendment) (Climate Emergency Measures) Bill 2018. Pub. L. No. No. 9 of 2018 (2018). https://data.oireachtas.ie/ie/oireachtas/bill/2018/9/eng/initiated/b0918d.pdf.

Oireachtas. Climate Action and Low Carbon Development (Amendment) Act 2021 (2021). https://data.oireachtas.ie/ie/oireachtas/act/2021/32/eng/enacted/a3221.pdf.

Piggot, G. (2017). The influence of social movements on policies that constrain fossil fuel supply. *Climate Policy, 18*(7), 942–954.

Piggot, G., Erickson, P., van Asselt, H., & Lazarus, M. (2018). Swimming upstream: addressing fossil fuel supply under the UNFCCC. *Climate Policy, 18*(9), 1189–1202. https://doi.org/10.1080/14693062.2018.1494535

Rempel, A., & Gupta, J. (2021). Equitable, effective, and feasible approaches for a prospective fossil fuel transition. WIREs Climate Change, n/a(n/a), e756. https://doi.org/10.1002/wcc.756.

République française. LOI no 2015-992 du 17 août 2015 relative à la transition énergétique pour la croissance verte (1). , Pub. L. No. 2015–992 (2015).

https://storage.googleapis.com/cclow-staging/lrrxae7jx2la8n4ryystii8bmz3s?GoogleAccessId=laws-and-pathways-staging%40soy-truth-247515.iam.gserviceaccount.com&Expires=1650595479&Signature=Kuzbe%2BnuD8CJEkBZon29qLBAQ%2B5fQVyRdFuQjIiOh6PZS0hV8mLJeOfx1a2xmeyNflFlzpVgyuGTfk%2FjMvRoPjS4UIA3f%2FY5OvkvzXrcRq2Q%2BbcKVs6PZbD6Dm3aKKdeMltuwsXM7t9%2F4lyPWnc2uq%2BvfzpgIFZy9OYThwI0vr%2Ba0TqJR0iukhBD%2FKrPB2sGILgeHx4L66fdhU2PfgTutB0aSCZrv3Pks1I3xA%2FII1ZVqZED1dTNy06633rkI0hz7NzfKEG9lPoplQCwTysXJd7NSHvU31w%2Bss8qUmKG5Ju9IdYNuW9ykhAE3JlaDc6meFEXCTK02s2mtdRDyq%2FCxA%3D%3D&response-content-disposition=inline%3B+filename%3D%22joe_20150818_0189_0001.pdf%22%3B+filename%2A%3DUTF-8%27%27joe_20150818_0189_0001.pdf&response-content-type=application%2Fpdf.

République française. Loi no 2021-1104 du 22 août 2021 portant lutte contre le dérèglement climatique et renforcement de la résilience face à ses effets (1). , Pub. L. No. 2021–1104 (2021).

SEI, IISD, ODI, E3G, and UNEP. (2020). The Production Gap: 2020 Special Report. https://productiongap.org/2020report.

Sperling, K., Madsen, P. T., Gorroño-Albizu, L., & Mathiesen, B. V. (2021). Denmark without Oil and Gas Production: Opportunities and Challenges (p. 35). Aalborg University. https://oilandgastransitions.org/wp-content/uploads/2021/11/Denmark-Oil-and-Gas-Report.pdf.

Szeman, I. (2019). *On petrocultures: globalization, culture, and energy* (1st ed.). West Virginia University Press.

Torney, D., & O'Gorman, R. (2019). A laggard in good times and bad? The limited impact of EU membership on Ireland's climate change and environmental policy. *Irish Political Studies, 34*(4), 575–594. https://doi.org/10.1080/07907184.2019.1647174

Trout, K., Muttitt, G., Lafleur, D., Van de Graaf, T., Mendelevitch, R., Mei, L., & Meinshausen, M. (2022). Existing fossil fuel extraction would warm the world beyond 1.5 °C. *Environmental Research Letters, 17*(6), 064010. https://doi.org/10.1088/1748-9326/ac6228

United Nations. (2019). Climate Action Summit Delivers Major Step-Up in National Ambition, Private Sector Initiatives on Pathway to Key 2020 Deadline. United Nations Meetings Coverage and Press Releases. https://www.un.org/press/en/2019/envdev1998.doc.htm.

United Nations. (2021). Secretary-General's statement on the IPCC Working Group 1 Report on the Physical Science Basis of the Sixth Assessment.

New York. https://www.un.org/sg/en/content/secretary-generals-statement-the-ipcc-working-group-1-report-the-physical-science-basis-of-the-sixth-assessment.1

United Nations. (2022, April 4). Secretary-General Warns of Climate Emergency, Calling Intergovernmental Panel's Report 'a File of Shame', While Saying Leaders 'Are Lying', Fuelling Flames | UN Press. Meetings Coverage and Press Releases. Press Release. https://press.un.org/en/2022/sgsm21228.doc.htm.

United Nations Framework Convention on Climate Change (UNFCCC). (2021). Glasgow Climate Pact. https://unfccc.int/sites/default/files/resource/cop26_auv_2f_cover_decision.pdf.

United Nations Secretary-General. (2019). UN Secretary-General's remarks at pre-COP25 press conference [as delivered]. https://www.un.org/sg/en/content/sg/press-encounter/2019-12-01/un-secretary-generals-remarks-pre-cop25-press-conference-delivered.

Welsby, D., Price, J., Pye, S., & Ekins, P. (2021). Unextractable fossil fuels in a 1.5 °C world. *Nature, 597*(7875), 230–234. https://doi.org/10.1038/s41586-021-03821-8

Yougova, D. (2021). *Climate action in France: Latest state of play (Briefing)* (p. 6). European Parliamentary Research Service.

Part III

Global South Case Studies

8

Extractive Policies in Mexico Under López Obrador: Bargains for Whom?

Darcy Tetreault

Introduction

López Obrador became president of México on 1 December 2018, after having won a landslide victory in the presidential elections that took place five months earlier. The former mayor of Mexico City (2000–2005) and third-time presidential candidate received over 30 million votes, representing more than half of the popular vote. In addition, the political party that he had formed in 2014—the National Regeneration Movement (*Movimiento de Regeneración Nacional*, MORENA)—secured a majority in both the Senate and the Chamber of Deputies, thereby giving López Obrador unhampered parliamentary support for his political agenda during the first half of his six-year mandate. This progressive agenda has been called "the fourth transformation" (4T), with reference to three transformative moments of social struggle in Mexican history:

D. Tetreault (✉)
Department of Development Studies, Universidad Autónoma de Zacatecas, Zacatecas, Mexico
e-mail: darcy.tetreault@uaz.edu.mx

P. Bowles, N. Andrews (eds.), *Extractive Bargains*, Frontiers of Globalization,
https://doi.org/10.1007/978-3-031-32172-6_8

independence from Spain (1810–1821), the War of Reform (1858–1861), and the Mexican Revolution (1910–1920). In this discourse, López Obrador's government seeks to transform Mexican society as profoundly as these three historical moments, only this time from above and without violence.

What roles have been assigned to the petroleum and mining sectors in the 4 T? What extractive bargains have emerged, under what terms, and for whom? These are the main questions that this chapter seeks to address. This is done by examining Mexico's extractive policies during the first three and a half years of López Obrador's presidency, through the lenses of extractivist bargains outlined in the introductory chapter of this book. This chapter begins with some brief observations of global extractivist trends and material flow patterns, and of the way in which Mexico fits into this larger picture (Sect. "Bargaining on Extractivism"). From there it goes on to examine the terms of the extractivist bargains that are currently under construction in Mexico, first on the national level (Sect. "The energy-Sovereignty Bargain on the National Level") and then with a focus on three groups of key stakeholders: *extractive capital* (Sect. "Bargains for Private Extractive Firms"), *labour* in extractive activities (Sect. "Stratified Labour Bargains"), and directly affected *rural communities* (Sect. "Directly Impacted Rural Communities"). The concluding section seeks to highlight the main contours of the extractivist bargains that are unfolding in Mexico under the current government of López Obrador and to distill their political, economic, and socioecological implications.

Bargaining on Extractivism

Extractivism has been defined as the removal of large quantities of material destined for export, with little or no processing (Gudynas, 2016). In the context of the primary- commodities boom that began in the first decade of the new millennium, governments from across Latin America sought diverse ways to increase the rate of extracting minerals, metals, hydrocarbons, and biomass, in order to stimulate economic growth and capture resource rents. In these strategies, different extractivist bargains were struck on the national level (Ellner, 2021). The progressive governments associated with the Pink Tide in electoral politics that coincided with this first super-cycle of the primary-commodities boom sought to garner for the state a greater share of resource rents derived from extractive activities, either directly through the strengthening and creation of state-owned enterprises or indirectly by imposing higher taxes and royalties on private and foreign companies. By contrast, conservative or "neoliberal" governments—such as those in Mexico and Colombia—continued to adhere to policies aligned with the (post-) Washington Consensus, including low taxation, simplified administrative procedures, and other measures meant to attract foreign direct investment (FDI) in the exploitation of subterranean resources (Veltmeyer & Petras, 2014). Herein lies what Maristella Svampa refers to as the "commodities consensus"; that is, irrespective of ideological leanings and of the different redistributive terms of the extractivist bargains in Latin America, there remains "a tacit or explicit agreement about the irresistible nature of the current extractivist dynamics, a product of the growing global demand for primary goods" (Svampa, 2019, p. 16).

Indeed, the rates of extracting materials from the Earth to enter into economic processing increased dramatically on the global level during the post-World War II period, and they have continued to accelerate since pro-market neoliberal reforms were imposed during the 1990s (Krausmann et al., 2009). Further, there have been significant changes in global patterns of material extraction and consumption since the 1990s, largely driven by high economic growth rates and rising material intensity in China and elsewhere in Asia. In just a 20-year period, China went from being a negligible importer of non-renewable resources to the largest in the world, followed by the United States, India, Brazil, and Russia (Muradian et al., 2012; Infante-Amate et al., 2020). Materials extracted from Latin America continue to flow to the United States and Europe, but increasingly to China and other Asian countries (Infante-Amate et al., 2020), including through increasing investments by Chinese companies in extractive activities in South America (Cypher & Wilson, 2015).

While primary commodities have come to dominate the value of exports for most South American countries since the first decade of the new millennium, Mexico's exports have continued to be dominated by manufactured goods in the cheap-labour maquiladora sector. Moreover, about 80% of Mexico's exports continue to flow to the United States. With this in sight, Cypher and Wilson (2015, p. 7) observe that "the socioeconomic impact of China's new role was much less in Mexico and Central America and in much of the Caribbean." Nevertheless, the overall rate of extracting materials from Mexico has increased dramatically since 1990, in the context of neoliberal structural reforms oriented to giving private and foreign capital greater access to the country's natural resources (Tetreault, 2022).

The aforementioned studies point to the interconnectivity between the expansion of the extractive frontier in Latin America and the acceleration of what has been conceptualized as the *social metabolism* of the world economy (Muradian et al., 2012), ultimately driven by the system's built-in orientation toward capital accumulation ad infinitum. From this view, the commodities consensus that emerged in Latin America over the desirability of accelerating material extraction rates stems from the need for the capitalist state to facilitate the accumulation of capital, while at the same time legitimizing the underlying social relations of production inter alia through redistributive social policies.

The conflicts that emerge from these contradictory functions encompass not only labour struggles but also those that revolve around the defense of indigenous and peasant territories, and more generally the defense of life.

In a growing body of critical literature, these latter struggles have been conceptualized in terms of Marx's explicative model of *primitive accumulation*, often with reference to Harvey's (2003) broader notion of *accumulation by dispossession* (Sacher, 2015), and sometimes employing an adapted version of Polanyi's double-movement theory (Castree, 2008). From this epistemological approach, the social-environmental impacts of large-scale extractive projects amount to enclosing the commons, leading in some cases to organized defense of the commons. In this frame, the commons refer not only to the land and natural resources that serve as a means of production for the subsistence of local populations, but also to the territory, symbolically significant landscapes, human-built infrastructure, and ecosystems that sustain collective social and cultural reproduction.

While extractivist bargains can be negotiated with labour and also with rural communities where the dominant current of organized struggle on the local level is to obtain more economic benefits and greater compensation for the environmental impacts of extractive activities; no bargain can be struck where local groups struggle to permanently block extractive activities, based on valuations of natural and human-built environments that emphasize the life-sustaining and cultural importance of specific territories. This is because these valuations—and more importantly the collective forms of self-governance and local organization that underpin them—are incommensurable and fundamentally at odds with the valuations of capital (ultimately oriented toward resource exploitation for profit) and with those of the state, which tend to project a "vision of natural goods as commodities, and, at the same time, as strategic natural resources" for national development (Svampa, 2015, p. 56).

In the face of resistance, agents of the state and capital can and often do resort to the use of diverse forms of violence to push forward extractive projects (Paley, 2015). Navarro (2015, p. 48) conceptualizes this violence along a continuum that moves in a crescendo along seven moments: institutional legality, consensus and legitimacy, capture and cooptation, disciplining and normalization, criminalization of protest, repression, and finally militarization and counterinsurgency. On the extractive frontier, Global Witness' annual reports indicate that of the 1992 land and environmental defenders murdered between 2002 and 2019, 1442 were in Latin America and 97 in Mexico (Global Witness, 2021).

The Energy-Sovereignty Bargain on the National Level

Ackerman (2020, p. 320) suggests that "Mexico's latecomer status [to the Pink Tide], along with the complex specifics of its political history and its contemporary role in the global economy, make it a particularly interesting case study and proving ground for progressive politics in the twenty-first century." As regards extractivism, this political history includes the nationalization of Mexico's petroleum sector in 1938 by the then-President Lázaro Cárdenas—in response to pressure from organized workers—considered to be an early landmark in the region for efforts to assert state control over natural resources (Gudynas, 2016, p. 103). During the post-World War II period, Mexico, like other Latin American countries, pursued a state-led development strategy geared toward import-substituting industrialization (ISI). This strategy included a form of resource nationalism that led to the consolidation of Pemex's monopoly in the petroleum sector and to greater state involvement in mining activities, through the expansion of parastatal companies and the imposition of tariffs and royalties on private mining activities. In 1961, the "Mexicanization of mining law" was promulgated, declaring that all mining companies operating in the country had to be at least 51% Mexican owned.

This strategy of resource nationalism began changing course in the 1980s. In the context of the debt crisis, Mexico became one of the first countries in the region to implement neoliberal structural adjustment programs. The mining sector was opened completely to private and foreign investment in 1992, after parastatal companies had been sold off with little transparency to well-connected Mexican businessmen (Delgado Wise & del Pozo Mendoza, 2005). In that year, a new mining law was established, giving mining precedence over all other productive uses of the land; as well as 50-year-long concession periods that can be extended for another 50 years through administrative procedures.

In the energy sector, incremental legal reform from 1992 onward allowed private and foreign companies to invest in downstream petroleum activities and to obtain service contracts to participate in upstream activities (Rousseau, 2017). The energy sector was finally opened completely via constitutional reform in 2013, with corresponding legal changes implemented the following year. In these ways, Mexico became exemplary of "classical extractivism" (Veltmeyer & Petras, 2014). At the same time, redistributive mechanisms in the mold of progressive neo-extractivism were paradoxically introduced in tandem with the energy reform, in both the mining and petroleum sectors, providing resource rents for social development projects in zones of extraction (Tetreault, 2020).

López Obrador criticized the energy reform every step of the way. As a presidential candidate in the lead-up to the 2018 election, he projected a discourse of energy sovereignty that included "rescuing" Pemex and using the energy sector as a "lever of development" (Moreno, 2017, p. 182). Three main corresponding lines of action emerged during the first three and a half years of his term: (1) actions to combat the stealing of hydrocarbons, (2) increased investment in drilling and infrastructure development, and (3) measures to strengthen Pemex financially, including a reduction in the main royalty paid by Pemex (called "shared utility rights"), the negotiation of loans from private banks to restructure its debt, and the injection of public resources to help the company make its debt payments (Tetreault, 2021).

Strengthened in these ways, Pemex has continued to play a central role in upstream activities, and increasingly in refining hydrocarbons. Before López Obrador became president, Mexico was importing from the United States almost three-quarters of the gasoline consumed in the country and 70% of the diesel (Pemex, 2019, p. 42). Originally, the plan was to increase Pemex's refining capacity from 612 thousand barrels per day (TBPD) in 2019 to 1470 TBPD by 2023, in order to meet 70% of the country's projected demand for gasoline and 93% of the demand for diesel (Pemex, 2019, pp. 188–9). To this end, López Obrador's government has been revamping the country's six existing refineries—which in 2019 were operating at under 40% of their combined total capacity—and it has also been building a new refinery at the port of Dos Bocas, in the state of Tabasco, which is expected to begin operating in 2023.

On 24 May 2021, López Obrador announced a deal to have Pemex buy Shell's 50% share of the Deer Park refinery in Texas to become the sole owner, at a cost of US$596 million. This deal was completed in January of 2022. Now, according to the president's discourse, the country is poised to become completely self-sufficient in gasoline and diesel production by 2023. At the same time, Mexico remains highly dependent on the importation of natural gas from the United States. In fact, in 2021

Mexico imported on average 5950 million cubic feet of gas per day, breaking a new record for the highest volume.[1]

The 4 T's energy-sovereignty initiatives have been extended to the electricity and mining sectors. In the mining sector, it is focused exclusively on lithium, whose price on the world market increased by a factor of over ten between January 2021 and March 2022. This speculative surge stems from the growing mainstream consensus that lithium constitutes a strategic mineral in transitioning away from fossil-fuel dependence, because of its use in the manufacturing of batteries for electric vehicles. On 1 October 2021, López Obrador sent a proposal to the Chamber of Deputies to make constitutional changes meant to strengthen the Federal Electricity Commission (*Comisión Federal de Electricidad*, CFE) and to put an end to the privileges afforded to private-sector producers of electricity by the 2013–2014 energy reform. The same proposal included changes to Article 27 of the Constitution to nationalize the country's lithium reserves, except for those that have already been granted through concessions to private firms. However, because MORENA lost its "qualified majority" in the Chamber of Deputies during the mid-term elections of 2021, opposition parties were able to block this proposal on 17 April 2022. The very next day, López Obrador's "plan B" was set in motion by sending to the Senate a proposal to reform Mexico's Mining Law, "to recognize that lithium is the patrimony of the Nation and its exploration, exploitation, benefit and use is reserved to favor the people of Mexico" (SEGOB, 2022: 1). This proposal also includes the creation of a state-owned enterprise for exploiting the country's lithium reserves. On 20 April 2022, it was approved by the Senate, where MORENA continues to hold a controlling majority. Time will tell how it will play out in practice.

To wrap up this section, it is worth pointing to some indicators of the degree to which mining and petroleum activities contribute to the national economy and public revenue. In 2020, the mining-metallurgical sector represented 2.3% of Mexico's Gross Domestic Product (GDP) and it was the fifth largest contributor of foreign currency earnings, at

[1] https://www.eleconomista.com.mx/empresas/Mexico-rompe-record-en-importaciones-de-gas-natural-de-EU-20220303-0019.html

US$18.4 billion (CAMIMEX, 2021, p. 29). According to data compiled by Mexico's Tax Administration Service, the effective income tax rate for mining companies in Mexico is below 7% and in practice they only delivered between 1% and 2% between 2016 and 2019 (Villanueva, 2022). In addition, since 2014 mining companies pay a royalty equal to 7.5% of their declared earnings, plus 0.5% of the income derived from the sale of precious metals, and these resources have been used to finance social development projects in mining regions (Tetreault, 2021).

As for the petroleum sector, it has long provided a significant percentage of the financing for public spending in Mexico. This has not only led to the progressive indebtedness of Pemex, but also allowed for the continuance of collecting relatively low taxes from private enterprises in other sectors of the economy.[2] Between 1994 and 2012, the national public purse received 31% of its income from Pemex, through a complex system of royalties and taxes (Puyana Mutis, 2015, p. 221). After oil prices plummeted in 2014, this contribution fell to below 20%; and in 2020, in the context of another fall in the price of oil due to the slowdown of interaction and mobility caused by the Covid-19 pandemic, Pemex's contribution to the national public purse fell to just 16.3% of the total.[3] In that year, foreign currency earning from Mexico's petroleum sector added up to US$17.4 billion (CAMIMEX, 2021, p. 29). While petroleum income represented 8.3% of Mexico's GDP in 2013, four years later it fell to just 3.8% (Fundar, 2018, p. 79).

Bargains for Private Extractive Firms

When López Obrador became president of Mexico, he put an end to the auctioning of oil fields to private firms. At the same time, he promised to respect the 112 contracts that were awarded to private firms through the three rounds of auctioning that took place between 2015 and 2018. In

[2] In 2020, Mexico ranked 38th out of 38 OECD countries in terms of the tax-to-GDP ratio. https://www.oecd.org/tax/revenue-statistics-mexico.pdf

[3] https://www.gob.mx/shcp/gacetaeconomica/es/articulos/las-finanzas-publicas-de-mexico-mantienen-fortaleza-destaca-el-importante-crecimiento-de-los-ingresos-presupuestarios?idiom=es

addition, he opened new avenues for private-sector participation in upstream activities via Integral Contracts for Exploration and Extractive Services. These contracts have a duration of between 15 and 25 years; Pemex maintains ownership of entitlements and continues as an operator, and private firms are remunerated through a fee in dollars per unit of hydrocarbon produced. According to Pemex's Business Plan 2019–2023, the government expects to attract 108 billion pesos of private investment through these contracts between 2020 and 2023 (equal to about US$5 billion) (Pemex, 2019, p. 192).

Another important opportunity for private investment in Mexico's petroleum sector is in the new refinery that is being built at the port of Dos Bocas, in the southern state of Tabasco. In July of 2019, it was announced that six firms had submitted successful bids and soon thereafter they were contracted to initiate the refinery's construction: Fluor Enterprises, ICA Fluor, Samsung Engineering, Asociados Constructores DBNR, Kellogg Brown and Root, and Constructora Hostotipaquillo.

As for the mining sector, López Obrador announced at the beginning of his term that his administration would not grant any more concessions to mining companies. At the same time, there has been no initiative to rescind the mining concessions granted by past governments, nor of changing their terms. The federal government granted over 45,000 mining concessions between 1994 and 2018, covering an area of approximately 105,000 hectares, equivalent to over half of the country's territory.[4] These include ten concessions granted to private firms during Peña Nieto's presidency to extract lithium from an area of 33,000 hectares (Nuñez Rodríguez, 2022, p. 62). Of these, the Sonora Lithium Project is the largest. With 1.67 million tons of proven reserves and almost twice that as probable reserves, it is considered to be among the largest in the world.[5] It is owned in equal shares by the English company Bancora and

[4] https://www.gob.mx/presidencia/prensa/que-sea-un-dia-de-solidaridad-y-fraternidad-con-los-que-sufren-expresa-presidente-en-visperas-de-navidad

[5] According to Bacanora's website on 14 October 2021: https://www.bacanoralithium.com/projects/sonora-lithium/

the Chinese company Gangfeng, with the latter in the process of acquiring 100% ownership.

Finally, it is important to point out that López Obrador government has given the green light to a number of new mega-mining projects that promise to bring billions of dollars of private investment to Mexico between 2021 and 2024.[6] In all, the "FDI in oil, gas and mineral extraction that Mexico received between January and September 2021 amounted to 3.468 billion dollars, the highest figure for a similar period since records have been kept" (Carbajal, 2021, p. 18).

Stratified Labour Bargains

Job creation is often at the centre of discourses that promote extractive activities. In 2019, before the Covid pandemic, mining and metallurgy employed 379,093 people in Mexico (SGM, 2021, p. 33). Of these, only 115,525 were in extractive activities per se; the rest were in the "fabrication of non-metallic mineral products" (143,655 jobs) and "basic metal industries" (119,840). In all, the mining and metallurgy sector provided jobs for 0.69% of Mexico's economically active population in 2019. Average wages in the sector were calculated to be 17,814 pesos per month in 2020, equal to about US$829, which is 44.8% higher than the national average (SGM, 2021, p. 32). At the same time, it is important to keep in mind that labour segmentation divides workers with "permanent" contracts from those with "temporary" ones, with the latter typically being offered to the local population during the initial stage of construction.

In the petroleum sector, Pemex registered 122,646 permanent employees in 2019 and 120,936 the following year (Pemex, 2021, p. 11). Wages for Pemex's unionized workers range from 6117 pesos per month (US$285) to 30,404 pesos per month (US$1415), depending on the employee's level, shift schedule, and type of work.[7] In addition, Pemex employs an estimated 17,000 "transitory workers" who do not have a permanent contract and associated benefits. On 27 April 2022, López

[6] https://miningmexico.com/10-prospectos-mineros/

[7] https://stprmnacional.org/Documentos/70%20I/Revision2020/SO_SIND_3.37.pdf

Obrador announced that these workers would be given permanent contracts, without consulting the Petroleum Workers' Union (*Sindicato de Trabajadores Petroleros de la República Mexicana*, STPRM). Even though legally the STPRM has the final say on hiring, this announcement provoked little resistance from the union's leaders and members.

Garza Toledo and Otero (2020, p. 1) suggest that, from the perspective of unionized workers, "the 4T has had positive effects, at least on the regulative realm." They point to the labour reform law that was published in the Official Newspaper of the Federation on 1 May 2019, which includes mechanisms to promote greater union democracy, representativity, and transparency. These changes, as the authors observe, respond to the exigencies of the US government in the renegotiation of NAFTA, eventually codified in Annex 23 of the United States-Mexico-Canada Agreement (USMCA), with the intention of providing Mexican workers with greater bargaining power to increase their wages and thereby lessen the comparative advantage that Mexico has in attracting FDI. Nevertheless, when the Petroleum Workers' Union (*Sindicato de Trabajadores Petroleros de la República Mexicana*, STPRM) was finally able to hold elections in January of 2022 after Covid-related postponements, the process was stained with widespread accusations of fraud from dissident groups alleging existing union bosses' control over the electronic voting system (Laureles, 2020). Indeed, even before Carlos Romero Deschamps—the notoriously corrupt leader of the STPRM since 1993—was forced to step down from his role as general secretary in October of 2019, there were expectations for greater representation from dissident currents within the STPRM and even a rival union, PETROMEX. The outcome, however, was for a group of close collaborators of Romero Deschamps to stay in control of the union, with long-time former treasurer Ricardo Aldana Prieto elected to the position of general secretary, in spite of his infamous involvement in the so-called Pemexgate scandal in 2000, among others (Pérez, 2017).

In the mining sector, Napoleón Gómez Urrutia, who since 2001 has been at the head of the National Union of Mining, Metallurgy and Steel Workers (*Sindicato Nacional de Trabajadores Mineros, Metalúrgicos, Siderúrgicos y Similares de la República Mexicana*, SNTMMSSRM), returned to Mexico in August of 2018 as a senator for MORENA through proportional representation, after having spent 12 years in Canada to avoid political persecution from previous governments. Since then, he has amassed political power by becoming president of the Senate's Labour and Social Welfare Committee, and president of the recently created International Confederation of Workers, which brings together more than 150 unions from diverse sectors of the Mexican economy. Under these political conditions, the SNTMMSSRM has won back collective contracts from rival unions at several mines in the states of Coahuila, Michoacán, Querétaro, Sinaloa, and Zacatecas; and it has negotiated significant wage increases at no less than 15 different mines and metallurgy plants across the country.[8]

Finally, it is worth noting the priority given to mining and hydrocarbon extraction in the context of the Covid-19 pandemic. When López Obrador's government announced on 31 March 2020 the immediate suspension of all non-essential activities in an effort to slow the propagation of the virus, petroleum extraction was exempt and continued uninterrupted, as did the construction of the refinery at Dos Bocas. Workers on offshore rigs were particularly vulnerable. By mid-November 2020, 356 Pemex workers had died from Covid-19, by far the highest number of any petroleum company in the world (Stillman, 2020).

Mining was initially classified as a non-essential activity, but in the context of soaring prices for gold and other minerals and under intense pressure from business groups, after six weeks López Obrador's government reclassified it as essential. In 2020, outbreaks of Covid-19 occurred at several mines in the country, including Equinox Gold's Los Filos mine in the state of Guerrero, Newmont and Goldcorp's Peñasquito mine in Zacatecas, and Great Panther's Topia mine in Durango.

Directly Impacted Rural Communities

Extractive activities inevitably reshape landscapes with the removal of materials, the construction of infrastructure, and—to one degree or another—the contamination of land, water, and air, especially in countries

[8] This count is based on a systematic review of news reports published in *La Jornada*.

like Mexico, where environmental laws are weakly enforced. This is explicitly acknowledged in Mexican policies designed to compensate for these negative impacts by channeling mining and petroleum rents to social development projects in zones of extraction, particularly the Fund for Hydrocarbon Producing States and Municipalities and the Fund for the Sustainable Regional Development of Mining States and Municipalities. These programs, which were created in conjunction with the 2013–2014 energy reform, constitute part of the extractivist bargain on the municipal and state levels. They have been analyzed elsewhere in terms of continuity and change during the first two years of López Obrador's government (Tetreault, 2020). Here, the focus is on directly affected rural communities on the sub-municipal level, where more than 500 social-environmental conflicts have emerged across the country since the turn of the millennium.[9] To be sure, not all of these conflicts involve organized resistance bent on stopping extractive activities. In the mining sector, a significant minority (42%) is oriented to negotiating better terms for the local population in exchange for accepting extractive projects or in some cases the focus is on demanding that promises made by the company be kept (Martínez Romero, 2020).

Garibay and his collaborators (2014) provide an anthropological analysis of the extractivist bargain for the rural communities directly affected by one of the largest open-pit gold mines in Mexico: Peñasquito, located in the central north state of Zacatecas and owned by Canadian-based company Goldcorp and US-based Newmont. The Peñasquito mine operates in an arid region in the northern municipality of Mazapil. The directly affected rural communities include Cedros, El Vergel, and Cerro Gordo, where smallholder farmers were—according to their own account—"tricked" into signing land-rental agreements in 2006, with promises of jobs and prosperity, and with little information about the environmental impacts of the mine (Garibay et al., 2014, p. 123). In 2009, at the height of job creation during the construction phase, when Goldcorp claimed to have directly created 8000 jobs, only about 70 local youths were working on the project, mostly as labourers, getting paid

[9] https://www.mexicoambiental.com/investigadores-de-la-unam-revelan-mas-de-500-conflictos-ambientales-en-mexico-y-construye-mapa-que-los-georeferencia-y-categoriza/

5000 pesos a month on average (equal to US$370 at the time). At the same time, the project destroyed the livelihoods of about 2000 people in the Mazapil Valley. Those affected have protested, saying they were misled. Indeed, in the initial agreement, rent payments, relocation costs, gifts, corporate social responsibility projects, and other transfers dispersed unevenly to the directly affected population only amounted to 0.012% of the project's anticipated net profits during the 22-year life expectancy of the mine. In 2009, after taking direct action to block entrances to the mine, organized groups of people from the affected communities managed to raise this figure to 0.108% (Garibay et al., 2014, p. 137). Since then, ongoing disputes between the impacted communities and the mine's operators and owners have led to the former blocking the mine's entrance on numerous occasions and over periods of time, with demands that range from respecting contracts for local material transporters to exigencies to repair overexploited aquifers that have resulted in the drying up of agricultural wells and springs used to provide drinking water (Uribe Sierra et al., 2020).

The most recent blockade led to the establishment of an agreement on 12 June 2020 between Newmont-Goldcorp and the affected population, brokered with the mediation of high-ranking representatives of the federal, state, and municipal governments. In spite of the massive environmental damage caused by the Peñasquito mine (as partially documented by Garibay et al., 2014 and Uribe Sierra et al., 2020), López Obrador publicly stated on 17 March 2021 that "there are companies that are exemplary, for example, the mining company in Mazapil, Zacatecas, which pays its workers well, helps the [local] communities, cares for the environment, and does not destroy territory" (cited in Aburto Zepeda, 2021).

López Obrador has repeatedly promised not to use violence to repress social movements. Nevertheless, the National Guard has been deployed to dislodge peaceful protestors. For example, on 23 November 2020, the National Guard forcefully dislodged indigenous opponents to a thermoelectrical plant in the central state of Morelos; and on 15 February 2022, it violently removed organized groups from the Nahua community of Santa María Zacatepec, in the bordering state of Puebla, who had taken over the installations of a bottled-water factory owned by Bonafont (Hernández Navarro, 2022).

While these expressions of state repression do not compare in brutality to some committed by past governments (e.g., the Nochixtlán massacre on 16 June 2016), it is disconcerting to note that the rate of murdering environmentalists and defenders of territory in Mexico increased during the first two years of López Obrador's presidency, with 18 in 2019 (Velázquez Hernández, 2020) and 30 in 2020 (Global Witness, 2021). In addition, the Mexican Centre for Environmental Law (CEMDA, 2021) recorded 104 attacks in Mexico against defenders of environment and territory in 2019 and 2020, including threats, physical attacks, criminalization of protests, intimidation, and murders. CEMDA (2020, p. 27) observes that the Mexican government, at one level or another (municipal, state, or federal), was allegedly responsible for over 40% of attacks in 2019, the first full year of López Obrador's presidency. In this context, it is no light matter that the President repeatedly denigrates "pseudo-environmentalists" who oppose and criticize his extractive policies and flagship projects.

Since López Obrador assumed the presidency, no significant changes have been made to the environmental laws that were established during the neoliberal era. In fact, the most important changes to environmental policy have to do with cuts to the budget and personnel of the Ministry of the Environment (*Secretaría de Medio Ambiente y Recursos Naturales*, SEMARNAT). Although López Obrador frequently underlines the importance of the environment in discourse, the resources allocated to SEMARNAT in 2019 were lower in nominal terms than any year since 2007 and less than half of this ministry's budget in 2015. SEMARNAT's budget in 2019 was 31 billion pesos (US$1.6 billion); it was further reduced, to just under 30 billion pesos in 2020; and it was allocated 31.4 billion pesos in 2021. In line with these budget constraints, all of SEMARNAT's state-level delegates and approximately 30% of its state-level administrative staff were let go without replacement (Madrid Ramírez, 2020, pp. 7–8). This, according to Madrid Ramírez (2020, p. 1), constitutes "the institutional dismantling of the environmental sector," which does not bode well for the peasant and indigenous communities whose territories are directly impacted by extractive projects.

Final Reflections and Conclusions

During the first three and a half years of López Obrador's presidency, the extractivist bargain in Mexico can be characterized on the national level in terms of *energy sovereignty*. This implies self-sufficiency in gasoline and diesel production, but not in the provision of natural gas. It implies strengthening the roles of state-owned energy companies, and at the same time policies to attract private and foreign investment to petroleum and mining activities. Energy sovereignty also finds expression in efforts to nationalize the country's lithium reserves.

The 4 T's extractivist bargain not only respects the terms of contracts and concessions granted to private petroleum and mining firms before López Obrador became president; it also provides the private sector with new opportunities to participate in the exploitation of Mexico's subterranean resources. At the same time, it gives continuance to the policies that were put in place in 2013 and 2014 to capture and redistribute resource rents, with some relatively minor changes, most importantly a reduction in Pemex's royalty payments and the elimination of focalizing mechanisms in mining regions.

The 4 T's energy-sovereignty bargain provides the federal government with resource rents to finance social policies. Moreover, by increasing Pemex's capacity to refine hydrocarbons and CFE's capacity to generate electricity (including by operating at a maximum its three coal-burning electrical power plants), López Obrador's government has largely been able to keep energy prices under control for domestic consumers at a time when international prices are rising rapidly in the context of the war in Ukraine and resumed economic activity and mobility in the wake of the ongoing Covid-19 pandemic.

The extractivist bargain under construction during López Obrador's presidency is oriented toward creating more relatively high-paying unionized jobs in mining and petroleum activities, even though these continue to represent a very small percentage of the country's economically active population. Although legal changes have been made to favor the democratization unions, this has not led to significant reconfigurations of union leadership in the mining and petroleum sectors. Big union bosses have either been incorporated into the political ranks of the 4 T (Napoleón Gómez Urrutia) or forced to step down (Carlos Romero Deschamps) to make way for a successor of the same political group (Ricardo Aldana Prieto), under conditions of political subordination. Pemex workers have maintained relatively high wages and, although their numbers were reduced by almost 4000 between 2018 and 2020, a much larger number of "transitory" workers will be given permanent jobs, in a way that bolsters political allegiance to the president himself, as opposed to union bosses. In the mining sector, workers affiliated with the union led by Napoleón Gómez Urrutia have gained bargaining power and achieved wage hikes in the context of high international prices. All of this speaks to the revival of some aspects of the corporativist political system that was constructed during the ISI period—and largely disarticulated during the neoliberal era—when state mediation of capital-labour relations worked through a network of party-affiliated and vertically integrated national-level unions.

Finally, it is important to consider that the 4T's energy-sovereignty extractivist bargain rests on the underlying objective of increasing the rates of extracting minerals, metals, and fossil fuels, in spite of the social-environmental risks and consequences that this implies for directly impacted rural communities and for contributing to climate change and other ecological crises on the global level. For the inhabitants of directly impacted rural communities, this means either accepting a certain level of contamination and destruction of territory in exchange for a broad range of relatively short-term compensatory economic benefits or organizing resistance and collectively constructing local-level (post-) development alternatives, as a growing number of (especially indigenous) communities in Mexico are currently doing, including Zapatista communities in Chiapas, Zapotecos and Mixes in the Sierra Juárez of Oaxaca, and Purépechas in Cherán, Michoacán.

In conclusion, the terms of the extractivist bargain currently under construction in Mexico are variegated and contradictory, with a certain orientation toward energy sovereignty on the national level. In this way, the bargain can be considered as a type of *independence bargain*, where—according to the terms outlined in the introduction to this book—resource extraction is promoted as a way to gain economic independence.

The 4 T's extractivist bargain also exhibits characteristics of a *social redistribution bargain*, by seeking to expand extractive activities in exchange for rents used to finance social policies, including public investment in zones of extraction. It seeks to provide low-cost energy for consumers and industries, lucrative investment opportunities for private-sector firms in the mining and petroleum sectors, and relatively high-paying jobs for unionized workers in extractive activities. Its negative impacts on the environment and on directly affected rural communities constitute its most glaring contradiction, not just in redistributive terms but also insofar as these impacts undermine the natural and social conditions of human (re)production on multiple scales.

References

Aburto Zepeda, M. M. (2021, March 19). Carta al Presidente sobre el desastre ambiente de la mina Peñasquito. *La Jornada de Zacatecas*. https://ljz.mx/19/03/2021/carta-al-presidente-sobre-el-desastre-ambiente-de-la-mina-penasquito/

Ackerman, J. M. (2020). The last surfer to hit the beach: Mexico and the "pink tide.". In S. Ellner (Ed.), *Latin America's pink tide, European integration and the post–cold war world* (pp. 319–342). Rowman and Littlefield.

CAMIMEX (Camera Minera de México). (2021). *Informe anual*. Retrieved June 8, 2022, from https://camimex.org.mx/index.php/publicaciones/informe-anual

Carbajal, B. (2021, December 5). Este año, récord en la inversión extranjera para el sector minero. *La Jornada*. https://www.jornada.com.mx/notas/2021/12/05/economia/este-ano-record-en-la-inversion-extranjera-para-el-sector-minero/

Castree, N. (2008). Neoliberalising nature: The logics of deregulation and reregulation. *Environmental Planning A: Economy and Space, 40*(1), 131–152. https://doi.org/10.1068/a3999

CEMDA—Centro Mexicano de Derecho Ambiental. (2020). Informe sobre la situación de las personas defensoras de los derechos humanos ambientales. CEMDA.

CEMDA—Centro Mexicano de Derecho Ambiental. (2021). *Informe sobre la situación en México de los derechos humanos ambientales en el contexto de megaproyectos*. CEMDA.

Cypher, J., & Wilson, T. D. (2015). Introduction China and Latin America: Processes and paradoxes. *Latin American Perspectives, 42*(6), 5–26. https://doi.org/10.1177/0094582X15599958

de la Garza Toledo, E., & Otero, G. (2020). Work and unionism in Mexico: Challenges for MORENA and the fourth transformation government. *Rupture Magazine*. https://rupturemagazine.org/issue-4/

Delgado Wise, R., & del Pozo Mendoza, R. (2005). Mexicanization, privatization, and large mining capital in Mexico. *Latin American Perspectives, 32*(4), 65–86. https://doi.org/10.1177/0094582X05278139

Ellner, S. (2021). Introduction: Rethinking Latin American Extractivism. In S. Ellner (Ed.), *Latin American Extractivism. Dependency, resource nationalism, and resistance in broad perspective* (pp. 1–28). Rowman & Littlefield.

Fundar. (2018). *Las actividades extractivas en México: minería e hidrocarburos hacia el fin del sexenio, anuario 2017*. Retrieved June 8, 2022, from http://fundar.org.mx/mexico/pdf/AnuarioExtractivas2017.pdf

Garibay, C., Boni, A., Panico, F., & Urquijo, P. (2014). Corporación minera, colusión gubernamental y desposesión campesina. El caso de Goldcorp Inc. en Mazapil. *Zacatecas. Desacatos, 44*, 113–142.

Global Witness. (2021). *Last line of defense. The industries causing the climate crisis and attacks against land and environmental defenders*. Retrieved June 8, 2022, from https://www.globalwitness.org/en/campaigns/environmental-activists/last-line-defence/

Gudynas, E. (2016). Natural resource nationalisms and the compensatory state in progressive South America. In P. A. Haslam & P. Heidrich (Eds.), *The political economy of resources and development: From neoliberalism to resource nationalism* (pp. 103–117). Routledge.

Harvey, D. (2003). *The new imperialism*. Oxford University Press.

Hernández Navarro, L. (2022, February 22). Altepelmecalli, la defensa del agua. *La Jornada*. https://www.jornada.com.mx/notas/2022/02/22/politica/altepelmecalli-la-defensa-del-agua/

Infante-Amate, J., Urrego Mesa, A., & Tello Aragay, E. (2020). Las venas abiertas de América Latina en la era del antropoceno: un estudio biofísico del comercio exterior (1900–2016). *Diálogos Revista Electrónica de Historia, 21*(2), 177–214. https://doi.org/10.15517/dre.v21i2.39736

Krausmann, F., Gringrich, S., Eisenmenger, N., Erb, K. H., Haberl, H., & Fischer Kowalski, M. (2009). Growth in global material use, GDP and population during the 20th century. *Ecological Economics, 68*, 2696–2705. https://doi.org/10.1016/j.ecolecon.2009.05.007

Laureles, L. (2020, January 23). La STPS da "golpe a la democracia" en la elección de petroleros, acusan disidentes. *La Jornada*. https://www.jornada.com.mx/notas/2022/01/23/politica/la-stps-da-golpe-a-la-democracia-en-la-eleccion-de-petroleros-acusan-disidentes/

Madrid Ramírez, L. (2020). *El desmantelamiento institucional del sector ambiental: Un balazo en el pie*. CCMSS.

Martínez Romero, U. P. (2020). *Continuo de conflictos megamineros en México: oposición y negociación en los casos de Cerro de San Pedro, Mineral de la Luz, Zautla y San José del Progreso*. Phd Thesis, FLACSO Mexico.

MORENA—Movimiento de Regeneración Nacional. (2017). *Proyecto de Nación 2018–2014*. Retrieved June 8, 2022, from https://transparencia.info.jalisco.gob.mx/sites/default/files/Plan-de-Nacion-de-Morena.pdf

Muradian, R., Walter, M., & Martínez-Alier, J. (2012). Hegemonic transitions and global shifts in social metabolism: Implications for resource-rich countries. Introduction to the special section. *Global Environmental Change, 22*, 559–567. https://doi.org/10.1016/j.gloenvcha.2012.03.004

Navarro, M. L. (2015). *Luchas por lo común. Antagonismo social contra el renovado cercamiento y despojo capitalista de los bienes naturales en México*. Bajo Tierra / BUAP.

Nuñez Rodríguez, V. (2022). *El Litio de México*.

Paley, D. (2015). *Drug war capitalism*. AK Press.

Pemex. (2019). *Plan de negocios de petroleros mexicanos y sus empresas productivas subsidiarias 2019–2023*. Pemex.

Pemex. (2021). *Anuario estadístico 2021*. Pemex.

Pérez, A. L. (2017). *PEMEX RIP. Vida y asesinato de la principal empresa mexicana*. Grijalbo.

Puyana Mutis, A. (2015). *La economía petrolera en un Mercado politizado y global. México y Colombia*. FLACSO Mexico.

Rousseau, I. (2017). *Tribulaciones de dos empresas petroleras estatales 1900–2014 (Trayectorias comparadas de Pemex y PdVSA)*. Colegio de México.

Sacher, W. (2015). Megaminería y desposesión en el Sur: un análisis comparative. *Íconos. Revista de Ciencias Sociales, 51*, 99–116.

SEGOB—Secretaría de Gobernación. (2022). *Decreto por el que se reforman y adicionan diversas disposiciones de la Ley Minera*. Retrieved August 19, 2022, from https://www.dof.gob.mx/nota_detalle.php?codigo=5649533&fecha=20/04/2022#gsc.tab=0

SGM—Servicio Geológico Mexicano. (2021). *Anuario Estadístico de la Minería Mexicana, 2020*. SGM.

Stillman, A. (2020, September 10). How AMLO's Crown Jewel became the world's deadliest covid company. *Bloomberg Businessweek*. https://www.bloomberg.com/news/features/2020-09-10/oil-producer-pemex-has-the-most-covid-19-deaths-of-any-company-in-the-world

Svampa, M. (2015). The 'commodities consensus' and valuation languages in Latin America. *Alternautas, 2*(1), 45–59.

Svampa, M. (2019). *Development in Latin America: Toward a new future*. Fernwood.

Tetreault, D. (2020). The new extractivism in Mexico: Rent redistribution and resistance to mining and petroleum activities. *World Development, 126*, 1–10. https://doi.org/10.1016/j.worlddev.2019.104714

Tetreault, D. (2021). Extractive policies in Mexico at the outset of López Obrador's presidency. In S. Ellner (Ed.), *Latin American Extractivism. Dependency, resource nationalism, and resistance in broad perspective* (pp. 149–165). Rowman & Littlefield.

Tetreault, D. (2022). Two sides of the same coin: Increasing material extraction rates and social environmental conflicts in Mexico. *Environment, Development and Sustainability*. https://doi.org/10.1007/s10668-021-02025-4

Uribe Sierra, S., Gómez Alonso, J., & Tetreault, D. (2020). Dos conflictos mineros en Mazapil, Zacatecas: entre la oposición, negociación y la colaboración. *Región y Sociedad, 32*, e1373. https://doi.org/10.22198/rys2020/32/1373

Velázquez Hernández, L. (2020). La defensa del ambiente en México, ¿cuestión de vida o muerte? *Diálogos Ambientales, 1*(1), 41–46.

Veltmeyer, H., & Petras, J. (Eds.). (2014). *The new extractivism. A post-neoliberal development model or imperialism of the twenty-first century?* Zed Books.

Villanueva, D. (2022, April 22). Empresas y asalariadospagan más de impuestos quemineras. *La Jornada*. https://www.jornada.com.mx/2022/04/22/economia/016n1eco

9

Colombia: Contradictions of the Territorial Peace Extractive Bargain

Jamie L. Shenk

Introduction

In May 2017, President Juan Manuel Santos gave the final remarks at that year's National Mining Conference in Cartagena. As he took to the podium less than a year after signing a peace agreement with the country's largest guerilla group—the Armed Revolutionary Forces of Colombia (*Fuerzas Armadas Revolucionariaas de Colombia*: FARC) —a small white dove stitched onto the left pocket of the president's shirt signaled his message to the country's mining leaders. Areas that were once inaccessible to investment because of the country's armed conflict were now open for business, Santos declared. Further, the industry's "legal mining activity—that attracts investment and generates employment—is and should be the key pillar of [the country's] post-conflict landscape" (Santos, 2017). Peace and mining were Colombia's future.

J. L. Shenk (✉)
Harvard Kennedy School, Cambridge, MA, USA
e-mail: jshenk@hks.harvard.edu

P. Bowles, N. Andrews (eds.), *Extractive Bargains*, Frontiers of Globalization,
https://doi.org/10.1007/978-3-031-32172-6_9

Recent expansion of extractive (mining and oil/gas) projects in Colombia, however, has not always been peaceful. The boom in foreign investment in the extractive sectors between 2000 and 2015 brought with it an attendant rise in protests and local conflicts (Dietz, 2018; García, 2017; Vargas, 2019). While subsequent national governments have promoted new mining and oil projects as potential drivers of economic development in conflict-affected areas (DNP 2014, 2018), local communities have pushed back against these plans as threats to their land and livelihoods. Without access to formal mechanisms for participation, these communities have relied on direct action, with resulting confrontations between protestors and State forces mirroring the contention of the country's decades-long internal armed conflict (Olarte-Olarte, 2019; Velasco, 2015; Vélez-Torres, 2014).

This chapter examines the interplay between extractive development, peace, and protest in Colombia as a way of illustrating the contradictions of the country's "territorial peace" bargain. The Colombian government's efforts to tie peace to extractive development could suggest the country is making efforts to strike an extractive bargain that might be seen as progressive on the normative axis, as discussed by Bowles and Andrews (Chap. 1 in this volume). This is further buttressed by the ideal of "territorial peace" outlined in the government's 2016 Peace Accord with the FARC. In practice, however, Colombia's extractive policy is best categorized as contradictory, veering into cognitive dissonance: while territorial peace privileges the voices of local communities most affected by armed conflict in discussions about economic development, the country's extractive framework silences those same communities.

The rest of the chapter proceeds as follows. The next section provides a short overview of Colombia's history of resource extraction. The bulk of the chapter then turns to present the visions and contradictions of Colombia's territorial peace bargain as a form of progressive extractivism. This analysis draws from a combination of documentary evidence, semi-structured interviews with local activists, academics, and NGO representatives, and fieldwork carried out in Colombia between 2019 and 2021. I conclude with a discussion of how Colombia might reconcile some of the contradictions between its extractive and peace policies.

A Brief History of Resource Extraction in Colombia

Natural resource development has a long history in Colombia. Gold extraction dates back to the pre-Columbian period, when indigenous groups panned for gold along the length of the Magdalena River to create *poporos*,[1] figurines, and other artifacts now on display at Bogotá's famed Gold Museum (Davis, 2020; Taussig, 2004; Tubb, 2020). When the Spanish conquistadors arrived in what is now Colombia in the 1500s, they embarked on numerous quests to find "El Dorado"—the legendary city of gold. None succeeded in discovering the mythical city, but the Spanish did find gold—an abundance of it in the mountains and rivers of the country's "gold belt" that runs along the central mountain range. The colonial gold trade, with its epicenter in the department of Antioquia, dominated Colombia's export economy as Gran Colombia became Spain's primary gold-producing colony (Bushnell, 2003, p. 17). For most of Colombia's history, gold and other mineral extraction has been conducted by small-scale, often-informal operations until the development of another resource—coal—introduced large-scale, multinational operations to areas in the country's North in the 1980s (Bolívar, Cesar, and La Guajira) (Botero Miranda, 2007; Rochlin, 2015; Ulloa, 2016; Ruiz Ruiz et al., 2018).[2]

Whereas gold and other mineral mining has been a consistent feature of Colombia's economy since pre-colonial times, the country's history of oil extraction is one of relative fits and starts. Oil fields were first discovered in the early 1900s, but extraction remained limited. This changed in the 1950s when the Rojas Pinilla regime led the Colombian state to assume a larger role in extraction through a process of nationalization. The government created the state-owned oil company, Ecopetrol, which

[1] Small bottles made to hold lime and crushed seashells that were used by indigenous peoples to activate the stimulating effect of chewing toasted coca leaves (See Taussig, 2004, pp. xi–xvi).

[2] See Daniel Tubb's (2020) *Shifting Livelihoods: Gold Mining in the Chocó, Colombia* and Michael Taussig's (2004) *my cocaine museum* for excellent ethnographies of informal gold-mining operations in the Colombian Pacific.

proceeded to take over the country's largest oil fields over the next decade. By 1969, the country had nationalized all oil reserves and passed a law introducing a new type of oil contract that would require foreign companies to partner with Ecopetrol for production under future contracts (Vasquez, 2014). Over the following two decades, investments in the oil fields of the country's eastern departments of Arauca and Casanare made Colombia a viable oil producer.

The scale of resource extraction in Colombia reached new levels in early 2000s, when a decline in domestic oil production combined with increasing prices for minerals during the commodity boom spurred the Colombian government to introduce regulatory reforms. Whereas the oil industry and mining operations had previously featured a relative balance of domestic companies, state-owned firms, and multinationals, the government's new policy oriented the extractive sector toward attracting foreign direct investment (FDI) (Garay-Salamanca et al., 2013; Vargas, 2019; Vasquez, 2014, ch. 4). The reforms, which included a full re-write of the country's mining codes, embraced neoliberal principles of privatization, free trade, and labor flexibility.

The reforms were reinforced by the Colombian government's simultaneous pursuit of free trade agreements with a variety of foreign governments, including the United States (signed in 2012), the European Union (signed in 2013), and importantly, Canada (signed in 2011). This final agreement facilitated the flow of investment into Colombia's extractive sectors from Canadian junior miners, in particular (Vélez-Torres & Ruiz-Torres, 2016). By 2013, the national government had approved mining and oil titles covering 5.6 million hectares of land with another 35 million hectares—one-third of Colombia's national territory—designated as "under mining interest" (Garcés Villamil & Rapalino Bautista, 2016; Negrete Montes, 2013).[3]

[3] Colombia was not the only country in Latin America to experience rapid growth in its extractive industries. The 2000s and 2010s saw the expansion of Latin America's "extractive frontier" across Peru, Ecuador, Bolivia, Chile, and Colombia, as new investments spurred the development of projects in areas outside of traditional mining hubs. Where these new projects sprang up, local conflict often developed (see Bebbington & Bury, 2013).

Territorial Peace and Colombia's Extractive Model

Colombia's national government tried to sell its citizens on its push into the globalized market as a way to finance the country's economic development, especially in rural areas hit hardest by decades of internal armed conflict. According to this extractive model, mining and oil projects would catalyze the construction of infrastructure in areas that had previously suffered from weak articulations to regional and national markets. Meanwhile, revenue from large-scale projects would trickle down to local communities through royalty payments distributed back to host communities. The promised influx of cash would help improve local government budgets for public expenditures in ways which resonate, although in a more limited way, with the social redistribution extractive bargains found across the continent (McNeish, 2017b; Ruiz Ruiz et al., 2018). In 2007, South Africa-based multinational AngloGold Ashanti publicly announced that it would begin developing what it claimed was one of the world's largest gold deposits in the mountains of Tolima (Colombia Solidarity Campaign, 2013). Meanwhile, national government officials repeated ad nauseam: extractives would serve as Colombia's "locomotor for development" (Santos, 2017).

The extractive bargain offered by the Colombian government, at least rhetorically, promised Colombians long-term economic growth and benefits to the nation as a whole in exchange for the loss of land of a select number of local communities. In this way, the Colombian government's narrative approximated the neo-extractivist model touted by other governments in Latin American during the commodities boom of the mid-2000s. That said, it is important to note that the Colombian government's bargain did not include institutional changes to facilitate redistribution, as was the case in other Andean countries, leaving the specific benefits of "progress" and "development" in neoliberal terms (Pérez-Rincón et al., 2018).

The tenor of Colombia's extractive bargain underwent a change after 2012, when the government publicly announced that it was pursuing peace negotiations with the country's largest guerrilla group, the FARC, to end the country's decades-long internal armed conflict. The FARC's demobilization promised to open areas of the country previously inaccessible due to the guerrilla groups' presence to new extractive projects and development (see Fig. 9.1). Meanwhile, the government needed a source of funding to pay for the hundreds of political reforms, social programs, and peacebuilding campaigns included in the final, 300-page agreement signed in November 2016. Seeing an opportunity to address both situations at once, Santos's administration repackaged extractive development as Colombia's "locomotor for peace" (Gutiérrez-Rodríguez, 2015). This shift in language reframed Colombia's extractive bargain as a "peace bargain"; extractive development would directly contribute to Colombia's post-conflict recovery.

The Contradictions of Colombia's Peace Bargain

Colombia's "peace bargain" presented mineral and hydrocarbon extraction as a building block for peacebuilding in the country, yet contradictions between the country's mining and oil practices and its vision for peace are evident on multiple levels. On the most fundamental level, Colombia's extractive policies and the text of the Peace Accord privileged different sets of actors whose priorities were often in direct opposition to one another.

An integral component of the 2016 accord's vision of a post-conflict Colombia centered around the concept of "territorial peace." The concept was first presented by High Commissioner for Peace Sergio Jaramillo, who referenced the term during a conference in 2014, and was later echoed by members of the FARC's negotiating team (Cairo et al., 2018). Territorial peace, as described by Le Billon et al. (2020, p. 304), "recognizes uneven distribution and experiences of violence across Colombia and seeks to achieve a positive and redistributive peace through the recognition, participation, and capacitation of marginalized groups, their relationship to diverse territories, and the enabling of new forms of bottom-up territorial development." In practice, the government, the FARC, and local communities have interpreted the concept to entail the empowerment of local communities to participate in policymaking about the economic development of their territories. Local communities would be called on to make the final decisions about the future of their land

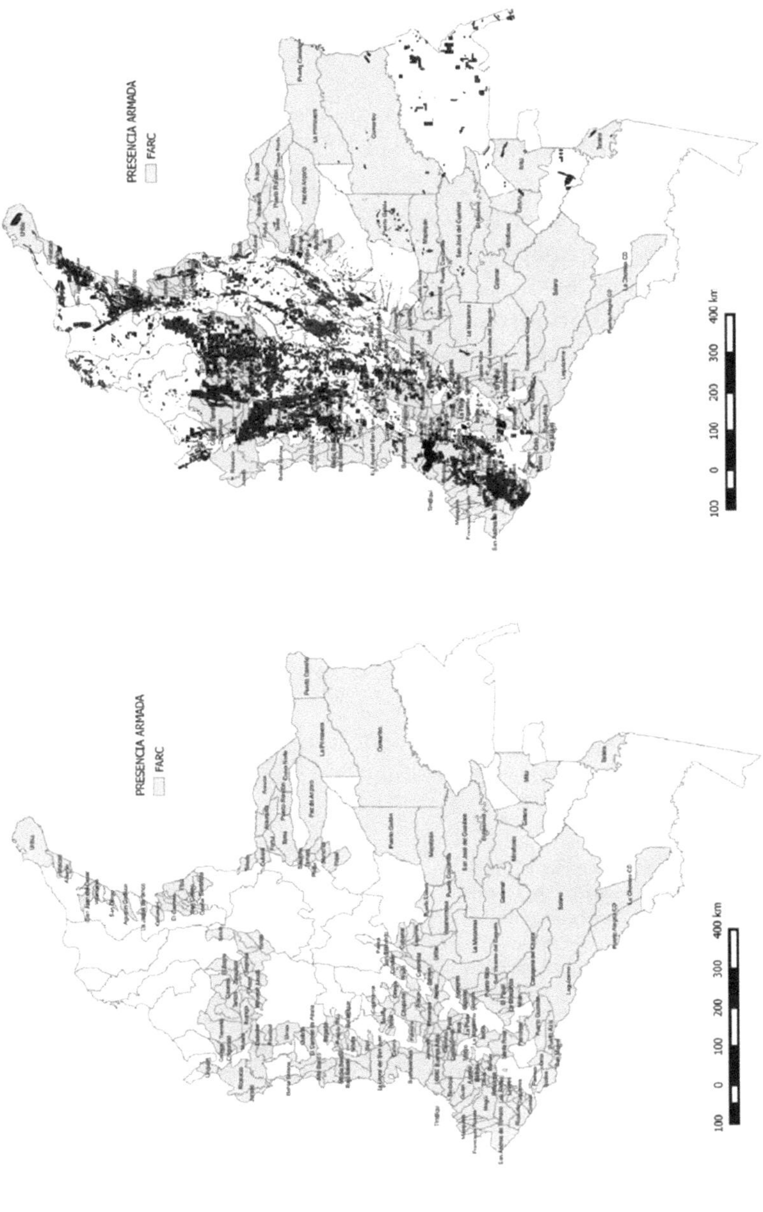

Fig. 9.1 Map of mining titles overlaid onto map of FARC presence. (Source: Author's elaboration with data from Fundación Pares and Tierra Minada. Areas shaded gray on both maps are municipalities formerly controlled by the FARC. Areas shaded in black in the map on the right are mining titles under review and/or granted by the National Mining Agency)

starting with 16 municipalities designated as the "hardest-hit" by the armed conflict but with the intention of covering all of the country's territory regardless of conflict experience (Cairo et al., 2018; Le Billon et al., 2020).[4]

The concept of "territorial peace" is built on the participatory and environmentalist character of Colombia's 1991 Constitution. In theory, the Peace Accord would expand guaranteed participation and consultation beyond the ethnic minority communities protected by ILO 169 and the limited number of *campesino* reserve zones (*zonas de reserva campesina*: ZRCs) created in 1994.[5] *Campesino* communities affected by armed conflict would also be prioritized in decision-making and would have a say in how their territory would be developed in the future. FARC negotiators expressed hope in interviews with a team of Colombian academics in 2017 that the concept would develop even further to resemble the indigenous worldview adopted by progressive governments in Latin America. The Ecuadorian philosophy of Good Living, *sumac kawsay,* or *buen vivir,* which promotes values of living in harmony with "Mother Earth," served as a reference point for this vision (Cairo et al., 2018, pp. 467–68). The 2016 Peace Accord would therefore usher in an era of environmental peace—where natural resources management serves as a space of cooperation and collaboration rather than conflict—as a component of positive peace (Galtung, 1996).[6]

On the surface, extractive development and territorial peace are not inherently in opposition. The Peace Accord's promise of territorial peace

---

[4] These municipalities were designated "PDET municipalities," as local communities were charged with writing Territorial Approach Development Plans (*planes de desarrollo con enfoque territorial*: PDET). The idea was that these plans would be used as a management tool for local, regional, and national government agencies to disperse funds and make decisions on productive projects in accordance with local communities' visions for development and rights as victims of the armed conflict. See https://participedia.net/case/5662

[5] In response to coordinated mobilization by some *campesino* communities demanding rights to FPIC during the 1991 constitutional convention, lawmakers passed a measure to create six *campesino* reserve zones (*zonas de reserva campesina*; ZRCs). Communities within these zones were afforded notable autonomy in deciding on issues related to economic development, including how to allocate land for agriculture and natural resource development (see Quijano-Mejía & Linares-García, 2017; Reyes Bohorquez, 2013).

[6] See Dresse et al. (2019) and Ide et al. (2021) for broader overviews of theories of environmental peacebuilding.

presented Colombia's post-conflict development plan as a kind of progressive extractivism; mining and oil revenues would play an integral role in financing the country's future of peace, *but only with the consent of local communities*. In practice, however, this final clause related to local communities' consent has proved to be a sticking point for Colombia's peace bargain. Rather than promoting peace and conflict resolution, the Colombian government's policies toward consultation and local resistance to extractive development have silenced communities in the service of private companies. Implementation of the 2016 Peace Accord was not accompanied by an overhaul of either the Colombian legal code or the government's attitudes toward protest, highlighting contradictions between the government's progressive rhetoric and its exclusionary practice.

Despite the progressive picture painted by mining executives and government officials in Bogotá, not all local communities welcomed extractive expansion into their territories.

Skepticism about the promise that projects would lead to economic and social wellbeing was central to local contention.[7] Many community leaders looked to the history of mining in Colombia and the Global South more broadly and saw examples of unfulfilled promises.[8] As Bowles and Andrews make clear in the introduction to this volume, the promised benefits of mining and hydrocarbon extraction have often failed to live up to communities' expectation once extraction begins. Mining and oil projects have often been associated with increased social and economic inequality, territorial dispossession, and "social problems" of alcohol consumption and prostitution (Ruiz Ruiz et al., 2018; Torres, 2014). Promised jobs most often go to well-educated workers from urban areas rather than residents of a mine's host community while those living near the mine site must bear the brunt of its environmental impacts (Ponce & McClintock, 2014).

Colombians also questioned the extent of the windfall that they would receive from royalties. Between 2007 and 2011, royalty rates the

[7] It is important to note that there exists a considerable degree of heterogeneity in opinions within communities—even those that are on the whole either supportive or opposed toward extraction (see, e.g., Conde & Le Billon, 2017, p. 685).

[8] Phone interview #3565 with environmental activist, August 2019.

companies were required to pay the Colombian government were the second lowest in Latin America. For every US dollar of revenue produced by mining operations, the state only received 16 cents—a fraction of that received by its neighbor, Ecuador (89 cents per dollar) (Ulloa, 2016). It did not help that communities oftentimes did not even find out about concessions given until they spotted company surveyors and equipment arriving on their land (Garcés Villamil & Rapalino Bautista, 2016). Overall, many in Colombia were skeptical that the Colombian government officials and private firms promoting extractive development would uphold their side of the peace bargain.

Anti-extractive protests steadily increased across the country from 2000 through the 2010s. Between 2000 and 2015, the Bogotá-based NGO *Centro de Investigación y Educación Popular* (CINEP) registered 263 protest events where participants made claims related to mining projects or mining-related policies. These raw numbers of protests may seem low compared to the explosion of protests documented in other Latin American countries from the 1990s onward (Almeida & Cordero, 2015; Alvarez et al., 1998; Escobar & Alvarez, 1992), but Colombia's ongoing armed conflict has historically put a damper on mass civil society movements (Archila, 2003; Velasco, 2015). Opponents of social movements in the government and private industry have often tried to stigmatize protesters by accusing them of collaborating with guerrilla groups. Such moves have made protest a high-risk activity for much of Colombia's history (Bautista, 2012; Lalinde Ordóñez, 2019; Van Isschot, 2015).

In rural municipalities where companies sought to break ground on new projects or expand existing sites, local activists and communities organized marches, roadblocks, and protests with the goal of restricting company access to proposed mining sites. Indigenous and Afro-Colombian groups filed *tutelas* claiming rights to land and protested that they had not been properly consulted (Jaskoski, 2020; Vélez-Torres, 2014). Informal gold miners were encouraged to register for titles post-hoc with the country's mining agency, but a backlog of cases and slow bureaucracy led many to join informal mobilizations against the growth of multinational investment (Rochlin, 2015). Government officials, in turn, responded to protests with repressive tactics familiar in areas plagued by decades of armed conflict—militarized policing and the criminalization of protest (Vélez & Lobo, 2019; Vélez-Torres & Ruiz-Torres, 2016). Where local communities, prioritizing territorial peace, resisted plans for new extractive projects the mismatches of these two visions of territorial post-accord Colombia were made clear. While the 2016 peace deal envisioned demilitarization of the countryside, the presence of Colombia's militarized, anti-riot police (*escuadrón móvil antidisturbios*: ESMAD) in rural areas increased significantly from 2012 onward in response to socio-environmental conflicts (Olarte-Olarte, 2019, pp. 31–34). Ironically, the enforcement of Colombia's "peace bargain" has contributed to, rather than disrupted, the country's cycle of violence in the countryside.

Putting the Peace Bargain in Perspective

How does the "peace bargain" in Colombia compare to other countries in Latin America and the other extractive bargains discussed in this volume? On the one hand, local resistance to extractive development in Colombia resembles other instances of protest and negotiations in other areas of Latin America's extractive frontier. Here, grievances against extractive development are not about "mining better"—improving the environmental and labor practices of existing projects—and instead question whether extraction should occur *at all* (Bebbington et al., 2013). Across Colombia, but also in the other Andean nations of Peru, Ecuador, and Bolivia, some of the strongest motivations for community resistance reflect residents' fear of dispossession. As Bebbington et al. (2013, p. 242) have previously noted, the prospect of new mining and/or hydrocarbon projects to a territory invokes the "generalized feeling of loss and dispossession of a way of living." From the perspective of these communities, disruption of their traditional industries and way of life is too high a price to pay for comparatively abstract promises of economic development for the country as a whole.

While themes of dispossession and local resistance are common across bargains along the global extractive frontier, what makes Colombia different from the cases mentioned so far is the role of the country's internal armed conflict in both creating and exacerbating tensions between communities and the state. Extractive development and violence related to Colombia's armed conflict have been deeply intertwined throughout the course of the country's decades-long internal armed conflict (see, e.g., Bernal-Bermúdez, 2017; Gutiérrez Rodríguez, 2018; Rettberg & Ortiz-Riomalo, 2018; Rettberg & Prieto, 2018). In some areas, active conflict facilitated the consolidation of land for the development of mega-projects. More often, guerrilla group presence precluded large-scale, corporate extractive development, as the state could not guarantee company security. The expansion of Colombia's extractive frontier in the past decades has therefore been predicated on the efficacy of the state's security apparatus in eliminating the threat of guerrilla group resistance.

These longstanding connections between the state, territorial development, and security lend a different tenor to contemporary conflicts to socio-environmental conflicts over extractive development in Colombia compared to other countries where protests have encountered violent state repression. Violence, in the words of scholars Irene Vélez-Torres and Guillermo Ruiz-Torres, "has become, in a sense, less of an expression of an incomplete or failed state, and more … part of the territorial administration of natural goods" (Vélez-Torres & Ruiz-Torres, 2016). In other words, state violence and repression as a response to citizen resistance to extractive development may be better understood as a continuation of state practice normalized by the country's armed conflict rather than an aberration. This practice manifests itself through the labeling of community members who resist extractive development as "subversives" and suggestions by government officials that guerrilla groups have infiltrated anti-extractive movements (McNeish, 2017a). By invoking the specter of guerrilla group presence, state agents are thus able to justify their securitized response to protest.

Control through violence has extended to the post-Peace Accord period and the government's shift toward the peace bargain of extractive development. Colombia continues to rank at the bottom (144 out of 163 in 2022) on the Institute for Economics and Peace's Global Index with no considerable improvements in standing since 2016.[9] This ranking is driven, in part, by consistently high scores in the likelihood of

[9] See https://www.visionofhumanity.org/maps/#/ for Colombia's ranking over time.

violent demonstrations and perceived criminality in society. One way to interpret this is that the rhetoric of territorial peace still has not translated to perceptions and practices of contention on the ground. The continued threat of violence is particularly acute for environmental activists who oppose extractive development.

Since 2016, Colombia has consistently ranked as one of the deadliest countries for social leaders and activists seeking to defend their land from mega-project development (Griffin, 2020). State agents have not been directly implicated in the murders of environmental defenders, but Iván Duque's presidential administration (2018–2022) has been widely criticized for at least not doing enough to protect those who mobilize against extractive development (El Espectador, 2021). In sum, the continued link between extractive development and violence further throws into question what kind of "peace" Colombia's peace bargain for extractives might mean.

Conclusion

Where does Colombia go from here? Colombia's plan for territorial peace sets out a framework for economic development that could approximate the normatively progressive bargain outlined in Chap. 1 of this volume. Extractive development could represent an important component of economic development to finance social justice and peacebuilding initiatives in the short term, but only with the consent of local affected communities. To begin moving toward territorial peace in practice, future governments must take two steps. First, they must begin to view extractive development as a *part* of territorial peacebuilding, rather than a financing mechanism. This would involve the development and implementation of more inclusive institutions to consult with local communities beyond FPIC and the re-writing of territorial development plans once every decade. Without access to formal mechanisms, *campesino* communities have made it clear that local conflicts over extractive development will continue. Furthermore, the provision of formal channels for participation, if accompanied by demilitarization of the state's response to local resistance, may begin to untangle the historical connection between land, development, and violence that has characterized interactions between the state and society in rural Colombia for so long.

Second, the Colombian legal apparatus must clarify the state's right to the subsoil.

Underlying the contradictions of the Colombian government's post-accord development plan—which purported to embrace "territorial peace" while promoting large-scale extraction—is a fundamental issue that the Peace Accord failed to fully address: who owns the land in Colombia? As in most countries around the world (the United States being one notable exception), Colombia's legal framework allows private individuals to own land above ground while maintaining the state's ownership of the subsoil. This allows the state to license land from private owners in order to develop mineral or other resource deposits found underneath the ground to create wealth "for the benefit of the nation" (Bebbington et al., 2013, p. 246; Hoetmer, 2017; Negrete Montes, 2013). The issue is that Colombia's constitution does not specify which state bodies take precedence in these decisions—whether the "state" should mean the national, regional, or local governments or a different actor altogether. This legal lacuna leaves two fundamental questions unanswered: who is the state? And who owns the subsoil?

Colombia's national government has maintained that the national executive is the proper representative of the state in decisions related to natural resource development. Its central argument is that the country cannot allow the preferences of a handful of individuals in isolated communities to make decisions that will impact the economic growth of the entire nation (McNeish, 2017b). This argument, of course, directly undermines the spirit of participatory democracy and territorial peace, which insists that local communities—no matter how remote—should be centered in decisions regarding their land.

Land and inequality have fueled violence in Colombia for decades (Palacios, 2006). It is therefore no surprise that confusion over what lies beneath the land's surface would contribute to the country's conflict. The justice system's approach to addressing conflict over the subsoil, however, should adopt the same territorial peacebuilding framework as applied to the land on top in order to maintain legal coherence.

There is reason to believe that the Colombian government may take at least some of these steps toward reconciling territorial peace and its extractive policies. In June 2022, Colombia elected Gustavo Petro as President. As Colombia's first leftist leader, Petro has explicitly stated his interest in shifting the country's extractive model toward a progressive, or even post—extractive bargain. Specifically, Petro's presidential campaign included promises both to ban fracking and the approval of large-scale, open-pit mining and to formally recognize and strengthen communities' access to processes of free, prior, and informed consultation (Anon, 2022). As of writing, it is far too early to tell how Petro's promises will translate to practice. The chapters of this volume, however, emphasize that extractive bargains are ever shifting.

Colombia's bargains, it is safe to assume, are no different.

References

Almeida, P., & Cordero, A. (Eds.). (2015). *Handbook of Social Movements across Latin America*. Springer.

Alvarez, S. E., Dagnino, E., & Escobar, A. (1998). *Cultures of Politics, Politics of Cultures: Re-Visioning Latin American Social Movements*. Westview Press.

Anon. 2022. *Programa de Gobierno: Colombia Potencia Mundial de La Vida 2022–2026*.

Archila, M. (2003). Idas y venidas, vueltas y revueltas: protestas sociales en Colombia, 1958–1990. In *Instituto Colombiano de Antropología e Historia : Centro de Investigación y Educación Popular*.

Bautista, S. C. B. (2012). Alternativas analíticas en el campo de la movilización social en Colombia: la acción colectiva de alto riesgo. Lecturas a propósito de la protesta campesina en el Tolima. *Estudios Políticos, 41*, 57–79.

Bebbington, A., Bebbington, D. H., Hinojosa, L., Burneo, M.-L., & Bury, J. (2013). Anatomies of conflict: Social mobilization and new political ecologies of the Andes. In A. Bebbington & J. Bury (Eds.), *Subterranean struggles: New dynamics of mining, oil, and gas in Latin America* (pp. 241–266). University of Texas Press.

Bebbington, A., & Bury, J. (Eds.). (2013). *Subterranean Struggles: New Dynamics of Mining, Oil, and Gas in Latin America*. University of Texas Press.

Bernal-Bermúdez, L. (2017). *The Power of Business and the Power of People: Understanding Remedy and Business Accountability For Human Rights Violations—Colombia 1979–2014*. University of Oxford.

Botero Miranda, A. (2007). *La ruta del oro: una economía primaria exportadora: Antioquia, 1850–1890* (1st ed.). Fondo Editorial Universidad EAFIT.

Bushnell, D. (2003). *The making of modern Colombia: A nation in spite of itself* (4. print). Univ. of California Press.

Cairo, H., Oslender, U., Suárez, C. E. P., Ríos, J., Koopman, S., Arango, V. M., Muñoz, F. B. R., & Quintero, L. Z. (2018). 'Territorial Peace': The Emergence of a Concept in Colombia's Peace Negotiations. *Geopolitics*.

Colombia Solidarity Campaign. (2013). *La Colosa: A Death Foretold: Alternative Report about AngloGold Ashanti Gold Mining Project in Cajamarca, Tolima, Colombia*. Colombia Solidarity Campaign.

Conde, M., & Le Billon, P. (2017). Why Do Some Communities Resist Mining Projects While Others Do Not? *The Extractive Industries and Society, 4*(3), 681–697. https://doi.org/10.1016/j.exis.2017.04.009

Davis, W. (2020). *Magdalena River of Dreams*. The Bodley Head.

Dietz, K. 2018. Consultas Populares Mineras En Colombia: Condiciones de Su Realización y Significados Políticos. El Caso de La Colosa. *Colombia Internacional*, (93), 93–117.

Dirección Nacional de Planeación. 2014. *Plan Nacional de Desarrollo 2014–2018, Todos por un Nuevo País*.

Dirección Nacional de Planeación. 2018. *Plan Nacional de Desarrollo 2018–2022: Pacto Por Colombia Pacto Por La Equidad*.

Dresse, A., Fischhendler, I., Nielsen, J. Ø., & Zikos, D. (2019). Environmental Peacebuilding: Towards a Theoretical Framework. *Cooperation and Conflict, 54*(1), 99–119. https://doi.org/10.1177/0010836718808331

El Espectador. 2021. *Gobierno Colombiano, Sin Voluntad Para Proteger a Líderes Ambientales*. Retrieved July 25, 2022 https://www.elespectador.com/colombia-20/conflicto/gobierno-colombiano-sin-voluntad-para-proteger-a-lideres-ambientales/

Escobar, A., & Alvarez, S. E. (Eds.). (1992). *The Making Of Social Movements In Latin America: Identity, Strategy, And Democracy*. Westview Press.

Galtung, J. (1996). *Peace by Peaceful Means: Peace and Conflict, Development and Civilization*. SAGE Publications.

Garay-Salamanca, L. J., Leal, M. C., Zamora, J. E. E., Morales, J. F., Negrete, R. E., Montes, L. Á., Becerra, P., Lleras, G. R., & Valencia, F. V. (2013). *Minería En Colombia: Fundamentos Para Superar El Modelo Extractivista*. Contraloría General de la República.

Garcés Villamil, M. Á., & Rapalino Bautista, W. G. (2016). La Consulta Popular como mecanismo de participación ciudadana para evitar actividades mineras. *Justicia juris, 11*(1), 52. https://doi.org/10.15665/rj.v11i1.617

García, M. C. 2017. *Protestas Relacionadas Con La Minería En Colombia 2000–2015*. Bogotá: CINEP/PPP. Country Report.

Griffin, O. (2020). *Colombia was deadliest country for land rights activists in 2019. Reuters*. Retrieved February 9, 2021 https://www.reuters.com/article/us-colombia-violence-environment-idUSKCN24U16G

Gutiérrez Rodríguez, J. D. (2018). The Connection between Oil Wealth and Internal Armed Conflicts: Exploring the Mechanisms of the Relationship Using a Subnational Lens. *The Extractive Industries and Society*. https://doi.org/10.1016/j.exis.2018.10.008

Gutiérrez-Rodríguez, J. D. (2015). Investing for Peace? On the Use of Resource Revenues to Finance an Eventual Post-Conflict Process in Colombia. *Revista Análisis Internacional, 6*(1), 221–250.

Hoetmer, R. (2017). 'There Is No Longer a Democracy...' Thoughts on the Local Referendums on Mining in Peru's Northern Frontier. In S. E. Alvarez, J. W. Rubin, M. Thayer, G. Baiocchi, A. Laó-Montes, & A. Escobar (Eds.), *Beyond civil society: activism, participation, and protest in Latin America* (pp. 179–198). Duke University Press.

Ide, T., Bruch, C., Carius, A., Conca, K., Dabelko, G. D., Matthew, R., & Weinthal, E. (2021). The Past and Future(s) of Environmental Peacebuilding. *International Affairs, 97*(1), 1–16. https://doi.org/10.1093/ia/iiaa177

Jaskoski, M. (2020). Participatory Institutions as a Focal Point for Mobilizing: Prior Consultation and Indigenous Conflict in Colombia's Extractive Industries. *Comparative Politics*. https://doi.org/10.5129/001041520X15757670821639

Lalinde Ordóñez, S. (2019). *Elogio a La Bulla: Protesta y Democracia En Colombia*. Dejusticia.

Le Billon, P., Roa-García, M. C., & López-Granada, A. R. (2020). Territorial Peace and Gold Mining in Colombia: Local Peacebuilding, Bottom-up Development and the Defence of Territories. *Conflict, Security & Development, 20*(3), 303–333. https://doi.org/10.1080/14678802.2020.1741937

McNeish, J.-A. (2017a). A Vote to Derail Extraction: Popular Consultation and Resource Sovereignty in Tolima, Colombia. *Third World Quarterly, 38*(5), 1128–1145. https://doi.org/10.1080/01436597.2017.1283980

McNeish, J.-A. (2017b). Extracting Justice? Colombia's Commitment to Mining and Energy as a Foundation for Peace. *The International Journal of Human Rights, 21*(4), 500–516. https://doi.org/10.1080/13642987.2016.1179031

Negrete Montes, R. E. 2013. Derechos, Minería y Conflictos. Aspectos Normativos. In *Minería en Colombia: fundamentos para superar el model extractivista* (pp. 23–57). Contraloría General de la República.

Olarte-Olarte, M. C. (2019). From Territorial Peace to Territorial Pacification: Anti—Riot Police Powers and Socio-Environmental Dissent in the Implementation of Colombia's Peace Agreement. *Revista de Estudios Sociales, 67*, 26–39. https://doi.org/10.7440/res67.2019.03

Palacios, M. (2006). *Between Legitimacy and Violence: A History of Colombia, 1875–2002*. Duke University Press.

Pérez-Rincón, M., Vargas-Morales, J., & Crespo-Marín, Z. (2018). Trends in Social Metabolism and Environmental Conflicts in Four Andean Countries from 1970 to 2013. *Sustainability Science, 13*(3), 635–648. https://doi.org/10.1007/s11625-017-0510-9

Ponce, A. F., & McClintock, C. (2014). The Explosive Combination of Inefficient Local Bureaucracies and Mining Production: Evidence from Localized Societal Protests in Peru. *Latin American Politics and Society, 56*(03), 118–140. https://doi.org/10.1111/j.1548—2456.2014.00243.x

Quijano-Mejía, C., & Linares-García, J. (2017). Peasant Reserve Zone: territorialities on dispute. *Revista de Trabajo Social e Intervención Social, 24*, 225–251.

Rettberg, A., & Prieto, J. D. (2018). *Conflicto crudo: Petróleo, conflicto armado y criminalidad en Colombia*.

Rettberg, A., & Ortiz-Riomalo, J. F. (2018). Minería de Oro, Conflicto y Criminalidad En Los Albores Del Siglo XXI En Colombia: Perspectivas Para El Posconflicto Colombiano. *Colombia Internacional, 93*, 17–63. https://doi.org/10.7440/colombiaint93.2018.02

Reyes Bohorquez, A. (2013). Las zonas de reserva campesina como figuras para el desarrollo rural colombiano Peasant reserve areas as figures for colombian rural development. *Perspectivas Rurales, 11*(22), 12.

Rochlin, J. (2015). Boom, Bust and Human Security in the Extractive Sector: The Case of Colombia. *The Extractive Industries and Society, 2*(4), 734–745. https://doi.org/10.1016/j.exis.2015.06.006

Ruiz Ruiz, N. Y., de Herrera, M. C., & Niño, K. F. (2018). *Geopolítica del despjo: Minería y violencia en Colombia*. Universidad Nacional de Colombia.

Santos, J. M. (2017, May 12). *Palabras Del Presidente Juan Manuel Santos En La Clausura Del Congreso Nacional de Minería 2017*. Presented at the Congreso Nacional de Minería.

Taussig, M. T. (2004). *My Cocaine Museum*. University of Chicago Press.

Torres, E. M. (2014). Conflictos y marcos de acción colectiva sobre y por territorios asociados con proyectos mineros a gran escala: Ecuador y Colombia. *Revista Colombiana de Sociología, 37*(2), 19–42.

Tubb, D. (2020). *Shifting Livelihoods: Gold Mining and Subsistence in the Chocó Colombia*. University of Washington Press.

Ulloa, A. (Ed.). (2016). *Extractivismos y posconflicto en Colombia: retos para la paz territorial* (Primera edición). CINEP/Programa por la Paz : Universidad Nacional de Colombia.

Van Isschot, L. (2015). *The Social Origins of Human Rights: Protesting Political Violence in Colombia's Oil Capital, 1919–2010*. The University of Wisconsin Press.

Vargas, G. A. (2019). Social Mobilisation in Colombia's Extractive Industries, 2000–2015. *The Extractive Industries and Society*. https://doi.org/10.1016/j.exis.2019.06.002

Vasquez, P. I. (2014). *Oil Sparks in the Amazon: Local Conflicts, Indigenous Populations, and Natural Resources*. University of Georgia Press.

Velasco, M. (2015). Social Movement Contention in Colombia, 1958–2014. In P. Almeida (Ed.), *Handbook of Social Movements Across Latin America*. Springer.

Vélez, M. A., & Lobo, I. (2019). Challenges of Organised Community Resistance in the Context of Illicit Economies and Drug War Policies: Insights from Colombia. *Journal of Illicit Economies and Development, 1*(1), 72–79. https://doi.org/10.31389/jied.15

Vélez-Torres, I. (2014). Governmental Extractivism in Colombia: Legislation, Securitization and the Local Settings of Mining Control. *Political Geography, 38*, 68–78. https://doi.org/10.1016/j.polgeo.2013.11.008

Vélez-Torres, I., & Ruiz-Torres, G. (2016). Extractivismo Neoliberal Minero Y Conflictos Socio-Ambientales En Perú Y Colombia. *Ambiente y Sostenibilidad, 5*, 3. https://doi.org/10.25100/ays.v5i1.4297

10

Embedded Extraction: The Chinese State's Response to the Local Resource Curse

Jing Vivian Zhan

Introduction

Natural resources, such as fuels and nonfuel minerals, are crucial for sustaining economic development and meeting industrial and energy consumption needs. However, resource extraction generates tremendous environmental damage in mining areas (Aragón & Rud, 2015; Epstein et al., 2011; Owen & Kemp, 2019), undermines the welfare of local citizens (Ardanaz & Caballero, 2016; Borge et al., 2015; Loayza et al., 2013), and causes frequent social conflicts between mining companies and local citizens (Arce, 2014; Arellano-Yanguas, 2008). Such adverse impacts of resource extraction, increasingly recognized as the local

J. V. Zhan (✉)
Department of Government & Public Administration, The Chinese University of Hong Kong, Hong Kong, China
e-mail: zhan@cuhk.edu.hk

P. Bowles, N. Andrews (eds.), *Extractive Bargains*, Frontiers of Globalization,
https://doi.org/10.1007/978-3-031-32172-6_10

resource curse (Aragón et al., 2015; Ogwang et al., 2019; Sexton, 2020),[1] plague many resource-rich countries and call for urgent solutions.

As a developing country that has a large variety of mineral resources, China strongly encourages mineral extraction to promote national and local economic development and industrialization. But like other resource-rich countries, it also suffers from the above-mentioned symptoms of the local resource curse. Under an authoritarian regime, China lacks an impartial judicial system and an autonomous civil society to effectively handle the negative externalities of extractive industries. As a result, it witnesses widespread resource conflicts in mining areas. Concerned about the threat to regime stability and legitimacy, the Chinese government from the top down has actively sought solutions to mitigate the local resource curse and quell social unrest.

Drawing on archival research of government policy papers, field research in mining areas, and secondary information sources such as media reports and scholarly publications, this chapter investigates the Chinese state's strategy to cope with the local resource curse. By searching legal document databases and official websites of the Chinese central and local governments, I collected more than 2800 policy papers regulating the operation of extractive industries and particularly their environmental, economic, and sociopolitical impacts in 244 officially recognized mineral-rich localities. The study of the central and local policies reveals a multitude of environmental, economic, social, and political measures through which the Chinese government attempts to embed extractive industries in local communities and mobilize them to address their negative externalities and contribute to local development and public welfare. I define such practices as embedded extraction and argue that it is a strategy for the Chinese government to pursue 'developmentalist extractive bargains with Chinese characteristics.' That is, the state promotes extraction to support national development goals such as increasing national income and raising citizens' living standards. Meanwhile, it

[1] Different from the vast literature on the resource curse (e.g., Auty, 1993; Fearon & Laitin, 2003; Ross, 2015; Sachs & Warner, 1995), which debates the macro-level impacts of mineral resources on the host country, the notion of local resource curse focuses on the micro-level and meso-level impacts on local citizens and communities which suffer from the negative externalities of extractive industries.

attempts to mitigate extraction's negative effects and address the unequal distribution of its benefits and costs in ways which also resonate with social redistribution bargains. Under the specificities of China's political economy and without the strong participation of civil society actors as seen in other countries, these bargains are struck between the state and extractive capital on behalf of the citizens. The findings highlight the active roles that the state can play to push extractive industries to address the concerns of local citizens. By establishing various linkages between mining companies and neighbouring communities, the Chinese government's policy of embedded extraction may provide a solution to the local resource curse.

The rest of this chapter is organized as follows. Section Two briefly reviews the changes and consequences of mineral extraction in China. Section Three discusses the Chinese central government's policy initiatives to address the environmental and socioeconomic problems associated with mineral extraction. Section Four examines in detail the resource-rich local governments' environmental, economic, social, and political measures of embedded extraction. The last section offers some concluding remarks.

China's Resource Boom and Its Consequences

Since the turn of the millennium, China has witnessed a sustained resource boom with both rising prices and increasing demand for mineral products. Despite some fluctuations, national mineral industrial output grew substantially between 1999 and 2017. At the highest point, mineral industrial output accounted for nearly 8% of China's GDP in 2010 (see Fig. 10.1). In particularly resource-rich areas such as Shanxi Province, Qinghai Province, and Xinjiang Uyghur Autonomous Region, mineral industrial output constantly accounted for 20% to 30% of provincial GDP throughout the 2000s and 2010s. The lucrative resource market attracted substantial investment in extractive industries. Although the strategically important mineral resources such as oil, gas, and rare earths are controlled by large state-owned enterprises (SOEs) or companies with a strong backing of state investment, most other minerals are open to

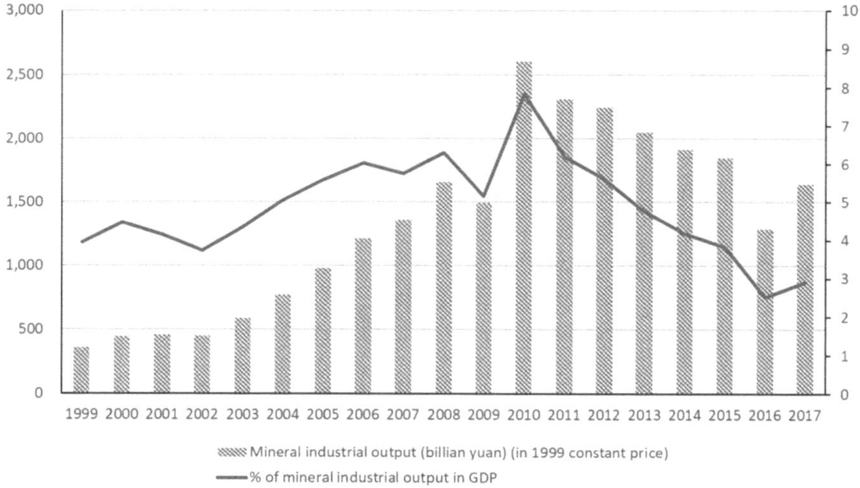

Fig. 10.1 China's National Mineral Industrial Output (1999–2017). Source: figure compiled based on statistics from *China Land and Resources Statistical Yearbook 2000–2018, Statistical Yearbook of China 2020,* and World Bank database (https://data.worldbank.org.cn/indicator/FP.CPI.TOTL.ZG?locations=CN). Note: mineral industrial output data include all provinces and offshore oil fields but exclude Hong Kong, Macao, and Taiwan

mining companies of all ownership types, including SOEs, collective-owned enterprises, private companies, and foreign-invested companies.

The zealous and chaotic resource extraction in many resource-rich Chinese localities has led to a multitude of environmental, economic, and sociopolitical problems. Mining-related environmental hazards such as air, water, and soil pollution, water shortage, and land collapse caused health problems, most notably pneumoconiosis, reduced agricultural productivity and damaged property, which imposed heavy financial and health losses on local citizens in mining areas and often forced them to relocate (Zhan & Zeng, 2017). While mining businesspeople enjoyed rapid accumulations of wealth, local citizens suffered from decreased job opportunities and suppressed incomes (Zhan, 2022). Due to the unequal distribution of benefits and costs, extractive activities have frequently led to conflicts (Chen, 2016; Yang & Ho, 2018; Zeng & Xia, 2013; Zhan & Zeng, 2017). Resource conflicts took the form of both labour disputes in the extractive sector and clashes between mining companies and neighbouring communities. The conflicts were of varying scales, ranging from a few participants to hundreds or even thousands of protestors. In one riot in a phosphorus-rich county in Guizhou Province in 2008, about 20,000 angry protestors went onto the streets and torched the government and police buildings (Zhan, 2013). Based on three datasets of social conflicts in China, namely the China Labour Bulletin (CLB) "Strike" dataset,[2] the "Collective Incidents" dataset collected by the Chinese Academy of Social Sciences (CASS), and the "China Strikes" dataset (Elfstrom, 2017), I identify 442 mining-related mass protests between 2003 and 2021.[3] Almost all Chinese provinces have experienced some resource conflicts.

Deeply concerned about the negative impacts on social stability and regime legitimacy, the Chinese government from the bottom up has anxiously and actively sought to address the local resource curse. Owing to the public ownership of mineral resources in China, mineral exploration and extraction are extensively regulated by various government departments such as land and resources, taxation, work safety, environmental protection, and industry and commerce. The state heavily intervenes in the processes of mineral prospecting, issuing of mining permissions, extraction, processing, transportation, and transactions of minerals. With such extensive administrative and political control, the Chinese state possesses strong bargaining power against the extractive industries and uses extractive bargains to mobilize mining companies to address their negative externalities and improve the welfare of local citizens, which may go beyond the normal scope of corporate social responsibilities (CSR). I call such practices embedded extraction and argue that it can avoid the many pitfalls of extractive enclaves that comparative studies have discovered, such as minimal benefits to local citizens (Akabzaa, 2009), inequality and marginalization of citizen groups

[2] China Labour Bulletin. https://maps.clb.org.hk/. Accessed 28 October 2022.

[3] It is important to note that these datasets all rely on media reports as major sources of information, which may not cover all incidents of conflicts, especially those in remote, rural areas and those that took place in earlier years when social media usage was low. Moreover, media reports on collective incidents are heavily censored in China. Hence, the statistics from these datasets are likely to undercount actual incidents of resource conflicts.

(Enns & Bersaglio, 2015), competition and conflicts (Côte & Korf, 2018), and weakened governance by the state (Ferguson, 2005). By building linkages between the extractive industries and local communities, embedded extraction can be an important strategy to cope with the local resource curse. The following sections will examine the concrete government policies to promote embedded extraction and the varied local practices on the ground.

Responding to the Local Resource Curse: Central Mandate

Since China's resource boom started in the late 1990s, the Chinese government has gradually realized the severity of the environmental, socioeconomic, and political costs of resource extraction. In 2013, the Chinese Central Government issued a major policy document entitled "The Plan for the Sustainable Development of Resource-Based Cities in China (2013–2020)" (the 2013 Plan hereafter) (State Council, 2013), in which the State Council clearly recognized 262 localities as resource-based cities (*ziyuanxing chengshi*).[4] Excluding the 18 localities that mainly rely on forest resources, there are 244 localities endowed with rich mineral resources including oil, natural gas, and solid metal and nonmetal minerals, most notably coal. This research focuses on these 244 mineral-rich localities.

The 2013 Plan heavily emphasized the need to promote sustainable development of the resource-based localities and required them to address a wide range of issues including environmental damage, poverty and unemployment of local citizens, public service provision, and social conflicts. Specifically, the 2013 Plan proposed the following policy goals with regard to the social, economic, and environmental well-being of the local citizens:

1. Creating employment and re-employment opportunities by fostering labour-intensive and service industries and facilitating the development

[4] The 2013 Plan referred to the 262 localities as cities, but they include prefecture-level cities, county-level cities, counties, and city districts.

of small and micro-scale enterprises. Priority should be given to unemployed mine workers, workers disabled due to mining accidents, and displaced residents and land-losing peasants due to resource extraction.

2. Renovating shantytowns in mining areas, constructing basic infrastructure such as water, heating, gas, electricity, roads, garbage treatment, schools, and hospitals, enhancing social management and community services in the newly constructed residential areas, and creating job opportunities for the relocated residents. Special attention is to be paid to residential areas and relocated residents suffering land subsidence caused by coal mining.
3. Improving the social security system covering senior care, medical service, work-related injuries, family planning, and so on, especially for laid-off and retired workers from mining companies, displaced peasants, and miners suffering work-related diseases. Enhancing the medical treatment of mining-related diseases such as pneumoconiosis, chronic gastritis, and skin disease.
4. Strengthening work safety regulations, enhancing emergency management of occupational and environmental hazards, and resolving social conflicts caused by resource extraction, land appropriation and displacement, restructure and bankruptcy of mining enterprises, environmental pollution, and so on, with the aim of creating a safe and harmonious working and living environment in mining areas.
5. Requiring mining companies to be responsible for treating their environmental damage such as land subsidence, open pit, goaf, drainage of underground water, and salinization of soil. The costs of environmental restoration in mined-out areas are to be borne by mining companies (*shui pohuai, shui zhili*). Strengthening environmental regulations on hazardous chemical discharge, especially heavy metals, and promoting energy saving and emission reduction by mining companies.

The issuance of the 2013 Plan suggests that the Chinese central government has been wary of the many environmental and socioeconomic problems associated with the extractive industries and was concerned about their damage to the citizens' livelihood and well-being as well as social stability in mining areas. It was also aware of the many problems accumulated throughout the decades of underregulated mineral extraction since the Maoist era, and thus it called for timely solutions to the accumulated problems. To achieve the multidimensional policy goals, the State Council required the resource-rich localities across China to step up their lawmaking efforts and design their own policies in accordance with the central mandate. In addition to the leading role of local governments, the State Council also emphasized the responsibilities of mining enterprises and the need to get them involved in the policy process (State Council, 2013).

Embedded Extraction: Local Practices

By scouring the government websites of the 244 officially recognized mineral-rich localities and searching Chinese legal document databases including PKU Law, Wanfang, and CNKI, I find that these localities have all issued their own regulations and policies to address the various symptoms of the local resource curse. I collected more than 2800 policy papers issued between 1999 and 2021 that regulate the extractive industries. Excluding those loosely related policies and those aiming to promote the overall development of the resource sector, I identified 2766 policy papers that explicitly mention measures to deal with the environmental, economic, and sociopolitical problems associated with mineral extraction. These policies explicitly or implicitly require or encourage mining companies to take part in and contribute financial or other resources to the policy process. Figure 10.2 shows the number of policies issued annually. We can see that while some localities took actions earlier than the central mandate, most localities were prompted into action afterwards, with a notable increase of issued policies in 2013, and 2016–2018 appear to be the most active years.

While local practices vary widely in terms of policy goals and concrete measures, two common goals as manifested by two key terms stand out: "green mining areas (*lvse kuangshan*)" and "harmonious mining zones (*hexie quangqu*)." The first term stresses the need for environmental protection to turn the normally broken, barren mining areas into green lands with ecological diversity. The second goal emphasizes the need to

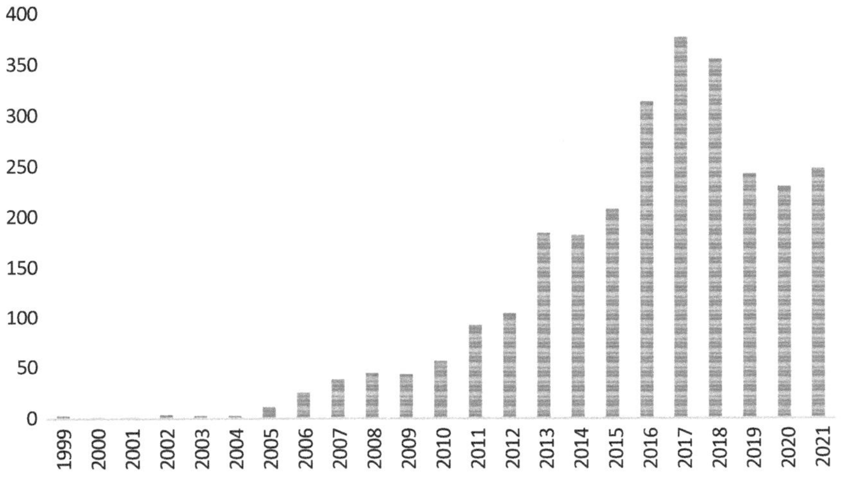

Fig. 10.2 Number of policies issued by resource-rich localities (1999–2021). Source: author's collection from PKU Law, Wanfang, and CNKI legal document databases and the government websites of resource-rich localities

maintain social stability in mining areas. This policy goal can be regarded as a new variant of the Chinese government's attempt to build a "harmonious society," which was first proposed by the Hu Jintao Administration in the mid-2000s and aimed at resolving mounting social conflicts in China.[5] But because social conflicts can arise from multiple causes, this goal is more elusive and requires multidimensional policies to achieve.

A thorough examination of the contents of the policy documents issued by the resource-rich localities reveals a large variety of local practices. To achieve the two key goals, local governments required mining companies to treat their environmental damage, contribute to local economic development and job creation, and enhance local citizens' welfare, which essentially created various linkages to embed the extractive industries in local communities. According to the specific policy goals

[5] The Central Committee of the Chinese Communist Party, 2006. "The Chinese Communist Party Central Committee's Decision on Several Major Issues Regarding the Construction of a Harmonious Socialist Society," http://www.gov.cn/gongbao/content/2006/content_453176.htm. Accessed 30 August 2022.

and measures, the local practices fall into four major categories, namely environmental, economic, social, and political measures.

Environmental Measures

Environmental issues have received by far the most policy attention from resource-rich localities. Among the 2766 policy papers collected, 1349 specifically deal with environmental protection and/or ecological restoration in mining areas. This is very much in line with the central emphasis on environmental protection. Although environmental issues had long taken a backseat when China pursued economic modernization and industrialization, since Xi Jinping came into power in 2012, environmental protection has become a highly prioritized and politicized policy area in China.[6] Along with the increasingly tightened environmental regulations nationwide, the resource-rich localities also stepped up their environmental standards and enforcement. Multiple localities have frequently launched environmental campaigns to fight air, soil, and water pollution. Most resource-rich localities promulgated policies to build "green mining areas" and set specific standards for mining companies to maintain the environmental and ecological systems in the mining areas.

Following the central principle that the costs of environmental protection and restoration should be borne by the perpetrators, the local governments commonly required mining companies to assume the responsibilities for minimizing and treating their environmental damage such as land subsidence and collapse. For example, to deal with land subsidence and collapse, which pose an imminent threat to the safety and livelihood of local citizens, the coal-rich Shanxi Province stipulated that mining companies must shoulder 30% of the costs of environmental restoration.[7] Many other resource-rich localities issued similar policies. In

[6] Xinhua Net. 2021. "Xi Focus: Toward people-nature harmony, Xi leads China's green action." http://www.xinhuanet.com/english/2021-06/04/c_139989249.htm. Accessed 30 July 2022.

[7] Shanxi Provincial Government, 2017. "The Notification of Shanxi Provincial Government Office on the Management of Comprehensive Treatment Fund for Collapsed Coal Mining Areas in

addition, local governments in resource-rich regions regularly collected administrative charges such as the Environmental Protection Deposit Fund (*huanjing baohu baozheng jin*), which later became the Ecological Environment Recovery Fund (*dizhi huanjing zhili huifu jijin*), from mining companies and used them for environmental protection and recovery measures.

To ensure mining companies take environmental protection seriously, local governments set concrete targets for them. For example, Datong City of Shanxi Province required mining companies to invest in afforestation, with the goal of covering at least 20% of the mining areas with greenery and restoring the ecosystem in at least 60% of the mined-out areas.[8] Some local governments attached environmental conditions to mining permissions. For example, Inner Mongolia Autonomous Region clearly required mining enterprises to set up specialized units and hire professional staff to deal with environmental protection and afforestation. In order to receive official permission for operation, mining companies need to design concrete plans to maintain and restore the ecological diversity of the mining and surrounding areas, which are subject to annual appraisals by local authorities.[9]

These measures attempted to reverse the long-term neglect of environmental protection in Chinese mining areas that relentlessly promoted mineral extraction for mainly economic purposes. Mining companies could no longer exploit the mineral resources at the expense of the environment and local citizens and had to take more serious measures and bear higher costs of environmental protection and recovery.

Shanxi." http://www.lc.gov.cn/ztzl/zcwj_3017/szcwj/201712/P020171230073843619046.pdf. Accessed 28 August 2021.

[8] Datong City Government, 2012. "The Notification on the Implementation Plan of Datong's Green Ecology Project," https://www.pkulaw.com/lar/406b525fd44f71df188c83f2ae818c02bdfb.html?keyword=%E6%B2%89%E9%99%B7%E5%8C%BA%20%E5%A4%A7%E5%90%8C%E5%B8%82. Accessed 11 September 2022.

[9] Inner Mongolia Autonomous Region Coal Industry Bureau, 2013. "The Opinions of Inner Mongolia Autonomous Region Coal Industry Bureau on Speeding up the Afforestation and Ecological Environment Management in Mining Zones (2013)," https://www.pkulaw.com/lar/59af3f4af1a59c0e1b6fa0e912180736bdfb.html?keyword=%E5%91%BC%E4%BC%A6%E8%B4%9D%E5%B0%94%20%E6%B2%89%E9%99%B7%E5%8C%BA%20. Accessed 30 August 2022.

Economic Measures

While not as emphasized as environmental protection in the local policy papers, economic growth continued to be a key goal for Chinese local governments, including those in resource-rich areas. As mining-induced environmental damage undercut agricultural productivity and led to the displacement and unemployment of local citizens, it hurt the prospects for economic growth in the affected areas. To recover economic losses and appease aggrieved citizens, the resource-rich localities desperately sought to create employment opportunities and increase the income level of the local citizens, and they actively involved mining companies in this process. One straightforward measure is to recover the farmlands lost to mining. After the extractive industries exhaust the mineral resources underground, the lands are often destroyed and deserted. The local governments have tried to recover the deserted lands and redistribute them to the peasants to increase their income. The recovery of farmlands often went hand in hand with the ecological restoration mentioned above, and mining companies were required to contribute to this cause. For example, Karamay City of Xinjiang Uyghur Autonomous Region issued an elaborate policy that required mining enterprises to allocate earmarked funds out of their operational costs on a monthly basis. The funds are owned by the enterprises but used under the supervision of the government to cover the actual costs of recovering the lands damaged by mining activities. If mining enterprises fail to comply, they are subject to administrative penalties including suspension or cancellation of mining rights and registration in the List of Enterprises with Serious Illegal and Dishonest Acts, which can lead to fines and even shutdowns. The local government can also bring the enterprises to court for failing to comply.[10]

[10] Department of Natural Resources, Department of Finance, and Department of Ecology and Environment of Xinjiang Uyghur Autonomous Region, 2022. "Notification on the Distribution of 'Mining Area Geological and Environmental Restoration Fund Management

In addition to recovering agricultural production, resource-rich localities strived to create job opportunities in the mining and other industrial sectors. In exchange for granting mining permissions, the resource-rich localities often required or encouraged the mining companies to hire the local labour force instead of migrant labour. For instance, Chifeng City of Inner Mongolia Autonomous Region encouraged the mining companies to prioritize hiring local peasants and herdsmen, especially from ethnic minorities. The government also provided vocational training for citizens with low labour skills to prepare them for industrial jobs. In 2017, the Chifeng government boasted of creating jobs for 706,000 peasants and herdsmen and providing 37,000 professional training sessions for its citizens.[11] In view of the fact that mining jobs tend to be limited due to the increasing mechanization of the extractive industries, the local governments also encouraged mining companies to use the local labour force for various services they need, such as catering, property management, transportation, and environmental recovery. An interesting model I observed through my field research in Inner Mongolia is that the village branches of the Chinese Communist Party set up village-based companies with the collective investment of the villagers and hired the villagers to provide transportation services to the mining companies operating in the villages. The village companies also provided professional training such as driving skills and start-up funds for the villagers to purchase trucks for transportation services. Because the mining companies used the village lands, the village party secretaries bargained with the companies and pressured them into using the services of the village companies instead of outside service providers.[12]

Scheme in Xinjiang Uyghur Autonomous Region'." https://www.pkulaw.com/lar/a102ad7edc1831ba216e80667f58e28fbdfb.html?keyword=%E6%96%B0%E7%96%86%E7%BB%B4%E5%90%BE%E5%B0%94%E8%87%AA%E6%B2%BB%E5%8C%BA%E7%9F%BF%E5%B1%B1%E5%9C%B0%E8%B4%A8%E7%8E%AF%E5%A2%83%E6%B2%BB%E7%90%86%E6%81%A2%E5%A4%8D%E5%9F%BA%E9%87%91%E7%AE%A1%E7%90%86%E5%8A%9E%E6%B3%95&way=listView. Access 29 August 2022.

[11] Chifeng City Government, 2017. "2017 Government Work Report of Chifeng City." http://222.74.76.11:8080/chfscsh/zwgk/xxgkzl/fdzdgknr/qtfdxx/gzbg/cfszf/201703/t20170317_430082.html. Accessed 27 March 2022.

[12] Author's interviews in Inner Mongolia, August 2012.

Furthermore, some resource-dependent regions also sought to diversify their industrial structure and create jobs in non-resource sectors. As a pioneer in this policy experiment, the Shanxi Provincial government launched a policy of "subsidizing peasants by coal (*yimei bunong*)" in 2006 and made it mandatory for coal mining companies to invest in non-coal businesses. The local governments in Shanxi all devised their own policies such as subsidies and favourable land and taxation policies to facilitate investment in non-coal businesses (Zheng, 2011, pp. 31–32). Thanks to the investment by coal companies, new businesses and employment opportunities gradually emerged. For example, 610 coal companies had set foot in the agricultural sector by 2008. One coal-turned-poultry company claimed to employ more than 3000 peasants, and another produce-processing company claimed to generate more than 50 million yuan of income for local citizens.[13] The Shanxi experience suggests that when given sufficient incentives and proper policy guidance, the mining companies could contribute to the diversification of industrial structures in resource-dependent areas and become new sources of employment opportunities for local citizens.

A new strategy emerged in recent years and became popular under Xi Jinping's high-profile anti-poverty campaign between 2016 and 2021. As one way to enhance the income of local citizens, some resource-rich regions encouraged villages in mining areas to use their collective assets to invest in mines and become shareholders of the mining companies. The profits from such investments would then be distributed to increase the villagers' incomes or provide social welfare benefits. For example, Kaiyang County of Guizhou Province, an underdeveloped region in southwest China, issued policies in conjunction with the anti-poverty campaign to encourage villagers living in poverty to invest in mining companies operating in the villages. Because the poor villagers lacked funds for such investment, they were allowed to pool the collectively owned lands for shares of the mining companies. In this way, instead of selling the lands to the mining companies and receiving one-off compensation, the

[13] China News Net, 2009. "Shanxi Subsidizes Peasants by Coal, 'Coal Bosses' Transform into 'Agriculture Bosses' (*Shanxi Yimei Bunog, 'Meilaoban' Bianshen 'Nonglaoban'*)," October 22, http://news.ifeng.com/mainland/200910/1022_17_1400633.shtml. Accessed 12 February 2020.

villagers could receive more sustainable income as shareholders.[14] Moreover, local governments in underdeveloped areas actively invited mining companies to invest in poverty villages by setting up collective businesses with the villagers. In return, the local governments gave them favourable policies such as prioritized allocation of mining rights and land supply.[15] By turning local citizens into investors and partners of mining companies, these measures essentially made mining companies deeply embedded in the rural economy and accountable to the shareholding villagers to a certain degree.

Social Measures

Mining companies have also widely provided public goods to local citizens in resource-rich regions. Under the Maoist command economy, state-owned mining companies had long provided public goods such as basic infrastructure, water, and power for not only their employees but also the general public in mining zones. Some mining companies even functioned as the de facto government, operating their own schools, hospitals, and police stations. In the post-Mao reform era, although a large number of nonstate-owned companies emerged in the resource sector, the Maoist legacies persisted. Both the government and the citizens continued to expect mining companies to shoulder social responsibilities, partly on the ground that they make profits out of the publicly owned natural resources and thus should pay back to the public.

Against this backdrop, both state-owned and private mining companies are commonly required to construct infrastructure such as roads, bridges, and irrigation systems for local communities. For example, state-owned oil companies in Daqing City of Heilongjiang Province and Dongying City of Shandong Province, both major oil fields in northeast China,

[14] Kaiyang County Government, 2021. "Notification on the Distribution of Kaiyang Green Mining Development Zone Construction Plan." https://www.kaiyang.gov.cn/zwgk/zfxxgk/fdzdgk/zcwj/kfbh/202109/t20210926_70544312.ht ml. Accessed 11 September 2022.

[15] Bijie Government, 2010. "Notification of Bijie Prefecture Administrative Office on the Distribution of Establishing Long-term Support Mechanisms of Mining Area Rural Development by Coal Mining Enterprises in Bijie Prefecture." http://d.g.wanfangdata.com.hk/Claw_D520011984.aspx. Accessed 20 March 2022.

were responsible for water, electricity, and heating supply and property management for residents around the oil fields. They also needed to sponsor hospitals and schools in the neighbourhood. By contrast, private mining enterprises may contribute to public services on a voluntary basis and in less institutionalized ways. Local governments tend to mobilize private companies to contribute to public projects through informal bargaining and using personal connections. Based on my field research in Shanxi and Jiangxi provinces, mining entrepreneurs usually tried to maintain good personal relationships with local officials in exchange for policy favours or protection from unfavourable policies. [16] Thus, mining entrepreneurs usually make financial contributions to infrastructural or charity projects, willingly or grudgingly. Overall, despite the differentiation between companies of different ownership types, mining companies in general would collaborate with local governments and share the costs of public goods provision.

One common problem that many mining areas face is the dismal living conditions and displacement of local citizens. Shantytowns widely existed in mining areas, which suffered from a lack of basic infrastructure and inadequate public services. To renovate the shanty towns and relocate the residents in areas suffering land subsidence, local governments often required mining companies, especially state-owned ones, to share the costs and even play leading roles in the renovation and relocation projects. In exchange, the local governments may offer favourable policies such as tax cuts as incentives.[17] For example, Datong City of Shanxi Province launched a campaign to renovate the shantytowns in its coal mines in 2006. Datong Coal Mine Group, a large coal mining company owned by Shanxi Provincial Government, played a leading role and shared 30% of the construction costs, while the residents, Shanxi Provincial Government, and Datong City Government shared 40%, 20%, and 10% of the costs,

[16] Author's interviews in Shanxi Province, October 2013; Jiangxi Province, May 2015.

[17] Yulin City Government, 2014. "Notification of Yulin City Government Office on the Distribution of the Implementation Method of Shanty Town Renovation in Yulin." https://www.pkulaw.com/lar/e8e2295ffad01d33aabef43b34def410bdfb.html?keyword=%E7%9F%BF%20%E6%A6%86%E6%9E%97. Accessed 14 April 2022.

respectively. By 2013, the project had constructed 11.3 million square metres of floor area and provided housing to 0.3 million people working or living in these areas.[18] By making such contributions way beyond the normal range of CSR, the mining companies essentially did the job that should have been taken up by the government.

Political Measures

A few resource-rich localities have explored political mechanisms to allow local citizens to participate in resource management so as to resolve or pre-empt resource conflicts. As an authoritarian country, China accommodates limited channels of political participation, and citizens have almost no say in the granting of mining permissions or the management of mining projects. Nevertheless, to deal with the frequent conflicts between the mining companies and local citizens, some local governments in Inner Mongolia Autonomous Region took steps to enhance citizens' participation in the governance of resource extraction. For example, Baotou City in Inner Mongolia decided in 2013 to publicize the details of proposed mining projects and hold public hearings on potentially controversial projects that could lead to serious environmental pollution or displacement on a large scale. Representatives of local peasants and herdsmen were invited to voice their opinions and raise their concerns, and the local government would then conduct assessments on the safety and feasibility of the projects and respond to the citizens' requests. After the establishment of the mining project, regular public consultations would be held to allow the local government, people's representatives, and mining companies to discuss and settle the disputes and conflicts arising from the extractive activities. If no agreement could be reached through consultation, the conflicting parties could resort to legal arbitration or litigation for conflict resolution.[19] Some other localities

[18] Xinhua Net, 2013. "The largest Shanty Town Renovation Project in Shanxi Approaches Completion, Benefiting 0.3 Million People." http://finance.people.com.cn/n/2013/0223/c70846-20577697.html. Accessed 11 September 2022.

[19] Baotou City Government, 2013. "Notification of Baotou City government on the Distribution of the Work Plan for the Construction of Pilot Harmonious Mining Zones in Baotou." http://www.baotou.gov.cn/info/egovinfo/1001/01xxgk/copy_2_xxgk_nry/BAO-001-00-0200000-2012-005.htm. Accessed 20 February 2022.

such as Kaiyang County in Guizhou Province also explored similar public consultation mechanisms.

Admittedly, there have been only sporadic attempts to change the political institutions and give local citizens more decision-making power in resource management. Most local governments largely took a top-down approach and dictated the process of resource extraction and conflict resolution. In comparison, environmental, economic, and social measures have been more extensively used to address the local resource curse in China.

Discussion and Conclusion

China's resource boom since the turn of the millennium has generated impressive economic growth in many of its resource-rich localities and contributed to national developmental goals. However, the aggressive and chaotic path of resource extraction has created environmental hazards, imposed health and financial losses on local citizens, and led to popular grievances and contentions. These problems seriously threatened regime legitimacy and stability and prompted the Chinese central and local governments to devise concrete policies to cope with the local resource curse.

By scrutinizing the government policy papers issued by 244 resource-rich localities and drawing on field research in selected mining areas and secondary information sources, this research finds that resource-rich local governments have adopted environmental, economic, social, and to a lesser degree, political measures to address the local resource curse from different angles, with key goals of building "green" and "harmonious" mining areas. One crucial element of these multidimensional measures is to encourage embedded extraction and make mining companies accountable and responsive to the needs of local citizens. Following the notion of "extractive bargains" proposed by Bowles and Andrews in Chap. 1, the Chinese practices can be regarded as extractive bargains between the state and the mining sectors to establish some sort of consensus with the local citizens and to compensate for their losses and improve their welfare. If effectively implemented, such policies may push mineral extraction towards a "progressive bargain," in which extractive industries can both contribute to developmental goals and meet social and environmental justice goals.

It is worth noting that the issued policies do not guarantee effective implementation of embedded extraction, which heavily depends on the capacity and incentive structure of the local governments, as the policy outcomes are achieved through bargaining and collaboration between local governments and mining companies. If the local governments possess weaker bargaining power than the mining companies, as in the scenario of large, powerful mining companies operating in poverty areas with dysfunctional local governments, the compliance of mining companies may be a problem. Even worse, if the local state is captured by resource interests, as indicated by many corruption cases involving local officials and mining businesspeople (Zhan, 2017), the situation may descend into "Faustian bargains" where short-term gains may be achieved for the state and business elites at the expense of the citizens.

Therefore, we need more empirical evidence in future research to assess the effectiveness of China's policies.

Although this chapter cannot draw definitive conclusions on the effectiveness of embedded extraction, we can have an initial assessment of the impacts of the Chinese government's measures by tracing the longitudinal trend of resource conflicts in China. Based on three Chinese social conflict datasets as mentioned earlier, I have identified a total of 442 resource conflicts between 2003 and 2021. As Fig. 10.3 shows, along with China's resource boom, the number of resource conflicts increased steadily from 2003 to 2015; but between 2016 and 2021, the number of resource conflicts declined continuously. Keeping in mind that the reported resource conflicts are likely an undercount of actual incidents (because many incidents may not be captured by the media, especially in the earlier years when social media was underdeveloped and reports on social instability are heavily censored in China), we should interpret the statistics with caution. Nevertheless, the decreasing trend since 2016, three years after the State Council issued the 2013 Plan and when the resource-rich localities actively issued policies to tackle the many problems caused by mineral extraction (see Fig. 10.2), suggests that the various measures of embedded extraction may have worked to a certain extent

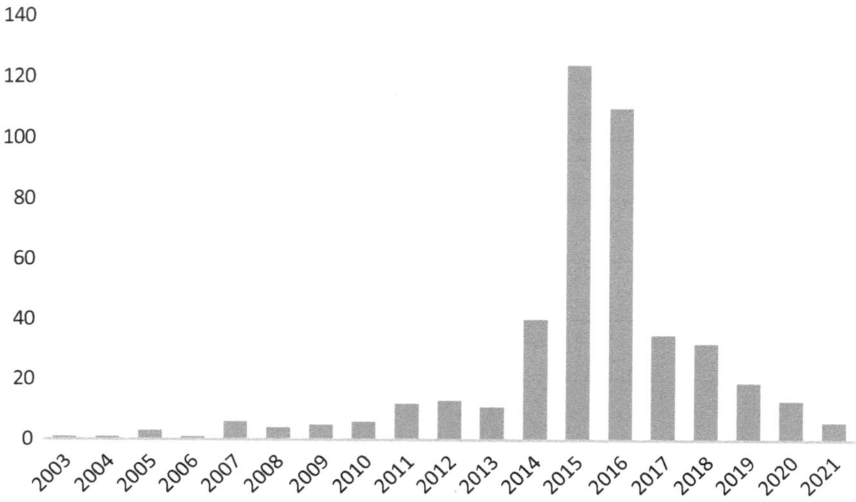

Fig. 10.3 Number of reported resource conflicts in China (2003–2020). Source: author's collection from China Labour Bulletin "Strike" dataset, the "Collective Incidents" dataset by the Chinese Academy of Social Sciences, and the "China Strikes" dataset by Elfstrom (2017)

towards the goal of building "harmonious" mining areas, assuming that the number of resource conflicts reported was not seriously distorted during this period.

The empirical evidence from China indicates that there are possible ways for the state to tackle the local resource curse through embedded extraction. If effectively implemented, embedded extraction can facilitate progressive extractive bargains and encourage extractive industries to meet both developmental goals and social and environmental justice goals. This finding makes both theoretical and empirical contributions. Theoretically, it contributes to the discourses of the resource curse and extractive bargains by pointing out the important roles that the state can play to address the adverse environmental and socioeconomic impacts of resource extraction. It also enhances our understanding of state-business relations by revealing the nuanced strategies that the state can use to intervene in the economy. Empirically, it generates policy implications for resource management not only in China but also in other resource-rich countries that suffer from the local resource curse.

Acknowledgement The author acknowledges the financial support from the Hong Kong Research Grants Council (GRF 14600722) and the National Social Science Foundation of China (19BGL204). She thanks Shiyuan Wang and Junru Wu for their excellent research assistance.

References

Akabzaa, T. (2009). Mining in Ghana: implications for National Economic Development and Poverty Reduction. In B. Campbell (Ed.), *Mining in Africa: Regulation and Development* (p. 25). Pluto Press/IDRC.

Aragón, F. M., & Rud, J. P. (2015). Polluting Industries and Agricultural Productivity: Evidence from Mining in Ghana. *The Economic Journal, 126*(597), 1980–2011.

Aragón, F. M., Chuhan-Pole, P., & Land, B. C. (2015). *The Local Economic Impacts of Resource Abundance: What Have We Learned?* The World Bank.

Arce, M. (2014). *Resource Extraction and Protest in Peru*. University of Pittsburgh Press.

Ardanaz, M., & Caballero, N. T. (2016). A Subnational Resource Curse? Revenue Windfalls and the Quality of Public Spending in Colombian Municipalities. *V JORNADAS IBEROAMERICANAS DE FINANCIAMIENTO LOCAL*, 1–29.

Arellano-Yanguas, Javier. 2008. "A Thoroughly Modern Resource Curse? The New Natural Resource Policy Agenda and the Mining Revival in Peru." *IDS Working Paper 300.*

Auty, R. M. (1993). *Sustaining Development in Mineral Economies: The Resource Curse Thesis*. Routledge.

Borge, L.-E., Parmer, P., & Torvik, R. (2015). Local natural resource curse? *Journal of Public Economics, 131*, 101–114.

Chen, X. (2016). *The Political Logic of Enterprise-driven Urbanization: A Case Study of Y Town in Shanxi Province*. Chinese Social Science Press.

Côte, M., & Korf, B. (2018). Making concessions: Extractive enclaves, entangled capitalism and regulative pluralism at the gold mining frontier in Burkina Faso. *World Development, 101*, 466–476.

Elfstrom, Manfred. 2017. *China Strikes*. Accessed March 21, 2021. https://chinastrikes.crowdmap.com.

Enns, C., & Bersaglio, B. (2015). Enclave oil development and the rearticulation of citizenship in Turkana, Kenya: Exploring 'crude citizenship'. *Geoforum, 67*, 78–88.

Epstein, Paul R, Jonathan Buonocore, Kevin Eckerle, Michael Hendryx, Benjamin M. Stout, Richard Heinberg, Richard W Clapp, et al. 2011. "Full cost accounting for the life cycle of coal in "Ecological Economics Reviews"." In *Annuals of The New York Academy of Sciences 1219*, by Robert Costanza, Karin Limburg and Ida Kubiszewski, 73–98.

Fearon, J. D., & Laitin, D. (2003). Ethnicity, Insurgency, and Civil War. *American Political Science Review, 97*(1), 75–90.

Ferguson, J. (2005). Seeing like an oil company: space, security, and global capital in neoliberal Africa. *American Anthropologist, 107*(3), 377–382.

Loayza, Norman, Alfredo Mier Teran, and Jamele Rigolini. 2013. "Poverty, inequality, and the local natural resource curse." *Policy Research working paper, no. WPS 6366.* Washington DC: World Bank Group.

Ogwang, T., Vanclay, F., & van den Assem, A. (2019). Rent-Seeking Practices, Local Resource Curse, and Social Conflict in Uganda's Emerging Oil Economy. *Land, 8*(4), 53–66.

Owen, J. R., & Kemp, D. (2019). Displaced by Mine Waste: The Social Consequences of Industrial Risk-taking. *The Extractive Industries and Society, 6*, 424–427.

Ross, M. L. (2015). What Have We Learned about the Resource Curse? *Annual Review of Political Science, 18*, 239–259.

Sachs, Jeffrey D, and Andrew M Warner. 1995. "Natural Resource Abundance and Economic Growth." NBER Working Paper 5398.

Sexton, R. (2020). Unpacking the Local Resource Curse: How Externalities and Governance Shape Social Conflict. *Journal of Conflict Resolution, 64*(4), 640–673.

State Council. 2013. "Quanguo Ziyuanxing Chengshi Kechixu Fazhan Guihua (2013-2020 Nian) (Sustainable Development Plan of Resource-based Cities in China (2013-2020)." November 12. http://www.gov.cn/zwgk/2013-12/03/content_2540070.htm.

Yang, X., & Ho, P. (2018). Conflict over Mining in Rural China: A Comprehensive Survey of Intentions and Strategies for Environmental Activism. *Sustainability, 10*(5), 1–18.

Zeng, M., & Xia, Y. (2013). Shehui Wending zhong de Ziyuan Zuzhou Xianxiang: Yi X Kuangqu Weili (The Resource Curse in Stability Maintenance:

A Case Study of X Mining Zone). *Wuhan Daxue Xuebao (Wuhan University Journal), 66*(5), 60–66.

Zhan, J. V. (2013). Natural Resources, Local Governance, and Social Instability: A Comparison of Two Counties in China. *The China Quarterly, 213*, 78–100.

Zhan, J. V. (2017). Do Natural Resources Breed Corruption? Evidence from China. *Environmental & Resource Economics, 66*(2), 237–259.

Zhan, J. V. (2022). *China's Contained Resource Curse: How Minerals Shape State-Capital-Labor Relations*. Cambridge University Press.

Zhan, J. V., & Zeng, M. (2017). Resource Conflict Resolution in China. *the China Quarterly, 230*, 489–511.

Zheng, Y. (2011). *Quanfu Jipin: Jujiao Lvliang Shijian (Poverty Relief by the Wealthy: Focusing on the Practices in Lvliang)*. China Social Science Press.

11

Creating a Gender-Sensitive Extractive Bargain in Tanzania Through Local Content and Women's Economic Empowerment

Jesse Salah Ovadia and Maud Esi Amoafo

Introduction

Tanzania's extractive industries involve a variety of minerals, including gold, diamonds, uranium, nickel, and natural gas (Hansen, 2013; Lange & Kinyondo, 2016). Tanzania's gold mining industry, the third largest in Africa after South Africa and Ghana, has been a critical contributor to the economy. In 2009, 20% of Tanzania's $4 billion export earnings were attributed to gold mining. According to the Bank of Tanzania (BOT), the 2020 export earnings of the minerals sector were 7,730,142.4 (million of TZS). This makes the sector the country's highest non-traditional export earner (BOT, 2020). Additionally, Tanzania's extractive industries attract $2 to $3 billion in FDI from global gold mining firms such as Barrick Gold, Anglo Gold Ashanti, and other extractive companies seeking to exploit these resources (Hansen, 2013; Hansen et al., 2016).

J. S. Ovadia (✉) • M. E. Amoafo
Department of Political Science, University of Windsor, Windsor, ON, Canada
e-mail: Jesse.Ovadia@uwindsor.ca; amoafo@uwindsor.ca

P. Bowles, N. Andrews (eds.), *Extractive Bargains*, Frontiers of Globalization,
https://doi.org/10.1007/978-3-031-32172-6_11

As a result of structural adjustment, privatization, the lack of awareness of local content until 2013, and the overly attractive concessions from government to mining companies through the 1998 Mining Act, government income and royalties became marginal, and this spurred sentiments amongst Tanzanian citizens that natural resources were being handed out for free to foreigners (Lange & Kinyondo, 2016). Therefore, despite high export earnings, government take from mining barely exceeded 20% of total revenues, and its contributions to the local economy were limited (Kambi & Kambi, 2017). Kweka (2009) argued that multinational corporations (MNCs) have been integrated into the Tanzanian economy to only a limited degree. In agreement with this, the Tanzanian Investment Authority (TIC) (2008) also highlighted that relatively major mining investments "have very insignificant sectoral linkage and multiplier effects" (see Hansen, 2013, p. 17). The 2009 Mining Policy, 2010 Mining Act, and particularly the Petroleum Act of 2015 signalled a revived government prioritization of local participation, community involvement, strong state ownership, and indigenization. Although they took some time to formulate into enforced regulations, these laws were also the beginning of the adoption of "hard" and "stringent" local content requirements, particularly in the gas sector (Jacob & Pedersen, 2018; Lange & Kinyondo, 2016; Ovadia, 2016b; Scurfield et al., 2017).

Notably, the enaction of new legal and regulatory frameworks in the gas sector was perceived by many Tanzanians as a "golden opportunity" and a "second chance" to right the wrongs of the previously enclaved mining sector while optimizing local participation in the oil and gas sector (Lange & Kinyondo, 2016; Mengi, 2013). However, the benefits and risks associated with resource extraction are unequally distributed among social groups. Social discontent with low employment opportunities in the mining sector coupled with the limited fiscal linkages in the sector engendered a wave of resource nationalism under President Magufuli (Jacob & Pedersen, 2018). For some, Magufuli's approach from 2015 to 2021, particularly to the artisanal and small-scale mining (ASM) sector, represented an attempted developmentalist extractive bargain. Magufuli's resource nationalism, driven by societal pressures for greater benefits and state interest in increased revenue, despite all its contradictions, can be interpreted as an attempt to create a new extractive bargain. However, that bargain still neglected the gender dimension. This chapter explores the possibility of designing a gender-sensitive developmentalist extractive bargain in Tanzania that is premised on the combination of local content and already existent Women Economic Empowerment (WEE) policies in its tentative framework. The following section reviews the literature on gender in Tanzania's extractive industries. Section 3 discusses local content. Section 4 introduces the notion of combining WEE and LCPs in a new gender-sensitive extractive bargain and Sect. 5 concludes the chapter.

Gender in Tanzania's Extractive Industries

Historically, mining is a male-dominated industry characterized by hypermasculinity, brotherhood, and "supernormal patriarchy" (Bradshaw et al., 2017; ILO, 2021; Lahiri-Dutt, 2011). Out of the more than 40 million individuals involved in ASM, 30% are women (World Bank, 2019). However, when it comes to formal employment in the extractive industries, extractive industry jobs usually comprise not higher than 10% female employment. Globally, resource extraction benefits men more directly than women, although women suffer disproportionately from its negative impacts, such as land destruction, displacement, and environmental pollution (Eftimie et al., 2009). The gendered impacts of mining range from increased sexual violence against women, discriminatory hiring processes, significantly lower wages, and limited employment opportunities for women (Eftimie et al., 2009; Jenkins, 2014). Similarly, in Tanzania, the benefits and risks of resource extraction are unequally distributed among different social groups.

Over the years, in addressing and re-examining the socio-economic and environmental impacts of resource extraction for host mining communities, particularly indigenous and tribal peoples unduly affected by mining activities, Indigenous-focused bargains and arrangements have attracted global recognition. With the adoption of the United Nations Declaration of the Rights of Indigenous Peoples (UNDRIP) in 2007, specific rights were enumerated to safeguard Indigenous rights (ILO, 2021). When it comes to mining in Africa, efforts to foster economic and social inclusivity/equity in extractive development in Africa are enshrined in the Africa Mining Vision (AMV), a collaborative product of the

African Union, African Development Bank, and United Nations Economic Commission for Africa. The AMV addresses gender equity and enumerates specific rights for women in mining by including empowerment in its tentative framework and explicitly calling for women to be included in the extractive sector. The document also urges all members, of which Tanzania is a part, to "initiate empowerment of women through integrating gender equity in mining policies, laws, regulations, standards and codes" (African Union, 2009, p. 32).

Both the Mineral Policy of 2009 and the National Energy Policy of 2015 acknowledged the predominant issue of gender inclusion and women's participation. The National Energy Policy of 2015 makes provision for women's participation in decision-making in the management and development of energy resources from all levels up to the grassroots levels. Currently, Tanzania's mining sector is governed by the 2010 Mining Act. As part of its progressive provisions, the act has included provisions that address gender dimensions, including women's roles and positions within decision-making processes (Majamba, 2021). However, due to the lack of numerical specificity and soft clauses, both the Mining Act of 2010 and the Mining (Local Content) Regulations of 2018 fail to engender action on women or gender issues.

Regarding employment and income, there are evident disparities as men enjoy significant benefits and higher profitability levels than women. However, initiatives to produce greater gender equity in Tanzania's extractive industries have been inadequate. For example, the Tanzania Women Miners' Association (TAWOMA) is a female miners' association founded in Tanzania to address the varied barriers facing women in the mining sector. According to the IGF, despite support from the State Mining Corporation (STAMICO) and African Minerals Geosciences Centre (AMGC) to provide technical training, TAWOMA, the organization has only achieved "isolated initiatives, and it is difficult to discern the contribution to the association as an institution. An integrated program of support with clear vision and objectives needs to be developed to help strengthen these associations, so they can deliver on their mandate" (IGF, 2018, p. 19).

Bradshaw et al. (2017) explore the fluidity and mobility of patriarchal relations of women in attaining economic survival in the extractive industries. In exploring the nuanced conceptualization of patriarchy, Bradshaw et al. (2017) emphasize the importance of not viewing women as mere victims of patriarchal relations or of forming presumptions on patriarchal relations and how they manifest. Rather, gender equality and resource wealth redistribution are enhanced through a deeper understanding of gender roles, supernormal patriarchal relations, and gender dynamics by policymakers to effectively address issues of gender in the extractive industries (Bradshaw et al., 2017).

Technology dependence and the reliance on extensive mechanization and industrialization procedures such as drilling and blasting have also perpetuated an association of mining machinery as men's work and reinforced masculinity in mining while concealing women's livelihoods in mining. A feminist rethinking, according to Lahiri-Dutt (2012), connotes a recognition and critical understanding of women's agency in mining beyond victimhood and as key actors in ASM, protesting and sustaining their communities through mining and also as economic agents outside mining contexts (home and domestic sustenance) (Lahiri-Dutt, 2012, p. 11).

In conceptualizing gender sensitivity in the extractive industries with reference to British Columbia, Sax and Tubb recount the "buzz phase" and expectations generated by the new petroleum find. This phase is usually accompanied by varied socio-economic, health, and environmental expectations, which may drown out voices calling for gender-sensitive approaches (Sax & Tubb, 2021). Also, Daley et al. (2018) note that Tanzania has measures to prohibit discrimination based on sex, gender, or marital status and to mainstream gender perspectives within policy-making in Development Vision 2025, the National Women and Gender Development Policy, and National Strategy for Gender Development of 2000, the 2004 Employment and Labour Relations Act and National Employment Policy of 2008, and the Mkukuta II (2018, 11). Thus, the failure of these policies to achieve greater gender equity in practice underscores the importance of revising existing legislation and policies as well as creating new and specifically targeted interventions to address the insufficiency of gender mainstreaming policies and to achieve better outcomes in one of the country's most important sectors.

Local Content in Tanzania's Extractive Industries

Considering the historically low government share of annual fiscal mineral revenues in many Southern and Eastern African mining regimes (i.e., Zambia, Zimbabwe, Tanzania), a shift from the overreliance on fiscal linkages (taxation) to the enhancement of backward, forward, and spatial linkages through local content development have been recommended to attain sustainable extractive-led growth (Anderson, 2011; Lundstøl et al., 2013). As stated by Tordo et al. (2013), the prime justification behind a state's commitment to LCPs is to increase domestic value addition through import substitution and generate local employment by replacing expatriates with domestic labour. In other words, countering the long-standing disconnect (enclavity) of the resource extraction and its limited employment opportunities requires local content implementation to optimize national value creation, in-country value retention, multiplier spillover effects on the domestic economy, and facilitate crucial backward and forward linkages along all levels of the value chain for the extractive industries (Ablo, 2015; Ovadia, 2014, 2016a, 2016b).

In ensuring the adoption of a more holistic local content strategy, Hilson and Ovadia emphasize the role of state-owned enterprises (SOEs) and state agencies in the public management of MNCs to attain public value creation. They champion a shift from soft and voluntary targets to a more aggressive and robust local content policy (LCP) implementation by SOEs with the involvement of stakeholders, MNCs, and oil communities (Hilson & Ovadia, 2020). Following lessons from the mining sector, the Tanzanian government established a local content strategy through the Natural Gas Policy of 2013, which dedicated a section to local content, and the National Energy Policy of 2015, which is now the government's primary policy document guide to local content in the energy sector (Scurfield et al., 2017). The finalization of the National

Energy Policy was followed by the enactment of the Petroleum Act of 2015.

Although the Petroleum Act, as well as the provisions of the PSAs, contained some more concrete requirements, the government's approach to local content only changed after 2016 with the publication of the Petroleum (Local Content) Regulations of 2017. These regulations set out minimum local content targets for employment of Tanzanians as well as for the use of Tanzanian goods and services (although the definitions of local company and local goods and services as well as the power granted to the Minister of Energy and Minerals to grant exemptions weaken their impact).

In anticipation of the global energy transitions towards decarbonization, LCPs must also encourage linkages to the service sector and focus on transferrable skills. Rather than focusing on local participation in highly specialized areas, it would be more beneficial and economically effective to concentrate on developing skills, goods, and services that are applicable to the non-gas economy or non-oil applications in Tanzania (Scurfield et al., 2017). Consequently, LCPs overlap with economic empowerment policies that are prevalent in many southern African countries, including Tanzania, where already existent WEE strategies exist in isolation from new local content legislations.

Combining Local Content and Economic Empowerment in Tanzania to Achieve a Gender-Sensitive Developmentalist Bargain

Various bargains ranging from climate bargains, indigenous-focused bargains, and post-extractive bargains have been adopted by governments to justify natural resource extraction despite extractivism's association with ecological crises, inequality, and social injustice. Resource extraction revenues are viewed as avenues to broad socio-economic transformation in many Global South countries. The justification for exploration grants lies in the promises of employment opportunities, local content, local procurement, and resource nationalism as a means to garner community engagement in resource governance (Poncian, 2021). Thus, this type of bargain can be thought of as a developmentalist bargain (Bowles and Andrews, Chap. 1 in this volume).

Tanzania's historical context of colonialism and socialist development culminated in its pursuit of economic empowerment strategies. A primary objective is to enable citizens of Tanzania to participate effectively in economic activities across a wide range of economic sectors. Ujamaa socialism and African models of economic development ideologies championed by Julius Nyerere after colonization served as inspirations for economic empowerment in Tanzania. The National Economic Empowerment Act of 2004 (URT, 2004) established the National Economic Empowerment Council (NEEC). NEEC has coordinated important female and youth empowerment programmes in Tanzania. Its Empowerment and Facilitation department carries out several programmes to enhance local participation in economic activities, such as its programme for women working in ASM, a joint project with the TAWOMA. Other youth programmes are also geared towards entrepreneurship training, mentoring, and financial access. However, most of its developmental activities occur in the gas regions of Lindi and Mtwara and popular mining areas such as Mwanza and Geita (Ovadia, 2016c).

Nearing the end of President Kikwete's administration, NEEC was tasked with the mandate of regulating and coordinating local content. A Local Content Department (LCD) in the NEEC was created. However, its efforts on gender and economic empowerment were not integrated into its work on local content. In theory, the LCD coordinates and monitors the government's local content policy with the different agencies and ministries that oversee local content (Ellis & McMillan, 2018). However, in practice, the Ministry of Energy and Minerals (MEM) has taken the lead so far in developing local content policies and laws (Scurfield et al., 2017). Therefore, the confusion over who is coordinating local content is part of why local content is not understood as connected to the core activities and interventions done in the name of economic empowerment, including the many interventions with a gender focus. This disconnect between agencies involved in LCPs and economic empowerment highlights the issue of a "confusing array of regulatory agencies" in the management, regulation, and interaction of efforts involved in LCPs.

Existent in the LCP institutional framework is the lack of clarity on how the different institutions would share responsibility in implementing LCP frameworks (Ovadia, 2017, p. 2).

Several development organizations involved in training and skills development, including the World Bank, United Nations Development Programme, DFID, VSO, and many others, often partner with the NEEC or the VETA. Additionally, these organizations work with the major international oil, gas, and mining companies to align training with the industry needs. NEEC has several programmes related to small and medium-sized enterprise (SME) development; however, SME development is generally considered not to be economic empowerment either and belongs to the Small Industries Development Organization (SIDO). This has often resulted in confusion and inconsistency between different SIDO and VETA when it comes to implementing projects within their specific mandates (Ovadia, 2017). Moreover, in Tanzania, local content experts, in their consultation with government on local content regulation, often overlook WEE initiatives. Historically, gender has consistently been excluded from local content despite the compelling overlap between women empowerment initiatives and local content policies (Ovadia, 2022).

According to the African Natural Resource Centre, "There are many potential benefits in promoting women's economic empowerment within O & G industries, such as more inclusive development, improved welfare for families, greater diversity and productivity, better corporate images of firms as gender champions, as well as more wealth and jobs staying in the host country" (ANRC, 2017, p. 7). Advancing WEE policies in extractive industry supply chains is championed as the best strategy towards the advancement of inclusive development, improved welfare, progressive diversity, and improved local participation. However, on local participation and WEE, Lambin and Nyyssölä have contrarily asserted that in Tanzania, "high levels of female labour force participation do not automatically imply greater levels of gender equality or women's empowerment" (Lambin & Nyyssölä, 2022, p. 3).

The abovementioned observations reveal that the process of increasing women's local participation in the extractive industries requires not only direct employment but also the adoption of a "hard" and "robust, comprehensive" approaches to local content and economic empowerment that requires binding quotas and targets to stimulate women's participation in the sector in a holistic way. Hence, following in the direction of other African countries that have enacted concrete targets and institutional regulations, the Tanzanian government appears to be making a shift from "watered down" "win-win" LCP approaches to more concrete regulations (Scurfield et al., 2017).

The exclusion of a gendered dimension in local content regulation, the lack of institutional clarity, absence of coordination on gender equality issues, the patriarchal customary societal system, and the inability to achieve the mandated female representation quotas on village councils connotes the need for more holistic gender bargains in Tanzania that is premised on the combination of LCPs that are gender-sensitive, and imbibes the already existent WEE in its framework. The design of this extractive bargain would maximize and optimize gendered benefits of resource extraction, correct the regulatory disconnect between WEE and LCPs, and facilitate an enabling environment to enable women to take advantage of set quotas and mandatory targets. In designing a bargain that prioritizes the inclusion of gendered dimensions into LCPs, initiatives ranging from TVET, SMEs development, local procurement of women-led businesses, and targets for direct employment are recommended in the Tanzanian context and explored further below.

A Gender-Sensitive Developmentalist Bargain: Skills Training, SME Development, and Hard Targets for Women's Employment and Procurement from Women-Led Businesses

In Tanzania, some extractive bargains have already been made with ASM miners. The third wave of resource nationalism under Magufuli's administration symbolized a shift from community resistance to resource extraction to a more "people centred natural resource governance" (Poncian, 2021, p. 9). The third wave of resource nationalism was characterized by improved opportunities for ASM miners to participate in shaping extractive policies and governance actively. In December 2016, President Magufuli gave the Vice President instructions to revoke a permit for large-scale mining and grant a mining concession to more than 5000 artisanal miners instead, steps aimed at establishing the ASM industry as a viable poverty alleviation sector for miners (Jacob & Pedersen, 2018; Kinyondo & Huggins, 2019). Despite the populist and antiliberal undertones to resource nationalism under Magufuli, his export bans on mineral concentrates, renegotiation of foreign mining contracts, returning mining blocks to ASM miners, and official presidential meetings with ASM stakeholders did lead to greater participation of ASM stakeholders (Jacob & Pedersen, 2018).

However, while the Tanzanian government has designed several strategies and open direct consultations to gain support from ASM miners for their government extractive policies, the gender dimension of the third wave of resource nationalism was rather inconspicuous. Generally, there was an overconcentration of government extractive bargains on positioning ASM on the same level as large-scale mining (LSM) for increased state fiscal benefits (Poncian, 2021). Poncian reiterated that "Neither do government measures to promote ASM seek to address exploitation, marginalisation and peripherisation of artisanal mining. They are, rather, measures aimed at recapitulating the sector for taxation purposes and for political legitimisation of government policies" (p. 15). Considering heavy mechanization in LSM, and its preference for male employment and workforce (Lahiri-Dutt & Macintyre, 2006), the labour intensiveness of ASM could have resulted in improved gender bargains for women in the ASM industry.

Most of the business training and microfinance projects spearheaded by extractive corporations and NGOs in Tanzania are targeted at women, believing that entrepreneurship can raise women out of poverty (Calkin 2015; McCarthy 2017, as cited in Lange & Wyndham, 2021). In the study on Mining for Equity, Eftimie et al. (2009) have demonstrated that women's empowerment can be promoted either economically or socially through literacy programmes, vocational training, business skills development, start-up grants for women, improved microcredit accessibility, and financial services amongst many others (Eftimie et al., 2009). In this vein, Mutagwaba et al. (2018, p. 82) in exploring education and WEE awareness in ASM in Tanzania indicated that "[s]kills and knowledge on entrepreneurship, investment and diversification into non-mining sectors would enhance women's roles in the community by promoting local content," and this can be championed through the NEEC facilitating partnerships with educational and vocational institutes through the VETA. However, in Tanzania, education, vocational training, skills, and SME development policies aimed at women's empowerment are not always understood as an integral component of LCPs (Ovadia, 2017).

Nonetheless, in most cases of the economies of sub-Saharan countries where informality is endemic (surpassing 70% in certain sectors in Tanzania), and where women are overrepresented in the informal sector despite the prevalent gender inequality, enhancing skills training through technical and vocational training among women is indicated to have double effects. These positive double effects include improving women's participation in informal employment, increasing female earnings, and offsetting gendered income inequality (Joseph & Leyaro, 2019; NBS, 2014, p. 46). According to Joseph and Leyaro (2019), TVET training "significantly improves males as well as females chances of entering into formal employment while at the same reduces their probability of working in informal, agriculture or being unemployed" (p. 1). Further evidence in support of TVET can be found in Ghana, where TVET is viewed as a critical social equalizer and a vital tool for women's empowerment. Through global policies and national policies initiated by the Government, such as Gender Responsive Skills and Community Development Project (GRSCDP), Women in Technical Education Department (WITED), and Girls Education Unit (GEU), a gender strategy and gender equality are being factored in all aspects of training in TVET institutions to address female unemployment (Morgan & Centers, 2013).

Few TVET institutions in Tanzania can accommodate women andgirls. This further exacerbates the already existent gaps in opportunities for women by inhibiting the accessibility of vocational education for women (Joseph & Leyaro, 2019). Thus, given that Article 12 of the Petroleum (local content) Regulation of 2017 already requires employment and training opportunities that would be provided by men and women, a gendered dimension can be inculcated in local content sub plans in Tanzania.

Aside from vocational and technical skill development, SMEs are a specific area of action for WEE and gender mainstreaming in government and other non-government assistance programmes. Improving local participation and building linkages between the extractive industries and the domestic economy should result in financial support and capacity building for SMEs to satisfy the goods and services needed at various levels of the extractive value chain.

When it comes to SME development in Tanzania, donors have already prioritized providing opportunities for women by spearheading initiatives such as the Tanzania Local Enterprise Development (TLED) projects. The project, mainly based in the oil hubs of Lindi and Mtwara, was launched in 2016 to provide gender-sensitive support to SMEs and their employees, increase the confidence of female entrepreneurs, and provide them with new markets. Through the TLED, Voluntary Service Overseas (VSO) plays an important role in developing skills and assisting small businesses in the oil, gas, and mining industries (Ovadia, 2016c). Although the TLED is a worthwhile initiative from the WEE standpoint, government officials responsible for local content do not generally view initiatives like this as local content (including NEEC, which is a partner in the project). Progressively, some policy circles have begun to shift their viewpoints on this issue. In their report on WEE, the ANRC stated that LCPs are an important tool for encouraging WEE and that "[t]he local content policy should identify specific entry points for SME engagement, including those sectors where women-owned firms are often found (hospitality services and retail trade)" (ANRC, 2017, p. 20).

Despite the ability of SMEs to form the basis of local procurement and supplier development programmes in Tanzania, Hansen (2013) reveals that SMEs are weakly developed and display the "missing middle" characteristics common in other African countries mainly due to the inexistent conducive business environment. The abandonment of the Barrick supplier development programme was an attestation of the inability of local suppliers (SMEs) to develop sustainable businesses from linkages and overcome the challenging national business climate (Hansen, 2013). Ownership and control of assets are critical constraints of women-based SMEs. Inaccessibility to finance also prevents women-led SMEs from participating in supply chains. According to Perks and Shultz (2020,

p. 381), an additional difficulty for women-led SMEs trying to enter supply chains is that they are typically low-profit investments with limited assets and capital. They have unique challenges in obtaining finance and are more vulnerable to market variability.

As have many developing countries, Tanzania has recognized the importance of female entrepreneurs in achieving economic growth. In response to the recognition, the government of Tanzania has established several policies and programmes aimed at increasing the start-up rates and performance of SMEs owned by women. Among them are women's banks, loan schemes, and agro-processing clusters developed by organizations such as SIDO (Isaga, 2018). However, still pertinent is Tanzania's cultural and customary practices that have unduly impacted the development of SMEs, particularly women-based SMEs. Socio-cultural impediments, financial performance, spouse interference, inadequate education and training, and customary land tenure systems retrogress women-led SMEs. It is perhaps due to these added challenges that the ANRC (2017) also argues that "[g]overnments and O[il] & G[as] companies could consider procurement provisions and policies to support SMEs, local businesses and women-owned firms" and explores the possibility of utilizing oil & gas companies' local procurement practices to create links between SMEs and the industry, including women-owned SMEs (p. 25).

Job creation, local procurement of goods and services, technology transfer, employment, and training and capacity building of local SMEs lie at the core of local content implementation and are requisite policies in attaining multiplier spillover effects from the enclaved extractive industries. While extractive bargains have been championed for ASM workers through resource nationalism policies, exclusion and marginalization are specific to women in the local community who relied on ASM before they were evicted from their land by transnational mining companies (Lauwo, 2018). As mining extraction and processing is generally masculine, large transnational mining companies in Tanzania often employ predominantly male forces, and job security for women in the mining sector is non-existent (Lauwo, 2018). When it comes to Tanzania's oil and gas industry, less than 20% of jobs are held by women, and women hold less than 10% of jobs requiring vocational training despite the designation of the First Schedule of Petroleum (Local Content) Regulations seeking 80% semi-skilled, and 100% unskilled workers localization within ten years.

The extractive industries generate indirect jobs in mining communities through local procurement and the development of businesses to service mines. In attesting to local procurement as a core component of local content, the ILO (2021) report asserts that most mining jobs are created by local procurement, which allows SMEs to provide services and manufacture inputs, creating employment spillovers for both men and women (ILO, 2021). Local procurement therefore provides avenues for large-scale mining to provide increased assistance and support for women-led SMEs in communities where extraction takes place. Through mechanisms of utilizing gender-responsive procurement, they can support SMEs owned and led by women by leveraging their buying power and supply chains (ILO, 2021). Commensurate with this, the IFC (2013) points out that large corporations stand to benefit from creating opportunities for women and young people from disadvantaged backgrounds. In local procurement, diversifying supplies to include under-represented groups improves quality and services and increases competition while increasing efficiency in the supply value chain (IFC, 2013). However, according to the Responsible Mining Index Report on 38 large mining companies' policies and practices globally, it was revealed that "only a small minority of companies take proactive measures to include women in their local procurement support measures, and without such measures, women will most likely be excluded" (RMF, 2020 as cited in ILO, 2021, p. 30).

In actuality, Tanzania's regulations only encourage CSR and a preference for local instead of advancing mandatory targets and policies (Nwapi & Andrews, 2018; URT, 2010, 2015). Thus, in examining the barriers to women's economic inclusion in Tanzania, with emphasis on barriers to markets and technology, Idris (2018, p. 12) highlighted that "although information about participation in government procurement is availed via government websites, there are currently no efforts to ensure that women entrepreneurs participate in the bidding/procurement process." Focus group meetings with blast committee members in selected mining communities in Tanzania also revealed that, "contrary to the mining companies' claim to promote local procurement and create employment, there is a lack of enterprising activities in local communities to support, promote or create employment for women who originally depended on artisanal mining" (as cited in Lauwo, 2018, p. 701). Therefore, it is clear that significantly more work is needed to create an approach to resource extraction in Tanzania that is both developmentalist and designed to promote greater gender equality.

Conclusion

The third wave of resource nationalism in Tanzania was characterized by extractivist policies, legislations, and meaningful engagements of ASM stakeholders to promote better extractive bargains for poor ASM miners. However, the absence of holistic gender approaches and the isolation of local content and WEE strategies has resulted in a system of contradictory bargains in Tanzania's extractive industries, where some elements of progressive bargains are being attained (TVET, SME development, local procurement, direct employment) and implemented while other government regulations/policies related to local content operate in a contradictory and opposite direction. The overlapping institutional authorities granted the regulatory power to implement local content and WEE, consisting of different ministries, private entities, and varied international donors, has lead to coordination difficulties, policy inconsistencies, and confusion in the country's extractive gender policy direction. Company initiatives, be it procurement plans or company CSR initiatives, are insufficient without the "hard" and "holistic" approach to stimulate practical action and implementation. A holistic approach to local content and gender equality requires all stakeholders to work together in one direction, guided by concrete targets and requirements. In South Africa, the 2002 Mining Charter Policy that included a 10% quota of women in the mining workforce by 2009 is indicated to have "proven successful, with South Africa now boasting some of the highest rates of female participation in mining in the world" (Perks & Schulz, 2020, p. 387). Fortunately, in Tanzania, there are precedents of affirmative action policies, and gender quotas to increase women's participation. This approach must be replicated across all extractive industry policies.

The disconnect of new local content policy frameworks and already existing WEE programmes has robbed Tanzania of an opportunity to create progressive gender bargains in its extractive industries and exacerbated the gender-based risks suffered in these deeply masculinized cultures of extraction. Consequently, the country's LCPs do not sufficiently address gender issues. WEE policies such as TVET, SME development, direct employment targets, and local procurement from local female suppliers are pursued separately, even though collectively, WEE strategies are critical areas in the promotion of local content and local participation in the extractive industries. By combining local content and WEE to capture the crucial strategies of TVET and SME development, among many others, local content in Tanzania would assume a more gender-sensitive stance and achieve much more significant strides towards gender equality in its extractive industries. The success of such a gender-sensitive developmentalist extractive bargain in Tanzania would require a new holistic approach that recognizes contemporary LCPs and the long-existing WEE strategies as part of one coherent policy objective.

References

Ablo, A. D. (2015). Local content and participation in Ghana's oil and gas industry: Can enterprise development make a difference? *The Extractive Industries and Society, 2*(2), 320–327. https://doi.org/10.1016/j.exis.2015.02.003

African Natural Resources Centre (ANRC). (2017). *Women's Economic Empowerment in Oil and Gas Industries in Africa*. African Development Bank.

African Union. (2009). *Africa Mining Vision, February 2009*. African Union Secretariat.

Anderson, C. (2011). *Creating a Legislative Framework to Govern Mining in Zimbabwe*. Revenue Watch.

Bank of Tanzania (2020/21). ANNUAL REPORT. Retrieved March 27th, 2022, from https://www.bot.go.tz/Publications/Regular/Annual%20Report/en/2021122922483700.pdf.

Bradshaw, S., Linneker, B., & Overton, L. (2017). Extractive industries as sites of supernormal profits and supernormal patriarchy? *Gender & Development, 25*(3), 439–454. https://doi.org/10.1080/13552074.2017.1379780

Daley, E., Lanz, K., Mhinda, A., Driscoll, Z., Ndakaru, J., Grabham, J., Kereri, E., & Mbise, E. (2018). Gender, Land and Mining in Pastoralist Tanzania. WOLTS Research Report No.2. *Mokoro Ltd & HakiMadini.*

Eftimie, A., Heller, K., & Strongman, J. (2009). Gender dimensions of the extractive industries: mining for equity.

Ellis, M., & McMillan, M. S. (2018). *Optimal local content for extractive industries: How can policies best create benefits for Tanzania?* (No. 2018/133). WIDER Working Paper. 10.35188/unu-wider/2018/575-6

Hansen, M. W. (2013). *Reaping the rewards of foreign direct investment: Linkages between extractive MNCs and local firms in Tanzania* (No. 2013: 22). DIIS Working paper.

Hansen, M. W., Buur, L., Mette Kjær, A., & Therkildsen, O. (2016). The economics and politics of local content in African extractives: lessons from Tanzania, Uganda and Mozambique. *In Forum for Development Studies* (Vol. 43, No. 2, pp. 201-228). Routledge. https://doi.org/10.1080/08039410.2015.1089319

Hilson, A. E., & Ovadia, J. S. (2020). Local content in developing and middle-income countries: towards a more holistic strategy. *The Extractive Industries and Society, 7*(2), 253–262. https://doi.org/10.1016/j.exis.2020.04.014

Idris, I. (2018). *Barriers to Women's Economic Inclusion in Tanzania, K4D Helpdesk Report.* Institute of Development Studies.

IFC. (2013). A guide to getting started in local procurement. IFC in collaboration with Engineers Against Poverty. Washington D.C.: Retrieved July 20, 2022, from http://engineersagainstpoverty.org/wp-content/uploads/2018/07/IFC-EAP_Local_Procurement_Guide.pdf

Intergovernmental Forum on Mining, Minerals, Metals and Sustainable Development (IGF). (2018). Women in Artisanal and Small-Scale Mining: Challenges and opportunities for greater participation. Winnipeg: IISD. Retrieved July 20, 2022, from https://www.iisd.org/publications/report/women-artisanal-and-small-scale-mining-challenges-and-opportunities-greater

International Labour Organization (ILO) (2021). Women in mining Towards gender equality. Sectoral Policies Department. Retrieved July 20, 2022, from https://www.ilo.org/wcmsp5/groups/public/---ed_dialogue/---sector/documents/publication/wcms_821061.pdf

Isaga, N. (2018). Start-up motives and challenges facing female entrepreneurs in Tanzania. *International Journal of Gender and Entrepreneurship*. https://doi.org/10.1108/ijge-02-2018-0010

Jacob, T., & Pedersen, R. H. (2018). New resource nationalism? Continuity and change in Tanzania's extractive industries. *The Extractive Industries and Society, 5*(2), 287–292. https://doi.org/10.1016/j.exis.2018.02.001

Jenkins, K. (2014). Women, mining and development: An emerging research agenda. *The Extractive Industries and Society, 1*(2), 329–339. https://doi.org/10.1016/j.exis.2014.08.004

Joseph, C., & Leyaro, V. (2019). Gender differential effects of technical and vocational training: Empirical evidence for Tanzania. *Journal of African Development, 23*(2), 294–321. https://doi.org/10.5325/jafrideve.23.2.0294

Kambi, B., & Kambi, M. (2017). Local Content Agenda: The Role of Institution Theory on Policy and Practical Challenges in Local Procurement Practice by Mining Entities in Tanzania. *Humanities and Social Sciences Letters, 5*(1), 1–10. https://doi.org/10.18488/journal.73/2017.5.1/73.1.1.10

Kinyondo, A., & Huggins, C. (2019). Resource nationalism in Tanzania: Implications for artisanal and small-scale mining. *The Extractive Industries and Society, 6*(1), 181–189. https://doi.org/10.1016/j.exis.2018.08.005

Kweka, J. (2009). The role of TNCs in the extractive industry of the United Republic of Tanzania. *Transnational Corporations, 18*(1), 93–123.

Lahiri-Dutt, K. (2011). The megaproject of mining: a feminist critique. In *Engineering earth* (pp. 329–351). Springer. https://doi.org/10.1007/978-90-481-9920-4_20

Lahiri-Dutt, K. (2012). Digging women: towards a new agenda for feminist critiques of mining. *Gender, Place & Culture, 19*(2), 193–212. https://doi.org/10.1080/0966369x.2011.572433

Lahiri-Dutt, K., & Macintyre, M. (Eds.). (2006). *Women miners in developing countries: Pit women and others*. Ashgate Publishing, Ltd. https://doi.org/10.4324/9781315233734

Lambin, R., & Nyyssölä, M. (2022). *Employment Policy in Mainland Tanzania: What's in It for Women?'* (No. wp-2022-67). World Institute for Development Economic Research (UNU- WIDER). https://doi.org/10.35188/unu-wider/2022/198-3

Lange, S., & Kinyondo, A. (2016). Resource nationalism and local content in Tanzania: experiences from mining and consequences for the petroleum sector. *The Extractive Industries and Society, 3*(4), 1095–1104. https://doi.org/10.1016/j.exis.2016.09.006

Lange, S., & Wyndham, V. (2021). Gender, regulation, and corporate social responsibility in the extractive sector: The case of Equinor's social investments in Tanzania. In *Women's Studies International Forum* (Vol. 84, p. 102434). Pergamon. https://doi.org/10.1016/j.wsif.2020.102434

Lauwo, S. (2018). Challenging masculinity in CSR disclosures: Silencing of women's voices in Tanzania's mining industry. *Journal of Business Ethics, 149*(3), 689–706. https://doi.org/10.1007/s10551-016-3047-4

Lundstøl, O., Raballand, G., & Nyirongo, F. (2013). Low government revenue from the mining sector in Zambia and Tanzania: fiscal design, technical capacity or political will? *Technical Capacity or Political Will.* https://doi.org/10.2139/ssrn.2411451

Majamba, H. (2021). Engaging Women in the Extractive Sector: A Review of Tanzania's Policy and Legislative Framework. *Tanzania Journal of Development Studies, 18*(1), 29–44.

Mengi, R.A. (2013). Local participation in the oil & gas industry in Tanzania. Paper Presented at the 2nd Tanzanian Oil and Gas Conference 23–24 October, Dar es Salaam Published in the Guardian 25.10.2013.

Morgan, G., & Centers, G. L. (2013). *Women in TVET: Input into Ghana's COTVET Gender Strategy Dialogue*. Global Learning Center.

Mutagwaba, W., Tindyebwa, J. B., Makanta, V., Kaballega, D., & Maeda, G. (2018). *Artisanal and small-scale mining in Tanzania–Evidence to inform an 'action dialogue'*. International Institute for Environment and Development.

National Bureau of Statistics (NBS) [Tanzania]. (2014). *Tanzania Integrated Labour Force Survey 2014*. NBS.

Nwapi, C., & Andrews, N. (2018). A "New" Developmental State in Africa? Evaluating Recent State Interventions vis-à-vis Resource Extraction in Kenya, Tanzania, and Rwanda. *Journal of Sustainable Development Law. MJSDL-RDDDM, 13*(2), 223–267.

Ovadia, J. S. (2014). Local content and natural resource governance: The cases of Angola and Nigeria. *The Extractive Industries and Society, 1*(2), 137–146.

Ovadia, J. S. (2016a). The petro-developmental state in Africa: Making oil work in Angola, Nigeria, and the Gulf of Guinea.

Ovadia, J. S. (2016b). Local content policies and petro-development in sub-Saharan Africa: A comparative analysis. *Resources Policy, 49*, 20–30. https://doi.org/10.1016/j.resourpol.2016.04.003

Ovadia, J. S. (2016c). *Local Content Situational Analysis in Tanzania in the Mining and Gas Sectors*. African Development Bank.

Ovadia, J. S. (2017). *Local Content in Tanzania's Gas and Minerals Sectors: Who Regulates?* CMI Brief.

Ovadia, J. S. (2022). Addressing gender inequality through employment and procurement: Local content in Tanzania's emerging gas industry. *The Extractive Industries and Society, 9*, 101028. https://doi.org/10.1016/j.exis.2021.101028

Perks, R., & Schulz, K. (2020). Gender in oil, gas and mining: An overview of the global state-of- play. *The Extractive Industries and Society, 7*(2), 380–388. https://doi.org/10.1016/j.exis.2020.04.010

Poncian, J. (2021). Resource nationalism and community engagement in extractive resource governance: insights from Tanzania. *Review of African Political Economy, 48*(170), 529–551. https://doi.org/10.1080/03056244.2021.1953975

Responsible Mining Foundation (RMF) (2020) Gender Inequality Runs Deep in Mining. Retrieved June 26, 2022, from https://www.responsiblemining-foundation.org/app/uploads/EN_Research-Insight-Gender-Inequality-June-2020.pdf

Sax, M., & Tubb, D. (2021). The buzz phase of resource extraction: Liquefied natural gas in Kitimat, British Columbia. *The extractive industries and society, 8*(3), 100938. https://doi.org/10.1016/j.exis.2021.100938

Scurfield, T., Woodroffe, N., & Olan'g, S. (2017). *Localizing Tanzania's gas sector: Determining optimal policies for an emerging producer* (pp. 1–21). Natural Resource Government Institute.

Tordo, S., Warner, M., Manzano, O., & Anouti, Y. (2013). *Local content policies in the oil and gas sector.* World Bank Publications. https://doi.org/10.1596/978-0-8213-9931-6

URT. (2004). *National Economic Empowerment Act.* United Republic of Tanzania.

URT. (2010). *The Mining Act (No. 14 of 2010).* MEM.

URT. (2015). Tanzania Mining Industry Investor's Guide. Dar es Salaam, Tanzania: MEM. Jun 2015.

World Bank Group (2019). State of the Artisanal and Small-Scale Mining Sector. Retrieved July 7, 2022, from https://delvedatabase.org/resources/state-of-the-artisanal-and-smallscale-mining-sector.

12

Contradictions of Privatized Developmentalist Bargains: Offshore Petroleum Extraction and Corporate Social Responsibility in Ghana

Moses Adjei and Nathan Andrews

Introduction

Ghana's discovery of oil in commercial quantities in 2007 and its subsequent production in 2010 have revived debates on the nexus between natural resource extraction and national development (Hilson, 2007; Oppong, 2018; Ovadia, 2012; Watts, 2004). This stems from the fact that while there have been fears of a possible resource curse from the experiences of countries like Nigeria, the experiences of countries such as Canada and Norway inspire hope for economic development, revenue

M. Adjei (✉)
School of Science and the Environment, Memorial University of Newfoundland, Corner Brook, NL, Canada
e-mail: amoses@grenfell.mun.ca

N. Andrews
Department of Political Science, McMaster University, Hamilton, ON, Canada
e-mail: nandrews@mcmaster.ca

P. Bowles, N. Andrews (eds.), *Extractive Bargains*, Frontiers of Globalization,
https://doi.org/10.1007/978-3-031-32172-6_12

generation and employment, among others (Ablo, 2015; Adunbi, 2020; Aryeetey & Ackah, 2018). Thus, the Ghanaian state has sought to justify ongoing extractive activities by appealing to its ability to support other goals such as social equity and economic development. This process of justification is what Bowles and Andrews (Chap. 1 in this volume) consider to be a quintessential aspect of the 'extractive bargains' that states promise various stakeholders in order to gain legitimacy in the host country of which Ghana is no exception. For instance, upon the discovery of oil, Ghana was thrown into a state of ecstasy as then-President John Agyekum Kufuor indicated as follows:

> *Even without oil, we are doing so well. With oil as a shot in the arm, we're going to fly. … My joy is that I'll go down in history as the president under whose watch oil was found to turn the economy of Ghana around for the better. (*BBC, 2007*)*

The remarks above show the high expectations and hope for economic development that the oil and gas sector was expected to bring to the country. Like the president, most Ghanaians especially inhabitants of the Western region were optimistic about the developmental potential of the oil, in terms of job creation, infrastructural development and improvement of their livelihoods to tackle some of the region's developmental setbacks (Oteng-Ababio, 2018; Obeng-Odoom, 2012, 2015). In addition to the government's promises to spur national development and fulfill community expectations, the petroleum extraction companies also promised jobs, infrastructural development and hospitality facilities especially for the 'host' communities (Andrews, 2013; DW documentary, 2020; Ovadia et al., 2020). However, to date the promises and expectations have not been realized. Rather, extant research shows that the *black gold* sector has had deleterious consequences on coastal communities and their livelihoods, especially fishing—an important occupation of the country's coastal population (Adjei & Overå, 2019; Obeng-Odoom, 2014; Ackah-Baidoo, 2013; Andrews et al., 2022).

Stemming from the limitations of state-backed extractive bargains, a key bargaining tool entailing Corporate Social Responsibility (CSR) programmes can be highlighted in Ghana and other resource-rich developing economies (Frynas, 2005; Hilson, 2007; Andrews, 2019; Adjei, 2021). Unlike the typical state-backed bargaining strategies, CSR refers to programmes and projects pursued by extractive companies to give back to society with emphasis on communities in close proximity to their operations as a way of addressing the negative impacts of resource extraction (Frynas, 2005; Hilson, 2007). Like most African countries, CSR programmes in Ghana are generally voluntary and often focus on community development through social, economic and environmental programmes (Osei-Kojo & Andrews, 2020; Adjei, 2021).

Quite different from other contributions in this volume, this chapter presents a case study that showcases extractive bargains beyond the state-society level. By introducing the idea of CSR into an understanding of extractive bargains, we hope to make a unique contribution that underscores the intricacies of a (quasi) privatized developmentalist bargain or what may be considered as 'privatized developmentalism'. Within this framework, the state is still responsible for making grand justifications for why extraction is needed. The difference, however, is that corporations are the main actors who are left with the extraction-related developmental outcomes promised by the state given that corporations themselves are eager to embed themselves in the societal space as a way to obtain a social licence to operate (Andrews, 2019, 2021). CSR therefore becomes a mechanism of intervention and a bargaining chip that often promises more than can be delivered in practice. This complexity surrounding the state- corporate-society relation is worth examining within the context of extractive bargains both at the analytical and normative levels. In the subsequent section, we provide a brief description of the extractive (developmentalist) bargain under focus and its connections with CSR. We then provide a brief account of the research methods for the study, which is followed by brief descriptions of interaction involving three main stakeholder groups in Ghana's offshore petroleum sector. The next section draws upon some primary data to contextualize our understanding of a (quasi) privatized developmentalist bargain, followed by concluding reflections.

Extractive Bargains and CSR: A Case of Privatized Developmentalism?

According to Bowles and Andrews (Chap. 1 in this volume), extractive bargains involve different approaches used by respective states to justify the continuation or intensification of natural resource extraction activities by highlighting the ability of the extractive sector to support economic development and other broader societal goals. Thus, the main goal of the bargaining process is to win support and shape the actions of different stakeholder groups including corporations, Indigenous groups, classes, social movements or 'public opinion' about natural resource extraction or conservation. This suggests that the concept of extractive bargains is largely state-centred, thereby pointing to the active role played by the state in terms of decision-making and policy framework around the resource-development nexus.

Amid the failures of Structural Adjustment Programmes (SAPs) to deal with the developmental needs of most African countries coupled with the 'miraculous' developmental experiences of state-centred East Asian states such as Singapore, Hong Kong and South Korea, many African countries have begun shifting towards regaining control over aspects of their development including the energy sector (Andrews & Nwapi, 2018). For instance, following the East Asian Tiger analogy, President John Agyekum Kufour touted Ghana to be an '*African Tiger*'—a development giant on the continent by virtue of its newly found oil and gas resources (BBC, 2007; Adjei, 2017). Beyond such statements, African states have shifted towards legislations and policies that advance developmentalism—culminating in what Ovadia refers to as a resurgence of 'petro-developmental states' on the continent (Ovadia, 2016). The Africa Mining Vision (AMV) which was promulgated in 2009 and its subsequent action plan in 2011 is one of the key policies aimed at re-centralizing the state in Africa's development (Andrews & Nwapi, 2018). Although AMV appears to focus on mining, this vision document has set the agenda to ensure greater state participation in the development of all mineral resources (Mkandawire, 2001).

The above-mentioned petro-developmentalism has been promoted primarily through local content policy (LCP) provisions in the energy sector, which seek to enhance local participation in the sector by promoting the use of local goods, services and expertise (see Andrews & Nwapi, 2017). The overall aim is to ensure that Ghanaians benefit directly from the petroleum sector in a manner that somewhat aligns with the aspirations of leading political figures (Ablo, 2015). To facilitate the active participation of Ghanaian businesses in the oil and gas sector, the Enterprise Development Centre (EDC) was established in 2013 through a collaboration between the government and partners of the Jubilee Oil Field (Ablo, 2015). The state-backed Public Interest and Accountability Committee (PIAC) was also established to ensure accountability and transparency in the use of petroleum revenue (Graham et al., 2019). In some sense, PIAC serves as a mechanism for elite instrumentalization of promised developmental outputs from resource extraction by showing that not only is the state taking practical policy steps than has been the case hitherto but it is also seeking to ensure resource revenue is used to the benefit of the general populace.

Notwithstanding, state-level developmentalist discourses do not often translate into the exercise of meaningful agency in practice. This is particularly true in the African context where states are unable (sometimes unwilling) to execute their stated developmental plans, making it largely ideological rather than practical. For instance, studies have shown that LCP provisions in Ghana have resulted in 'local elite' capture instead of supporting state promises around broad-based developmental benefits (Adjei, 2021; Andrews & Nwapi, 2017, 2018). In instances where locals are employed in the petroleum sector, offshore labour practices and relations show new forms of carceral spaces being created to 'depotentialise' the local labour force (see Ablo, 2022, p. 8).

Mkandawire identifies two components of the developmental state: structural and ideological (Mkandawire, 2001). The structural component highlights a state's capacity (within the context of institutional, technical, administrative and political set-up) to effectively implement its developmentalist policies. The ideological component points to a state that is 'developmentalist' in its orientation, particularly one that conceives its core mission to be that of ensuring economic development but lacks the requisite capacity, human resources or even political will to advance the said agenda (Andrews & Nwapi, 2018). In Ghana, despite President Kufour's optimism and the ambitious statements made about Ghana's developmental potential upon the discovery of oil and gas, a few years after the commencement of commercial oil production shows that the impacts of oil exploitation had largely failed to be translated into developmental gains (Oppong, 2018; Ackah-Baidoo, 2013). Rather, studies show that spending patterns of the state have changed (Aryeetey & Ackah, 2018). For instance, spending from the government's oil revenue, which is dedicated to longer-term development programmes in strategic areas, such as agriculture, is rather diverted for shorter-term political goals (see Aryeetey & Ackah, 2018).

The above discussion confirms Routley's (2014) conclusion that the developmental state concept in Africa often works more as a buzzword than a real model. This assertion questions what may be considered as a developmentalist bargain according to the framework proposed by Bowles and Andrews (Chap. 1 in this volume). To complicate the framing even further, the introduction of Corporate Social Responsibility (CSR) tends to shift the pendulum of a state-society bargain out of the hands of the state into those of corporations who are then expected to deliver societal goods and services. As the findings below show, various developmental projects spanning from education to infrastructure among others have been undertaken by extractive companies through their CSR programmes. This presents a serious contradiction in terms of what state-society bargains mean in practice and how extractive bargains generally in this context involve some degree of 'scapegoating' for the limited development visible in host communities. In other words, the societal embeddedness that CSR programming results in serve as a function of corporate benevolence in a manner that augments the corporation's goal of being viewed as a 'good neighbour' or 'corporate citizen' while also permitting the state to delegate (or entirely neglect) its core developmental functions. This is what we characterize as a quintessential aspect of 'privatized developmentalism'. The so-called developmentalist bargain is therefore suspicious and the messy intermingling of state, corporate and societal forces in the Ghanaian example points us to its contradictory position on the normative spectrum of extractive bargains. The empirical section to follow expands further on this framing.

Methods

This chapter is the outcome of long-term research on Ghana's petroleum sector examining how CSR programmes and projects undertaken by petroleum companies have transformed the lives of coastal communities. The study involved a series of qualitative data collection from Axim, Sekondi-Takoradi and Accra between May 2014 and December 2019. Data were produced through in-depth interviews, informal discussions and participant observation. In-depth interviews with a total of 39 participants were conducted using interview guides. Twelve of the participants were fishers (canoe owners, crew members and fish traders) and seven were traditional leaders in Axim. In addition, three petroleum company officials, fourteen government officials and three officials from civil society groups were interviewed in Axim, Sekondi-Takoradi and Accra. The informants were selected through purposive and snowball sampling. The data consisted of audio-recorded transcribed interviews and field notes that were analysed through a process of coding and text analysis. In addition to the series of fieldwork, official documents, reports, newspaper articles and web pages were analysed.

Main Stakeholders in Ghana's Offshore Petroleum Sector

The key stakeholders actively engaged in Ghana's offshore petroleum extraction include the petroleum companies (e.g., Jubilee Partners), local community groups (e.g., fisherfolk) and the national/regional/local governmental regulatory authorities. In this section, we show that the different stakeholder groups have different interests in the petroleum sector and the marine space where the resource is extracted, which leads them to employ different forms of bargaining to pursue their interests. The first stakeholder group to briefly examine is state regulatory bodies and institutions. The Ghanaian state's interest in developing its petroleum sector began in the 1980s with the establishment of the Ghana National Petroleum Corporation (GNPC) as the central body responsible for managing the sector (Mohan et al., 2018). Upon oil discovery in 2007, more robust regulatory mechanisms, policies and institutions emerged including the Petroleum Commission (Act 821 of 2011)—which resulted in the transformation of GNPC into a state-owned oil company—the Petroleum Revenue Management Act (PRMA) (Act 815 of 2011), a local content bill (LI2204 of 2013) and PIAC which was established under the PRMA.

On paper, these state institutions do contribute to transparency and accountability, but a critical scrutiny of their roles shows major deficiencies as alluded to in earlier sections of this chapter. According to Mohan et al. (2018, p. 7), one of the reasons for such structural deficiencies is the 'bipartisan nature of Ghanaian political power that underpins them and the need to secure informal patronage networks' which results in these institutions being undermined. The state institutions are hampered by limited resources to effectively monitor and ensure compliance with the offshore petroleum extraction rules and ocean space utilization (Adjei, 2017; Obeng-Odoom, 2014). A study by Adjei (2021) shows that due to limited resources, state regulatory bodies mostly rely on the equipment provided by oil companies such as speedboats for monitoring the activities of the same companies offshore. He concludes that such overreliance of the state on companies coupled with limited onsite checks are likely to lead to faulty assumptions and incorrect decisions by government regarding the potential impact of petroleum extraction. Additionally, it elevates the corporation as a key development actor which tends to take the place of the state in delivering needed societal goods.

Aryeetey and Ackah (2018) also suggest that one of the biggest challenges in negotiating oil agreements is how to take adequate care of the interests of host communities which may face challenges such as pollution, loss of livelihood, increased living cost and sometimes death resulting from exploration and extractive activities. If these challenges are not adequately addressed, they may result in the conflicts and tensions found in many developing economies including Ghana (Osei-Kojo & Andrews, 2020; Adjei & Overå, 2019; Ackah-Baidoo, 2013). Despite its developmentalist orientation, the point here is that the structural deficiencies of Ghana's petroleum legislation suggest that these regulations are largely ideological with limited real developmental impact at the national and local levels. This notwithstanding, understanding the role of the state in petroleum extraction is critical as it determines the extent and forms of extractive activities which take place within the country (Chagnon et al., 2022).

Secondly, local communities are key players in the petroleum sector as they are often considered the custodians of the natural resource (Hilson, 2007). In Ghana's offshore petroleum extraction, the 'local community' is also known as the 'zone of influence' (Ackah-Baidoo, 2013, p. 153). It consists of the six coastal districts of the Western region demarcated as areas likely to be negatively impacted by exploration and extraction activities and in the specific case of accidents. By virtue of their historical dependence on the sea for livelihood, the small-scale fisherfolk especially in the South-western coast of Ghana are important stakeholders in Ghana's offshore petroleum extraction and bargaining processes. Although the petroleum and fishery industries have different resource interests, the activities occur within the same ocean space where fishers fish for livelihood and petroleum companies explore and extract petroleum resources for profits. The general state-level rhetoric around what may be regarded as a developmentalist extractive bargain can be placed within the context of local contestations, offshore conflicts and resistance to the activities of petroleum extractive companies (see Ackah-Baidoo, 2013; Adjei & Overå, 2019; Andrews et al., 2022). For instance, most coastal fishing communities blame offshore petroleum companies for the dwindling fish stock in the ocean (Owusu & Adjei, 2021). These contestations point to the government's inability to fulfil its promises of job creation, improved livelihood and economic prosperity to Ghanaians as indicated in the early years of petroleum extraction. Amid these contestations and tensions, the CSR of petroleum companies is considered an important compensatory mechanism to ensure that the potential negative impacts of petroleum extraction especially on coastal communities are minimized.

Offshore petroleum companies represent the third group of stakeholders to be briefly discussed here. The main offshore petroleum companies in Ghana include Tullow Oil Ghana Limited (40%), Kosmos Energy (20%) and the remaining 40% share for other companies such as Anadarko Petroleum, GNPC, Aker Energy and Petro SA (Adjei & Overå, 2019; Tullow Oil, 2015). Through the GNPC, the Ghanaian state is not only a regulator, but also a key player in the petroleum sector. In general, petroleum extractive activities are a major source of revenue to the government through exports, royalties and taxations. A developmentalist bargain may be touted based on the expectation that the more the resource rents emerging from taxes and royalties accrue, for instance, the likelier it would be for the country to attain its socio-economic objectives. Yet instead of direct state-society bargain, we see CSR as serving as an important bargaining chip not only for the companies involved but also the state primarily due to the state's limited capacity relative to the international oil companies or unwillingness to address developmental needs and increasing local agitations, resistance and conflicts (Adjei, 2021; Andrews & Siakwah, 2020).

Some mainstream scholarship reinforces the idea that CSR activities by extractive companies can (and probably should) support developmental efforts in host countries especially in areas such as education, health and other general community infrastructure (Dartey-Baah et al., 2015). Yet, evidence from recent studies suggests that CSR even in its 'progressive' form is hampered by a myriad of constraints—what Osei-Kojo and Andrews (2020) refer to as the 'dark forces'—which limit the overall impact of such privatized developmentalist extractive bargains (see also Adjei, 2021). These 'forces' include misplaced priorities and duplication of projects on the part of companies, high expectations from affected communities and limited involvement of beneficiaries among others as discussed in the following sections (Ofori & Ofori, 2014; Osei-Kojo & Andrews, 2020). While scholars have itemized these dark forces, the processes through which they emerge are still unclear. In the next sections, we analyse the scope and contradictions entailed in seeing privatized or corporate-led CSR as part of extractive bargains. As alluded to previously, it is obvious that CSR does not represent a typical form of extractive bargain. However, the oil companies' operationalization of such programmes coupled with the state support for the petroleum companies suggest that CSR may be considered as a 'quasi' extractive or privatized developmentalist bargain which merits attention. Such an assessment also shifts the discussion of extractive bargains from state-led justifications for resource extraction to corporate-led bargaining.

Contextualizing CSR as a Privatized Developmentalist Bargain

As noted earlier on, what we characterize as a privatized developmentalist bargain manifests itself in the societal embeddedness of CSR programming. On the one hand, the state makes bold proclamations and justifications (such as '*with oil as a shot in the arm, we're going to fly*' as noted earlier) that it cannot practically see to fruition. On the other hand, petroleum companies are seeking to present themselves as 'good citizens' by rolling out a variety of initiatives that are meant to directly benefit the populace. The state therefore relinquishes its developmental obligations to communities in the neighbourhood of extractive activities (even sometimes society at large) based on the hope that multinational corporations will step in to serve people's needs. By becoming so embedded in the daily lives and wellbeing of people, the extractive bargains around development shift to corporations which then gain the influence to determine and 'give sense' to what sort of development communities need (see, for instance, Andrews, 2021). In this section of the chapter, we touch briefly on educational, social and infrastructural interventions.

On its website, a major shareholder of Ghana's offshore petroleum sector, Tullow Oil, identifies the provision of developmental infrastructure especially in host communities as one of its key areas of concern. CSR is considered an important means of delivering such projects. Such projects are intended to maintain good relations with affected communities and possibly to ameliorate the negative effects of their activities. As an oil company official indicated in an interview, '*CSR is more philanthropic; we [oil companies] do it to try and maintain a good neighbourhood*'. This interview excerpt shows that while petroleum companies are expected to undertake community development projects, such deliveries are not compulsory but rather considered as a form of corporate 'good will' which has a dual purpose of helping them obtain some form of social licence to operate. An acceptance of their operations in the host country and community also gives such companies good image intentionally (Wanvik, 2016; Adjei, 2021). As such, these companies focus on CSR projects which are more tangible and visible within the shortest possible time. Interviews revealed that such projects do not often benefit local community groups such as fisherfolk whose lives may be negatively affected by extractive activities (see Andrews et al., 2022).

The educational sector is one of the key areas of petroleum extraction companies' CSR deliveries. Such deliveries include provision of scholarship, construction of school blocks, provision of textbooks as well as vocational and technical training programmes for communities especially within the zone of influence. For instance, Tullow Oil Ghana has sponsored the construction of a dormitory for Axim Girls High School to house over 600 students (interview with company official, Takoradi). The GNPC also provides scholarships to brilliant but needy Ghanaian students in primary and high schools within the six coastal districts of the Western region. Such educational programmes are intended to give back to host communities especially those who mainly depend on the sea for subsistence. However, interviews with fisherfolks in Axim indicated that the target groups within these communities such as the children of fisherfolk who are of school-going age do not usually receive these scholarships due to what is often considered on paper as their lower academic standing. As a fish trader indicated:

> *It [the scholarship] does not get to our children. The real fishermen and fish traders who are negatively affected by petroleum activities and supposed to benefit from this [scholarship] do not mostly get it. It is the politicians and their friends who benefit.*

The above interview excerpt suggests that the scholarship distribution is characterized by local elite capture. As indicated by the fish trader, powerful individuals and groups who may not be negatively impacted by petroleum extraction but are politically connected tend to benefit from the scholarships provided by the petroleum companies. Interview with an oil company official in Takoradi indicated that while the aim of the scholarship is to help lessen potential impact of their activities on host communities, the fisherfolk are not necessarily primary targets. Rather the aim of such delivery is to support the entire host communities. Supporting the entire community may mean that those who bear the highest cost of petroleum extraction activities such as fisherfolk may not benefit from the sector.

Another important aspect of petroleum companies' CSR delivery is the provision of various infrastructural developments. These include the supply of potable drinking water to communities by drilling wells and boreholes, and community centres, among others for host communities. Amid the government's limited capacity to provide these social amenities to all needy areas, CSR has become an important mechanism of corporate intervention to address such government shortcomings. Such corporate benevolence is well displayed with huge signposts at the entrance of recipient communities and project sites in addition to their virtual display on the companies' websites. Yet, due to lack of maintenance after their installations and ongoing government neglect, these tangible developmental outputs become short-lived. In an interview with a fish trader in Axim, she indicated: '*They [oil companies] only do grand opening of their projects. What happens after is none of their business.*' A fisherman in Axim also indicated: '*[T]he only time I saw water flowing through that pipe [pointing to the pipe born water installation] was the first day it was opened by the companies*'. The state was also blamed for not undertaking its role of providing social amenities such as good drinking water, schools and for allowing corporations to take charge of these roles. A chief fisherman indicated that, '*since government knows that the oil companies will do it [provide social amenities], no major [developmental] project has been undertaken*'. This not only tends to give the petroleum companies power over the local communities in times of disagreements and conflicts but also allows the companies to realize some leverage with and favour from the government. For instance, in response to the concerns of fisherfolks about the negative impact of petroleum extraction activities, a government official in Accra indicated:

> *The fishermen should even appreciate the oil company's efforts. They have provided schools, portable water and even scholarships. Let me tell you something, this is not compulsory. They [oil companies] are only doing it to support us. We need to appreciate them rather than complain about everything.*

Clearly, petroleum companies seem to have the support of the government official by virtue of their CSR provisions, irrespective of community concerns around negative impacts and the unequal distribution of benefits. Through CSR, the government's responsibility or 'burden' of providing such essential services to these communities becomes reduced or almost non-existent (Frynas, 2005; Osei-Kojo & Andrews, 2020). Rather, studies show that spending patterns of the state have changed (Aryeetey & Ackah, 2018). For instance, spending from the government's oil revenue, which is dedicated to longer-term development programmes in strategic areas, such as agriculture is rather diverted for shorter-term political goals (see Aryeetey & Ackah, 2018).

The evidence here reveals a contradictory outcome of an extractive bargain—in fact, a supposedly developmentalist bargain—that has been touted by government and political elites operating at different levels. In the normative sense, we place Ghana's extractive bargains on the contradictory side of the spectrum for two reasons. First, if we examine local content provisions on face value one would argue that there is a clear commitment to align resource extraction with some 'progressive' vision (i.e., long-term, and broad-based developmental goals). Yet, in reality, research abounds to show that not as many 'local' people are benefiting from such endeavours (see Ablo, 2015, 2020; Andrews & Nwapi, 2018). Also, local content is something corporations are expected to embark upon and report on without the government ensuring that the workforce has the capacity for the ambitious procurement and recruitment targets. Second, there is a stark contradiction between proclaimed policy objectives in key documents such as AMV and what occurs in practice. To be sure, the AMV can be considered as a form of renaissance for resource nationalism (Besada & Philip, 2015) or petro-developmentalism (Ovadia, 2016) but the contradiction dwells in the reliance on corporations to deliver development to needed communities instead of a progressive (perhaps 'Tiger') state that is both structurally and ideologically equipped to pursue and deliver core development targets. To sum up this section, it must be noted that the position of the GNPC (a state-owned company) as part of the Jubilee Partners presents an opportunity which could be realized if the multinational partners (e.g., Tullow and Kosmos) did not maintain more than 60% of shares and decision-making power over developmental projects undertaken through the partnership.

Discussion and Concluding Reflections

As alluded to in the introduction, this chapter examines the form of extractive bargain that prevails in Ghana with emphasis on the petroleum sector. In particular, we have highlighted the importance of accounting for the dissonance or dialectical relationship between what is proclaimed/promised and what materializes in practice for beneficiary communities and society at large when conceptualizing extractive bargains at the state level. From the findings presented in this chapter, corporations seem to have taken over the implementation of extractive bargain that is negotiated by the state. This manifests in what we have characterized as a (quasi) privatized developmentalist extractive bargain that involves a laissez-faire approach where the state's developmentalist agenda, which serves as justification for sustained resource extraction, is primarily led by private petroleum companies. The challenge here is that the delivery of development by the private sector with government playing a mere supportive role leads to elite capture and misplaced projects with limited impact on communities that have been negatively affected by offshore extraction, including the broader society.

A question we can briefly examine here is why Ghana appears to have adopted a quasi-privatized model despite its outward developmentalist rhetoric. There are several factors to explain this but Andrews (2021) has pointed to three aspects of what he calls the 'politics of sensemaking and sensegiving' that may offer some insights. The first aspect is the prevalence of private authority within the Ghanaian space, which is sustained by a free-market ideology that empowers extractive corporations in a manner that is often not comparable to the power of the state itself. This presence and power give corporations a 'degree of normative flexibility' that permits them to play an active role in developmentalism while simultaneously self-determining the parameters of their role (Andrews, 2021, p. 227). Second, a history of overreliance on international financial institutions such as the IMF and World Bank has ensured that the industry remains liberalized enough to promote corporate-led development instead of one that may solely be state-engineered. The permissiveness that is made possible by the two factors noted above leads to a third aspect—the deliberate neglect of government's developmental responsibility—which is not a function of the absence of active social forces but rather the presence of civil society groups that are less inclined to be politically antagonistic to dominant power structures and elite coalitions as compared to examples in Latin America for instance (Block, 2008). These three points present an interesting picture of how historical trajectories intersect with ongoing socio-political culture and some deliberate choices to explain what we have characterized as a (quasi) privatized developmentalist extractive bargain in Ghana.

Clearly, our findings suggest that CSR is unlikely to (and should not) replace state-led developmentalism. Apart from the fact that companies would almost always pursue projects that would enhance their profitability and external acceptability irrespective of local concerns (Adjei, 2021; Frynas, 2005), they are not equipped to address the developmental challenges of host communities and stakeholder groups because that is not the main reason why they are in business. As argued by Osei-Kojo and Andrews (2020), community needs are extremely varied—ranging from building toilets to providing monthly monetary handouts for impacted people such as fisherfolk. In addition, it is sometimes difficult to decide on who the impacted populations are and what kinds of compensation or benefits might be deemed sufficient (Osei-Kojo & Andrews, 2020; Ackah-Baidoo, 2012). Government's reluctance to strictly guide the operations of petroleum companies could stem from the benefits they derive from their CSR programmes and the country's quest to remain an internationally competitive ground for foreign direct investment in the oil and gas sector (Andrews & Nwapi, 2018). Similarly, states are subject to various international pressures. Operating in the global capitalist market amid their limited power means that there are conditions and constraints to Ghana's extractive policy options (Bowles and Andrews, Chap. 1 in this volume). As alluded to above, compelling historical processes that precede natural resource domination of the economy have weakened institutions in the global south while promoting elites' interests and thereby undermining how the resource sector can encourage growth and development (Rosser, 2006). These external dark forces tend to position the developmental state idea in Ghana, like many developing countries, more as a buzzword than a model that is strategically implemented (Routley, 2014).

The above-mentioned points suggest the need to bring back the state into Ghana's developmentalist agenda where the respective state institutions at the national, regional and municipal/district levels take charge of community development. Ghana could take a cue from the East Asian developmental model by taking a central role in its developmental agenda but perhaps with a democratic orientation where different stakeholder groups could contribute to the state-led developmental process. It is therefore important for political leaders to ensure that the various existing state regulatory mechanisms and developmental trajectories are pursued irrespective of their political ideologies. This would make them accountable to local beneficiaries of development initiatives rather than relying on profit-oriented corporate bodies which tend to act on whim and discretion.

Ultimately, and even if CSR were to play some complementary role in community-based development, the state needs to ensure that it maintains oversight responsibility. Focusing on Ghana's mining sector, research by Andrews and Essah (2020) has pointed to an 'open, prior and independent deliberate discussion' (OPIDD) as a grassroots initiative that can help entrench government's fiduciary role in long-term community development while enabling host communities to negotiate better arrangements with corporations. This process also entails undertaking extensive community needs assessment that can inform policymaking and strategic planning. What this means is that purported extractive bargains could only materialize if the state entity that does 'development talk' intentionally takes practical steps to deliver development, provided there is sufficient consensus among key decision-makers to do so and if host communities are directly engaged by their government(s). Mere talk is cheap.

To conclude, this chapter has shown that more work can fruitfully be done in further exploring the extractive bargains idea across multiple contexts, scales and issue areas. Indeed, several chapters in this volume cover interesting case studies. While extractive bargains (extractivism in general) remains an important area of research worthy of further examination, there is also a possible future where social forces who resist all forms of resource extraction will emerge as a formidable group to undermine the broader societal acceptance of rhetorical or even enforceable state-sanctioned extractive bargains. Ayelazuno (2019) argues that such grassroots mobilization which has a long history in the context of Latin America, for instance, has not been realized in Ghana despite the fact that the same socio-economic deprivation and uneven development that give birth to and sustain such movements are present in Ghana, including the rest of sub-Saharan Africa (see also Conde & Le Billon, 2017). This geographically differentiated experience with 'resistance from below' is quite puzzling and not fully understood but within the context of the negligible benefits accruing to impacted (host) communities of capitalist extractivism, one cannot rule out this future possibility of sustained grassroots mobilization and resistance which would push Ghana towards a 'post-extractive bargain' in some sense.

References

Ablo, A. D. (2015). Local content and participation in Ghana's oil and gas industry: Can enterprise development make a difference? *The Extractive Industries and Society, 2*(2), 320–327.

Ablo, A. D. (2020). Enterprise development? Local content, corporate social responsibility and disjunctive linkages in Ghana's oil and gas industry. *The Extractive Industries and Society, 7*(2), 321–327.

Ablo, A. D. (2022). Carceral labour: Offshore work relations, conflicts and local participation in Ghana's oil and gas industry. *Political Geography, 93*, 102556.

Ackah-Baidoo, A. (2012). Enclave development and 'offshore corporate social responsibility': Implications for oil-rich sub-Saharan Africa. *Resources Policy, 37*(2), 152–159.

Ackah-Baidoo, A. (2013). Fishing in troubled waters: Oil production, seaweed and community- level grievances in the Western region of Ghana. *Community Development Journal, 48*(3), 406–420.

Adjei, M. (2017). *Governing the ocean space for the coexistence of fishery and petroleum industry in Ghana's Western Region*. Master's thesis, The University of Bergen.
Adjei, M. (2021). Dealing with social acceptance: The strategies of offshore petroleum extraction companies and stakeholder attitudes in Ghana. *The Extractive Industries and Society, 8*(3), 100922.
Adjei, M., & Overå, R. (2019). Opposing discourses on the offshore coexistence of the petroleum industry and small-scale fisheries in Ghana. *The Extractive Industries and Society, 6*(1), 190–197.
Adunbi, O. (2020). Extractive practices, oil corporations and contested spaces in Nigeria. *The Extractive Industries and Society, 7*(3), 804–811.
Andrews, N. (2013). Community expectations from Ghana's new oil find conceptualizing corporate social responsibility as a grassroots-oriented process. *Africa Today, 60*(1), 55–75.
Andrews, N. (2019). *Gold mining and the discourses of corporate social responsibility in Ghana*. Palgrave Macmillan.
Andrews, N. (2021). Corporate social responsibility as sensemaking and sensegiving in a hydrocarbon industry. *Business & Society Review, 126*(2), 211–234.
Andrews, N., Amongin, S., & Dery, I. (2022). Oil, fish, and livelihoods: Narratives of hydrocarbon benefits and gendered relations in Ghana. *Energy research and social. Science*. (in print).
Andrews, N., & Nwapi, C. (2017). A "new" developmental state in Africa?: Evaluating recent state interventions visa-vis resource extraction in Kenya, Tanzania, and Rwanda. *McGill International Journal of Sustainable Development Law and Policy, 13*(2), 223–267.
Andrews, N., & Essah, M. (2020). The sustainable development conundrum in gold mining: Exploring 'open, prior and independent deliberate discussion' as a community-centered framework. *Resources Policy, 68*, 101798.
Andrews, N., & Nwapi, C. (2018). Bringing the state back in again? The emerging developmental state in Africa's energy sector. *Energy Research & Social Science, 41*, 48–58.
Andrews, N., & Siakwah, P. (2020). *Oil and development in Ghana: Beyond the resource curse*. Routledge.
Aryeetey, E., & Ackah, I. (2018). The boom, the bust, and the dynamics of oil resource management in Ghana. *Mining for Change*, 97–118.
Ayelazuno, J. A. (2019). *Neoliberal globalisation and resistance from below: Why the subalterns resist in Bolivia and not in Ghana*. Routledge.
BBC News. (2007, June 19). Ghana will be an African tiger. http://news.bbc.co.uk/2/hi/africa/6766527

Besada, H., & Philip, M. (2015). Mining codes in Africa: Emergence of a 'fourth' generation? *Cambridge Review of International Affairs, 28*(2), 263–282.

Block, F. (2008). Swimming against the current: The rise of a hidden developmental state in the United States. *Politics and Society, 36*(2), 169–206.

Chagnon, C. W., Durante, F., Gills, B. K., Hagolani-Albov, S. E., Hokkanen, S., Kangasluoma, S. M., Konttinen, H., Kröger, M., LaFleur, W., Ollinaho, O., & Vuola, M. P. (2022). From extractivism to global extractivism: The evolution of an organizing concept. *The Journal of Peasant Studies, 49*(4), 760–792.

Conde, M., & Le Billon, P. (2017). Why do some communities resist mining projects while others do not? *The Extractive Industries and Society, 4*(3), 681–697.

Dartey-Baah, K., Amponsah-Tawiah, K., & Agbeibor, V. (2015). Corporate social responsibility in Ghana's national development. *Africa today, 62*(2), 71–92.

DW Documentary. (2020). *Oil promises—How oil changed a country*. Retrieved January 10, 2021, from https://www.youtube.com/watch?v=b58b-BvWEpo

Frynas, J. G. (2005). The false developmental promise of corporate social responsibility: Evidence from multinational oil companies. *International Affairs, 81*(3), 581–598.

Graham, E., Gyampo, R. E. V., Ackah, I., & Andrews, N. (2019). An institutional assessment of five years of the public interest accountability Committee in Ghana's oil and gas sector. *Journal of Contemporary African Studies, 37*(4), 316–334.

Hilson, G. (2007). Championing the rhetoric? 'Corporate social responsibility in Ghana's mining sector. *Greener Management International, 53*, 43–56.

Mkandawire, T. (2001). Thinking about developmental states in Africa. *Cambridge Journal of Economics, 25*(3), 289–314.

Mohan, G., Asante, K. P., & Abdulai, A. G. (2018). Party politics and the political economy of Ghana's oil. *New Political Economy, 23*(3), 274–289.

Obeng-Odoom, F. (2012). Natural resource abundance and eminent domain: A case study from Africa. *Local Economy, 27*(4), 319–325.

Obeng-Odoom, F. (2014). Black gold in Ghana: Crude days for fishers and farmers? *Local Environment, 19*(3), 259–282.

Obeng-Odoom, F. (2015). Global political economy and frontier economies in Africa: Implications from the oil and gas industry in Ghana. *Energy Research and Social Science, 10*, 41–56.

Ofori, D. F., & Ofori, A. T. (2014). Mining sector CSR behaviour: A developing country perspective. *African Journal of Management Research, 22*(1), 62–84.

Oppong, N. (2018). Negotiating transparency: NGOs and contentious politics of the extractive industries transparency initiative in Ghana. *Contemporary Social Science, 13*(1), 58–71.

Osei-Kojo, A., & Andrews, N. (2020). A developmental paradox? The "dark forces" against corporate social responsibility in Ghana's extractive industry. *Environment, Development and Sustainability, 22*(2), 1051–1071.

Oteng-Ababio, M. (2018). 'The oil is drilled in Takoradi, but the money is counted in Accra': The paradox of plenty in the oil city, Ghana. *Journal of Asian and African Studies, 53*(2), 268–284.

Ovadia, J. S. (2012). The dual nature of local content in Angola's oil and gas industry: Development vs. elite accumulation. *Journal of Contemporary African Studies, 30*(3), 395–417.

Ovadia, J. S. (2016). *The petro-developmental state in Africa: Making oil work in Angola, Nigeria and the Gulf of Guinea*. Hurst.

Ovadia, J. S., Ayelazuno, J. A., & Van Alstine, J. (2020). Ghana's petroleum industry: Expectations, frustrations and anger in coastal communities. *Journal of Modern African Studies, 58*(3), 397–424.

Owusu, V., & Adjei, M. (2021). Politics, power and unequal access to fisheries subsidies among small-scale coastal fisherfolk in Ghana. *Ocean & Coastal Management, 214*, 105920.

Rosser, A. (2006). *The political economy of the resource curse: A literature survey.* https://opendocs.ids.ac.uk/opendocs/bitstream/handle/20.500.12413/4061/Wp268.pdf

Routley, L. (2014). Developmental states in Africa? A review of ongoing debates and buzzwords. *Development Policy Review, 32*(2), 159–177.

Tullow Oil. (2015). *Tullow oil PLC 2015 corporate social responsibility report.* Retrieved November 27, 2016, from http://www.tullowoil.com/Media/docs/default-source/5_sustainability/tullow-oil-2015-corporate-responsibility-report.pdf?sfvrsn=2

Wanvik, T. I. (2016). Governance transformed into corporate social responsibility (CSR): New governance innovations in the Canadian oil sands. *The Extractive Industries and Society, 3*(2), 517–526.

Watts, M. (2004). Resource curse? Governmentality, oil and power in The Niger Delta, Nigeria. *Geopolitics, 9*(1), 50–80.

13

Extractive Bargains Reconciling Postcolonial Pluralism? Plural Economies in Bolivia and Ecuador

Isabella M. Radhuber, Marie Jasser, and Diego Andreucci

Introduction

Indigenous organisations have put forth unique proposals for plural economies in Bolivia and Ecuador that were constitutionally recognised in 2008–2009. Yet, in extractivist settings, diverse re/productive forms

I. M. Radhuber (✉)
Department of Political Science, University of Vienna, Vienna, Austria
e-mail: isabella.radhuber@univie.ac.at

M. Jasser
ViennaDepartment of Development Studies, University of Vienna, Vienna, Austria

Instituto de Investigación Científica y Social, Universidad Nur, Santa Cruz de la Sierra, Bolivia
e-mail: marie.jasser@univie.ac.at

D. Andreucci
Department of Economic History, University of Barcelona, Barcelona, Spain
e-mail: diego.andreucci@ub.edu

P. Bowles, N. Andrews (eds.), *Extractive Bargains*, Frontiers of Globalization,
https://doi.org/10.1007/978-3-031-32172-6_13

continue to be undermined, raising questions about the extractive bargains offered by these plurinational states. In this chapter, we analyse the development of plural economies and the tensions that arise in the context of tin mining in Huanuni (Bolivia) and copper mining in Intag (Ecuador). We focus on the period from the 1990s to 2017. We argue that Bolivia's and Ecuador's original extractive bargains, which sought to reconcile postcolonial pluralism with extractivism, was an important step, yet insufficient to protect diverse re/productive forms.

The proposal for "plural economies" envisions empowering diverse re/productive activities, especially communitarian modes of re/production based on diverse small-scale and subsistence activities. It has been brought forth by indigenous organisations defending their own communities' subsistence and territorial integrity, organisations that have built an alliance with peasant unions, NGOs, intellectuals, the ruling party and others since the early 2000s. Visions for plural economies have been embedded into plurinational state projects aimed at embracing various nations and indigenous-peasant peoples as well as their re/productive forms (Augsburger, 2021; Chávez et al., 2008; CONAIE, 1994, 2012; Garcés, 2010; Radcliffe & Radhuber, 2020; Ruales & Zaragocin, 2020; Tapia, 2019a, 2019b).

Plural economies have been a central claim by indigenous organisations in both countries since then. Bolivia and Ecuador have undergone significant social unrest in the past years, where by progressive as well as conservative governments[1] were implicated in weakening indigenous organisations through co-optation, control and division (Delgado, 2017; Farthing, 2019; Vela-Almeida et al., 2020). Both countries' indigenous organisations have maintained their claim for more plural economies; and Ecuador's movement has also regained its organisational capacity, as has been demonstrated in the 2019 and 2022 mass mobilisations

[1] Since the mid-2000s, both countries took a sharp turn to the left, in the wake of an intense cycle of mobilisations sparked by years of dismal socio-economic conditions caused by neoliberal governments. Since 2006, Evo Morales's Movement to Socialism (MAS) party has been in power in Bolivia, interrupted by the conservative Añez government between November 2019 and the end of 2020; it is now in its fourth mandate, with President Luis Arce. In Ecuador, Rafael Correa's progressive party Alianza PAIS was in power between 2007 and 2017, followed by a return to conservative neoliberalism; at the time of writing, the conservative and extreme right Movement CREO party of Guillermo Lasso holds the presidency.

(CONAIE, 2022). This chapter explains successes and limits in Andean plurinational development, contributing to understanding the socio-political dynamics that enable (or not) extractive bargains which recognise and promote the coexistence of diverse re/productive activities.

The analysis is based on 63 qualitative interviews[2] conducted in Bolivia and Ecuador from 2012 to 2017 with representatives of state companies; state institutions at local, departmental and national levels; national leaders of indigenous organisations; local producers in the two case study locales; and other relevant organisations. In addition, we have analysed indigenous documents and political economic data from central banks' databases. The data has been supplemented by secondary literature and internet sources.

Theorising Different Pluralisms Vis-à-Vis Extractivisms

In order to understand the limits of Andean plurinational development, and the specific extractive bargain which aspires to reconcile extractivism with postcolonial pluralism, we draw on Latin American theoretical debates on plurinationalism. René Zavaleta is one of Latin America's most prominent intellectuals who theorised the state in postcolonial settings, emphasising that various modes of production and historical temporalities co-exist within national territories in terms of an overlapping or motley social formation (*formación social abigarrada* in Spanish). These modes of production are only partially articulated, resulting in an overlapping, disjointed social formation. While for Zavaleta, the condition of disjointed, overlapping societies has been considered a deficiency to be overcome (as it was seen as an obstacle both to capitalist and socialist development and therefore a problem), later scientists and socio-political movements have positively valued and politicised this condition (Augsburger, 2021; Zavaleta, 2011). Bolivian political scientist Luis Tapia has developed this notion further, speaking of "overlapping societies" (Tapia, 2019b), highlighting capitalist and colonial development

[2] All interviews, unless explicitly stated otherwise, were conducted by Isabella Radhuber.

beneath the coexistence of such societies in conditions of inequality and exploitation:

> Coexistence does not automatically translate into functionalisation and modernisation towards capitalism, but rather there is a long coexistence of colonial nature with a set of economic, social, political and cultural institutions that claim superiority over the rest, and demand them [the rest] tribute to finance the reproduction of this type of formation and domination. (Tapia, 2019a, p. 24, own translation[3])

In plurinational states, re-defining autonomous regions at regional, departmental, municipal and territorial levels has been considered a milestone, as these have included indigenous autonomous areas. Sovereignty arrangements are the other key area identified by indigenous organisations to enable decision-making capacity over their territories (on the novel proposals to pluralize sovereign arrangements through plurinational statehood, see Radhuber & Radcliffe, 2022; cf. Postero & Fabricant, 2019; Simpson, 2014). However, the impacts from extractivism have continued to drastically affect people, territories and states.

Extractivism has been discussed in terms of its differential impacts, intersecting with gender and race inequalities in the region (Gargallo, 2021; Rodriguez Fernandez, 2020). The intensification of extractivism in Bolivia since 2006 and its advance into indigenous territories and protected areas have led to social destructuring and what we have elsewhere called "political dispossession," that is, the expropriation of political voice and spaces for decision-making and participation (Radhuber et al., 2021). Women figure prominently in anti-extractivist protest movements and movements in defence of territory across Latin America—also because indigenous women appear to be one of the most aggrieved by mining activities (Chavez & López, 2018; Gago & Gutiérrez, 2018; Jenkins, 2015; Muñoz & Villareal, 2019).

---

[3] The Spanish original is:

"La coexistencia no se traduce en automática funcionalización y modernización hacia el capitalismo, sino que se da una coexistencia larga de carácter colonial en la que hay un conjunto de instituciones económicas, sociales y políticas y culturales que reclaman superioridad sobre el resto y a partir de esto exigen tributo para financiar la reproducción de ese tipo de formación y dominación."

We will show how indigenous and other local groups target not only industries but also their respective states when negotiating extractive projects and self-determination (Horowitz et al., 2018). Postero and Fabricant (2019) argue that a contradiction exists when indigenous actors have to negotiate their self-determination with the state. Rodriguez Fernandez (2020) analyses how indigenous peasant-women in charge of subsistence production and social reproduction are particularly affected by extractivism in Oruro, Bolivia. Billo (2020) demonstrates how women in Intag, Ecuador, challenge patriarchal relations perpetuated through extractive relationships, offering a gendered decolonial analysis of everyday state formation as a site of resistance. Anthias (2018) points to the limits of state recognition in the case of land titling that have been experienced in indigenous struggles for self-determination. Here, we will show how indigenous organisations re-negotiated plural economies in Bolivia and Ecuador's plurinational states, and analyse the tensions and contradictions that arise when plural economies are implemented in practice.

Plural Economies: From Indigenous Proposals to Constitutional Recognitions

Since the 1990s, indigenous groups have brought forward proposals for strengthening plural economies with the aim of recognising and articulating diverse livelihoods, with particular emphasis placed on their re/productive activities. A former leader of Ecuador's indigenous organisation CONAIE specifies the claim for a plural economic model as follows:

> [O]ur political project is to transform the Ecuadorian state according to the vision of a plurinational state; so, the government system, the economic system shall no more be one sole system that dominates the others. Regarding the economic system, the best, strongest and richest system must comprise various economic systems, because we are talking about various nations. We can also say pluralism, so it is about economic pluralism. (Interview, Quito/Ecuador, 12/2012)

He furthermore explains how the design of a plural economy helps to remediate tensions from economic crises:

> These systems will also help us to get out of any economic crisis, and any crisis of the development model that is on the table since the capitalist system. (…) That will not function anymore, we are already in a crisis, and for us the alternative is to propose these economic systems [in the plural]." (Interview, Quito/Ecuador, 12/2012)

The "Political Project of CONAIE" from 1994 (and the slightly modified 2001 project) had an extensive section on a "New Economic Model for a Plurinational State: An Ecologically Planned Communitarian Economy." Alongside co-ownership of resources, it foresaw the coexistence of diverse economic forms based on personal-familiar, communitarian-self-managed, state and mixed ownership. Envisioning "economic, political, cultural, technological and scientific equality of the nationalities and people and other social sectors of the national society" (CONAIE, 1994, 2001, 2012), priority was given to the communitarian organisational forms of the indigenous people and nationalities.

In Bolivia, a former head of highland indigenous confederation CONAMAQ explains that, for them, a plural economic model implies strengthening a variety of economic forms in different economic activities. In contrast to Ecuador's organisations, CONAMAQ also envisions direct indigenous participation in extractive economies. The example given is that of

> communitarian mining, which would only work with a so-called shared management (*co-gestión* in Spanish), but with communitarian firms leading, it could be led by the populations of the places in which these resources are found. They can take over, they can take the company, but in shared management with the state. So we would have to see, how much does the state contribute? And how much the communitarian firm? And how they can industrialise. … So it is almost the same, but with originary nations on top. (Interview, La Paz/Bolivia, 06/2013)

Co-ownership of lands and natural resources has also been a central claim when indigenous, originary and peasant organisations formed a common alliance, the so-called Unity Pact, in 2004. With the participation of the above-mentioned organisations as well as the support of experts (*técnicos*) and allied NGOs, the Unity Pact elaborated a Constitutional proposal that was first proposed to the Constitutional Assembly on 5 August 2006 (Garcés, 2010). Based on these organisations' ideas, the Unity Pact proposed a social communitarian economy that comprises six economic forms: two different communitarian forms—one more penetrated by market logics than the other[4]—as well as cooperativist,[5] state, private and mixed economic forms (Garcés, 2010, p. 210f.).[6] In both countries, indigenous organisations claimed that communitarian economic forms should be strengthened[7] and diverse forms of ownership recognised within a plural economic model.

Following long periods of discussion and deliberation within and among indigenous-peasant organisations as well as in both countries' constitutional assemblies (for an ethnography of these processes see Schavelzon, 2015), these proposals were recognised in Bolivia's and Ecuador's Constitutions of 2009 and 2008 respectively, as follows:

> Article 306—I. The Bolivian economic model is plural and oriented towards improving the life quality and towards good living (*vivir bien*) of all Bolivians. II. The plural economy is constituted through the communitarian, the state, the private and the social cooperative economic form of organisation (Bolivia 2009, own translation). III. The plural economy articulates the different economic organisational forms by means of the principles of complementarity, reciprocity, solidarity, redistribution, equality, legal security, sustainability, balance, justice and transparency. The

[4] These are small-scale urban/rural production inspired by communitarian principles and the community economy, which includes peasant, indigenous and native economic organisations and other associations (Garcés, 2010).

[5] The term "cooperative" in Bolivia usually refers to small, self-organised mining companies. The creation of cooperatives was a survival strategy for unemployed miners after massive dismissals from the state company occurred during the 1980s (for further details, see, e.g., Andreucci & Radhuber, 2017).

[6] The communitarian economic forms fall into what Polanyi termed "substantive economies," that is, an "institutionalised interaction between humans and their natural surroundings in satisfaction of their material wants (…) in other words, the way people go about securing their livelihood" (Holmes, 2014, p.532).

[7] Community-managed projects have also been defended in the tourist sector, in this case against agricultural projects (Colloredo-Mansfeld et al., 2018).

social and communitarian economy complements the individual interest with the collective *vivir bien*. (Bolivia., 2009, own translation)

In Ecuador:

Art. 283. The economic system is social and solidary; it recognizes the human being as subject and as end; it aims at a dynamic and balanced relationship between society, state and market, in harmony with nature; and it has as objective guaranteeing the production and reproduction of the material and immaterial conditions that enable the good living (*buen vivir*). The economic system is integrated through the public, the private, the mixed, the popular and solidary economic forms of organisation alongside others determined in the Constitution. The popular and solidary economy is regulated according to the law and includes the cooperative, the associative and the communitarian sector. (Ecuador, 2008, own translation)[8]

However, the Constitution cannot be taken as a point of arrival, but constitutes a mere starting point, a horizon for struggle in the words of Bolivian researcher Oscar Vega Camacho:

Here there is a very important issue, I would say the Constitution should be read as a political program, right? That would be the other dispute, it is not a legal document, it is a political program and this makes it a living Constitution, in force. (Interview by Diego Andreucci, La Paz/Bolivia, 03/2014)

In theory, therefore, an extractive bargain was struck between the central state and indigenous and peasant organisations in which extraction would continue but within the context of constitutionally protected and promoted plural economies. In the following section, however, we will show how plural economies have suffered severe backlashes in practice, which is most visible when resource extraction projects are implemented detrimental to the existing re/productive forms.

[8] The Superintendent of Popular and Solidary Economy states that, apart from diversifying economic sectors such as empowering agriculture, the economic organisational forms through which such diversification can be achieved play a crucial role (Interview, Quito/Ecuador, 10/2012).

Mining Activities Versus Diverse Re/productive Forms in Huanuni (Bolivia) and Intag (Ecuador)

In this section, we trace the practice of plural economies in the context of mining activities in Huanuni (Bolivia) and Intag (Ecuador).

Suspension of Fundamental Rights in the Context of Tin Mining in Huanuni (Bolivia)

While the Posokoni mountain in the municipality and town of Huanuni represents Bolivia's biggest tin mine, diverse re/productive activities are practised in the region. The mountain's peak reaches 4945 metres above sea level and it is located in the Andean mountain range just southeast of La Paz. In the department of Oruro, the history of mining dates back to 1604. The first operations in Huanuni were documented just before 1900 (López et al., 2010, p. XVII). Today, 44% of the municipality's population is dedicated to mining, while the relationship between mining and other activities in this area is hybrid (López et al., 2010, p. 32; Instituto Nacional de Estadística, 2017). A member of the Centre for Ecology and Andean Peoples (CEPA) explains that "many families dedicated to agriculture also work in mining, they are called *agromineros*" (Interview, Oruro/Bolivia, 03/2016; 01/2017).

In October 2006, tin mining in Huanuni has been (re)nationalised through Supreme Decree 28901, due to pressure by local cooperative miners that turned into violent conflict, which was finally solved by employing them in the mine. Some years later, the manager of the Huanuni Mining Company complained that "we are inflated with personnel, we are a social company, we'd need 1,500 workers but we have 4,700 workers" (Interview, Huanuni/Bolivia, 05/2013). The director of the historical archive of Bolivia's public mining company COMIBOL said that it would be in the region's nature to be a mining and oil extraction zone (Interview, La Paz/Bolivia, 01/2017). The director himself comes from a family of miners, used to work as a labourer in the mines and now counts 48 years of service in the company. However, the department of Oruro also has a number of small-scale and community-based activities: 30% of the population engages in subsistence or semi-subsistence agriculture, livestock, hunting and fishing, and another 7% in artisanal manufacturing (National Statistics Institute, 2017).[9] In this context, the socio-ecological impacts of mining have always threatened communitarian modes of re/production and livelihoods.

In 2009, indigenous-peasant groups achieved a great success in defence of their livelihoods, as Supreme Decree 0335 declared the Poopó Lake basin, where Huanuni is located, an "environmental emergency zone" (Arias, 2015; Decreto Supremo 335, 2009, p. 7). This milestone was achieved by a protest march organised by the "Coordination for the Defence of the Basins of the River Desaguadero, the Lake Uru Uru and the Lake Poopó" (CORIDUP)—a 2008 founded organisation of local campesinos, who are allied with organisations affiliated with CONAMAQ and politically self-identify as indigenous (Arias, 2015, p. 36f). CORIDUP's president said that Decree 0335/2009 awoke much hope for farmers, animal-breeders and fishers, who mobilised to defend their re/productive activities. But, over 10 years on, the decree's objectives were not met (Interview, Oruro/Bolivia, 01/2017; Technical support and expert staff CEPA, Interview, Oruro/Bolivia, 01/2017). For instance, the tailings dam of the Huanuni mine that should have been completed by 2011 has only been partially constructed in 2022 (CEPA, 2022), and the contamination of waters and soils continued unabatedly. Hence Decree 0335 remains a success on paper, not translated into concrete improvements on the ground.

Subsistence farming, animal breeding and fisheries are severely affected by contamination.[10] A mother and daughter dedicated to small-scale

[9] Ethnic diversity is also high in the region: In the municipalities of Huanuni and Antequera, 73% of the population belong to Quechua, Uru and Aymara indigenous nations in the department, and the poverty rates amount to over 64%.

[10] In Huanuni, only about 6% of the extracted materials are tin concentrates, whilst the rest are waste and emissions (López et al., 2010, p. 46). 20,000 tons of sulphate and two tons of arsenic and lead are discharged every year into the waters of the Huanuni sub-basin (ending in Lake Poopó). The Vice Ministry of the Environment proved that the levels of zinc and cadmium in the waters are above the permitted level. This contamination is due to the presence of 300 mines. The Bolivian Programme for Strategic Research (PIEB) has furthermore studied genotoxic harm to children and mothers exposed to polymetallic contamination (close to the San José mine in Oruro) and neurotoxic effects of heavy metals, as well as a reduced intellectual coefficient and mental functions. In addition, atmospheric contamination provokes disorders, especially in children and adolescents (Ribera, 2010, p. 191-207, cf. Andreucci & Gruberg Cazón, 2015).

cultivation of mainly potatoes, quinoa and corn and animal breeding in San Agustín de Puñaca (a rural community downriver from Huanuni) explained that "there is no water for irrigation, only the water from the rain ... we don't have water here ... the Huanuni mine is the one that contaminates most ... the River Poopó, it is all red" (Interview, Poopó/Bolivia, 01/2017). Moreover, sheep and cows died as "the animal breeders now take the water from the contaminated well" (Interview, Poopó/Bolivia, 01/2017). The president of the fishing cooperative of Sora Sora explained that they lived off Lake Uru Uru and Lake Poopó (Interview, Oruro/Bolivia, 01/2017). Most of them usually dedicated six months a year to agriculture and animal breeding and another six months to fishing. The president of the departmental fishing federation, which is composed of 700 fisherpeople of Lake Poopó and Lake Uru Uru, said that mining undermines fishing (Interview, Oruro/Bolivia, 01/2017). In the region of Huanuni, where waters are severely contaminated, communities struggled for closing the water cycles of mining and for the construction of a tailings dam, alongside medium- and long-term strategies for remediation (Mongabay, 2017; cf. Perreault, 2013).

A leading member of the Departmental Service of Agriculture and Animal-Breeding SEDAG added that "long-term remediation plans are needed, we are still addressing these problems like firemen, be it draughts or contamination" (Interview, Oruro/Bolivia, 01/2017). SEDAG's director also confirmed that the contamination of Lake Uru Uru threatened agriculture, animal breeding and fishery: "each time we are losing more soil instead of recuperating it ... we have a hard time recuperating it" (Interview, Oruro/Bolivia, 01/2017). Lake Poopó, until recently the second water body in Bolivia after Lake Titicaca, was declared evaporated in December 2015 and has only partially recovered since then. It had been described as the de facto tailing dam of mining in Huanuni by an expert staff of the organisation Centre of Ecology and Andean Peoples CEPA: "[Mining] has moreover killed and dried the Lake (Poopó), which has taken away a source of work from the fishers" (Interview, Oruro/Bolivia, 01/2017; also see: Oruro's secretary for the Environment, Water and Mother Earth, Interview, 01/2017). The secretary for the Environment,

Water and Mother Earth of Oruro said that "this contamination dates back 500 years, it persists since colonial times, and today we are facing degraded soils" (Interview, Oruro/Bolivia, 01/2017).

"Shielding mining companies" in Intag (Ecuador)

In Ecuador's Intag region, copper exploration dates back to the early 1990s. The organisation Ecological Defence and Conservation of Intag, DECOIN, was founded in 1995. Resistance to mining intensified from 1997 to 2002. Copper exploration has been repeatedly interrupted by local populations who have burnt down exploration camps in 1997 and 2005 (DECOIN, 2017; Latorre et al., 2015). The municipality Cotacachi, for example, declared itself an Ecological County that forbids mining and other conservation-threatening activities.

Communities in the Intag region of Ecuador prevented copper mining activities from starting for 18 years, arguing that these would thwart the re/productive activities of the region. Located amidst a mega diverse cloud forest between 1800 and 2800 metres above sea level, it is one of the world's 25 biodiversity hotspots (Myers et al., 2000). Environmental impact studies have revealed that the exploitation of copper would entail severe social and ecological consequences. According to the 2008 Constitution, Intag is one of the regions that comprise important water sources and species at risk of extinction as well as primary forest, in which mining activities should not take place (Billo, 2020; Davidov, 2014).

The defence of productive diversity has been a major motivation for rejecting mining activities in the region.[11] Today's main economic activities include organic coffee cultivation (alongside tropical fruit, coffee, cacao, corn, beans, potatoes, tree-tomatoes, sugar cane and bananas). Also, ecotourism, rural communitarian tourism projects as well as artisanal production of cosmetics grew strong in the region. Small-scale agriculture and animal breeding, for example, absorb 70% of the workforce

[11] The region counts a population of 13,102 (2010), of which 82.3% identify as mestizos, 6.6% as afro, black and mulata (6.6%) and 5.7% as indigenous (Latorre et al., 2015, p. 26).

and non-salaried or subsistence activities employ 41%. Many of these forms are now registered by the Superintendence of Popular and Solidary Economy (Latorre et al., 2015, p. 23, 30; Representative of Cotacachi's municipality, interview, Cotacachi/Ecuador, 01/2017). As many of these activities depend on clean water, indigenous-peasant movements have started a local, small-scale project whereby "hydroelectric plants should generate resources for the conservation of the hydric basins" (President of Consorcio Toisán, interview, Cotacachi/Ecuador, 01/2017). Unlike mining, the use of water would be at a smaller scale and without any contamination (Co-founder of the project, interview, Cotacachi/Ecuador, 01/2017). The Hidrointag project intends to build small-scale hydroelectric plants that should provide income for supporting other re/productive activities. Social and productive diversity of the region was a major reference point, around which resistance against mining emerged.

The local cattle-breeding association of Alto Chalguayaku (Intag) states in its internal regulations that they are against any mining. Their president explains that, as small-scale cattle-breeders, they provide for the country; agriculture is always more important, and mining destroys it all: "after mining, all would end, and we would have to go to a different place," he says. "[Therefore, we have to] defend what is ours because it is ours ... the good and productive earth, the calm environment, this paradise" (Interview, Junín/Ecuador, 04/2016).

A member of the Women's Coordination of Intag explains (Interview, Junín/Ecuador, 04/2016) how her opposition to mining stems from her knowledge of how mining undermines existing forms of living and economic activities. She recounts how in the very beginning—when Mitsubishi entered the territory in 1992 and employed people—everybody supported the mining activity, but nobody knew about mining and their rights. The impact of mining—she explains—is especially severe for women:

> We women will always be more affected as mothers of our families, as housewives in these places. It affects us, for example, through the water issue, the issue of the social impact through mining and the violence (...) the problem is that the men go to work, and the woman stays here, she remains more defenceless than before.

> Mining activity is not good in territories like ours, because we have the luck to have productive lands, we have primary forests, we enjoy a lot of water, have a big water reserve, and this is what we don't want to get destroyed, to end. We would rather collaborate so that it gets better each day—if it is clean now, it should be even cleaner for our future generations so that they can also enjoy it. (Interview, Junín/Ecuador, 04/2016; Muñoz & Villareal, 2019)

The president of the cattle-breeding association in Intag explains how extractive activities attempt to destructure societies by causing social division. He specifies that the social impacts on families during this exploration phase are due to tense relations between different economic forms:

> [T]hey call the kids, and say: 'come one, we will give you work, you know? We will pay you well', so then they go on and on … let's say, you are my daughter, it goes on, and you say, 'oh daddy, let me go work for the company' and I tell you 'no, don't go, because that is not good [for our productive activities]', and that's where the social impact starts. It is considerable, and tremendous problems come up … tremendous, I tell you, within one family, some are in favour, some against. (Interview, Junín/Ecuador, 04/2016)

In Intag, the population continuously responded to a state agenda that has declared Intag as a mining zone (Billo, 2020, p. 7; Avcı, 2017; Arellano, 2022). A representative of the National Secretary of Development and Planning (SENPLADES) explained that "the strategic sector generally has to be administered by public companies (…); the mining company [ENAMI] is one of the new companies created and supported by the state, mainly by the state-owned petroleum company" (Interview, Quito/Ecuador, 03/2013). The local population's resistance culminated in the extinction of all mining concessions in the exploration stage, alongside a 70% reduction of the mining industry workforce, imposed through the Mining Mandate (in 2008). However, after 2008 the Ecuadorian state strengthened its role in resource extraction: Before the mandate, 9.000 mining concessions were given to private Canadian and US companies. After a two year pause, about 80% of those concessions were reverted to Ecuadorian state entities, particularly the Ecuadorian Mining Company (ENAMI) founded in 2010. (Latorre et al., 2015, p.30; Varela, 2010, p.134)

However, despite strong opposition that aimed at defending re/productive diversity, the Ecuadorian mining company managed to break the resistance in 2009. Amidst rising copper prices (Dossier, 2015, p. 221), the Ecuadorian and Chilean state mining companies ENAMI and CODELCO signed an agreement, which was formalised two years later under the name "project Llurimagua" (CODELCO, 2011; Latorre et al., 2015, p. 37). The companies' delegates were backed by national security in order to break resistance and violently enter the zone. Social leaders associated with resistance were legally persecuted; most paradigmatically, Junín Javier Ramírez, then president of the community, was detained and held for 10 months in 2014, accused of rebellion and sabotage. Amnesty International and other organisations expressed their concern regarding human rights (see Amnesty International, 2013, also see Human Rights Watch, 2015). Nevertheless, the next steps for mining exploration were taken.

A member of Intag's Women Coordination complains that they were suffering a tenacious attack by the government, that their rights and the Constitution itself were not respected, and that the environmental impact assessment was based on a series of mistakes (Interview, Junín/Ecuador, 04/2016; cf. DECOIN, 2017). An authority of Cotacachi's municipality government lays out that they have exhausted all possibilities for participation. The municipality wanted to carry out popular consultations, but this possibility was taken away from them through a Constitutional change in December 2015. Over 80 observations they had made to the environmental impact assessment were not taken into account (Interview, Cotacachi/Ecuador, 04/2016). They also tried to conform a citizen oversight committee, but "finally the company surpassed us, and they formed their own committee" (Interview, Cotacachi/Ecuador, 04/2016; 01/2017; also see: member of ACRI and Consorcio Toisán, interview, 01/2017; on the committee see Empresa Nacional Minera, 2015). Democratic rights for participation in decision-making around resource exploitation have been plainly suspended.

A member of Intag's Women Coordination explains that there is no possibility to actually participate in political decision-making:

> In the face of this, we feel impotent, defenceless, there are no laws that protect us. [...] The law is just being implemented when it is for the miners, it is not applicable for the peasants. The municipality is well intentioned, but the government decides from above. (Interview, Junín/Ecuador, 04/2016)

The authority of Cotacachi's municipal government concludes that this constitutes a "shielding of mining companies" that they experience in Intag. He explains:

> They are taking away all your legal possibilities to work. [They] have achieved an interweaving, a legal structure that shields [mining companies]. ... I am progressively realising that, no matter what you do, they have a sort of shield around the mining companies. Around them, there can happen a thousand things, but they are impermeable, they go ahead with their work, their plans, nothing affects them, nothing perturbs them. The mining companies have a lot of experience for creating this interweaving, and here they have found the perfect form with a government with popular support [referring to the progressive government of Correa, then in charge] that could break the resistance of the people in Intag. (Interview, Cotacachi/Ecuador, 01/2017)

Moreover, there was a direct and blunt employment of police or military violence, as police and paramilitary interventions were used to enforce copper exploration in Intag. Police presence negatively affected local productive forms, most visibly communitarian tourism. In 2022, various communities maintained legal disputes against different mining projects in Intag to ensure the rights to environmental consultation and protection (Mongabay, 2017; Sotalin, 2022).

Concluding Reflections: Extractive Bargains to Reconcile Postcolonial Pluralism?

In Bolivia and Ecuador, indigenous movements have tackled postcolonial legacies by articulating plans to pluralise national economies in a way that suits the existence of diverse re/productive activities in the countries. They have achieved unprecedented success—at least on paper—as indigenous-peasant organisations' demands for plural economies have been inscribed in their respective countries' Constitutions.

Indigenous agendas for plural economies have sought to address colonial legacies of social inequality. According to Tapia (2008, pp. 29–36), postcolonial contexts are characterised by "overlapping societies" (*sociedades abigarradas*): one (dominant, colonial) society lives off the others, it consumes them, it uses up the time and resources required for their self-development. In other words, capitalist-colonial developments perpetuate an unequal articulation between diverse modes of production. Indigenous agendas for plural economies aim at tackling postcolonial extractivist legacies by empowering diverse (subaltern, colonised) economic forms, especially communitarian modes of re/production. Yet the defence of such diversity is hindered by the permanent dominating role of extractivism even in highly diverse, variegated, societies.

In Huanuni, Bolivia, indigenous-peasant movements have designed their strategies in response to the violation of their fundamental rights to physical and psychological integrity, water and food security. Yet, they faced power structures that have sustained extractivism since colonial times. In Intag, Ecuador, as movements and their political allies attempted to make use of existing and newly introduced mechanisms to facilitate citizen participation, they encountered hard power structures referred to as a mechanism of "shielding mining companies" by an interviewee. This rendered impossible their partaking in decision-making and social control of extractive activities.

Our analysis has revealed how mining operations entail the violation of fundamental and political rights rooted in power structures that have built up since colonial times, and mechanisms of "shielding mining companies" that have been backed by the states' executive forces. A look at the plurinational legal instruments created during the 1990s and early 2000s explains the strength of these structures only partially. Here, we argue that the time frame for analysis has to be broadened in order to capture the historical accumulation of power that has perpetuated such extractivist political economic, and highly transnationalised, structures since colonial times. What plurinationalism has changed is that it has attempted to institutionalise plural sovereignty claims (Radhuber & Radcliffe, 2022) linked to diverse modes of re/production, unveiling a perduring capitalist-colonial core of the state in its political economic dimension and state-society relations.

For the conceptualisation of extractive bargains in the context of post-colonial (often highly plural) contexts, this means that the power structures that have existed since colonial times must be taken into account if these agreements are to deliver on their promises. Although their demands were recognised in the constitutions of both countries, the implementation of plural economies encountered obstacles stemming from the intertwined colonial and capitalist relations that unfolded in specific ways on the ground. Therefore, the displacement of diverse re/productive activities is closely intertwined with the continuous recreation of a constitutive capitalist and colonial moment.

In many Latin American "pink tide" countries the extractive bargain is/was to allow extractive activity to continue and expand in exchange for increase in state revenues which would be used to reduce poverty and advance social redistribution goals. In Ecuador and Bolivia, the extractive bargain has gone beyond this in theory. It proposed allowing extractivism to continue, but only as a part of plural economies which permit, facilitate and encourage the existence and expansion of other economic sectors and forms of social organisation, including non-capitalist ones. This has been added to the Constitutions of these countries and reflects the underlying reality of these states as plurinational, that is, as comprising multiple, autonomous, sovereign nations within a single state space.

In practice, however, extractive activity has undermined, rather than co-existed with, other plural economies, and generated resistance as a result. This is because the logic of the colonial-capitalist extractive sector is incompatible with respecting the rights of others to use land in a different way. As a result, the central state has intervened on behalf of mining capital, sometimes with force, and has, in effect, fallen back on demanding acceptance of the extractive bargain offered in other "pink tide" states.

The Andean indigenous-peasant movements' proposals for a more plural and just extractive bargain aimed to empower non-extractivist and communitarian modes of re/production. But this has not happened in practice. What is needed, therefore, is to strengthen the power of the plurinational organisations which would enable them to effectively contest the decisions of the central state.

Nonetheless, the constitutionally recognised proposal for "plural economies" holds the potential to create more equality between and among different re/productive forms when such power dynamics are taken into account. And last but not least, they hold the potential to balance tensions that build up in (economic) crises arising from capitalist-colonial dynamics.

References

Amnesty International. (2013). *Ecuador: Temor por la seguridad de activistas medioambientales.* . Retrieved from http://bit.ly/1Nb0rg6.

Andreucci, D., & Gruberg Cazón, H. (2015). *Evaluación de la gestión socio-ambiental del sector minero en Bolivia. El caso de la Cuenca del Lago Poopó.* CENDA. Retrieved from http://ambiental.net/wp-content/uploads/2016/05/AndreucciGruberGestionSocioAmbientalMineraBolivia16.pdf

Andreucci, D., & Radhuber, I. M. (2017). Limits to "counter-neoliberal" reform: Mining expansion and the marginalisation of post-extractivist forces in Evo Morales's Bolivia. *Geoforum*, vol. 84, https://doi.org/10.1016/j.geoforum.2015.09.002

Anthias, P. (2018). *Limits to decolonization: Indigeneity, territory, and hydrocarbon politics in the Bolivian Chaco.* Cornell University Press.

Arellano, A. (2022, February 10). Ecuador: comunidades de Íntag demandan al Estado para proteger a la naturaleza de la minería. *Mongabay.* Retrieved from https://es.mongabay.com/2022/02/ecuador-comunidades-de-intag-demandan-al-estado-para-proteger-a-la-naturaleza-de-la-mineria/

Arias, C. J. (2015). *Coridup. Una organización social en defensa de la Madre tierra.* CEPA/ Red Umavida.

Augsburger, A. (2021). The plurinational state and Bolivia's formación abigarrada. *Third World Quarterly, 42*(7), 1566–1582. https://doi.org/10.1080/01436597.2021.1899803

Avcı, D. (2017). Mining conflicts and transformative politics: A comparison of Intag (Ecuador) and Mount Ida (Turkey) environmental struggles. *Geoforum, 84*, 316–325.

Billo, E. (2020). Patriarchy and progressive politics: gendered resistance to mining through everyday social relations of state formation in Intag, Ecuador. *Human Geography, 13*(1), 16–26.

Bolivia. (2009). *Constitución Política del Estado: promulgada el 7 de febrero de 2009*. Congreso de Bolivia.

CEPA. (2022, April 11). *Empresa del Estado trabaja al margen de la normativa ambiental.* CEPA. Retrieved from https://cepaoruro.org/empresa-del-estado-trabaja-al-margen-de-la-normativa-ambiental/

Chavez, M. & López, C. (2018). *Women Rebel in Tariquía. NACLA Report on the Americas,* 50(4):408–410. CEDIB (2013). Retrieved June 27, 2017, from https://www.cedib.org/wp-content/uploads/2013/08/Tabla-Poblacion-Indigena1.pdf

Chávez, P., Mokrani, D., & Tapia, L. (2008). *Coloquio Poder y Cambio en Bolivia 2003- 2007*. PIEB.

CODELCO. (2011). *Firma de acuerdo Codelco-Enami EP de Ecuador, 28.11.2017*. Retrieved June 27, 2017, from https://www.codelco.com/firma-de-acuerdo-codelco-enami-ep-de-ecuador/prontus_codelco/2011-11-28/122201.html

Colloredo-Mansfeld, R., Ordoñez, A., Paltán, L. H., Quick, J., Quiroga, D. & Williams, J. (2018). Conflicts, Territories, and the Institutionalization of Post-Agrarian Economies on an Expanding Tourist Frontier in Quilotoa, Ecuador. *World Development 101*. https://doi.org/10.1016/j.worlddev.2016.11.001

CONAIE. (1994). *Proyecto Político de la CONAIE*. CONAIE.

CONAIE. (2001). *Aprobado en el I Congreso Nacional de las Nacionalidades y Pueblos Indígenas del Ecuador*. REDCI.

CONAIE. (2012). *Proyecto Político de la CONAIE*. CONAIE.

CONAIE. (2022, June 22). *Demandas de la movilización nacional, popular y plurinacional*. Retrieved from https://conaie.org/2022/06/20/demandas-de-la-movilizacion-nacional-popular-y-plurinacional/

Davidov, V. (2014). Land, copper, flora: Dominant materialities and the making of Ecuadorian resource environments. *Anthropological Quarterly, 87*(1), 31–58.

DECOIN. (2017). *Breve historia de la resistencia a la minería*. Decoin. Retrieved June 27th 2017 from http://www.decoin.org/breve-historia-de-la-resistencia-a-la-mineria/

Decreto Supremo 335. (2009). *Bolivia: Decreto Supremo N° 335, 21 de octubre de 2009*. Lexivox. Retrieved on June 28, 2017 from: http://www.lexivox.org/norms/BO-DS-N335.xhtml.

Delgado, A. C. (2017). The TIPNIS Conflict in Bolivia. *Contexto Internacional, 39*(2), 373–392. https://doi.org/10.1590/s0102-8529.2017390200009

Dossier Estadísticas. (2015). *Dossier Estadísticas del Sector Minero Metalúrgico 1980-2014*. Ministerio de Minería y Metalurgia & Estado Plurinacional de Bolivia.

Ecuador. (2008). *Constitución de la República del Ecuador*. Registro Oficial 449.

Farthing, L. (2019). An Opportunity Squandered? Elites, Social Movements, and the Government of Evo Morales. *Latin American Perspectives, 46*(1), 212–229. https://doi.org/10.1177/0094582X18798797g

Gago, V., & Gutiérrez, R. (2018). Women Rising in Defense of Life. *NACLA Report on the Americas, 50*(4), 364–368. https://doi.org/10.1080/10714839.2018.1550978

Garcés, F. (2010). *El Pacto de Unidad y el Proceso de Construcción de una Propuesta de Constitución Política del Estado: Sistematización de la experiencia*. Centro Cooperativo Sueco, retrieved from https://redunitas.org/wp-content/uploads/2019/04/PACTO_UNIDAD.pdf

Gargallo, F. (2021). *Feminismos desde Abya Yala: ideas y proposiciones de las mujeres de 607 pueblos en nuestra América*. Universidad Autónoma de la Ciudad de México.

Holmes, C. (2014). Introduction: A post-Polanyian political economy for our times. *Economy and Society, 43*(4), 1. https://doi.org/10.1080/03085147.2014.955700

Horowitz, L. S., Keeling, A., Lévesque, F., Rodon, T., Schott, S., & Thériault, S. (2018). Indigenous peoples' relationships to large-scale mining in post/colonial contexts: Toward multidisciplinary comparative perspectives. *The Extractive Industries and Society, 5*(3), 404–414.

Human Rights Watch. (2015, August 27). *Environmentalists Under Siege in Ecuador*. Human Rights Watch. Retrieved from https://www.hrw.org/news/2015/08/27/environmentalists-under-siege-ecuador

Instituto Nacional de Estadística. (2017, February). 236 años Oruro. *INE*. Retrieved from https://siip.produccion.gob.bo/noticias/files/BI_170220171e8fc_FOLLETO_DE_ORURO_2017.pdf.

Jenkins, K. (2015). Unearthing Women's Anti-Mining Activism in the Andes: Pachamama and the "Mad Old Women". *Antipode, 47*(2), 442–460. https://doi.org/10.1111/anti.12126

Latorre, S., Walter, M., & Larrea, C. (2015). *Íntag, un territorio en disputa. Evaluación De Escenarios Territoriales Extractivo Y No-extractivo*. Universidad Andina Simón Bolívar-Abya-Yala.

López, E., Sempértegui, Á. C., Tito, S. L., Lara, E. M., & Molina, P. (2010). *El costo ecológico de la política minera en Huanuni y Bolívar*. PIEB.

Mongabay. (2017). *Décadas de contaminación: ríos cargados de metales pesados recorren las comunidades de Oruro en Bolivia*. Mongabay. Retrieved June 28th 2017 from https://es.mongabay.com/2017/03/rios-contaminacion-relaves-medio_ambiente-pueblos_indigenas-recursos_naturales-bolivia/; http://www.lapatriaenlinea.com/?nota=256251

Muñoz, E., & Villareal, M. C. (2019). Women's Struggles Against Extractivism in Latin America and the Caribbean. *Contexto int, 41*(2), 303–325. https://doi.org/10.1590/S0102-8529.2019410200004

Myers, N., Mittermeier, R. A., Mittermeier, C. G., Da Fonseca, G. A., & Kent, J. (2000). Biodiversity hotspots for conservation priorities. *Nature, 403*(6772), 853–858.

Perreault, T. (2013). Dispossession by accumulation? Mining, water and the nature of enclosure on the Bolivian Altiplano. *Antipode, 45*(5), 1050–1069.

Postero, N., & Fabricant, N. (2019). Indigenous sovereignty and the new developmentalism in plurinational Bolivia. *Anthropological Theory, 19*(1), 95–119.

Radcliffe, S. A., & Radhuber, I. M. (2020). The political geographies of D/decolonization: Variegation and decolonial challenges of/in geography. *Political Geography, 78*, 102–128.

Radhuber, I. M. & Radcliffe, S. A. (2022). Contested Sovereignties: Indigenous disputes over plurinational resource governance. *Environment and Planning E: Nature and Space*, DOI: 25148486211068476.

Radhuber, I. M., León, M. C., & Andreucci, D. (2021). Expansión extractivista, resistencia comunitaria y'despojo político'en Bolivia. *Journal of Political Ecology, 28*(1), 205–223.

Ribera, M. O. (2010). *El sector minero: análisis crítico y problematicas socioambientales de: megaproyectos Mutún, Cuenca del Poopó, Cuenca del Pilcomayo, Megaproyecto San Cristobal Actualización 2009-2010. Serie de estudios de caso sobre problemáticas de socio ambientales en Bolivia (No. 2)*. LIDEMA.

Rodriguez Fernandez, G. V. (2020). Neo-extractivism, the Bolivian state, and indigenous peasant women's struggles for water in the Altiplano. *Human Geography, 13*(1), 27–39. https://doi.org/10.1177/1942778620910896

Ruales, G., & Zaragocin, S. (2020). De-géneros y territorios ¿Tiene género la tierra? In D. T. Cruz & M. Bayón (Eds.), *Cuerpos, territorios y feminismos: compilación latinoamericana de teorías, metodologías y prácticas políticas* (pp. 303–313). Abya Yala.

Schavelzon, S. (2015). *Plurinacionalidad y Vivir Bien/Buen Vivir: dos conceptos leídos desde Bolivia y Ecuador post-constituyentes*. Abya Yala.

Simpson, L. B. (2014). Land as pedagogy: Nishnaabeg intelligence and rebellious transformation. *Decolonization: Indigeneity, Education & Society, 3*(3), 1–25.

Sotalin, K. (2022, February 14). Íntag apelará fallo que negó acción para consulta minera. *El Comercio*. https://www.elcomercio.com/actualidad/politica/intag-fallo-consulta-mineria-corte.html.

Tapia, L. (2019a). *La ley del valor y América Latina*. Autodeterminación.

Tapia, L. (2019b). History and Structure in the Thought of René Zavaleta. *Historical Materialism, 27*(3), 127–135.

Varela, M. (2010). Las actividades extractivas en Ecuador. *Ecuador Debate, 79*, 127–150.

Vela-Almeida, D., Zaragocín, S., Bayón, M., & Arrazola, I. (2020). Imaginando territorios plurales de vida: una lectura feminista de las resistencias en los movimientos socio-territoriales en el Ecuador. *Journal of Latin American Geography, 19*(2), 87–109.

Zavaleta, R. (2011). *Obras completas*. Plural Editores.

Part IV

Beyond the National: Bargains at Other Scales

14

Global Extractive Bargains for Green New Deals

Paul Bowles and Nathan Andrews

Introduction

Many political parties, national governments and regional bodies in the Global North have advanced various versions of 'Green New Deals' (GNDs) designed to cut carbon dioxide emissions to meet climate change objectives and a variety of social objectives associated with a just transition. While they differ in form and content, taken together, these Green

We are grateful to Walsham Tenshak for providing research assistance which was invaluable in the writing of this chapter.

P. Bowles (✉)
Global and International Studies, University of Northern British Columbia, Prince George, BC, Canada
e-mail: paul.bowles@unbc.ca

N. Andrews
Department of Political Science, McMaster University, Hamilton, ON, Canada
e-mail: nandrews@mcmaster.ca

P. Bowles, N. Andrews (eds.), *Extractive Bargains*, Frontiers of Globalization,
https://doi.org/10.1007/978-3-031-32172-6_14

New Deals would involve a significant shift away from fossil fuels and an increase in energy from renewable solar and wind sources as well as an expansion of 'clean' forms of transportation such as electric vehicles (EVs).

In this chapter, we examine some prominent GNDs to see if and how they address the issue of the global governance of the extraction of the minerals which will be needed to expand solar, wind and EVs. We argue that accompanying any GND will need to be a global extractive bargain governing the continuing extraction of the minerals powering the 'clean' energy transition. In the next section we provide an overview of ten GNDs and point to their implications for solar, wind and electricity storage including EVs. We identify the minerals, and their sources, which will be needed to support the expansion of these three energy types. We also examine the extent to which the GNDs explicitly or implicitly recognize the need for new methods of global mineral governance.

As we will show, many GNDs are silent on the global governance mechanisms that will be necessary to support the mining of, and international trade in, critical minerals. This silence suggests that one form of global extractive bargain is to separate the GND objectives from the means necessary to implement them and to delegate mining governance to existing separate and parallel negotiations of global mining frameworks and international norms. We analyse these 'parallel bargains' in the Section on "Scenarios for Global Extractive Bargains". We also argue that in order to move in the direction of a progressive global extractive bargain we need to rethink and recalibrate the aims and mechanisms of global mineral governance. In this regard, we argue that while the Global North evokes the language of the 1930s to advocate for GNDs for the twenty-first century, the countries of the Global South may need to evoke the language of the 1970s to advocate for a 'Green New International Economic Order' (GIEO) if they are to benefit from the twenty-first-century energy transition. The prospects for such a Global Extractive Bargain are, however, not high.

Green New Deals

The original New Deal, of course, was designed to address the capitalist crisis of the 1930s in the US and, later, informed post-1945 reconstruction in Europe. The idea was the forging of a new social contract in which economic growth would be spurred by government spending and by policies which addressed the needs of the unemployed and the working class more generally.

The calls for GNDs in the contemporary period generally echo the concern with addressing social inequality but add to it the need to promote economic growth which is compatible with environmental sustainability and the energy transition away from fossil fuels in particular although there are also debates over whether "green degrowth" might be a better path (Hickel, 2021). The calls for GNDs come from a range of generally centrist and leftish political parties, governments, institutions and think tanks all concerned with charting a more socially equitable and environmentally sustainable future. Within them we might expect to find therefore some exposition of forms of extractive bargains especially if we consider the roles that will need to be played by renewable energy sources.

To consider this further, we summarize in Table 14.1 below the energy goals in a sample of ten recent GNDs and highlights the implications for solar, wind and EV production. The Table also indicates whether the implications for mining and international trade regulations form part of the GND under consideration.

As might be expected all the proposals surveyed provide goals for GHG emission reductions. These are variously expressed as targets for emission reductions from 2005 levels consistent with the COP process, and/or for net zero emissions. For example, the European Commission for a Green Deal calls for net zero GHG emissions by 2050, an emissions goal also set by US Congress Resolution 109 although with no date attached. Other proposals call for the rapid phase out of fossil fuels (e.g., Labour for a Green New Deal) while others aim to "decarbonize" the economy (e.g., Democracy in Europe Movement 2025) or growth (Boston University and UNCTAD). These are moving targets and the transition in Europe, for example, is being speeded up through the

Table 14.1 Summary of Green New Deals for the energy transition and governance

Green New Deal proposal	Energy goals	Mineral and/or trade governance	Special features
Labour for a Green New Deal (UK) (2019)	Zero carbon emissions by 2030 Rapidly phase out all fossil fuels Large investment in renewables Increase public transport not private vehicles	"Development of renewables, particularly solar PV, is reliant on the extraction of rare earth metals which are, at present, often sourced in an environmentally and socially unjust manner. ... Thus, in order to ensure a Green New Deal is internationally just and environmentally sound, the mass deployment of renewable energy must be done without contributing to environmental degradation or, critically, to human exploitation in the supply chain." Advocates general trade principle: "Supporting developing countries' efforts to challenge unjust, neocolonial and unsustainable economic structures and ensuring the Green New Deal does not replicate these, particularly in the extractive sector".	Welcome climate refugees
European Commission for a Green Deal (2019)	Net-zero GHG emissions by 2050 Maximize the use of renewables to decarbonize Europe's energy supply	"Recovery and recycling of raw materials will be of particular importance in those sectors and technologies where new dependencies might emerge, such as a reliance on critical materials like cobalt, rare earths or graphite, whose production is concentrated in a few countries outside Europe. But also strengthened EU trade policy has a role to ensure sustainable and secure supply of these materials to the EU."	
Korea's New Deal proposed by former President Moon Jae-In (Govt. of Republic of Korea, 2020)	20% energy from renewable sources by 2030 Wind power test sites in at least 13 cities Support solar installation costs. 1.13 m EVs target	None	Build a "green industrial cluster" Develop EV parts production, hydrogen fuel cell systems, fuel for eco-friendly vessels

US Congress Resolution 109 introduced by Alexandria Ocasio-Cortes, co-sponsored by 94 members of Congress (US Congress, 2019)	Net-zero GHG emissions. Meeting 100% of the power demand in the United States through clean, renewable, and zero-emission energy sources, including (1) by dramatically expanding and upgrading renewable power sources and (2) by deploying new capacity	"Enact and enforce trade rules, procurement standards, and border adjustments with strong labor and environmental protections (1) to stop the transfer of jobs and pollution overseas; and (2) to grow domestic manufacturing in the United States."	"Promote justice and equity by stopping current, preventing future, and repairing historic oppression of … 'frontline and vulnerable communities'."
Mission: Possible-The Green Climate Action Plan by the Green Party of Canada (2019)	60% reduction in GHG emissions by 2030; zero emissions by 2050 Increase renewables All new vehicles to be EVs by 2030; all vehicles on roads must be EVs by 2040	None	"Establish an inner cabinet of all parties: Modelled on the war cabinets of Mackenzie King and Winston Churchill, parties will work together to ensure that climate is no longer treated like a political football."
Green New Deal proposed by Democracy in Europe Movement 2025 (DiEM25, 2019)	Decarbonize the economy. Establish the Green Public Works (GPW), a public investment agency that will channel Europe's resources into green transition projects	Intervene in the design of global prudential standards to introduce punitive capital requirements for investments in fossil fuel heavy and environmentally destructive projects and businesses in the Basel framework	Strong focus on environmental justice within Europe

(continued)

Table 14.1 (continued)

Green New Deal proposal	Energy goals	Mineral and/or trade governance	Special features
A Green New Deal Policy report by Data for Progress (US) (Carcock et al., 2018)	100% clean and renewable energy by 2035 Zero net emissions from energy by 2050 100% zero-emission passenger vehicles by 2030 100% fossil-free transportation by 2050	None	
Green New Deal proposed by US Green Party (n.d.)	100% clean energy by 2030. "Build a nationwide smart electricity grid that can pool and store power from a diversity of renewable sources, giving the nation clean, democratically-controlled, energy."	None	"End destructive energy extraction and associated infrastructure. … Halt any investment in fossil fuel infrastructure. … End all subsidies for fossil fuels and impose a greenhouse gas fee/ tax to charge polluters for the damage they have created."

Geneva Principles for a Green New Deal (Boston University and UNCTAD) (Gallagher and Kozul-Wright, 2019)	Decarbonize growth	Global rules should be calibrated towards environmental sustainability; "States share common but differentiated responsibilities to advance global public goods and protect the global commons."	Green industrial policy Policy space for states to pursue national development strategies
A People's Green New Deal (Ajl 2021)	Ecosocialist planning to reduce emissions; "controlled industrialization"; reduced transportation; wind and solar-powered shipping, trains, and factories	Unclear—based on Cochabamba Declaration (2009)	Climate-debt reparations. National solutions

RePower Europe initiative designed to rapidly reduce reliance on imports of natural gas in particular from Russia in the wake of the latter's invasion of Ukraine.

There is also widespread support in the GNDs for the expansion of "clean energy" and for the use of renewables. In this regard, wind and solar power are frequently identified as energy sources to be expanded for residential and commercial buildings as well as for transportation. EVs also figure prominently although some proposals put more emphasis on public transportation rather than private modes of transportation. Data for Progress in the US, for example, targets 2030 for zero-emission vehicles, the same date as the Green Party of Canada. Under the European Commission's Green Deal, individual EU member states may introduce their own policies and some have already announced dates for the elimination of the sale of new gasoline engine cars. Former President Moon Jae-In's proposal for South Korea also involved a large increase in EV production and use. Labour for a Green New Deal places the emphasis squarely on public transportation which is perhaps not surprising given that leading scientists argued that to meet UK EV targets for 2050 would require "just under two times the total annual world cobalt production, nearly the entire world production of neodymium, three quarters the world's lithium production and 12% of the world's copper production during 2018" (Natural History Museum, 2019).

Given this estimate based just on the UK's demand, it is clear that taken together the various GNDs will require a substantial, perhaps impossible, increase in the mining of critical minerals and metals needed for wind, solar and EV production and energy storage and the transition to renewable energy sources. If, taken together, the goal of the GNDs is to keep the increase in global temperatures to under 2 degrees Celsius, then a World Bank (2017, p. xii) study provides some estimates of the orders of magnitude that this implies: renewable energy will have to increase from its current 14% of the global energy mix to 44%. This implies a 1000% increase in the demand for the metals used in electric storage batteries, a 250% increase in those used in wind technologies and a 300% increase for those used in solar technologies (World Bank, 2017, pp. 12–17). As a first look at this issue, we provide in Table 14.2 a list of

Table 14.2 Minerals and metals used in three renewable energy types

Solar	Wind	EVs and Energy Storage
Bauxite	Bauxite	Bauxite
Copper	Copper	Copper
Nickel	Nickel	Nickel
	Iron	Iron
Lead	Lead	
	Rare Earths	Rare Earths
	Manganese	Manganese
Silver		Silver
Molybdenum	Molybdenum	
Indium		Indium
Zinc	Chromium	Titanium
Tin		Cobalt
Selenium		Graphite
Tellurium		Lithium

Source: World Bank (2017: 75) and authors.

Note: The terms" rare earths" refers to17 different elements, often found together in the Earth's crust. Of the 17, three are of particular importance to the development of green energy technologies: dysprosium, neodymium and praseodymium.

Key:

Used in all three energy types

Used in any two energy types

Used in one energy type

the main minerals and metals needed in production for these three renewable energy sources.

These minerals and metals are found in many parts of the world including many in the Global South as well as in settler colonial states of the Global North. Table 14.3 provides details of which countries are the main producers; by how much demand for these minerals and metals

Table 14.3 Main sources of selected minerals and metals required for solar, wind, EV and energy storage (by country, 2015, in order of production importance)

Minerals and Metals	Main Sources
Bauxite	Australia, China, Malaysia, India, Guinea, Jamaica
Copper	Chile, China, Peru, China, US, DR Congo, Australia, Russia, Canada, Zambia
Iron Ore	China, Australia, Brazil, India, Russia
Lead	China, Australia, US, Peru, Mexico, India
Zinc	China, Australia, Peru, US, India, Mexico, Bolivia
Nickel	Canada, Australia, New Caledonia, Indonesia, China, Colombia, Cuba, South Africa
Cobalt	DR Congo, China, Canada, Russia, Australia, Philippines, Cuba, Madagascar
Silver	Mexico, China, Peru, Australia, Chile, Russia, Bolivia, Poland
Lithium	Australia, Chile, Argentina, China, Zimbabwe
Titanium	China, Australia, Vietnam, South Africa, Mozambique, Kenya

Source: World Bank XE "World Bank" (2017)

increases depends on many factors including the speed of the shift towards renewables, rates of global economic growth and the technologies adopted, but we can expect that there will be a substantial increase in their extraction in these countries over the coming decades. The ways in which domestic extractive bargains are being formulated in many of these countries are thoroughly examined in other chapters in this volume. In this chapter, we focus on extractive bargains at the global level given that for the GNDs listed in Table 14.1 to have any chance of being successfully implemented, a substantial increase in critical mineral production in, and trade with, the countries listed in Table 14.3 will be needed.

This raises the question of the global conditions under which such extraction and trade will take place. In particular, what sort of global extractive bargains might be envisaged that would enable the energy transition to be undertaken in ways which facilitate the attainment of environmental and social justice goals? It is to this question that we now turn.

Scenarios for Global Extractive Bargains

At the global level, the adoption of GNDs and the energy transition may play out in a number of ways not all of which would constitute global extractive bargains. Two such 'non-bargains' are worthy of brief consideration here. The first is a return to colonial forms of resource extraction in which mining companies from the Global North extract resources under little scrutiny or international regulation. Arguably, this occurs in the present especially in countries where governance is weak, where security has been militarized and partly privatized and where state elites and mining companies have formed pacts for mutual self-enrichment. While not denying that this is a reasonable characterization of some locations, we do not examine this further here since the basic requirements for a bargain—a state-society arrangement designed to provide at least some level of legitimacy to mineral extraction—is absent. A second scenario reflects not a global bargain but geoeconomic rivalry more along East-West lines as China, a major source of critical minerals and rare earths, seeks to use its resources for its own purposes and blocks their export to other countries. An example of this has already been provided when China blocked the export of rare earth elements to Japan in 2010 in an ongoing dispute over territorial claims. In 2021, tensions with the US caused both countries to consider halting trade in rare earth elements between them with China not wanting to supply a hostile power and the US not wanting to be dependent on imports from China for materials used in military production. It is possible that trade in rare earths and other critical minerals will be subject to the dictates of geopolitics and geoeconomics where international power rivalries will determine their production and international distribution. This scenario, too, is by no means impossible or even unlikely but we again explore it no further here and focus on two scenarios which are more consistent with the idea of a global extractive bargain. We call these the 'parallel' and the 'GNIEO' bargains.

Parallel Bargains

Many of the GNDs proposed in the Global North make no mention of the global trade and mineral governance regimes needed to support them. Where mention is made, it is often with the interests of the Global North in mind—the need for EU trade rules to ensure mineral security in the European Commission proposal and for protecting US jobs and manufacturing potential in US Congressional Resolution 109. The majority of the GNDs analysed in Table 14.1 are therefore inward-looking, designed to appeal more to domestic populations, despite their global implications. In confronting global climate change it seems that many GND proposals are decidedly insular in their foci. In the absence of being addressed in the proposals, the default position is that mineral extraction will be considered in other fora and through other parallel international initiatives; that is, existing international norms are to be relied upon to fashion a global extractive bargain capable of governing the energy transition.

There is a plethora of parallel international norms that serve as corporate codes of conduct in the area of extraction and beyond, including the UN Global Compact, Global Reporting Initiative (GRI), Extractive Industries Transparency Initiative (EITI), the Voluntary Principles on Business, Security and Human Rights (VPs), UN Guiding Principles on Business and Human Rights (UNGPs), and the International Organization for Standardization (ISO) suite of international standards among others. Although not all of them have an emphasis on environmental sustainability per se, which will align with prospects of GNDs, they all support this apparent shift in corporate orientation towards a triple bottom line that includes people, planet and profits. We can argue that this shift in corporate orientation is due to both the urgency of the climate crisis and its impact on companies' bottom lines. Putting in place a climate protocol and other climate mitigation strategies at sites of operation and throughout the supply chain, for instance, imagines a future (potentially 'greener') world where mining still plays a role in the global political economy.

As noted previously, the global extractive bargain that will support energy transitions will be fuelled by further resource extraction in different parts of the world. If the same or similar multinational corporations whose behaviour these existing norms are expected to govern are to be the ones in charge of 'greener' extractive activities, one would expect these norms to maintain some prominence over time. For instance, business and human rights (BHR) norms such as the VPs and UNGPs are intended to ensure that people's rights are protected and that corporations are not able to get away with human rights violations that could result from the energy transition. Given that National Action Plans for BHR are emerging in different jurisdictions (see Rivera, 2019) and scholars are also beginning to explore the connection between "human rights due diligence" and "climate due diligence" (Macchi, 2021; Bright & Buhmann, 2021), there is some potential in envisioning the promise of implementing these norms.

As climate-related financial disclosures from companies become an aspect of corporate reporting and sustainability accounting, the EITI and GRI will continue to be international benchmarks for such activities. It must be noted that these parallel international initiatives have their own limitations especially given that majority of them are voluntary and do encounter significant challenges in practice (see Sovacool & Andrews, 2015; Andrews, 2019, 2020; Wettstein, 2021). Yet, there is perhaps something to be said about their potential for all these initiatives to work together in some fashion to help construct a global extractive bargain. The UN Global Compact in particular, which is considered as the world's largest corporate social responsibility initiative, has the potential to play a leadership role in this area despite its current shortfalls (see Rasche & Waddock, 2014).

The International Finance Corporation (IFC), an arm of the World Bank, has a set of eight Performance Standards on Environmental and Social Sustainability that are noteworthy. These standards also serve as an important parallel bargain because companies that receive financial support from IFC are required to use them as a benchmark for managing environmental and social risks (IFC, 2012). This means that it is not as voluntary as some of the corporate-led self-regulatory initiatives because maintaining continuous investment in a mining project is dependent on the ability of the mining company to show that it has met the basic criteria established by the standards. One aspect of the standard is the focus on companies seeking the 'free, prior and informed consent' (FPIC) of local and Indigenous populations in areas of operation, thereby aligning with other international instruments such as the United Nations Declaration on the Rights of Indigenous Peoples (UNDRIP). This reflects the need to uphold the three forms of justice (i.e., distributive, procedural, recognition) that underpin energy transitions (Williams & Doyon, 2019). Thus, one would expect the global extractive bargain to entail serious considerations for FPIC and the general involvement of people who are typically marginalized from such activities (Armstrong, 2021).

The OECD principles of corporate governance constitute an aspect of the parallel international initiatives that are meant to improve corporate governance practices in both OECD and non- OECD countries. These general principles connect with the OECD Guidelines for Multinational Enterprises, which contain specific best practices for responsible corporate conduct in areas of human rights and labour rights, information disclosure, environment, bribery, consumer interests, science and technology, competition, and taxation (OECD, 2011). The guidelines on the environment in particular focus on sound environmental management and generally reflect the principles and objectives of the Rio Declaration on Environment and Development (Agenda 21). The guidelines also partially focus on what responsible business conduct means for climate change—which involves the private sector being proactive in, firstly, reducing GHG emissions and the overall impact of their activities on people and the planet, and secondly, strengthening the resilience of their wider supply chains in order to adapt to and tackle climate change. The understanding that informs this bargain is the idea that companies that are able to reduce emissions and transition to net-zero will be better placed to satisfy consumer and investor expectations, maintain a social licence to operate, and increase their overall competitiveness and bottom line.[1]

For something specific on energy transitions, the OECD in early 2022 published a policy document that examines a framework to decarbonize

[1] For more details, see http://mneguidelines.oecd.org/rbc-and-climate-change.htm

the economy (D'Arcangelo et al., 2022). While recognizing the differences across the various member-states of the organization, the framework focuses on a policy mix that has three key components: "(1) emission pricing policy instruments; (2) standards and regulations; (3) complementary policies to facilitate the reallocation of capital, labour and innovation towards low-carbon activities and to offset the adverse distributional effects of reducing emissions" (D'Arcangelo et al., 2022, p. 6). The redistributive aspect of the framework seeks to ensure that the transition to a low-carbon economy does not disproportionately impact low-skilled workers and low-income households in order to build the social and political support needed for decarbonization policy packages. This is a clear manifestation of the 'inclusion' narrative that informs these parallel global bargains. It is noteworthy that the decarbonization framework aligns with other efforts such as the OECD International Programme for Action on Climate (IPAC), which serves as a benchmark to support member-states in achieving the objectives of the Paris Agreement by evaluating specific national and international policies aimed at net-zero GHG emissions by 2050.[2]

One of the central instruments for twenty-first-century broad-based global environmental governance is the UN Sustainable Development Goals (SDGs) with a 2030 timeline in focus. The SDGs represent an important parallel bargain because the 17 goals attempt to capture aspects of the development thinking that has informed post-1945 economic endeavours while also envisioning a post-2030 world that is both sustainable and inclusive with the contested catchphrase of "leaving no one behind" (Weber, 2017; Sénit, 2020). Arguably, it may even be regarded as an epitome of the collaborative governance needed to sustain any form of bargain towards the global governance of energy transitions especially when one considers its multi-stakeholder approach. For example, many extractive corporations are now reporting on specific SDG benchmarks in their operations and specifically how they contribute to the attainment of the 17 goals (see ElAlfy et al., 2020; Shayan et al., 2022). While many of the goals are intertwined, SDG7 (affordable and clean energy) and SDG13 (climate action) in particular are more directly concerned with the

[2] See https://www.oecd.org/mcm/IPAC%20brochure.pdf

objective of energy transition and net-zero emissions. One striking point is that most of the initial targets stipulated in the current GNDs (see Table 14.1), which entails cutting GHG emissions by 60–100% or attaining 100% clean energy by 2030, coincides with the expiry of the SDGs.

It has been widely acknowledged that the ability to advance the other SDGs largely depends on energy (United Nations, 2021). Yet, the objective to make substantial progress towards SDG7 by 2025 remains rather ambitious. We can postulate, however, that with the vision for a decarbonized energy system by 2050, the new formulation of these global goals after the current SDGs expire in 2030 may be prominently focused on different aspects of sustainable transitions that are core to recent iterations of the GND proposals. One reason for viewing the SDGs as a parallel bargain is their recognition of the need "to translate this global picture into nuanced regional, national, and subnational plans to ensure that the transition is just and leaves no one behind" (United Nations, 2021, p. 9). The point here is that there is potential for the UN and future formulations of the SDGs to transform the current insular focus of GNDs to one that may become widely embraced globally.

There is also a role for regional parallel bargains. The Africa Mining Vision (AMV), which was endorsed by the African Union (AU) in 2009, is a crucial policy document that seeks to facilitate "transparent, equitable and optimal exploitation of mineral resources to underpin broad-based sustainable growth and socio-economic development" (African Union, 2009, p. v.). The vision document recognizes the rich endowment of many African countries and pushes an agenda that helps specific governments to take development back into their own hands, which scholars have pointed to as a return to a 'new' developmental state (see Ovadia, 2016; Nwapi & Andrews, 2017; Andrews & Nwapi, 2018). Although it serves as a parallel regional governance framework for mineral extraction, the AMV's contribution to what we have conceptualized in this chapter as a GND is not explicit. Program cluster 7 of the AMV Action Plan focuses on environmental and social issues but deals more with the impacts of mining in communities than on sustainable transitions (African Union, 2011).

Despite what is lacking in Africa's regional mining framework, the AU has an Africa Energy Transition Programme (2020–2025), driven by AU

Agenda 2063, SDGs and the Paris Agreement on climate change. Although Africa is estimated to produce less than 4% of global GHG, the AU's energy transition programme has some bold plans towards decarbonization. For instance, EV for collective transportation systems (e.g., taxis, buses) in large cities in particular are deemed feasible in the short term (African Energy Commission, 2019). After the preparatory phase in 2019 and 2020, phase two of the programme (2021–2024) is expected to be implemented in five countries followed by a third phase (2023–2026) which will broaden implementation to additional countries. It is notable that the staggered and gradual approach to implementing the programme is likely to ensure buy-in is sought from key stakeholders involved in the extractive bargain at the regional level. To be sure, it will not be straightforward to expect oil-dependent states such as Nigeria, Libya, Angola and Algeria to immediately opt into this GND. The different workings of the AMV and the energy transition programme present an interesting parallel that underpins the extractive bargain on the continent, which reflects a tension between the quest to exploit natural resources for broad-based development and the need to show some commitment to transitioning away from these same resources that are meant to sustain socio-economic growth.

It is noteworthy that in terms of mechanisms that are facilitating the global extractive bargain capable of governing the energy transition, there are cross-country exchanges and cross-institutional learning in different regions of the world. In the Asia-Pacific, for instance, in 2021 South Korea hosted a regional seminar on GND projects with an emphasis on climate finance, technology and entrepreneurship.[3] The seminar involved several countries from the region, including some of those listed in Table 14.3 as having key minerals needed for energy transition. The ten-member states of the Association of Southeast Asian Nations have been recently called upon to develop a GND given the impact of climate change in the region in terms of weather- related disasters (The ASEAN Post, 2021). A similar bold vision is expected to emerge from Latin America if countries in the region are to make meaningful progress

[3] See https://gggi.org/asia-pacific-regional-seminar-on-green-new-deal-projects-climate-finance-technology-entrepreneurship/

towards energy transition (see Palacios & Cárdenas, 2022). This suggests that even in the absence of concrete frameworks or 'deals' at some regional levels in the Global South, there are initiatives and policy conversations contributing to the bargains needed to govern the energy transition.

These parallel bargains see an energy transition as necessary and seek to regulate extractive industries through a series of voluntary and implicitly involuntary codes of conduct designed to ensure that human rights are respected, social sustainability enhanced and environmental and climate goals met. This form of global bargain—continued extraction to meet climate goals but within a framework of international norms designed to spread the benefits and limit the costs—can be considered as occupying the contradictory position on the spectrum identified in Chap. 1. On the one hand, some of the aims of the parallel bargains are clearly desirable from a sustainability—in all its dimensions—perspective. There is recognition of the need to reign in corporate behaviour which violates human rights and leads to excessive environmental harm. At the same time, much of this is predicated on the need to continue with capitalist development, privilege private capital and view agents as 'stakeholders' whose interests need to be mediated by the adoption of international norms. These norms do not challenge dominant modes of extraction and face large and continual enforcement problems. As such, these parallel bargains may be thought of as a promising change but often lacking the boldness and enforcement mechanisms necessary to achieve it. To paraphrase a term used by a UN study of Structural Adjustment policies in the 1970s, the contemporary global institutional parallel bargains can be described as offering "extractivism with a human face". As a step in the direction of a more progressive global bargain, we consider what might be termed a Green New International Economic Order bargain.

Concluding Reflections: A GNIEO Bargain?

The fact that many of the GNDs proposed in the Global North do not explicitly recognize, much less address, the need for a global extractive bargain as part of the energy transition is in part revealed by the use of the term 'New Deal' itself. As noted in the Introduction, this term resonates with policies adopted in the US in the 1930s and in post-1945 Europe and the use of the term itself denotes the primacy of domestic social contracts put in place during those periods in the Global North. This Global North focus can be illustrated by considering some Canadian contributions. For example, the Green Party of Canada invokes the historic experience of a 'war cabinet' as an example of the way in which climate action should be depoliticised. Klein (2020) similarly invokes the wartime experience as a way of galvanizing Canadian society against an existential threat and examines how that experience can be used to good effect now. The Green Party of the US (n.d.) strikes a similar note in arguing that a Green New Deal "starts with a WWII-type mobilization". The Green Party of Canada's proposal title 'Mission: Possible' of course invokes a popular Hollywood film series but also resonates with Mariana Mazzucato's *Mission Economy* (2021) in which she invokes the 1960s moon landing as providing an example of the type of public-private synergies that are capable of producing spectacular results and argues that similar synergies are needed now to confront climate change. But whether it is New Deals, wartime efforts, or moon landings, the popular imaginaries and historical reference points are all drawn from the Global North. The Global South is entirely absent despite the fact that, as we have seen, mining its minerals will be critical to the success of the energy transition.

Some of the GNDs surveyed in Table 14.1 do provide a starting point for including the Global South, however. The Geneva Principles advanced by UNCTAD and Boston University's Global Development Policy Centre highlight the need for policy space and green industrial policies in the Global South. This resonates with Nem Singh's analysis discussed in Veltmeyer's chapter. Perhaps unsurprisingly the developmentalist potential for energy transitions is also highlighted in Former President Moon Jae-In's proposal for South Korea. Arl's 'People's Green New Deal' highlights the important role that "climate debt" may need to play in reaching a just global climate bargain. He too focuses on national autonomy, the "national question" as he puts it, but leaves underexplored how these national and local autonomous units will work together to produce global climate solutions. The most explicit discussion is provided by the UK's Labour for a Green New Deal which identifies the environmental and human exploitation present in existing mineral extraction and calls for challenging unjust global economic structures. In so doing, it allows the invocation of a different historical reference point, one advanced by the countries of the Global South, namely, the New International Economic Order (NIEO) of the 1970s. By choosing a different historical starting point, we may be provided with a new window into what a progressive global extractive bargain might look like in the contemporary period, to avoid the situation where, as Vergara-Camus (2022, p. 319) puts it, "the development of renewable energy often reproduces dynamics that are reminiscent of colonial and postcolonial extractivism".

The NIEO was a comprehensive framework for multilateral trade governance advanced by the Group of 77 developing countries to ensure that they benefitted more from the global trading system. It called for, *inter alia*, commodity price stabilization and indexation, technology transfer to enable greater industrial production in the Global South, binding codes of conduct on transnational corporations, debt relief and greater representation in international organizations, especially the international financial institutions (Snyed, 2016). Of course, the world has changed in many ways since the NIEO was proposed in the 1970s. The North-South divide has been eroded by the economic rise of some countries from the Global South with the result that the world has become multipolar or multicentric, commodity prices have been on a two-decade upward trajectory making the 'terms of trade debate' less relevant, and there have been four decades of neoliberalism which have stripped away regulations even as the liberal trading system itself has been increasingly undermined by a variety of nationalist economic programmes. Notwithstanding these changes, might the elements of a GNIEO be gleamed from its predecessor and provide a basis for a more progressive global extractive bargain than that implied by the parallel bargains discussed in 3.1?

Reconsidering the NIEO highlights three critical areas which a global extractive bargain will need to address in a progressive GNIEO for the twenty-first century. These three areas are technology, codes of conduct and representation.

With respect to technology, this operates at a number of levels. The issue of technology transfer is relevant for countries mining the minerals used in renewable energy sources and for the users of those sources themselves. For the producers of the minerals it means having access to the best technology in mining and remediation. It also means for countries in the Global South having access to the technology which allows adding value to the minerals rather than being confined to being raw material exporters. It means for the users of renewable energy sources in the Global South that they have access to the minerals and to the technologies utilizing them.

Having "access"is, of course, a vague term and it is the terms on which such access is granted that is key. It is here that the creation of a Global Green Technology Bank, for example, can play an important role as the repository of the technical data and scientific blueprints necessary for the global energy transition. Technologies developed in the Global North should be placed for free in this Bank as part of the payment of its climate debt. Compensation could be paid to technology developers from the Global South. Users would be able to access the Bank, and associated expertise, without payment. This is not an example of simply a techno-fix but rather a call for a political re-bargaining of how technology is owned and distributed.

To ensure that the best technologies are used, global rules requiring their use in all new projects could be established. But codes of conduct need to go far beyond this to ensure that environmental and social justice objectives are met in the global energy transition. This means that in colonial settler states, for example, UNDRIP, and its inclusion of FPIC, go beyond its status as an aspirational Declaration applied to states and written into law at all levels of government. It means that enforceable, legally binding standards are applied to all extractive industries globally; transnational corporations must be legally accountable for their operations worldwide in ways in which they are not now.

This requires a new global architecture premised on allowing all countries to have unrestricted access to the best technologies, to operate within a global system where transnational corporations are held to account, and where the rights of local populations are real. At the same time it must be an architecture which allows for rising incomes in the Global South consistent with an effective energy transition. To create such an architecture will require many architects; it cannot be the preserve of the Global North to dictate its features as it has been in the past. Global governance systems which guarantee effective representation and voice by all countries will be needed.

By picking up on three key themes of the NIEO advanced some half-century ago, namely, technology, enforceable codes of conduct and representation we can see what is missing from many contemporary discussions of GNDs. An energy transition that is socially and environmentally just must have an international dimension. The current practice of relying on what we have termed parallel bargains falls well short of what is required. Reflecting on what a GNIEO might look like shines the light on some key unaddressed issues of the global governance architecture. Reframing the historical lens, away from New Deals and to the NIEO, is useful in identifying blind spots in the current proposals and for opening up a dialogue of what might be required even if the prospects of getting even this far remain decidedly low.

References

African Energy Commission. (2019). *Designing the African Energy Transition.* Retrieved April 7, 2022, from https://au-afrec.org/sites/default/files/2022-02/4%20AFREC%20Designing%20the%20African%20Energy%20Transition.pdf

African Union. (2009). *Africa Mining Vision.* Retrieved April 7, 2022, from https://au.int/sites/default/files/documents/30984-doc-africa_mining_vision_english.pdf

African Union. (2011). *Action Plan for Implementing the AMV.* Retrieved April 7, 2022, from https://au.int/sites/default/files/documents/31003-doc-action_plan_final_version_jan_2012_2.pdf

Ajl, M. (2021). *A People's Green New Deal.* London: Pluto Press.

Andrews, N. (2019). Normative Spaces and the UN Global Compact for Transnational Corporations: The Norm Diffusion Paradox. *Journal of International Relations and Development, 22*(1), 77–106.

Andrews, N. (2020). The UN Global Compact: An Overview of the Promise and Pitfalls. *The Palgrave Handbook of Corporate Social Responsibility,* 1–21.

Andrews, N., & Nwapi, C. (2018). Bringing the State Back in Again? The Emerging Developmental State in Africa's Energy Sector. *Energy Research & Social Science, 41*, 48–58.

Armstrong, J. H. (2021). People and Power: Expanding the Role and Scale of Public Engagement in Energy Transitions. *Energy Research & Social Science, 78*, 102136.

Bright, C., & Buhmann, K. (2021). Risk-Based Due Diligence, Climate Change, Human Rights and the Just Transition. *Sustainability, 13*(18), 10454.

Carcock, G. et al. (2018). *A Green New Deal: A Progressive Vision for Environmental Sustainability and Economic Stability*. Data for Progress.

D'Arcangelo, F., Levin, I., Pagani, A., Pisu, M., & Johansson, Å. (2022). *A Framework to Decarbonise the Economy*. OECD Economic Policy Papers, No. 31. OECD Publishing. https://doi.org/10.1787/4e4d973d-en

DiEM25. (2019). *The Green New Deal for Europe*. Democracy in Europe Movement 2025.

ElAlfy, A., Darwish, K. M., & Weber, O. (2020). Corporations and Sustainable Development Goals Communication on Social Media: Corporate Social Responsibility or Just Another Buzzword? *Sustainable Development, 28*(5), 1418–1430.

European Commission. (2019). *Communication of the Commission: The European Green Deal*. Brussels: European Commission.

Gallagher, K., and Kosul-Wright, R. (2019). *A New Multilateralism for Shared Prosperity: Geneva Principles for a Global Green New Deal*. UNCTAD/Boston University.

Government of the Republic of Korea. (2020). *Korea's New Deal: National Stategy for a Great Transformation*. Seoul: Government of Reublic of Koreak.

Green Party (US). (n.d.) *Green New Deal: For A Clean, Renewable and Sustainable Future*. Available at gp.org.

Green Party of Canada. (2019). *Mission: Possible—The Green Climate Action Plan*. Green Party of Canada.

Hickel, J. (2021). *Less is More: How Degrowth Will Save the World*. Penguin Random House.

IFC. (2012). *Performance Standards on Environmental and Social Sustainability*. Retrieved April 8, 2022, from https://www.ifc.org/wps/wcm/connect/24e6bfc3-5de3-444d-be9b-226188c95454/PS_English_2012_Full-Document.pdf?MOD=AJPERES&CVID=jkV-X6h

Klein, S. (2020). *A Good War: Mobilizing Canada for the Climate Emergency*. Toronto: ECW Press.

Labour for a Green New Deal. (2019). *A Green Jobs Revolution*.

Macchi, C. (2021). The climate change dimension of business and human rights: the gradual consolidation of a concept of 'climate due diligence'. *Business and Human Rights Journal, 6*(1), 93–119.

Natural History Museum. (2019). Leading scientists set out resource challenge of meeting net zero emissions in the UK by 2050. *Press Release*. June 5.

Nwapi, C., & Andrews, N. (2017). A "New" developmental state in Africa?: Evaluating recent state interventions vis-a-vis resource extraction in Kenya, Tanzania, and Rwanda. *McGill International Journal of Sustainable Development Law and Policy, 13*(2), 223–267.

OECD. (2011). *OECD Guidelines for Multinational Enterprises*. OECD Publishing. https://doi.org/10.1787/9789264115415-en

Ovadia, J. S. (2016). *The petro-developmental state in Africa: Making oil work in Angola, Nigeria and the Gulf of Guinea*. Hurst & Publishers Ltd.

Palacios, L., & Cárdenas, M. (2022). A Bold Plan to Finance Latin America's Energy Transition. *Americas Quarterly*. Retrieved April 7, 2022, from https://www.americasquarterly.org/article/a-bold-plan-to-finance-latin-americas-energy-transition/

Rasche, A., & Waddock, S. (2014). Global sustainability governance and the UN Global Compact: A rejoinder to critics. *Journal of Business Ethics, 122*(2), 209–216.

Rivera, H. C. (2019). National action plans on business and human rights: Progress or mirage? *Business and Human Rights Journal, 4*(2), 213–237.

Sénit, C. A. (2020). Leaving no one behind? The influence of civil society participation on the Sustainable Development Goals. *Environment and Planning C: Politics and Space, 38*(4), 693–712.

Shayan, N. F., Mohabbati-Kalejahi, N., Alavi, S., & Zahed, M. A. (2022). Sustainable Development Goals (SDGs) as a Framework for Corporate Social Responsibility (CSR). *Sustainability, 14*(3), 1222.

Snyed, A. (2016). *New International Economic Order (NIEO)*. Available at https://www.academia.edu/20932190/New_International_Economic_Order_NIEO_

Sovacool, B. K., & Andrews, N. (2015). Does transparency matter? Evaluating the governance impacts of the Extractive Industries Transparency Initiative (EITI) in Azerbaijan and Liberia. *Resources Policy, 45*, 183–192.

The ASEAN Post. (2021). *ASEAN Needs A Green New Deal*. Retrieved April 7, 2022, from https://theaseanpost.com/article/asean-needs-green-new-deal

United Nations. (2021). *Theme Report on Energy Transitions: Towards the Achievement of SDG 7 and Net-Zero Emissions*. Retrieved April 7, 2022, from https://www.un.org/sites/un2.un.org/files/2021-twg_2-062321.pdf

US Congress. (2019). *H. Res. 109 - Recognizing the Duty of the Federal Government to Create a Green New Deal*. Washington DC: US Congress.

Vergara-Camus, L. (2022). The Energy Transition and the Global South. In H. Veltmeyer & P. Bowles (Eds.), *The Essential Guide to Critical Development Studies* (2nd ed., pp. 319–326). Routledge.

Weber, H. (2017). Politics of 'leaving no one behind': contesting the 2030 Sustainable Development Goals agenda. *Globalizations, 14*(3), 399–414.

Wettstein, F. (2021). Betting on the Wrong (Trojan) Horse: CSR and the Implementation of the UN Guiding Principles on Business and Human Rights. *Business and Human Rights Journal, 6*(2), 312–325.

Williams, S., & Doyon, A. (2019). Justice in energy transitions. *Environmental Innovation and Societal Transitions, 31*, 144–153.

World Bank. (2017). *The Growing Role of Minerals and Metals for a Low Carbon Future*. The World Bank.

15

Conclusion: Debates and Extractive Bargains at Different Scales

John P. Hayes, Clifford Gordon Atleo, Raphael Deberdt, Jeff Geipel, Alem Cherinet, and Margot W. Parkes

Introduction

John P. Hayes

This closing chapter is based on a roundtable at the workshop in Prince George in May 2022 which served as the launchpad for this edited volume. The closing roundtable featured experts from academia, non-governmental organizations, the mining industry, and mining industry watchdogs. As a group, we reflected on and debated the core questions: how does the notion of 'extractive bargains' feature in your own work or

J. P. Hayes (✉)
Department of Political Science, McMaster University, Hamilton, ON, Canada

The School of Public Policy, University of Calgary, Calgary, AB, Canada
e-mail: hayesj1@mcmaster.ca

C. G. Atleo
School of Resource and Environmental Management, Simon Fraser University, Burnaby, BC, Canada
e-mail: clifford_atleo@sfu.ca

P. Bowles, N. Andrews (eds.), *Extractive Bargains*, Frontiers of Globalization,
https://doi.org/10.1007/978-3-031-32172-6_15

research? In what ways is the state-society nexus important for how we understand extractivism today and in a likely post-extractive world? Finally, how do distinctions between 'public' and 'private' spheres—which can be false, misleading, or perhaps useful in some cases—help to (dis)organize our understanding of extractivism? The following forum-style chapter explores each expert perspective in turn.

While chapter contributions examine cases of state-led construction and managing of the extractive bargain, this roundtable sought to showcase how different stakeholders in the academic, NGO, and industry spaces are engaging the possibilities and improbabilities of state-led natural resource development that lies at the core of the extractive bargain. Given the importance of state-led bargain making, scale was a recurring theme in the roundtable discussion, because the sector each participant is in brings with it a myriad of institutional interactions with other actors and organizations from the local to the global level. In turn, the various levels of state authority (or lack thereof) over the public sphere inform one's outlook on the possibilities and limitations of the bargain between stakeholders. Following the co-editors' argument that states and social actors are subsumed in the dialectics of negotiation and consensus

R. Deberdt
Department of Anthropology, University of British Columbia, Vancouver, BC, Canada

Mining Governance (CEGEMI), Catholic University of Bukavu, Bukavu, South Kivu, Democratic Republic of the Congo
e-mail: raphael.deberdt@alumni.ubc.ca

J. Geipel
Mining Shared Value initiative of Engineers, Vancouver, BC, Canada
e-mail: jeffgeipel@ewb.ca

A. Cherinet
University of Calgary, Calgary, AB, Canada
e-mail: atcherin@ucalgary.ca

M. W. Parkes
School of Health Sciences and Northern Medical Program, University of Northern British Columbia, Prince George, BC, Canada
e-mail: Margot.parkes@unbc.ca

building, so too are the scholars, practitioners, and activists embroiled in a similar process over the bargain between economic development prospects of extraction and the myriad risks and downsides. Reaching definitive answers within this dialectic process can be distilled into control over knowledge production, disciplinary traditions, and epistemic communities within professional disciplines.

As experts in divergent professions, each roundtable participant brought with them a positionality, unique concerns, assumptions, and distinct questions to ask in the search for answers about the realities of the extractive bargain across varieties of social-environmental contexts. Hajer and Vertsteeg (2005) and Darier (1999) explain that Foucault's governmentality is useful in analysis of ecological discourse, because it helps unpack the discursive strategies of population control through the introduction of new forms of knowledge to steer the extractive bargain debate in the public sphere. There is a tacit responsibility to interrogate these dynamics and how they permeate knowledge production as well as our respective institutional vantage points. In the organization of this chapter, the roundtable hosted competing discourses and epistemologies about measuring winners and losers in different contexts of extractive bargains, contestations over what constitutes good governance, what constitutes sufficient free, prior, and informed consent, what is determined to be acceptable ecological clean up, and other debates familiar to the study of social dimensions of extractivism. As representatives of various institutions, our work challenges, but also might be informed by, our academic, non-governmental, community, or industry affiliations—all of which have predeterminations to showcase definitive answers and disseminate findings on the winners and losers of extractivism.

Selling the Bargain: Mining, 'Sustainable Extractivism,' and Public Discourses in Emerging Resource Economies

John P. Hayes

Government ministers and staff routinely consult experts in marketing and public opinion to not only run effective campaigns to sell the bargain of extraction, but also to shape the fundamental discursive nature of how citizens discuss these controversial projects. In other words, there is a state-led attempt to not only sell an extractive bargain and cast the widest net of consent possible, but also to instil faith in the citizenry that, despite the widely understood risks, extraction can be done sustainably. Further, personal observations from meeting multiple countries' government ministries of environment, energy, and mining, along with the Canadian foreign service, affirm the co-editors' statement that 'states are designing and promoting "extractive bargains", a search for an acceptance by a wide range of social actors.' In line with that argumentation is a need for selling the bargain via discursive shaping of public opinion.

In my work, I have observed a discernible pattern wherein state agents are forthcoming in informing stakeholders seen as sympathetic to industry that they are actively shaping how their citizens discuss extractivism. It might not come as a surprise that these state actors are selling the extractive bargain to the public in two main ways: first, as a sustainable and environmentally safe enterprise, by highlighting ongoing technical innovation and engagement with foreign, mainly Canadian, experts to mitigate against risk. Second, and as pointed out elsewhere in this volume, a wider climate bargain is at stake, whereby clean resource development is linked to supplying to the world its raw materials for a post-carbon, clean energy economy, meaning, 'critical minerals' and 'green metals.' However, what is less observed in the state-led public debate of extraction is how states are obscuring and confusing what the object of the bargain is. Obfuscating concepts like green energy, net-zero emissions, or sustainable extraction erase from public discourse the difference between the *act* of subsoil extraction and the *outcome* of extraction—a renewable energy output such as an EV battery, wind turbine, or solar panel—which in turn paints both the raw material extraction as one and the same as the clean energy item it produces, and is therefore inherently driving a tacit understanding of resource extraction as a 'good,' low-risk activity.

States appear to be acutely aware that obfuscation is beneficial, and that social acceptance for extraction comes from public dissemination of innovative solutions for mitigating the negative impacts of industry in all its forms (see Government of Canada XE "Canada", 2021). Public relations and marketing funded by governments, industry research institutes, and firms all zone in on sharing the good news that there is historically unprecedented investment in net-zero solutions, while simultaneously preserving the status quo of ongoing extractivism. Cox et al. (2022) fuse progressive public policy and extractivism in a study that proves why carbon taxes are advantageous to the mining industry, because carbon-pricing will help mining firms gain competitive advantage in supplying critical minerals that the energy industry needs for their products to move away from fossil fuels. Hydrogen powered mine haul trucks and even selenium eating bacteria to mitigate against water supply contamination are also being promoted by Canadian media (see Steen, 2022). It is for this reason that I suggest we are far from a post-extraction world and should instead be talking about the prospects of a 'post-carbon world,' as that will be the first phase of state-society consensus that moves heavy industry, transportation, agriculture, and other core economic activities away from fossil fuels, yet wholly reliant on mining critical minerals.

Beyond innovation discourses, 'catching up' is happening at a remarkable rate in resource-rich jurisdictions outside the OECD. Among many examples of catching up are clear cases of small states emerging as global leaders in carbon-intensive extractivism. Guyana is now poised to be the fourth largest producer of offshore oil and gas, surpassing the United States by 2035, and hosting 32% of new oil discoveries worldwide since 2015 (Blackmon, 2022). Ghana is expanding from offshore into onshore oil and gas exploration, along with public investments into new geological technical training programmes to bolster the mining industry. Likewise, Mexico's legal reforms since 2018 have reversed the liberalization of their oil and gas market, disincentivized new sources of capital investment into modernizing refineries, and the federal electricity authority have rolled back plans to move away from burning heavy-grade crude bitumen for the nation's energy grid (El Universal, 2021). Brief examples such as these indicate that some jurisdictions are actively asserting sovereign expansions over their subterranean resource endowments, with or without the participation of corporate capital and without impactful pushback from international environmental authority.

Public and private spheres are also becoming increasingly interlocked as states seek to balance feeding emerging markets for critical minerals, transitions to more clean energies, and court the financial power of oil and gas. In Canada, there is a close linkage between the state and extractive industries in expanding global leadership, technical knowledge, and investment in new subsoil ventures in oil, gas, and mining. An important dimension in the state-industry relationship is how the private sphere has been reshuffling investment in the most egregious extractive activities to align with federal policy objectives. Notably, the recent shift in ownership of dirty, carbon-intensive industries from publicly traded companies to private equity is fuelled by publicly traded firms scrambling to enhance their public image and improve their ESG scores among institutional investors. Private equity, on the other hand, operates without the ethical constraints of shareholder scrutiny (Monga, 2022). Despite this divestment by publicly traded companies under the pressures from environmentally focused shareholders, the distinction between public and private spheres remains embroiled in the ongoing extraction of some of the most carbon-intensive activities, because public pension funds remain major clients of private equity and publicly traded companies (Braich, 2021; Rowe et al., 2019).

State-owned enterprises (SOEs) also remain an important topic for focus in the extractive bargain. SOEs, especially under resource nationalist regimes, are also implicated in not keeping pace with green transition. While some may sympathize with state-ownership for its redistributive aims, it is worth recognizing that those outcomes may come with negative ramifications. Dispossession of land from non-extractive activities, poorly designed environmental regulations, and a lack of capital investment into technical upgrades to minimize ecological damage are not behaviours reserved for one type of ownership over another. In the search for consensus over extractive bargains, there are varieties of capitalism and varieties of engagement between states, society, and industry. Yet, a glaring pattern of discursive power wielded in shaping public opinion is steadfast and rooted in a state-led objective to reach a utilitarian end, despite the endurance of groups in resistance and opposition to the fundamental concept of an extractive bargain.

Asserting Indigenous Self-Determination in an Era of Decarbonization and Reconciliation in Canada

Cliff Atleo

I was asked by the editors of this volume to reflect on how the notion of 'extractive bargains' might be understood in my own research, particularly as it relates to Indigenous communities and their engagements with settler states and multinational corporations. I will do this by first situating myself as an Indigenous researcher and then discuss my research. Both of my parents are Indigenous from the west coast of British Columbia, Canada. I am Tsimshian on my mother's side from the community of Kitselas from the House of Niishaywaas where I carry the names Kam'ayaam and Sm'oogyit Niis Na'yaa. I am Nuu-chah-nulth-aht on my father's side where I carry the name Čačim'mułnii from the House of ƛaakišpiił. My Indigenous names and kinship affiliations might not mean much outside of my communities, but they are vital with respect to my research relationships. My names and familial affiliations indicate my place within these communities, including my responsibilities and relations of accountability. I have engaged in research within my home communities as well as neighbouring Indigenous communities. I am expected to act with respect and foster relations of reciprocity.

My research has mostly focused on Indigenous governance and a variety of resource sectors including fisheries, forestry, mining, and oil and gas. I have recently begun to focus on Indigenous leadership in renewable energy and sustainable transport (land, sea, and air). I look at these issues through several interconnected lenses: (a) Indigenous self-determination; (b) settler-colonialism; (c) environmental politics; (d) neoliberal capitalism; and (e) Indigenous feminism. It has been my goal to develop a more nuanced understanding of resource issues, considering Indigenous perspectives and priorities. I believe that this analytical approach can aid in the understanding of 'extractive bargains' as posited by Bowles and Andrews (Chap. 1 in this volume).

While there is a stereotype of Indigenous peoples being the 'original environmentalists' and always opposing development, I would argue that

Indigenous nations in the Western Hemisphere have always tried to negotiate to protect their jurisdictions, peoples, and the land even before the arrival of Columbus in 1492. None of this is to suggest that Indigenous peoples are not environmentally minded, but that their relations with land and animals are more complex than how we currently understand simplified notions of conservation and environmentalism. Bruce Braun (2002), Lynne Davis (2011), and Paul Nadasdy (2005) have all made nuanced contributions to understanding Indigenous peoples and environmentalists.

A resource-extractive dependent settler state like Canada has long made 'extractive bargains' often defying treaties and evoking charges of environmental racism and the acceptance of sacrifice zones (Bullard, 1993; Lerner, 2010; Preston, 2013). The notion of sacrifice for the greater good was exemplified when Canadian Prime Minister Justin Trudeau stated: 'We are going to get the pipeline built. It is a project in the national interest. This project will go ahead' (Snyder, 2018). Shortly thereafter, Canada bought the Trans Mountain pipeline for $4.5 billion. Much has been made of the impact benefit agreements signed by First Nations along the pipeline route, but as Atleo et al. (2022) note, most Indigenous leaders felt like they had no choice. Despite Canada finally adopting the UN Declaration on the Rights of Indigenous Peoples (UNDRIP) and even passing UNDRIP legislation in 2021, a robust interpretation of the concept of free, prior, and informed consent (FPIC) outlined in multiple articles of the declaration remains elusive. A scenario where a First Nation can negotiate but never say 'no' is not a genuine choice.

Indigenous peoples are accustomed to negotiating against overwhelming odds, yet they remain steadfast in utilizing a variety of tools to assert their self-determination. Climate change is no longer abstract: In my part of the world, heat waves, forest fires, and 'atmospheric rivers' that cause catastrophic flooding are becoming increasingly normal. And this environmental imbalance has been exacerbated by the COVID-19 pandemic. And while these myriad crises create daunting challenges, they may also present us with opportunities. We can think about our relations with land and (economic) relations with each other differently. Indigenous peoples and lands have borne the brunt of negative consequences from unrestrained capitalism. As we decarbonize our economies, we must be mindful of UNDRIP obligations and respect for Indigenous lands and peoples.

Extractive Bargains and the Role of Downstream Supply Chain Actors

Raphael Deberdt

For decades now, the study of mineral extractive industries has centred around the mine site and the relationships between states and the mining companies and communities surrounding the operations. This state-centric approach is particularly valuable to assess how it seeks to shape the behaviour and practices of other actors, from companies to classes or racial groups. I argue that extending the bargain behind the state to include supply chain actors, in particular downstream companies, proves to be a productive way to examine another way to engage with social and economic actors. Downstream companies include both brand companies with direct relationships with individual customers as well as their direct suppliers. While much focus is on the social licence to operate and the widespread resistance to extractivism, the new corporate supply chain citizenship complicates the landscape.

The involvement of downstream companies at the extractive site, directly through engagement with mining companies and communities (artisanal miners in particular), and indirectly through supply chain management systems, is a recent trend. Mostly located in the Global North, these companies structure their involvements in Global South countries with a focus on states with weak forms of governance, for example, the Democratic Republic of the Congo (DRC). Affected by the increasing pressure to responsibly source raw materials and to secure critical supplies, brand companies extend their reach to the furthest part of their value chains and engage in a new form of extractive bargain including the private sector, governments, and civil societies. The securitization of supplies, in particular in the context of the green transition away from fossil fuels, is echoed by states' release of strategic minerals lists. Nickel, cobalt, or lithium used for electric vehicle batteries and tantalum and tungsten for the high-tech sector are only a few of these now deemed critical minerals. While states push for the creation of national or regional supply of key materials, or their extraction in allied countries, downstream companies use their economic strength to sign supply deals directly with mining companies.

On the other side of this extractive bargain, the notion of responsible sourcing also resonates as a powerful dynamic driving downstream companies' behaviour in the upstream sector. Responsible sourcing is defined by the OECD as 'the process enterprises should carry out to identify, prevent, mitigate and account for how they address these actual and potential adverse impacts in their own operations, their supply chain and other business relationships' (2018, 15). Applied in a downstream-upstream framework, responsible sourcing begins by creating links and power relationships between brand companies and mining enterprises. Spurred by reputational risks often raised by independent research on the abuses occurring at the upstream level, growing pressure led brand companies to address their impacts throughout their supply chains. The development of responsible sourcing processes, informed by due diligence efforts, led to bargains being transferred from the responsibility of the extractive state to downstream companies. In this context, downstream companies aim at defining what are the different forms of resource extraction for 'good,' as described by Bowles and Andrews (Chap. 1 in this volume).

I do not argue that downstream companies have replaced the state in the bargaining occurring at the extractive site. In many ways, including in states considered 'failed,' the state remains the main interlocutor in the process that involves social actors as part of the search for consensus around certain extractive bargains (Bowles and Andrews, Chap. 1 in this volume). However, I propose to address the development of a parallel form of bargain using supply security and responsible sourcing as the core frameworks for its conduct. While visible in a series of extractive sites across the globe, the DRC provides a vibrant example of downstream interest in regulating and bargaining on extractivism's impacts, benefits, and limitations. Hence, I provide avenues through which exploring the extractive bargain as downstream companies negotiate around responsible sourcing and supply security simultaneously.

Walking on this rope, downstream economic actors embrace a role of enforcers of norms, standards, and frameworks to achieve the 'good' of resource extraction while brokering deals to receive a so-called clean supply of raw materials. The bargain then becomes a complex set of dynamics transcending downstream companies' individual roles to include civil societies, upstream companies, states, international organizations, and their customers often located in the Global North. The potential for positive developments and the optimism surrounding natural resource endowment and extraction is reflected in this notion of supply security combined with responsible sourcing. Deeply rooted in corporate social responsibility (CSR) discourses, far removed from the extractive site, and with a regulatory aspect based on voluntary frameworks, this new extractive bargaining aims at reconciling conflicting dynamics of capital extraction. The tensions of capitalistic extraction are then rendered manageable from a downstream risk mitigation perspective by participating in the extractive bargain.

Developmental Prospects of an 'All of Systems' Local Procurement Approach

Jeff Geipel

Our work with the non-profit Mining Shared Value initiative of Engineers Without Borders is to encourage and help the global mining sector procure more goods and services in the host countries where extraction takes place. We work as a resource, convenor, and champion for the issue, using systems change as a lens to lock-in self-reinforcing best practices for company processes, government policies, and all other system components that influence whether local procurement takes place.

When it comes to the concept of 'extractive bargains,' in effect, we are trying to reshape the bargain between investing mining companies and host countries so that more of the potential economic benefits of mineral extraction stay in host countries. The premise of our work is that in most developing countries, as well as in many remote regions within advanced countries, the current arrangement is ultimately unbalanced, and more economic benefits should stay closer to where mining takes place. This is not to say that in such cases mining companies are deliberately avoiding creating economic benefits through procuring goods and services, but rather that such outcome are the results of systems that need to be shifted.

Crucially, host countries that obtain more economic benefits from mining through effective local content regulations does not mean that the investing company loses. Unlike other elements of the overall bargains between mining companies and host countries where one side tends to benefit at the expense of the other—such as taxation and environmental regulation—local procurement is much more of a mutually beneficial phenomenon. Mining companies generally prefer to procure more locally where possible, as local labour costs are often lower, and having suppliers nearby reduces lead times. We are thus trying to create a new bargain for the issue of local procurement that benefits both.

Where there is conflict however is in the short term, where host governments desire to build up suppliers to the mining sector and dislodge existing procurement from international suppliers. This often raises procurement costs for mining companies in the short term as they have to accept higher priced goods and services, often with quality and reliability concerns, until supplier businesses can strengthen their capacity to be competitive with international suppliers.

When governments use local content regulations that require mining companies to give preference for domestic suppliers, they are trying to force a shift in the bargain. Even if most mining companies realize that a strong domestic supplier base will benefit them in the long run, it is also understandable they would oppose government interventions that raise costs in the short term.

As such, while we believe that governments do need to intervene in some way to dislodge existing procurement patterns, we advocate in our work an 'all of system' approach, where all actors in the system have an interest in supporting local suppliers. Increasing local procurement cannot be left to only one actor, such as a progressive mining company implementing effective local procurement processes, or a government effectively supporting suppliers. The reality is that mine sites change owners, and governments shift to new leaders and parties, and so the only way to truly change the system is to create a new 'bargain' where many actors as possible have a self-interest in increases in local procurement, and work together to achieve this. Our goal with the Mining Shared Value initiative is to make systemic change to achieve this bargain.

Informal Institutions and the Bargains Not Bargained For

Alem Cherinet

The Extractive Resource Governance Program (ERGP) resides within the School of Public Policy, University of Calgary. In our line of work, where policy meets practice, we engage with actors across the spectrum of extractive resource governance and development. Whether working with world governments, industry, community, or academia, we encounter cause and effect in ways that are multifaceted, always deeply rooted in context and reflecting trade-offs from the macro level of the state to the micro level of communities. As and when extractive bargains are struck, we are often called on as advisors, to shepherd key processes, help resolve critical issues, and support capacity building initiatives.

This workshop brought together a series of case studies, offering a deep dive into how state and non-state actors are grappling with the challenges of today, and making decisions about tomorrow. Many of the studies presented reflected the types of focus areas and projects we engage with, from social, political, and economic topics to technical and international themes. My own reflections on the concept of extractive bargains drew me to considering those which are unintended: the types of outcomes we do not bargain *for* but nevertheless *produce*, and which go on to shape realities for state and society, with radiating impact. A project is hailed for its level of community participation and sets a local precedent, later leveraged into new legislation. A state chooses to nationalize a critical mineral and inadvertently triggers opportunities for illicit markets. A country in conflict uses the promise of resource development as an instrument of peace, but underestimates historical struggles for land tenure, leading to a new form of national conflict. A mining company enhances its commitment to environmental practice but unintentionally opens space for coercion or violence against activists at the community level. Whether positive outcomes or negative moral hazards, these dynamics inevitably and constantly emerge in resource governance, with a great deal of our efforts aimed at trying to anticipate these effects (Leonard & Grovogui, 2017). We want to aim for the positive, and think strategically enough to mitigate the negative.

I see the nexus between state and society as a highly iterative process, where the connections between public and private spheres can be clearly defined, top-down structures, but also crucially (and necessarily) collaborative with far fewer rigid contours. Especially where results may be negative, and where the potential for harm and conflict exists, it is imperative that state and society are able to work in partnered ways.

The formality of the state is necessary from a regulatory perspective, to be sure, and it sets the tone in governance. But the informal relationships, the transactions between and among state and non-state actors carry vital influence. Like the mass beneath the tip of the iceberg, the informal processes and networks are far less visible but can be incredibly determinant. For this reason, when examining the state-society nexus, and in considering *the bargains we do not bargain for*, I view the state today as requiring a responsively adaptive posture, essential for keeping step with shifting realities, actors, interests, and circumstances since state policies do not always produce intended outcomes (Policzer, 2012). The same is true for industry. And the need manifests regularly in my field.

Public Health and Well-being Implications of Extractive Bargains

Margot W. Parkes

This contribution offers brief reflections on the public health and well-being implications of the notion of 'extractive bargains,' the state-society nexus as a pathway to understanding extractivism, and the interaction of public and private spheres in addressing these issues. These reflections are framed by several important influences. My perspective reflects my experience as someone who grew up living in Ngai Tahu territories of the South Island of Aotearoa/New Zealand. This influences how I think about governance, Indigenous contexts, about resources in general, as well as the very notion of extractivism and our relationships with that which is being 'extracted,' whether 'natural resources,' or the ecosystems and living systems we depend on for health and well-being (Parkes, 2020; Parkes, 2022). A related consideration is that I have only lived in my current context, in northern BC, on the unceded territories of the Lhiedli T'enneh First Nation since 2009, meaning that my insights are heavily influenced by the role that brought me here. I came to UNBC in 2009, as a Canada Research Chair in Health, Ecosystem and Society, and this trio of interests and connections weaves throughout my reflections. My remarks also reflect my foundational training as a medical doctor, who has subsequently developed a research portfolio that prioritizes working and learning with others—across regions, cultural contexts, disciplines, and sectors—to foster better understanding of land, water, and living systems (ecosystems) as foundational for health, equity, and well-being; and to strengthen collaborations that reflect these connections. This applied orientation also means that I am interested in understanding 'What?' (are the issues), as well as the reflective questions of 'So what?' and 'Now what?' and in particular the question of 'Who needs to do what differently?' in order to decrease harm to the health of humans and other species (Parkes, 2020). I see these questions as especially important when considering extractivism and extractive bargains in terms of their implications for eco-social approaches to health and well-being.

Reflections on the relevance of extractive bargains to my work draw especially on insights arising within a national and international collaboration known as the Environment, Community, Health Observatory (ECHO) Network that focuses on strengthening intersectoral capacity to understand and respond to the cumulative environment, community, and health impacts of resource extraction and development (Parkes et al., 2020; Sloan Morgan et al., 2020). Attention to the health implications of extractivism focuses not only on particular illnesses and disease outcomes, but also on the ways that upstream changes in landscapes and eco-social contexts result in a cascade of downstream effects and impacts, including equity and ecological impacts raised by other contributors, with far-reaching consequences for health and well-being (Aldred et al., 2021; Brisbois et al., 2019, 2021; Gislason et al., 2018; Parkes, 2016).

These integrative considerations are especially important when considering public health in relation to the state-society nexus and public-private spheres. In particular the ways that communities, actors, and agencies focused on health and well-being have potential to have important implications for the 'new alliances' that others have discussed in relation to the social and ecological consequences of extractive bargains with some powerful and challenging questions about the 'unusual allies' (Parkes et al., 2020), and lines of accountability that need to be invoked to prevent harm in these spaces (Sloan Morgan et al., 2020). Beyond the specific challenges of COVID-19, 'public health' has a long history of engaging with complex, messy social and environmental issues, working across the state-society nexus in order to create a 'fence at the top of the cliff, rather than the ambulance at the bottom' to improve the health of society, in ways that demand renewed attention in the context of the Anthropocene (Buse et al., 2018). This work has always demanded engagement across different sectors and agencies and, in the context of extractivism, creates the potential for new kinds of conversations with actors that may not traditionally have seen public health as relevant to their work. Increased attention to 'wellbeing economies' in relation to extractivism could, for example, find new allies with those working to enact the recent Geneva Charter on Well-being (WHO 2021).

Understanding the relationships between extractive bargains and public health also demands attention to the complex dynamics of scale from the global to the local and the deeply personal and experiential (Buse et al., 2018; Buse et al., 2019; Parkes et al., 2020). In grappling with these issues, increased attention is being given to ways of knowing with a focus well beyond linear pathways to disease, and renewed emphasis on integrative, interconnected, and holistic conceptualizations of health that have been an ongoing strength within Indigenous knowledge systems (Aldred et al., 2021; Redvers, 2018; Redvers et al., 2022). These contributions are re-invigorating attention to interrelationships that are often rendered invisible by intentionally siloed sectors and knowledge systems, evident from public health to extractive industries and beyond. Given that a strength of attention to extractive bargains conversation may be to make visible dynamics that have previously been invisible, these more integrative perspectives can offer important reminders of the need for attention to who is included in extractive bargains, who and what perspectives are being excluded, and how making these dynamics more visible could create windows to shift how bargains are negotiated.

A final reflection picks up on the value, mentioned by others, of shifting our scholarly attention from critical analysis around what has gone wrong, and what is deeply broken, to the active pursuit of what is going right and how to do more of that. This co-benefits orientation is an increasing focus of my work and those across the ECHO Network, recognizing the limits of only focusing attention on negative, hazardous, damaging, and harmful pathways, and the value of focusing research and policy attention on what is creating positive pathways to health, environment, and community, and the potential of new coalitions and alliances that can contribute to those co-benefits. The expansion of co-beneficial conversations helps to move beyond abstracted analyses and create a more informed understanding of who can do what differently, to contribute to co-beneficial pathways? In this context Indigenous leadership continues to shift conversations in ways that foster a more integrative sense of the overall direction, with an emphasis on preventing harm and promoting reciprocal benefit across environmental, equity, and health goals. Although such conversations have a long way to go, they have potential to shift conversations about extractivism in ways that can also fuel integrative, eco-social approaches to a more healthy, equitable, and ecologically coherent future.

Conclusion

The interdisciplinarity of natural resource governance scholarship, public policy analysis, activism, solidarity, and technical work across the extractive supply chain all feature in the roundtable. There is profound interconnectedness in the variant backgrounds of the experts, which reflect a world of actors linked together by a collective imminence of ecological crisis and the climate transition. This roundtable brought together a small sample of experts from different organizations that share in a dedication to asking questions and seeking positive solutions to the extractive bargain for communities at the forefront of extraction. Broadly defined, these are matters of distribution and of ecological impact that are driven by state actors in conjunction with a myriad of other stakeholders. Finding answers often boil down to positionality, epistemic communities, and ontologies. In turn, causal inference, affirmation, or rejection of foundational debates in the study of extractivism (e.g., resource curse (Auty, 1993), tragedy of the commons (Hardin, 1968), or accumulation by dispossession (Harvey, 2003)) are informed by these underlying understandings of relationships in the state-society-nature nexus. Reaching across divergent methodological and epistemic communities to seek measurable conclusions of the winners and losers, or, positive and negative outcomes, brings out a range of debates and conclusions in determining the possibilities and improbabilities of extractive bargains.

References

Aldred, T.-L., Alderfer-Mumma, C., de Leeuw, S., Farrales, M., Greenwood, M., Hoogeveen, D., O'Toole, R., Parkes, M. W., & Sloan Morgan, V. (2021). Mining sick: Creatively unsettling normative narratives about industry, environment, extraction, and the health geographies of rural, remote, northern, and Indigenous communities in British Columbia. *The Canadian Geographer / Le Géographe Canadien, 65*(82–96). https://doi.org/10.1111/cag.12660

Atleo, Clifford Gordon (Niis Na'yaa/Kam'ayaam/Chachim'multhnii), Tyla Crowe, Tamara Krawchenko and Karena Shaw. 2022. "Indigenous Ambivalence? It's not about the Pipeline: Indigenous Responses to Fossil Fuel Export in Western Canada." In *Public Responses to Fossil Fuel Export: Exporting Energy and Emissions in a Time of Transition,* edited by Hilary Boudet and Shawn Hazboun. : Elsevier.

Auty, R. (1993). *Sustaining Development in Mineral Economies: The resource curse thesis.* Routledge.

Blackmon, David. 2022. "New Oil Power Guyana On Pace To Surpass U.S. Offshore By 2035," *Forbes,* July 28, 2022. https://www.forbes.com/sites/davidblackmon/2022/07/28/new-oil-power-guyana-on-pace-to-surpass-us-offshore-by-2035/?sh=4d4dd9ea6c06.

Braich, Baneet. 2021. "Canada's biggest public pensions heavily investing in fossil fuels, new report suggests," *CBC News,* August 13, 2021. https://www.cbc.ca/news/canada/pension-fund-investments-fossil-fuels-1.6138550.

Braun, B. (2002). *The Intemperate Rainforest: Nature, Culture, and Power on Canada's West Coast.* University of Minnesota Press.

Brisbois, B. W., Reschny, J., Fyfe, T. M., Harder, H. G., Parkes, M. W., Allison, S., Buse, C. G., Fumerton, R., & Oke, B. (2019). Mapping research on resource extraction and health: A scoping review. *The Extractive Industries and Society, 6*(1), 250–259. https://doi.org/10.1016/j.exis.2018.10.017

Brisbois, B., Hoogeveen, D., Allison, S., Cole, D., Fyfe, T. M., Harder, H. G., & Parkes, M. W. (2021). Storylines of research on resource extraction and health in Canada: A modified metanarrative synthesis. *Social Science & Medicine, 277*, 113899. https://doi.org/10.1016/j.socscimed.2021.113899

Bullard, R. (1993). The Threat of Environmental Racism. *Natural Resources and Environment, 7*(3 (Winter)), 23–26.

Buse, C. G., Oestreicher, J. S., Ellis, N. R., Patrick, R., Brisbois, B., Jenkins, A. P., McKellar, K., Kingsley, J., Gislason, M., Galway, L., McFarlane, R. A., Walker, J., Frumkin, H., & Parkes, M. (2018). Public health guide to field developments linking ecosystems, environments and health in the Anthropocene. *Journal of Epidemiology and Community Health, 72*(5), 420–425. https://doi.org/10.1136/jech-2017-210082

Buse, C. G., Smith, M., & Silva, D. S. (2019). Attending to scalar ethical issues in emerging approaches to environmental health research and practice. *Monash Bioethics Review, 37*(1–2), 4–21. https://doi.org/10.1007/s40592-018-0080-3

Cox, B., Innis, S. S., Kunz, N. C., & Steen, J. (2022). The mining industry as a net beneficiary of a global tax on carbon emissions. *Communications Earth & Environment, 3*(17), 1–8. https://doi.org/10.1038/s43247-022-00346-4

Darier, E. (1999). Foucault and The Environment: An Introduction. In E. Darier (Ed.), *Discourses of the environment.* Blackwell publishers.

Davis, L. (2011). Home or Global Treasure? Understanding Relationships between the Heiltsuk Nation and Environmentalists. *BC Studies, 171*(Autumn), 9–36.

El Universal. 2021. "Ductos Obsoletos otro de los riesgos en pemex." November 2, 2021. https://www.eluniversal.com.mx/cartera/ductos-obsoletos-otro-de-los-riesgos-en-pemex.

Gislason, M. K., Morgan, V. S., Mitchell-Foster, K., & Parkes, M. W. (2018). Voices from the landscape: Storytelling as emergent counter-narratives and collective action from northern BC watersheds. *Health & Place, 54*, 191–199. https://doi.org/10.1016/j.healthplace.2018.08.024

Government of Canada 2021. "Canada sets a world standard for sustainable mining." https://www.tradecommissioner.gc.ca/canadexport/0003604.aspx?lang=eng.

Hajer, M., & Vertsteeg, W. (2005). A Decade of Discourse Analysis of Environmental Politics: Achievements, Challenges, Perspectives. *Journal of Environmental Policy & Planning, 7*(3), 175–184.

Hardin, G. (1968). The Tragedy of the Commons. *Science, 162*(3409), 1243–1248.

Harvey, David. (2003). "Accumulation by Dispossession," *The New Imperialism*, 137-182. Oxford: Oxford University Press.

Leonard, L., & Grovogui, S. N. (Eds.). (2017). *Governance in the Extractive Industries: Power, Cultural Politics and Regulation* (Vol. 1, 1st ed.). Routledge.

Lerner, S. (2010). *Sacrifice Zones: The Front Lines of Toxic Chemical Exposure in the United States*. MIT Press.

Monga, Vipal. 2022. "One of the World's Dirtiest Oil Patches Is Pumping More Than Ever," *The Wall Street Journal,* January 13, 2022. https://www.wsj.com/articles/oil-sands-canada-dirty-carbon-environment-11642085980?reflink=share_mobilewebshare.

Nadasdy, P. (2005). Transcending the Debate over the Ecologically Noble Indian: Indigenous Peoples and Environmentalism. *Ethnohistory, 52*(2 (Spring)), 291–331.

Parkes, M. W. (2016). Cumulative Determinants of Health Impacts in Rural, Remote, and Resource-Dependent Communities. In P. M. Gillingham, R. G. Halseth, J. C. Johnson, & W. M. Parkes (Eds.), *The Integration Imperative: Cumulative Environmental, Community and Health Effects of Multiple Natural Resource Developments* (pp. 117–149). Springer International Publishing. https://doi.org/10.1007/978-3-319-22123-6_5

Parkes, M. W. (2020). Working together for WHOLE systems: approaching well-being and health, while oriented to living-systems and equity. In C. Stephens (Ed.), *Animals, Health, and Society Health Promotion, Harm Reduction, and Health Equity in a One Health World* (1st ed.). Taylor and Francis Group.

Parkes, M. W. (2022). River conversations: A confluence of lessons and emergence from the Taieri River and the Nechako River. *River Research and Applications, n/a*(n/a). https://doi.org/10.1002/rra.3907

Parkes, M. W., Poland, B., Allison, S., Cole, D. C., Culbert, I., Gislason, M. K., Hancock, T., Howard, C., Papadopoulos, A., & Waheed, F. (2020). Preparing for the future of public health: Ecological determinants of health and the call for an eco-social approach to public health education. *Canadian Journal of Public Health, 111*(1), 60–64. https://doi.org/10.17269/s41997-019-00263-8

Policzer, P. (2012). A Complex Adaptive State System: Networks, Arms Races And Moral Hazards. *Revista de ciencia política (Santiago), 32*(3), 673–685. https://doi.org/10.4067/S0718-090X2012000300010

Preston, J. (2013). Neoliberal settler colonialism, Canada and the tar sands. *Race and Class, 55*(42), 42–59.

Redvers, N. (2018). The Value of Global Indigenous Knowledge in Planetary Health. *Challenges, 9*(2), 30. https://doi.org/10.3390/challe9020030

Redvers, N., Celidwen, Y., Schultz, C., Horn, O., Githaiga, C., Vera, M., Perdrisat, M., Mad Plume, L., Kobei, D., Kain, M. C., Poelina, A., Rojas, J. N., & Blondin, B. (2022). The determinants of planetary health: An Indigenous consensus perspective. *The Lancet Planetary Health, 6*(2), e156–e163. https://doi.org/10.1016/S2542-5196(21)00354-5

Rowe, James K., Steph Glanzmann, Jessica Dempsey and Zoë Yunker. 2019. "Fossil Futures The Canada Pension Plan's failure to respect the 1.5-degree Celsius limit." *Canadian Centre for PolicyAlternatives.* https://policyalternatives.ca/sites/default/files/uploads/publications/BC%20Office/2019/11/ccpa-bc_FossilFutures.pdf.

Sloan Morgan, V. S., Hoogeveen, D., Farrales, M., Gislason, M. K., Parkes, M. W., & Harder, H. G. (2020). Resource extraction and intersectoral research: Engaging accountable relations in the Environment Community Health Observatory Network. *Environment and Planning C: Politics and Space*, 2399654420951805. https://doi.org/10.1177/2399654420951805

Snyder, Jesse. 2018. "'We are going to get the pipeline built': Trudeau begins federal talks with Kinder Morgan to guarantee Trans Mountain." *National Post*, April 15, 2018.

Steen, John. 2022. "Selenium-eating bacteria could help fight pollution created by the mining industry: BRIMM director," BNN Bloomberg. https://www.bnnbloomberg.ca/video/selenium-eating-bacteria-could-help-fight-pollution-created-by-the-mining-industry-brimm-director~2374754.

Index[1]

[1] Note: Page numbers followed by 'n' refer to notes.

P. Bowles, N. Andrews (eds.), *Extractive Bargains*, Frontiers of Globalization,
https://doi.org/10.1007/978-3-031-32172-6

Kolibri 360 GmbH
Ferdinand-Jühlke-Straße 7
99095 Erfurt, Deutschland
produktsicherheit@kolibri360.de